Gendering the Nation-State

Edited by Yasmeen Abu-Laban

Gendering the Nation-State
Canadian and Comparative
Perspectives

UBCPress · Vancouver · Toronto

17 16 15 14 13 12 11 10 09 08   5 4 3 2 1

Printed in Canada with vegetable-based inks on ancient-forest-free paper (100% post-consumer recycled) that is processed chlorine- and acid-free.

Library and Archives Canada Cataloguing in Publication

Gendering the nation-state : Canadian and comparative perspectives / edited by Yasmeen Abu-Laban.

Includes bibliographical references and index.
ISBN 978-0-7748-1465-2 (bound); ISBN 978-0-7748-1466-9 (pbk.)

1. National state. 2. Power (Social sciences). 3. Citizenship. 4. Feminism – Political aspects. I. Abu-Laban, Yasmeen, 1966-

HQ1236.5.C2G42 2008   305.4201   C2008-900779-4

Canadä

UBC Press gratefully acknowledges the financial support for our publishing program of the Government of Canada through the Book Publishing Industry Development Program (BPIDP), and of the Canada Council for the Arts, and the British Columbia Arts Council.

This book has been published with the help of a grant from the Canadian Federation for the Humanities and Social Sciences, through the Aid to Scholarly Publications Programme, using funds provided by the Social Sciences and Humanities Research Council of Canada.

Printed and bound in Canada by Friesens
Set in Stone by Artegraphica Design Co. Ltd.
Copy editor: Deborah Kerr
Proofreader: Stephanie VanderMeulen
Indexer: David Luljak, Third Floor Research and Reference

UBC Press
The University of British Columbia
2029 West Mall
Vancouver, BC V6T 1Z2
604-822-5959 / Fax: 604-822-6083
www.ubcpress.ca

Contents

Contributors

Yasmeen Abu-Laban is Associate Professor in the Department of Political Science at the University of Alberta.

Caroline Andrew is Dean of Social Sciences and Professor of political science at the University of Ottawa.

Janine Brodie is Professor and holds the Canada Research Chair in Political Economy and Social Governance in the Department of Political Science at the University of Alberta.

Louise Chappell is Senior lecturer in the School of Economics and Political Science at the University of Sydney, Australia.

Maya Eichler is a doctoral candidate in the Department of Political Science at York University.

Jane Jenson is Professor and holds the Canada Research Chair in Citizenship and Governance in the Department of Political Science at the University of Montreal.

Paul Kershaw is Assistant Professor in the Faculty of Graduate Studies at the University of British Columbia.

Judy Rebick holds the Canadian Auto Workers Sam Gindin Chair in Social Justice and Democracy at Ryerson University, and is past president of the National Action Committee on the Status of Women.

Marian Sawer is Professor of political science in the Research School of Social Science at Australian National University.

Francesca Scala is Assistant Professor in the Department of Political Science at Concordia University.

Jackie F. Steele is a doctoral candidate in the Department of Political Science at the University of Ottawa.

Linda Trimble is Professor and Chair of the Department of Political Science at the University of Alberta.

Jill Vickers is Chancellor's Professor in the Department of Political Science at Carleton University.

Shauna Wilton is Assistant Professor of political studies at Augustana Faculty, University of Alberta.

Acknowledgments

This volume originated in a full-day workshop titled "Gendering the Nation-State" held at the Canadian Political Science Association (CPSA) meetings in Winnipeg, Manitoba, on 3 June 2004. The workshop brought together a number of scholars, both Canadian and international, to share theoretical and empirical insights into how and why gender, and gender in conjunction with other forms of difference, matters in understanding the nation-state today.

A volume such as this owes a great deal to a great many people and organizations. I would like to thank the CPSA for support given to me, as the 2004 section head for women and politics, in developing this workshop; David Laycock, the 2004 CPSA program chair, for his vision and encouragement; and Michelle Hopkins, CPSA executive director, for her galvanizing work connecting political scientists across Canada. At the University of Alberta, I would like to signal my appreciation for the work of E. Anne Mackenzie (Research Services Office) and her ongoing commitment to facilitating the research that takes place across faculties at the university; the funding given by the Research Services Office to support indexing this volume; the computing assistance of Lenise Anderson; the work of Leslie Robertson, who compiled an integrated bibliography while also teaching and doing her own research; and the library assistance of Alexa DeGagne, a master's student in the Department of Political Science. I would like to acknowledge the financial assistance of the Canadian Federation for the Humanities and Social Sciences and its Aid to Scholarly Publications Programme, which made this volume possible. I am grateful to Emily Andrew, senior editor of UBC Press, for skilfully guiding this project from its inception; and to production editor Anna Eberhard Friedlander and copy editor Deborah Kerr for their skilled and valuable work in the final stages. Not least, I also thank the anonymous reviewers for their insightful and constructive comments.

This volume arises out of the larger ongoing feminist struggle for justice, equality, and analytic understanding. Challenges to traditional ways of

understanding the nation-state demand a rethinking of past understandings; they foster new ways of thinking, new forms of questions, and new
linkages that frequently transcend disciplinary boundaries. These original
essays, written specifically for this book by senior and junior academics,
social activists, and graduate students, illustrate the dynamism and multiplicity of the struggle as it unfolds across generations, across geographic
space, and across genders and other forms of social divide.

I would particularly like to thank the contributors for their passion and
their dedication in this quest and for their commitment to ensuring that
this volume reached fruition.

Yasmeen Abu-Laban

Gendering the Nation-State

Gendering the Nation-State: An Introduction

Yasmeen Abu-Laban

The idea of a world without borders, a world in which the state was not all-powerful, captured the popular imaginary at the end of the twentieth century. This could be seen in the 1990 bestseller *The Borderless World* by corporate strategist Kenichi Ohmae, in the frequent invocation by business, media, and political elites, in all major world languages, of the idea of globalization (Held et al., 1999: 1), and even in the unfounded fear that Y2K computer glitches would have worldwide apocalyptic consequences (Kingwell, 1996; Swerdlow, 1998). Yet, despite all the anxiety, particularly in North America, the year 2000 came and went without the global disasters some predicted. More to the point, the early years of the twenty-first century are rife with examples of how much we are still collectively impacted by political processes in which states, national citizenship, and nationalism remain powerful forces.

Perhaps the most striking reminder of the continued import of these political processes comes from the fallout and response to the September 11, 2001 attacks in New York and Washington. In very real terms the "war on terrorism" has involved states – hence, the American-led war in Afghanistan in 2001, and the American-led invasion of Iraq in 2003. Across Western countries the rapid passage of anti-terrorist legislation, as well as renewed attention to policing borders in the name of national security, speaks to the relevance of national citizenship in the twenty-first century. Both the anti-terrorist legislation and the focus on borders have served to differentially target and restrict the rights and liberties of non-citizens (visitors, immigrants, asylum seekers) (Macklin, 2001; Fenwick, 2002; Cole, 2002-03; Haubrich, 2003; Abu-Laban, 2004). Amidst the surge in US sales of American flags and the renewed popularity of Huntington's (1993, 1996) essentialist argument about a "clash of civilizations," the immediate aftermath of September 11 does not suggest a post-national world. Rather, what has been underscored is the continued currency of Orientalist discourses that differentiate the civilized "us" (a community in which women have purportedly achieved autonomy and social equality) and the barbarian "them" (where women are unequal) (Said, 1979; Abu-Laban, 2001).

Feminist analyses, attuned to the playing out of notions of masculinity and femininity, have much to add to our understanding of why state-led military violence came to be viewed by many Americans as the best response to the events of September 11 (Cohn and Enloe, 2003: 1203-5). Cynthia Enloe (Cohn and Enloe, 2003: 1201) notes feminist analyses also have much to say about the manner in which "national security" has assumed a prominence over other conceptions of security since September 11, and, moreover, that a feminist understanding of Orientalism can reveal how the oppression of women "has been used as a measure of how enlightened a society is, without a much deeper commitment to deprivileging masculinity." More broadly, feminist analyses have much to add to our understanding of the nation-state both before and after September 11.

This volume takes as its focus "gendering the nation-state" by bringing the insights of feminism front and centre to show how socially constructed notions of both masculinity and femininity play out in relation to nation and state processes in Canada, in other countries, and internationally. The central thesis guiding this book is that a comprehensive approach to the theoretical and empirical study of political life in the twenty-first century demands that explicit analytic attention be given to gender. Specifically, current feminist scholarship draws attention to how gender matters for understanding relations of power, and therefore the ongoing contestation over the allocation of both symbolic and material resources in which nation-states are implicated historically and today. Consequently, when one approaches the major issues now dominating social science and political science research, such as the challenges posed by globalization to the nation-state and its autonomy, gender is a critical consideration.

Eschewing the assumptions about the "borderless world" that underpinned much popular discussion in the 1990s, feminism is, by definition, attuned to boundaries. This has specifically involved attending to the manner in which the historically and culturally specific drawing of boundaries around "the public" and "the private" have differential implications for men and women (Lamphere, 1993). Moreover, by the 1990s feminist theorizing and feminist praxis began to increasingly, as well as explicitly, consider the manifold ways in which the experiences of both women and men vary by class, race, ethnicity, religion, and disability, among other forms of difference. Of course there remains a lively debate among feminists about how best to recognize difference in light of the dangers inherent in essentialism, in light of present (if not growing) economic inequalities, and in light of the status of the project of eradicating gender oppression (McLaughlin, 2003: 7-22). Chandra Talpade Mohanty's *Feminism without Borders* (2003) epitomizes the spirit of one contemporary response to this debate by arguing that in fact difference must be acknowledged before change and justice can exist across social divides. Mohanty remarks that "Feminism without borders is not the same thing as 'border-less' feminism. It acknowledges the fault lines, conflicts, differences, fears and containment that borders represent. It acknowledges that there is no one sense of border, that the lines between and through nations, races, classes, sexualities, religions, and disabilities, are real – and that a feminism without borders must envision change and social justice work across these lines of demarcation and division" (2). Mohanty's articulation of a feminism without borders, insofar as it involves the recognition and crossing of divides, is useful for thinking not only about the social but also the disciplinary borders that are traversed in the chapters of *Gendering the Nation-State*.

Crossing Divides: Scope and Goals

Contributors to this volume use the insights of feminism to reveal the manner in which the nation-state – a central organizing unit in the modern world and thus equally central in modern social science and especially political science – is variously encoded by gendered assumptions, which in turn produce gendered outcomes. The book's central thesis, that the serious study of social and political life requires attending to gender, unfolds in separate sections devoted to gender and nation, gender and state processes, and gender and citizenship. Here political scientists come together to address how and why gender matters by examining constructions and reproductions of "the nation," the differential impact of state and international institutions and policies on specific groups, and access to rights and forms of participation and belonging.

At a very basic level, this collection illustrates the theoretical and empirical importance of engaging with gender. The chapters speak to the contributions multidisciplinary and interdisciplinary gender analysis makes to the discipline of political science by broadening the definition of the political through politicizing the public and the private. As a package, this collection also shows the import of addressing both "nation" and "state." The variety of nationalisms and the complexity of state processes are particularly relevant for understanding a multinational and federal country such as Canada, which was founded on settler-colonialism and still receives immigrants. However, the placement of Canada in a comparative frame of reference illustrates that political outcomes at international, national, subnational, and local levels are also related to power relations infused by gender and other forms of difference. It is this kind of attention that paves the way for better understanding such diverse issues explored in the book as the formation of nation-states (Chapter 1), the collapse of nation-states (Chapter 2), neoliberalism (Chapter 8), globalization (Chapter 12), the international criminal court (Chapter 7), public policy (Chapters 5, 6, 9, and 10), elections, parties, and representation (Chapter 4), and immigration (Chapter 3). It is also this kind of attention that can inform our understanding of the past so as to envision a different future (Afterword).

The chapters in this collection, in their engagement with theory and empirical evidence, reflect current developments. However, in a very real sense, *Gendering the Nation-State* builds on extensive work that has been done for well over three decades in the multidisciplinary and interdisciplinary areas of gender/women's studies, as well as within the field of women/gender and politics in the discipline of political science. Indeed, in the past decade alone, Canadian and international scholars have made a number of contributory interventions to the study of gender, diversity, and politics, including the state and gender, as well as nation and gender.[1]

Yet, despite the large body of feminist scholarship that has been and continues to be produced, the discipline of political science as a whole has yet to fully acknowledge and engage the implications of this work. Put differently (and to extend the observations of Mohanty), there is no "political science without borders" when it comes to feminist scholarship. Rather, it appears that disciplinary biases, assumptions, and practices have discouraged analytic attention to gender (see Vickers, 1997). Thus, writing in 1999, Jane Arscott and Manon Tremblay suggested that in both Quebec and Canada outside Quebec, the absorption of feminist scholarship within the discipline, and within the major disciplinary journals, was at best a work in progress. For many years, there have been sections within the Australasian Political Studies Association, the American Political Science Association, and the Canadian Political Science Association that aim to showcase scholarship in the field of gender by recognizing the best of it. One example that comes to mind is the 2003 introduction of the Jill Vickers Prize for the best paper on women, gender, and politics given at the Canadian Political Science Association's annual meeting (Sawer, 2004). However, as recently as 2004, Marian Sawer's analysis suggested that not only has the discipline of political science remained male-dominated in most parts of the world, but the impact of feminist scholarship on curricula and the field as a whole "remains additive rather than transformative" (563). Sawer contrasts this with the more decisive impact that feminist scholarship has had on such related areas as sociology and history in the scholarly work undertaken by both men and women in those disciplines (553-60).

Therefore, by bringing feminism front and centre, *Gendering the Nation-State* is a response to a disciplinary incompleteness in political science; thus, the focus on the nation-state is deliberate. Even in the face of increasing discussions about globalization, it has been noted that the study of the state provides the most unified focus for the various subfields within political science (O'Lary, 1996; Katznelson and Milner, 2002). Yet, at the same time, the way in which gender and feminist analyses have contributed to the study of the state and citizenship remains at best only partially recognized and minimally integrated into work in the discipline. Moreover, within much Canadian and international political science literature, discussions of nation and nationalism have tended to be separated from those pertaining to the state and citizenship. Additionally, much theorizing on nation, nationalism, public policy, and citizenship has ignored gender relations, with the consequence that gender is treated as marginal or even irrelevant. This collection, however, brings together political scientists who engage with the multidisciplinary and interdisciplinary study of gender in relation to the traditional concepts of the state, citizenship, and nation. The overt focus on the nation-state is used to reinforce both the challenge and the contribution feminist scholarship poses to what arguably remains the central organizing unit within the discipline of political science.

In addition, though much work has crossed disciplines in the areas of gender and electoral politics, gender and citizenship, gender and public policy, and gender and nationalism, with some notable exceptions (e.g., Yuval-Davis, 1997), these areas are treated in separate volumes. This book takes up all these areas, with the intent of interrogating and integrating the theoretical and empirical importance of addressing both "nation" and "state." This provides a unique window into the dynamism and diversity that gender analysis engages in terms of methodology, theory, and foci; in addition, it shows the distinct contribution that feminist analysis brings to the study of what, in different ways, remains a key unit of analysis across contemporary social science – the nation-state.

Keeping the traditional core of the discipline of political science and its disciplinary interstices in mind, the following sections will frame the insights that gender analysis brings to the concepts of state, citizenship, and nation.

The Contribution of Feminist Scholarship

Gendering the State

The development of modern social sciences in the nineteenth century introduced the concepts of "state" and "society" into the shared lexicon, though these have been utilized differently across time and disciplines. Within political science, the 1950s and 1960s were characterized by a retreat from the concept of the state, a result of both the popularity of pluralist approaches to understanding power and the development of "systems theory," explicitly designed by David Easton to replace the state concept (Easton, 1957; Almond, 1997).

The 1960s and 1970s saw a revived interest in the study of the state, initially among scholars working in the Marxist tradition, particularly in Europe (Miliband, 1969; Althusser, 1971; and see Blackburn, 1972: 238-62, for the debate between Ralph Miliband and Nicos Poulantzas). The state also came to be studied, mainly by American scholars, in relation to Max Weber's understanding of it as an organization. The cry to "bring the state back in" was a call to view the state as capable of pursuing goals – either in periods of crisis or even more generally – independent of the pressures of classes and/ or social groups (Skocpol, 1979, 1985; Nordlinger, 1981). The type of abstract theorizing found in the Marxist and neo-institutionalist debates around state autonomy in the 1970s and 1980s no longer characterizes contemporary research, but the insights generated by feminist scholarship beginning in this same period cannot be ignored in any adequate account of the state today (Jessop, 2001). It is in relation to both the Marxist and the Weberian traditions that feminist scholarship has posed key challenges and opened new avenues of theory and research.

Weber posited the state as an organization that has a monopoly over the "legitimate" use of force in a given territory. However, feminist scholarship has drawn attention to a number of issues that show the limitations of Weber's perspective. Consider, for example, violence, its expression in both public and private spheres, and by non-state actors. As Catherine MacKinnon (1989: 169) has bluntly put it, Weber's monopoly over coercion "actually describes the power of men over women in the home, in the bedroom, on the job, in the street, through social life." Attention to the expression of militarized violence and, relatedly, the international system, has also shown the value of attending to gender in relation to war (Elshtain, 1987; Goldstein, 2001) and in international relations theory (Enloe, 1989; Peterson and Runyan, 1993; Whitworth, 1994; Pettman, 1996). As well, Weber's state as an organization has been unpacked, leading to the development of a feminist case – attuned to the experience of many women who undertake caring work – against hierarchically administered societies (Ferguson, 1984) as well as debate about the possibilities of state feminism (Chappell, 2002). More broadly, a focus on the state as an organization has given rise to a healthy women-in-politics literature dealing not only with the civil service but also with political parties, legislatures, and courts. In fact, the creation of an online "women in politics bibliographic database" by the Inter-Parliamentary Union and the United Nations Development Programme is a testimony to the proliferation of literature on these topics pertaining to countries across the globe (see http://www.ipu.org).

Feminist theorizing has also drawn from Marxism and the critical questions that emerge from key themes raised by Marx, including power, class, exploitation, ideology, and praxis. These themes in particular raise critical questions in relation to the supposed neutrality of the liberal state, and have inspired and continue to inspire much feminist theoretical scholarship sensitive to the uneven outcomes experienced by subordinate classes and groups (Barrett, 1980; MacKinnon, 1989; Brown, 1995; Bannerji, 1995).

Yet it must be noted that feminist state theorizing has also grapp[
Marxism, revealing tensions between Marxist and feminist thought
the centrality of Marxism in the post–Second World War revival of interest
in the state, it is perhaps not surprising that in the 1970s much feminist
work on the state engaged with and adopted methods of theory construction similar to those in Marxist writings of the same period (Jessop, 2001:
157). A key example might be Mary McIntosh's (1978: 259) intervention
arguing that class domination (and the capitalist nature of the state) is more
"fundamental" than gender domination.

By the late 1980s, new responses were being formed. On the one hand,
attempts were made to further modify state theory in light of the complex
and variable role played by women as carers and wage earners, as well as
the complex and variable role played by different states (historically and
cross-nationally) in reproducing gender inequality (as the development of
"state feminism" might suggest) (Sassoon, 1987: 15-42). As Anne Showstack
Sassoon's introduction to her important anthology *Women and the State* maintains in explaining the inspiration of the collection, "What became obvious
was that the actual situation of the mass of women had gone beyond the
terms of the domestic labour debate ... Yet this debate and most Marxist
analysis tried to move directly from the theoretical category of mode of
production to the socially and historically constructed family. The questions posed became narrowed to how the family helps reproduce the capitalist
mode of production, and in particular, how it physically reproduces the
working class. Women's role was reduced to their role in the family" (17).
On the other hand, some feminists warned against even attempting to develop a theory of the state insofar as it involved engagement on political
terrain – whether liberalism or Marxism – that differed from feminism. In
the view of Judith Allen (1990: 21, 22), "the state" was not an "indigenous"
concept of feminist theory: "'The state' is a category of abstraction that is
too aggregative, too unitary, and too unspecific to be of much use in addressing the disaggregated, diverse and specific (or local) sites that must be
of most pressing concern to feminists." Allen urged that empirical and theoretical attention be given not to "the state" but to concepts such as policing,
law, medical culture, the body, sexuality, violence, and masculinity (22).

In the ensuing years, certain of the concepts identified by Allen have
proven to be important and fruitful loci for feminist theory, one major example being the body (see Carson, 2001). Yet the call to completely abandon the state as a concept was never wholly accepted, in large part because
it ran counter to evident developments including, as Wendy Brown (1995:
194) notes, the growing number of women who were dependent on the late
capitalist state. As she puts it, "While the state is neither hegemonic nor
monolithic, it mediates or deploys almost all the powers shaping women's
lives – physical, economic, sexual, reproductive and political – powers

wielded in previous epochs directly by men." Moreover, as Jacqueline Stevens (1999: 52) has observed, though it may be that "it is the marked 'feminist' political scientist, i.e., the professional other, who is taking up serious work on dynamics of the family," whereas "the unmarked political scientist writes about the state," it should not be forgotten that the state is a membership organization. As Stevens's rich account demonstrates, the state has rules of inclusion and exclusion based on (variable) kinship practices and kinship anxieties that in turn reveal a sex/gender system (267-80).

Rather than abandoning the state as too abstract a category, many recent attempts to theorize it reflect greater historical and cross-cultural sensitivity – a feature also evident in more recent accounts criticizing patriarchy as a concept or theory when it is used ahistorically to speak of a universal and homogeneous social system (Dahlerup, 1987; Pilcher and Whelehan, 2004: 94-96). Thus, more recent articulations addressing gender and the state view gender relations as dynamic and suggest that the state plays a key role in regulating, generating, and even – especially in periods of crisis – transforming the gender order (Connell, 1990). Additionally, since the 1990s increased attention has been given to complexity and multiplicity – in part an outcome of the insights of postmodernism (Flax, 1990). This has led to more focus on the articulation of social relations around gender, race, and class in specific state structures and policies (Anthias and Yuval-Davis, 1993; Stasiulis and Yuval-Davis, 1995; Abu-Laban and Gabriel, 2002), as well as to an interest in how specific constructions of masculinity and femininity come to be privileged in state discourses, state institutions, and state practices (Jessop, 2001: 159). As increasing attention in the 1990s and 2000s has been paid to themes of globalization, neoliberalism (with its stress on markets as efficient allocators of goods and services, cuts to social spending, and individual self-reliance), and regionalism (as seen, for example, in the widening and deepening of the European Union, or the North American Free Trade Agreement), it is also feminist literature that has drawn attention to their gendered impact (Bakker, 1994; Gabriel and Macdonald, 1994; Kelly, Bayes, and Young, 2001; Bayes et al., 2006).

Gendering Citizenship
Like the state, citizenship has been a major focus in modern social science research, political science, and especially the field of political philosophy. Indeed, in its connection to themes of community, belonging, and participation, it is also a concept that animated the writings of the classical philosophers of the Western canon such as Aristotle (Pocock, 1992: 38). It has continued to inspire philosophers into the present. Additionally, citizenship has been approached from the vantage point of rights, especially in the post–Second World War period with the development of the welfare state in advanced capitalist countries. When one considers the concept of

citizenship from the perspective of belonging and participation as well as from the perspective of rights, it is clear that feminist theorizing has drawn systematic attention to the manner in which women have been excluded from citizenship. Increasingly since the 1990s, feminist theorists have also examined the implications of gender and other forms of difference at both national and global levels, revealing in turn the ongoing tension around treating "woman" as a unified subject versus addressing differences arising from identity/culture or from membership in marginalized or privileged groups based on class, race, ability, heteronormativity, and so on.

One of the most thoroughgoing critiques of the exclusion of women from the participatory promise of citizenship comes from Carole Pateman (1988b), who argues that membership in the "public sphere" is based on fraternity, which serves to both exclude and subordinate women in the "private sphere." In this way, Pateman challenges the rights and freedoms that supposedly derive from the social contract as envisioned by modern theorists such as Locke, Hobbes, and Rousseau, who neglected to consider a prior sexual contract. However, it is the sexual contract, argues Pateman, that allows for the patriarchal control of men over women; its contemporary iterations are to be found in contracts concerning marriage, prostitution, and surrogate mothering. Pateman's attention to women's differential treatment and exclusion from citizenship has also been central to work that took as its focus the development of rights, including in relation to the welfare state.

The pathbreaking post-war account of citizenship was provided by T.H. Marshall (1964). Marshall's evolutionary account of the development of rights in Britain argued that civic rights (relating to the rule of law) developed in the eighteenth century, to be followed in the nineteenth century by political rights (voting) and subsequently, with the advent of the welfare state in the twentieth century, by social rights. Much of the debate about Marshall's work in the 1960s, 1970s, and even the 1980s concerned the implications of the welfare state for understanding class-based conflict and consciousness (see Barbalet, 1988). However, the development of feminist scholarship, with its attention to the private sphere, the sexual division of labour, history, and cultural variability, served to illuminate new avenues of research and theory.

Feminist theorists have also demonstrated how women, precisely because of their relegation to the private sphere, have experienced rights acquisition that differs from that described by Marshall. Thus, for example, even in addressing the history of Britain itself – the focus Marshall took in his work – Sylvia Walby (1994) finds that women's entrance into rights not only occurred later but also followed a very different trajectory, with political rights actually preceding civil rights. As well, standard definitions of political rights, with their emphasis on voting, fail to capture some of the distinct ways in which women participate in politics (Vickers, 1997: 48).

Addressing the sexual division of paid and unpaid labour suggests that women have experienced citizenship rights and obligations differently. As Ruth Lister (1993: 4) puts it, by and large, men "are free to be full-time wage-earning citizens, and, if they so choose, active political citizens" because they are unencumbered by obligations of care for children and/or adults that characterize the experience of many women. Such insights have raised questions about the gendered nature of the welfare state itself, with its foundational assumptions about male breadwinners (Pateman, 1988a), and spawned new theorizing regarding how care can be better valued in relation to citizenship and social policy (Fraser, 1994; Hankivsky, 2004). As well, cuts and reformulations in state spending are being examined for their distinct impact on men and women (Bakker, 1994; Dobrowolsky and Jenson, 2004).

The attention feminist theorists have given to gendering citizenship feeds, in distinct ways, into a larger ongoing and unresolved debate in political philosophy about whether equality is best achieved through the same treatment or differential treatment (Taylor, 1992b). There is, however, no clear unanimity on this issue among feminist scholars, an issue that has become increasingly complicated when one considers the gender implications of calls for a multicultural citizenship by theorists such as Will Kymlicka (1995). Thus, for example, though the late Iris Marion Young (1989: 251) argued for a differentiated citizenship for women, as well as minorities and other historically disadvantaged groups, "since the inclusion and participation of everyone in public discussion and decision-making requires mechanisms for group representation," other feminist philosophers, such as the late Susan Moller Okin (1998), have argued that a multicultural citizenship will undermine the rights of female minorities. This has generated its own forms of criticism about the nature of the evidence used by Okin and others in presenting their claims (Phillips, 1997; Honig, 1999). Attempting to escape the "cul de sac" of the debate over same and differentiated citizenship, Ruth Lister (1993, 1997) has united the two forms; her approach recognizes that women are not a monolithic group and that their experience as citizens is mediated by such factors as race, ethnicity, class, age, and sexual orientation. This formulation bears some resemblance to Chantal Mouffe's (1992) call to abandon a focus on the unitary subject and to consider a fuller multiplicity of relations.

Not least, in attending to gender and other forms of difference, progressively more feminist theorists of citizenship have considered the possibilities and limits of discussions of global citizenship (Archibugi, Held, and Köhler, 1998) as well as forms of regional citizenship such as European Union citizenship (Meehan, 1993). Insights into levels beyond the national state have been aided by addressing gender and other forms of difference in global migration and the negotiation of national borders. Thus, such work also considers citizenship in its most formal sense as a status that allows the right of entry into a state (Yuval-Davis, 1991; Dobrowolsky and Tastsoglou, 2006), serving to highlight again how the state is a membership organization.

Gendering Nation

As with that regarding citizenship and the state, feminist work on nationalism has challenged the long-standing failure of much existing literature to consider gender. Indeed, from the early post–Second World War work of Karl Deutsch (1953), who attempted to use the scientific method to predict and control nationalism, to the idealist account of Elie Kedourie (1960), and to Michael Ignatieff's post-Cold War era international bestseller *Blood and Belonging* (1993), there has been a weighty silence about gender and nation. At its most basic level, therefore, feminist work on nationalism draws attention to this silence. Additionally, feminist theorizing on nationalism challenges existing findings that have traditionally animated debates over nationalism, with the consequence that the very evidence used to support competing claims in the literature is brought into question.

One major area of debate within mainstream work on nationalism has been whether nationalism is a primordial force or a product of modernity (Anthony D. Smith, 1998). Those who find the roots of nationalism in modernism variously attribute its rise and spread to the role of intellectuals and ideas (Kedourie, 1960), the uneven development caused by capitalism (Nairn, 1977), industrialization and the system of mass education (Gellner, 1983), and the advent of the printing press (Anderson, 1991). However, attention to gender has served to challenge the foci of these debates, showcasing the important role played by women as "bearers of the nation." As Deniz Kandiyoti (1994: 376-77) puts it, "Women bear the burden of being 'mothers of the nation' (a duty that gets ideologically defined to suit official priorities) as well as those who reproduce the boundaries of ethnic/ national groups, who transmit the culture and who are the privileged signifiers [in terms of dress and behaviour] of national difference." In particular, feminist accounts have underscored that it is women (rather than schools or intellectuals, for example) who are central in the intergenerational transmission of cultural traditions and customs (Yuval-Davis, 1998). Moreover, there are dialectical relations between state, nation, and family that rest on distinctions between sex and gender (Stevens, 1999). In this sense, whether nationalism is viewed as a primordial force, a modern force, or some combination of the two, attention to gender brings with it a very different explanation for the persistence and/or rise of nationalism.

Additionally, analytic consideration of gender has brought with it new ways of answering another question that has influenced non-feminist theorizing – whether nationalism is best viewed as a progressive or reactionary force (Apter, 1989). This question became especially pertinent in moving beyond the universalizing focus of many early post–Second World War accounts that considered only European experiences and tended to homogenize these experiences. For instance, the focus on gender in the work of Kandiyoti (1994) and McClintock (1995), among others, raises questions about the extent to which specific social and political structures and belief systems can keep women in subordinate positions in both colonial and post-colonial contexts.

Not least, in attending to difference, feminist accounts have shown that in fact nations are complex and internally differentiated. In this way, different nations and expressions of nationalism can produce diverse constructions of femininity and masculinity; women and men of different races, classes, religions, and sexualities are privileged differentially within any nation; and, moreover, those with relative privilege may act to preserve it (see Blom, Hagemann, and Hall, 2000; Dhruvarajan and Vickers 2002; Bhattacharya, Gabriel, and Small, 2002). The importance of these findings can hardly be overestimated, given that nationalism remains a potent force in the twenty-first century.

Gendering the Nation-State: This Volume

The chapters in this volume draw from, engage with, and build upon a number of themes, debates, and recent developments found in the feminist contributions to gendering the nation, state, and citizenship described above. As such, they frequently employ insights that cut across a number of theoretical concerns. These chapters are also in conversation with each other, as some authors offer contrasting perspectives and alternative ways of viewing the contemporary period and engaging with theory. This book is organized into three parts followed by an afterword.

In Part 1, the contributors examine gender and nation, using aspects of the comparative method to address several distinct contexts for the formation of the nation-state and the playing out of nationalism These include countries of the global North, anti- and post-colonialism in the global South, communist and post-communist Russia, and the current context of global migration, which has ensured that countries of both North America and Europe are "immigrant-receiving nations," even though their responses to this reality may differ due to different welfare state practices. This effort to uncover both similarities and differences across space and time is in keeping with much current scholarship on nationalism, which has shied away from the early post-war attempt to generate a universal theory of nationalism. The comparative approach employed throughout Part 1 also highlights certain themes identified in feminist theorizations of nation. These include the roles played by women in state-formation and national movements, the manner in which various national expressions reflect distinct constructions of masculinity and femininity, and the dialectical relation-ship between state and nation, which has much to do with socially con-structed difference (gender, race, class).

In Chapter 1, Jill Vickers notes that discussions of gender and the forma-tion of modern nation-states remain rare. She calls for gendering the hy-phen in "nation-state" to account for the diversity of women's experiences and women's participation both in the formation of core Western nation-states and in modernizing anti-colonial national movements. In explicat-ing some of the differences between these two contexts, Vickers' historical analysis shows that as the core nation-states formed, women were denied political and civil rights in them, whereas in anti- and post-colonial con-texts women and men typically achieved these citizenship rights simultan-eously. Vickers' account is sensitive to variability in a number of ways. She notes that the public-private divide may have less pertinence in many coun-tries of the South where, for instance, the family has a distinct political role recognized in many constitutions. As well, she points out that the perfor-mative nature of gender and the biological markers of sex take on different meaning depending on time and space. This leads her to address how sex/gender regimes affect nation-state processes and vice versa. Ultimately, Vickers finds that though outcomes do differ, one area that appears con-stant in the making and remaking of nation-states is the duality of women's roles as citizens (when achieved) and their family roles as structured by marriage laws.

In Chapter 2, Maya Eichler seeks to rectify the way that scholars, examin-ing the post-communist transformation of Russia, overlook the gendered character of economic, political, and social changes. Taking this fundamen-tal transition as a temporal marker, she addresses the intersections between nation and gender in the making of the Soviet/Russian transformation. Eichler overviews how the 1970s were characterized by increased academic and scholarly debate about the Soviet gender order. She notes that the tran-sition begun during perestroika involved economic reforms and the legiti-mization of market ideology, as well as the promise to revert to a more "natural" Western gender order in which women returned to the private sphere and men "regained their masculinity." Yet, with the global spread of neoliberalism, in practice the retreat of women from employment has proved possible only for Russia's new capitalist class, provoking new criticisms of capitalism and the West in some quarters. As well, the re-traditionalization of gender roles, in the form of militarized masculinity, has proven to be contested when it comes to the Chechen wars.

In Chapter 3, Shauna Wilton draws from the literature on gender and nation, as well as debates over multiculturalism, to address how both the Canadian and Swedish states are involved in projecting an image of the nation to immigrants. In both countries, national state agencies engage in producing literature, in various languages, for potential new members of the national political community. Underscoring the manner in which the state is a membership organization, this socialization literature presents an image of a "good citizen," a process that Wilton argues is gendered and that interacts with race and class, just like immigration policy itself. Her analysis of the images and text of the English-language versions of this literature in Sweden and Canada suggests that the welfare state and women's equality are most emphasized in Sweden, whereas Canada lays greater emphasis on ethnic and racial diversity and individual self-reliance. In both cases, however, the discussions of gender and/or gender equality are framed within the private sphere of the family, while other spheres (such as the workplace) are ignored.

Part 2 of the book is devoted to gender and state processes. Here, con-tributors take as their focus various state institutions and processes (the legislature and the bureaucracy) as well as institutions and processes that involve the interface between state and society (political parties) and the state and the global community (the International Criminal Court). Along with the foci, the specific method employed by individual authors varies (from content analysis to qualitative interviews), as does the specific theory engaged (from critical mass to transnational activism). However, despite these differences, analysts in Part 2 speak collectively to the relevance of specific structures and/or specific ideas in accounting for outcomes. These include the significance of differing legislative systems for understanding the impact of female and male elected officials, the constraints imposed by bureaucratic culture on feminist policy researchers, the negative impact of the "new populism" on equity-seeking groups, and the important, though understudied, impact of the agendas pursued by official state delegations at the international level. The state does not emerge as neutral in any of these accounts, but in keeping with the move away from abstract theorizing around state autonomy that characterized much work of the 1970s and 1980s, these chapters explicate how specific institutions and processes shape, and may sustain or transform, social relations.

In Chapter 4, Linda Trimble focuses on women in politics – that is, on their presence in legislatures and their impact on policy formation. She notes the continuing numerical under-representation of women in legisla-tive assemblies across the globe, as compared to their numbers in the popu-lation. However, Trimble departs from the assumptions of such number-based theories as "critical mass" (which posits that incorporating a certain thresh-old number of women will transform a policy-making environment), choos-ing instead to interrogate the extent to which a direct relationship exists between descriptive (or numerical) representation and active (or substan-tive) representation. In keeping with much recent feminist theorizing that highlights the complex and intersecting nature of identity, Trimble questions the extent to which there is actually a coherent set of "women's interests" that can be represented. Additionally, she reminds us of the variable impact of legislative systems on elected officials, stressing that parliamentary governance itself, with its strict party discipline, poses constraints on all of them.

The emphasis on the constraints that organizational structures and cultures pose is continued in Chapter 5 by Francesca Scala. This examines the bureaucratic demands for objective and impartial policy advice in Canada. Taking as its focus the contentious issue of reproductive technologies, Scala's chapter addresses the tension between feminist analysis and mainstream policy analysis as the work of Canada's Royal Commission on New Reproductive Technologies, created in 1989, evolved. She argues that the commission's inherent quantitative research bias and the dichotomization of policy analysis versus policy advice proved incompatible with the vision of feminist policy researchers. As a result, this particular commission failed to seize the opportunity to move beyond the scientific and medical realm of reproductive technologies to address their social impact on women, including minority women and women with disabilities.

The emphasis on the relevance of ideas is continued in Chapter 6 by Marian Sawer. This chapter also draws attention to the role of political parties as important carriers of ideas in their distinct interface between state and societal actors. Sawer engages in a systematic comparative examination of both Canada and Australia since the 1990s, focusing on the manner in which the policy-making arena has been transformed by the impact of populism on party and electoral politics at the national level in both countries. Unlike the rural populism of the past that targeted the financial elites of large cities, the new populism of today constructs a divide between taxpayers and a welfare state elite. Thus, in both Canada and Australia, the public discourse has shifted with negative consequence for feminists, femocrats, and other equality-seeking groups who have been increasingly delegitimized in the policy-making arena.

In Chapter 7, Louise Chappell addresses what has been an important site for the engagement of transnational feminist activists. Specifically, in the context of developing the International Criminal Court, these activists attempted to establish an international definition of gender, urged the inclusion of forced pregnancy as a new crime in international law, and sought to address sexual violence in the family. This agenda, however, was contested by another transnational grouping consisting of Vatican representatives, political elites of certain Islamic states, and representatives of North American "pro-life" organizations. Chappell's analysis of the mixed outcome of this struggle highlights the need for the literature on transnational activism to consider more closely the role played by official state delegations in pursuing normative agendas at the international level, as well as the fact that what constitutes success for some actors may be the preservation of the status quo. Her analysis also draws attention to how the argument about a "clash of civilizations" is contradicted by the fact that conservatives in the West and the "Muslim world" share a desire to maintain control over women's bodies, and that, in contrast, there are both Muslims and Catholics who supported the goals articulated by the transnational women's movement.

Part 3 of the book more explicitly considers the connection between gender and citizenship, with specific, though not exclusive, attention to the Canadian context. In keeping with much recent feminist citizenship literature that discusses citizenship at levels other than simply the national, the analysts address multiple levels: from the personal to the local to the national and even the global. Reflecting on the long-standing tradition of addressing citizenship in relation to the welfare state, contributors in Part 3 are particularly concerned with understanding policy outcomes over time. However, far from presenting an evolutionary and teleological account in the tradition of Marshall, these assessments are concerned with understanding change; indeed, throughout the chapters there emerges a sense that the rights and participation attached to citizenship are not static, especially when it comes to the ideal of gender equity. Nonetheless, the nature of the theory used by the authors in Part 3 varies, giving rise to a lively debate over neoliberalism (and whether this is an adequate way of understanding social policy in Canada today) and bringing into sharper relief how citizenship (whether differentiated or not) shapes and is shaped by social relations.

Taken together, Chapters 8 and 9 present a debate around neoliberalism versus post-neoliberalism. Chapter 8, by Janine Brodie, echoes Marian Sawer's Chapter 6 assessment of Canada and Australia, agreeing that since the 1990s virtually all equality claims have been erased from the policy discourses and practices of the Canadian state. However, her chapter traces the reason for this primarily to the ascendancy of neoliberalism, which she suggests has created a state governing project that is markedly different from the post-war Keynesian welfare state. Reflecting directly on the Canadian context, and drawing on the comparative welfare state and citizenship literature, Brodie emphasizes that neoliberalism is both anti-statist and anti-social. The erasure of gender from the policy agenda in favour of a focus on individuals sits uneasily with what Brodie identifies as the increased feminization of poverty, growing stress levels among women who combine unpaid care work with paid labour, and a commodification of the work of caring that has intensified racial and class disparities between women. In light of the dominance of neoliberalism, Brodie issues a call for feminists to bring both the state and gender back in.

In Chapter 9, Jane Jenson continues the conversation around accounting for the disappearance of gender from the social policy sphere in Canada. Jenson introduces the idea of a "citizenship regime" both to describe the designated beneficiary of social policy and to underscore the relevance of accounting for change, in this case the change in Canada's social-spending patterns. Although social spending of the 1930s to the 1960s focused on the male worker, that from the 1960s to the 1980s concentrated on women and other marginalized groups, such as ethnic minorities. For Jenson, neo-liberalism has been a more momentary state response, with the period from the late 1990s effectively represents a post-neoliberal period characterized by new social spending and a new target. Specifically, in Canada the influence of a social investment perspective has provided a new rationale and logic encouraging directing monies to poor children. However, as Jenson notes, a citizenship regime with a child-centred definition of equality has as a consequence hidden the need for adult citizens to make claims on the state and to contest inequality.

In Chapter 10, Paul Kershaw draws on the logic of much of the feminist welfare state and citizenship literature, which has stressed how women experience citizenship differently precisely because of the sexual division of labour. Simultaneously, he turns on its head the logic of a citizenship duty to work that is advocated by conservative commentators. Noting that a central theme in feminist and welfare research is the need to transform the behaviour of men in relation to primary care work, his chapter outlines what Canadians might learn from the experiences of other countries, and how the state may utilize its power to encourage a more equitable distribution of child care work as one duty of citizenship.

Chapter 11, by Jackie F. Steele, takes up the continued existence of the institution of marriage to address the implications for citizenship of different marital naming policies in Quebec and the rest of Canada. She addresses how the liberal rhetoric of "choice" serves today to mask the old idea that women and their offspring are the property of male household heads, fragments of which remain in the marital naming laws in Canada outside Quebec. Drawing from mainstream philosophical discussions of liberty in liberalism and republicanism, Steele argues that, of the two, the republican tradition is more likely to promote laws that are in keeping with many feminist goals.

Part 3 concludes with Chapter 12, by Caroline Andrew, which is situated within a growing body of work, in response to globalization, that examines scales of political action. These scales of political action can operate at different levels – from the body, to the household, to the local, to the national, to the regional, and even to the global. Andrew therefore advocates the relevance of gendering the city-state as both part of and separate from gendering the nation-state. The gendering of the city-state in Canada illustrates the importance of women's urban citizenship. Using a case study of urban decision making and women's access to municipal services in Ottawa, Andrew underscores the potential that exists at the urban level for diverse groups of women to effect change. In a way not necessarily replicated at other levels, urban citizenship allows some greater possibilities for addressing equity issues stemming from the intersections of gender, ethnocultural diversity, immigration status, class, and age.

In examining the theoretical and empirical understandings advanced by gender analysis in the areas of the nation, the state, and citizenship, this work has clearly been invigorated by the work of feminist activists. Canadian scholars commonly see three different waves of feminist mobilization: the first, running from the late nineteenth to the early twentieth centuries, focused on formal political equality; the second, beginning in the 1960s, concentrated on eliminating sex discrimination and implementing equity in areas relating to employment; the third, emerging in the 1980s, concerned itself with multiple identities. In the Afterword to this volume, Judy Rebick addresses the recent history and trajectory of feminism, suggesting the ongoing need to engage with the state, but noting, as implied in the expression "the personal is political," that the sites of resistance are manifold. Rebick outlines struggles of the past and looks at the future of gender equality in light of the challenges, many described by authors in this volume, as well as the opportunities for resisting domination at personal, state, and global levels.

Rebick's contribution reminds us of the continuing reality of gender inequality in the family, the workplace, the street, and through the dominant culture. Given the reality of persisting gender inequities, it is critical that political science better attune itself to gender analysis and redress the disciplinary insufficiency. Although, admittedly, not all change necessarily requires engagement with the state, at the same time the state cannot be ignored. By examining the gendered and gendering nature of the nation-state, a concept so central to the discipline's core, political scientists, as this volume shows, can enrich our understanding of how many inequities are created, perpetuated, augmented, and even potentially undermined. There is a synergy between political science, interdisciplinary and multidisciplinary gender studies, and feminist praxis that has yet to be fully potentiated. This volume (re)affirms the relevance of mobilizing this synergy for political change and for the analysis, critique, and understanding of politics in the twenty-first century.

Part 1
Gender and Nation

1

Gendering the Hyphen: Gender Dimensions of Modern Nation-State Formation in Euro-American and Anti- and Post-colonial Contexts

Jill Vickers

Western feminists tend to view nationalism with suspicion, believing that "all nations are gendered, all are invented and all are dangerous ... representing relations to political power and to the technologies of violence" (McClintock, 1993: 61). Elsewhere, however, many women have combined feminist and national projects. Globally, nationalism mobilizes more women than any other form of politics (Bystydzienski, 1992). Moreover, women's participation in national liberation movements has often gained them citizenship simultaneously with men. In some cases the resulting gains for women were short-lived, but elsewhere they have been more long-lasting. In the large, powerful Western countries, most feminists consider states to be inherently male-dominated and oppressive; therefore, they believe that women who participate in them are co-opted or duped. Because "nations" are conflated into the modern nation-state form, they too are viewed as inherently male-dominated and linked to violence. Even in the West, some women achieved feminist goals by participating in national projects. Many women in Quebec, for example, believe feminist goals are best achieved this way, challenging the idea that nationalism is always bad for women. In Finland, organized women's active involvement in the struggle to gain freedom from Russia not only achieved their citizenship, but also let them "get in on the ground floor" of the new democracy, resulting in a more women-friendly state as a result (Vickers, 2006a, 2006b). Why does involvement in national projects have different consequences for women in different situations? How can women know when to avoid involvement and when to embrace it?

In this chapter, I explore the significance for women of the *hyphen* that joins "nation" (representing solidarity) to "state" (representing organized force). Nationhood is not just another dimension of identity politics; nor is nationalism just another social movement. Because nationalism and nationhood are central in creating and restructuring modern nation-states, exploring their gender aspects can help explain women's current relations with (or alienation from) political institutions and state politics. Women's experiences with nations and nationalisms range from positive alliances to alienation to exclusion. The key to gender/nation diversity lies in whether women participated in or were excluded (or alienated) from nation-state founding, and/or nation/state restructuring.[1] Where women organized themselves and participated in national movements to found or restructure nation-states, especially democracies, they could involve themselves in the initial development of political institutions. Given the *path-dependent* nature of such institutions, this early entry facilitated women's greater integration into state politics. Especially where women became a critical mass in state institutions, nation-states could become more women-friendly. Women could also influence the founding national discourses. Even where they did not experience early entry, being mobilized by national movements to restructure their nation-state could also provide opportunities for their integration. This chapter shows that nation-state making had different outcomes for women, depending in part on how a specific nation-state was formed. I explore gender/nation relations in two contexts: the first is that of the original Western nation-states, where the model of modernity was created; the second is that of post-colonial states, where modernizing national liberation movements often recruited women (Jayawardena, 1986). These are not the only contexts in which gender/nation relations differ (see Vickers, 2002), but I focus on them in this account.

Both nationalism and feminism are ideologies and movements able to mobilize women: when do they combine and why? In the first wave of modern nation-state making, in western European countries, they rarely combined, which resulted in a "long-standing tendency of Western feminism ... to reject nationalism as an emancipatory framework" (Jacoby, 1999: 513). This reflects (and supports) gender/nation relations in which feminism is detached from (even opposed to) national movements. Most Western women see feminism as a universalist ideology, one associated with pacifism and socialism. As a result, "women ... [seemed] to be more local, more global and less national in their political agendas than men" (Walby, 1997: 19). Those who affiliated with national projects were rare because "feminism and nationalism" were "almost always incompatible ideological positions" (Kaplan, 1997: 3).[2] In fact, Tami Jacoby (1999: 513) claims that "the merging of feminism and nationalism [is] ... a precise starting point for distinguishing nonwestern feminists from their Western counterparts." It was feminist scholars in (or from) post-colonial states (or encapsulated nations such as Quebec) who challenged the dominant Western feminist view that nationalism is always bad for women. In fact, comparative research shows that gender/nation relations vary *within* Western (colonial) and non-Western anti- and post-colonial contexts, as well as between them (Vickers

2006a). By comparing modern nation-state formation and restructuring in both contexts, I identify the gender dimensions of these two nation-state models as related to one another through colonialism.

Are francophone feminists in Quebec right in believing that their nation would be more woman-friendly if it had more autonomy? If women can open up space for feminist activism in some nationalist movements, why can't they in others? Why does women's nationalist activism only sometimes result in more women-friendly nation-states? To address this complex puzzle, the chapter has five parts: first, I outline my conceptual framework, providing key definitions; second, I explore some of the mainstream literature on nations and nationalism to show the limits of gender-blind theory; third, I make the case for gendered accounts of nation-state making and restructuring; fourth, I explore gender/nation relations in Western versus anti-colonial and/or post-colonial contexts; and fifth, I offer some preliminary theorizing of gender-nation relationships.

Conceptual Framework

National phenomena, in my conception, span public, communal, and domestic spheres. I explore how sex/gender regimes affect nation-state processes *and* how they are affected by national phenomena. I explore how sex/gender regimes and gender scripts shape nation-states and the nation-state system. I emphasize the path-dependent nature of political institutions and its effect on gender/state relations. I begin by providing definitions for these key concepts.

A *sex/gender regime* designates the norms and social practices that regulate sexual relations between men and women. Such regimes have two parts: *sex/gender arrangements* and *gender scripts.* The concept draws on Sylvia Walby's (1997) idea of a "gender regime," which she conceptualizes as different forms of patriarchy "in which men dominate, oppress and exploit women." This takes place within six structures: household production, paid work, the state, male violence, sexuality, and cultural institutions. "Patriarchal" here means systematic or institutionalized male dominance. I modify Walby's usage in three ways. First, though all the sex/gender regimes explored by Walby, and the examples discussed in this chapter, are patriarchal, I do not assume that all are of this type. If systematic male dominance were eliminated, some normative (agreed to) structures regulating relationships among people concerning sexuality, household, and reproduction would probably still exist; so I assume the theoretical possibility of non-patriarchal sex/gender regimes. Second, I conceptualize all institutions as composed of two parts – social structures and the ideas that legitimize them – so I distinguish between the gender scripts, or ideas that legitimize sex/gender practices, and the practices themselves. Third, I use *sex*/gender because there is more than one possible relationship between the bodily and discursive aspects of sex/gender, especially when modified by technology.[3] My usage is also influenced by R.W. Connell's (1990: 523) idea that each nation-state has a "gender regime" that is "the historically produced state of play in gender relations" or "the precipitate of [that institution or state's] social struggles" around gender relations. I understand states to be composed of multiple institutions in which gender regimes may vary. For example, a country's legislature could even have a majority of women representatives, while its military institutions remain male-dominated.

Nation is one of the most controversial terms in scholarship and politics. Scholars conflict over whether nations are products of European modernity or more enduring phenomena that existed previously.[4] Definitions of the modern state conflate nation with state because the two are so intertwined. But I understand *nations* to be entities that can exist apart from states, though they may also be the creations of states. For example, the Polish nation existed through long periods of partition among three foreign powers without a state of its own; Quebec has a quasi-state within Canada; and India is a nation constructed by its post-colonial state, the British imperial state, and partition. A simple common definition is not possible because nations played different roles at different stages in state formation, consolidation, and restructuring. The idea of "the nation" was appropriated by modern state elites as the focus of nationalist ideology in state and nation building, which aimed to create a single homogeneous culture within each state by making nation and state boundaries coincide. Roland Axtmann (2004: 260, emphasis added) believes that by the nineteenth century "the notion of the 'nation'-state came to stand for the idea that legitimate government could only be based upon the principle of national self-determination *and that state and nation ought to coincide*. The nation became understood as the 'unitary body within which sovereignty resided.'" But he notes that both nations and states pre-existed the invention of the modern nation-state form, although not all states were blessed with a pre-existing nation they could appropriate to consolidate their claims to rule. In many "civic" nation-states, which supposedly base citizenship within a territory on a shared relationship between citizens and state institutions, the dominant national culture infuses those institutions, likely alienating any minority nations subject to them. I understand nations to be political and cultural collectives of peoples *who consider themselves distinct* because of their history, language, destiny, origins, faith, and creations, and because of their association with specific territories.[5] They can exist apart from states, but modern states are also active creators of a common national identity (nationhood) and suppressors of the identities of any encapsulated minority nations.

Gendering the hyphen also involves how feminism was constructed and how it relates to nationalism. In the original Western countries, which also were colonial/imperial powers, feminism was a distinctive, modern emancipatory project. In many anti- and post-colonial contexts, and in minority and dominated nations in the West, however, feminism often became entwined with national liberation and nation building. Nationalism associated with modernizing anti-colonial national projects "empowered millions of women" (Bystydzienski, 1992: 20). Why were most Western feminists alienated from nationalism, whereas in anti- and post-colonial contexts feminism and nationalism often emerged together?[6] Nayrereh Tohidi (1993: 110) believes that Western feminism was unique because it developed in relation to industrial capitalism and representative democracy. She asserts that its capacity to sustain autonomous organizations resulted from the "fierce struggle [of Western feminists to] ... extend ... democratic and civil rights to the female part of the population." Although some Third World women reject feminism as a product of Western domination, others insist on its indigenous origins. For example, *feministas* combined campaigns for gender justice (including citizenship) with anti-colonial, nationalist activism in the Philippines from the late nineteenth century to the present day.[7] A similar context existed for women on the margins of the West. Finnish women combined feminist campaigns with the struggle to free their country from Russian rule. Half of Norway's women mobilized to vote in a woman's referendum regarding separation from Sweden (Vickers, 2006a, 2006b). In both the Third World and marginal Western contexts, feminism was associated with national liberation movements.

Finally, I understand political institutions to be path dependent. Once set up, they will follow the path established for them unless and until something powerful shifts them from it. Paul Pierson (2000, 2004) argues that this occurs because the collective action required to create institutions entails high setup costs, and that the longer people do things in a particular way, the greater the effort needed to change them. Institutions also tend to favour the power status quo. The structural arrangements come to seem natural, and a self-reinforcing feedback loop develops over time, creating a stable equilibrium. Gender regimes are part of institutional design, so getting in on the ground floor matters. If women are excluded when an institution is founded (or restructured), ideas legitimizing their exclusion will be incorporated into the feedback loop, making resistance to their subsequent entry especially strong. Consequently, by making exclusionary ideas an integral part of institutionalized state power, the path-dependent nature of state institutions solidifies gender regimes that deny women power and access to decision making and subsequently marginalize them, even after legal access is achieved.

The Limits of Gender-Blind Theory
Below, I explore the gender dimensions of modern nation-state formation in two contexts: the original (first-wave, Western) nation-states, and the

anti- and post-colonial nation-states that adopted the Western model of modernity, or had it imposed on them through colonialism. Many theorists believe the modern nation-state form originated with the French Revolution (Hall et al., 1996). But others see its origins much earlier, in the centralization of states by monarchies and in the centuries-long development of a stable nationhood (Canovan, 1996). Erica Benner (2001) explains its origins in the international system of relationships that developed in western Europe in early modernity and was then extrapolated worldwide. Misolav Hroch (1993) identifies a number of different ways in which nations became fused with states, even in Europe. I have explored how this diversity affected gender/nation relations (Vickers, 2002, 2006a). In the original nation-states, the modern state model entailed excluding women from the state as citizens, as bearers of civil rights, and as owners of property. They remained excluded for at least a century – from the French and American Revolutions and the Great Reform Act (1832) into the twentieth century. This launched nation-state institutions and processes of purported democratization from which women were excluded. Moreover, because of their path-dependent nature, these nation-state institutions often still marginalize most women, since male dominance was built into institutional designs.

Can we relate this model of the original modern nation-states to the concept of "the West"? My concept of the West is not so much geographic as in terms of countries that share a paradigm for organizing society and legitimizing political power (Vickers, 2006a). As Saud Joseph (1997: 75) points out, the West is characterized, in part, by the idea of a "public/private divide" that "serves as an enabling metaphor" along with "other state-elaborated notions of boundary," the individualized citizen, the social and sexual contract, citizen rights, civil society, and democracy. For example, the original Western states used discourses about citizenship that justified excluding women from exercising public power, and from the power of property, by restricting the power of kinship in politics and attempting to limit potentially influential women to the new private family. The gendered private/public divide also delegitimized dynastic and extended-family claims in the public realm. Mainstream theorists of nationalism also stress the effects of removing religion as the main legitimizer of Western political rule (see, for example, Anderson, 1991). So, in theory, the Western, modern paradigm represented the victory of secular states over competing ways of organizing and legitimizing state power based on kinship and religion. In practice, the goal was to remove religious (sectarian) conflict from politics, mainly by removing the sway of religious authority from modern governments. Alternatively, the goal also could be achieved by requiring all citizens to adopt the monarch's faith, by setting up a new state church headed by the monarch, by removing all marks of religion from the public sphere ("secularization"), or by "pillarization," in which all the religions recognized by the state had their own public institutions. But religion continued to be a force in politics, especially in laws governing women's lives and personal status. Countries that developed this paradigm most fully were among the most successful colonial powers.[8]

The new international system spread these state characteristics, although not all states discarded kinship or religion from their governments. Many "modernizing" elites tried to impose the paradigm but often were only partly successful. Often, "personal status" arrangements governing marriage, divorce, inheritance, adoption, financial support of wives, sexual relations, and reproduction were not subject to state regulation in new post-colonial countries and remained governed by religious authorities in some. Exploring the extent to which the classic paradigm of Western modernity was adopted or imposed, therefore, is one important way of understanding why gender/nation relations vary. To the extent that anti-colonial nationalism involved a strand that valorized tradition, elites seeking national liberation frequently differed on the acceptability of this aspect of the modern, or Western, paradigm.

In the original modern nation-states, women were denied political and civil rights, but middle- and upper-class women took on new roles as "citizen-mothers" (Vickers, 2003) or "republican-mothers" (Kerber, 1980). Women were expected to reproduce the nation in the family, and these new ideologies valorized their roles within families and legitimized their exclusion. Nationality, substituting for religion and kinship to legitimize and organize political power, freed up individualized men for a market economy. Male economic elites used the new nation-states to expand markets and to consolidate power and profit through nation-building, colonial, and imperial projects. Women lost status, economic independence based on property ownership or guild membership, and political power. Although less privileged women continued to work for wages, married women lost control of property, including their own wages. By contrast, in many post-colonial countries, women and men became citizens simultaneously (Jayawardena, 1986), and women's participation in national movements often gained them civil and property rights in the new states. In some cases, elite women were also recruited for nation building; however, some feminists doubt that nationalist feminism can succeed in the long term, because it is often frustrated by the tendency of male nationalists to take advantage of women's mobilizations around national projects, only to delay or abandon feminist projects after national liberation is achieved (Herr, 2003). Others (such as Moghadam, 1994) believe that changes in both nationalisms (increasingly anti-modern and revivalist) and feminisms make it unlikely for an alliance that was productive for many women a century ago to succeed in the current conjunction. In both Western and post-colonial contexts, however, women were expected to reproduce citizens and collective identities, and to mediate between traditional values associated with the nation (including language and religious values) and modern norms associated with the state and market economy.[9] In some anti-colonial and marginal Euro-American countries, such as Finland, however, women were already organized and able to use their alliances with national liberation causes to promote more women-friendly nation-states.

First-wave nation-state making followed a new path that was theorized as universal and normative in gender-blind modernist accounts. The original modern nation-state form actually emerged before nationalist *ideology and movements,* built on existing stable nationhood and centralized states (Canovan, 1996). The sex/gender regime based on women's political exclusion became part of the model that others then imitated, or had imposed on them. Euro-American women were also expected to bridge the public/private split that characterized the model by mediating between tradition and faith at home and modern, rational secularism in the public sphere. This constrained women's choices and agency but became an ideal promoted around the world concerning how modern women should live and behave. An elaborate ideological system developed in the "cult of true womanhood," which valorized women's spirituality and (unpaid) domestic work.

To explain women's diverse experiences with national phenomena, we need a *gendered* analysis of how nation-states emerged. Some countries invented the modern nation-state model; others imitated it or had it imposed on them. The gender implications of each context differed: women were privatized and denied participation for a century or more in the original Western nation-states, whereas they often participated, and sometimes were allies, where societies joined together to liberate themselves from foreign rule. Context also affected democratization and the creation or restructuring of (path-dependent) political institutions. In the first context, women were citizens solely through their physical and cultural reproductive activities and came to resist the constraints this imposed; in the second, they often gained citizenship when men did and could sometimes promote their goals as women within national projects. Where militarism was involved, however, women's opportunity for agency was usually more limited. Through the concept of gendering the hyphen, therefore, we can explore how the roles women played in creating and restructuring nation-states differed and how they were the same.

Gendering Accounts of Nations and Nationalism

The diversity of women's experiences with nation-states poses a tough theoretical challenge because feminist ideas, objectives, and strategies are intertwined with different socioeconomic, cultural, and political conditions in different parts of the world. Even within each country the experiences of majority-culture and minority-culture women differ. Anthony D. Smith

(1998: 210) believes that "gender-nation theories" must "provide a more comprehensive causal analysis of [how] the complex interrelations of gender and nation contribute to the formation of nations and the spread and intensity of nationalism." By addressing how "the complex interrelations between gender and nation" contribute to the formation and restructuring of nation-states, I propose to insert gender into mainstream theories of nations and nationalism, while also demonstrating their importance for feminist scholarship. Many sociological accounts of "modern" society consider gender arrangements in which men are the breadwinners and mothers remain home to be functional. Although mainstream theorists of nationalism rarely include gender as a category of analysis, most assume that this model is natural. Moreover, this aspect of the model of modernity played a key role in creating and maintaining nation-states by legitimizing the privatizing of kinship. Modern nation-states sought to control how women reproduced national identity (including language and religion) by socializing their children and promoting identity through food, dress, music, crafts, and festivals. Privileged majority-culture women's activity in their communities sustained collective identities and, through their charity and other "good works," mediated between traditional/religious values and modern values of state and market. Women loyal to minority nations within modern state territories, however, can undermine the national identities created by states and promoted by schools, the media, and so on. Instead, they can reproduce minority identities or ethnicities, even helping politicized nations persist.

The nation itself mediates between modern and traditional, secular and spiritual (Canovan, 1996; Chatterjee, 1986, 1989; Nairn, 1974, 1977). Partha Chatterjee (1989) believes affluent Indian women were mobilized by nationalists in part to perform the work of mediation he believes was essential to adapting nationalism as an ideology to an anti-colonial project. In Margaret Canovan's (1996) terms, women became the shock absorbers when values clashed in modernization. Women's dual roles as citizens (once they achieved political citizenship) and as mothers/wives/daughters in their families, as structured by marriage laws and the demands of kinship, are a constant in how women participate in making and remaking nation-states. Even women's work outside the family changes this very little unless women earn enough to buy care work from other women to replace their own. Western and post-colonial nation-state making involved parallel processes. Affluent women were assigned to affective domestic roles. But in anti-colonial movements, women also had to symbolize modernity in the public sphere to demonstrate their country's worthiness for independence because colonial rulers claimed that their rule was justified because traditional indigenous societies oppressed their women. They were to be educated and modern "new women" at school or work, but – like Western women

– they were also expected to preserve domestic traditions (including male dominance) and spiritual values at home. In both contexts, market and state were to be secular and rational, but the family was to be a haven where children, elders, the sick, and men received women's care. Women were to provide the emotion and charity drained from the efficient, rational, and impersonal public sphere and economy. Their unpaid care work in the family (and poorly paid care work for others in public institutions subsequently) made modern nation-states function. In both contexts, privileged men and women shared an ideal of companionate marriage that represented the new conjugal relationship associated with Western modernity. Rejecting the idea that most women mobilized by nationalism were merely tools of male political ambitions, Aparna Basu (2000: 168) concludes that "most women joined the [Indian] freedom struggle because ... they were inspired by nationalist ideas and wanted to see the end of foreign rule." Although only a minority of the female population became involved, "nationalism became a permitted area for women's participation" (167); their participation gained the women citizenship rights that nationalist leaders promised (and delivered) on independence.

The dominant explanation of nations and nationalism in both contexts is modernist. Smith (1998: 224) asserts that "modernists ... derive both nations and nationalism from the novel processes of modernisation, ... [and] show how states, nations and nationalism, and notably their elites, ... mobilized and united populations in novel ways to cope with modern conditions." For Smith, "modern conditions" are those necessary for rationalized economies and societies, including the homogeneous culture modernists believe industrialism requires. Most modernists believe that nations are *created by* nationalism or "imagined" by elites. Anthony D. Smith (1991: 4), the only major Western scholar of nations and nationalism to address gender, considers it the most difficult aspect of human identity around which to create collective mobilization because women are "geographically separated, divided by class and ethnically fragmented." Consequently, Smith believes, if one is "to inspire collective consciousness and action," gender cleavages "must be allied to ... more cohesive identities," such as nationalism. Other modernist theories ignore sex/gender regimes altogether, reflecting either the view that the impact of modern nation-states is the same for men and women or that gender has no impact. The exclusion of women as active citizens, bearers of rights, and owners of property clearly had a profound impact on the original nation-state model, however much women's loss of political and economic power was dressed up with ideological redefinitions of motherhood and family. By excluding the female half of a country's potential citizens, state elites could more easily control nation-state building and restructurings such as democratization (franchise expansions).

Were women even considered part of the nation in the original modernist model? Liah Greenfeld (1992), writing about the "roads to modernity" in five such countries, argues that national*ism* came to exist only when *most of a country's population* identified with "the nation," which she believes first occurred in sixteenth-century England. Did women identify with the nation, despite being excluded from citizenship, rights, and property ownership? Functionalist theory associates women with modern society's expressive or affective needs (emotions), but Greenfeld doesn't see families as sites where, as I have argued, nations are made or survive.[10] Modernists think "the nation" signifies *those who consent to political rule,* which would seem to exclude women as long as they were denied civil, economic, and citizenship rights. In France, for example, women were denied the vote for 155 years after the revolution; the model modern nation-state operated for 156 years before a single woman was ever elected. Walker Connor (1994: 98-9) believes the enfranchisement of "most" of the population, *explicitly including women,* was necessary before a country became a nation-state, which would deny France nationhood before 1945. Smith rejects Connor's thesis, but does not follow his own logic to its (gendered) conclusion. In the original Western nation-states, the concept that "the people" were to provide democratic legitimation through consent excluded women for many generations. Except in some marginal Western countries such as Finland and Norway, women were not involved in the genesis of state institutions. As a result, the discourses that for many years had been used to legitimize their exclusion continued to bar their participation long after they gained legal rights. (Note that I am not addressing the white settler colonial state context here.)

Although Greenfeld's analysis never explicitly considers whether women were members of the nation, her characterization of "modernity" sheds light on the question. She theorizes three features of modern societies, those relating to class, state, and growth. Greenfeld (2000: 39) asserts that modern nations have an "open system of stratification referred to as class structure" in which the *individual* is the bearer of status, *transferable resources* such as wealth and education are its basis, and *social mobility* occurs. By contrast, she describes "non-modern nation-states," which she associates with "traditional societies," as characterized by a "rigid family form," a "non-transferable resource-based stratification," and a situation in which "social mobility is an abnormality." Greenfeld believes that a "modern" society requires a "modern family form" in which *individuals* are divorced from religious and family identities and destinies, and must make their own destiny. Imbued with social ambition, they compete for status, power, and resources since achievement, not ascription, locates them. Greenfeld (41, emphasis added) concludes that "as a result [of the principle of equality of membership in the nation] the individual becomes independent from the group in which he *or she* is born, and status, necessarily [becomes] separated from ascriptive group-characteristics." Despite Greenfeld's politically correct "or she," women continued to be ascribed gender-specific roles through marriage laws, even when freed from their birth family by the modern sex/gender regime. Women were not allowed to be competitors for status or for economic or political power, as she describes, until long after the original nation-states were founded and their model of modernity created, except in the final years of the old order when high-born women still commanded some political and economic power. Western modernity subjected all married women to gender ascription. And currently, even after most legal inequalities have ended, a majority of Western women still perform domestic and reproductive roles without pay and mediate in many ways between private and public to stabilize nation-states. Women cannot be "individuals" in the modern, Western sense as long as their sex assigns them to gendered roles and unpaid (or poorly paid) care work, even after they became legally free to compete. Women were eventually incorporated as individuals in the competitive modern world, but many still find it hard to overcome the effects of these gendered roles and tasks and the biases in public institutions against women's participation that stem from the long exclusion of their sex from public affairs.

Greenfeld believes that nationalism *created* modern states (not the reverse). This is key because it makes the national principle (of equal membership of citizens) central to the concept of popular sovereignty, a concept upon which the legitimacy of the impersonal, abstract, and legal-rational powers of modern states rests. Eventually, Western women, especially the most privileged, benefited from the nation-state's internal stability, solidarity, and economic growth, and from colonial exploitation, through longer lives, reduced mortality due to childbirth, greater access to education and self-development, greater capacity for self-organization, work in the helping professions, and eventually citizenship and rights. However, excluded from the abstract, "rational" world of power and administration, and from owning property, women remained associated with care work and with the empathy and emotion removed from the public sphere, rather than with states, citizenship, and power. Greenfeld also sees economic growth and competition among nation-states as essential aspects of modernity, replacing ethics, emotion and kinship-based obligations in political and economic relationships. But women still mediated between the economic rationality of capitalism and traditional obligations to care for kin. Increasingly, they also worked as volunteers outside their homes, providing charity to those without family support. The value of this work done without monetary cost also contributed to the success of these Western nation-states, at women's expense. Even in international relations, many women played the role of peacemakers acting against wars they considered male in origin.

Feminist scholars believe that nations and nationalism are gendered. But because nations and nationalism have a propensity for violence and exclusion, many in the West see them as part of institutionalized male dominance and dismiss variations in gender/nation relations as irrelevant. However, Floya Anthias and Nira Yuval-Davis (1989: 87) focused attention on women's roles in reproducing ethnic and national projects as biological reproducers, reproducers of boundaries between ethnic/national groups, ideological reproducers and transmitters of culture, signifiers of ethnic/ national differences, and participants in national, economic, political, and military struggles. While they concentrate mainly on ideological phenomena, others focus more on the political dimensions. V. Spike Peterson (1999), L. Pauline Rankin (2000), and others also maintain that nationalism legitimizes compulsory heterosexuality by mandating heterosexual marriage and valorizing motherhood as women's contribution to nation making – indeed, as their only respectable role. Another charge is that nationalists, whom feminists assume are always pro-natal, value women only for their reproductive capacity, which they try to control.

These critiques help illuminate why women's relations with nation-states and nationalist movements vary. As the modern nation-state became the main focus for political mobilization, Western women were increasingly excluded from the public realm. Although less affluent women continued to work for wages, those who previously wielded the power of property were denied this form of economic power. Axtmann (2004: 260-61) believes "the success of the modern nation-state ... rested on acceptance of its claim to be able to guarantee the physical security, the economic well-being, and the cultural identity of its citizens." But the modern nation-state did *not* "guarantee physical security" to women and children (McClintock, 1993: 61).[11] Although it claimed a monopoly on the legitimate use of force, until very recently it did not use it to provide security for women (or children or elders) by "interfering" in violent relationships in the home, at school, or at work. Private "disciplining" of women and children by their male guardians was sanctioned by law. The new nation-state form of government did deliver the security to foster economic development, from which privileged women gained, but it would not use its power to protect women. Excluding women from citizenship and property ownership made it possible for governments to negatively affect them (and to tax them) while simultaneously ensuring that women could not hold them accountable.

This new nation-state model was spread widely through imitation and colonialism; it was also legitimized by theories of popular sovereignty based in "the nation" and eventually by democracy itself (Benner, 2001). Governments were seen as legitimate to the extent that they effectively represented "the nation" and could therefore claim to act according to the will of the people. Theories developed to legitimize women's exclusion were built on Enlightenment ideas borrowed from ancient Greece. Early democratization often acted against women, as it did when laws that expanded the franchise to new groups of men explicitly denied the vote to all women. Gendered accounts of recent democratization waves are revealing: "Evidence drawn from ... around the globe suggests that *democratization* produces gendered redistributions of resources and responsibilities that *make women worse off*" (Hawkesworth, 2001: 223-24, emphasis added). For example, as they virtually disappeared from decision making, women in eastern Europe were *re-privatized*, lost access to public child care, and often lost reproductive rights. They were "drastically underrepresented" in decision making in the new "modern democracies."[12] The first wave of nation-state making and the eventual transition to democracy of the original modern nation-states took several centuries to complete, blurring our perception of its effects on women. Nonetheless, we do know that women's loss of public, civic, and property rights was not an accidental feature of nation-state making and consolidation, but actually central to it. Moreover, the first wave of democratization, in which these states were restructured, had women's struggles for citizenship at its core. Only when women started to use their citizenship did feminists begin to see the modern public/private divide as a problem for women everywhere.

Western versus Colonized/Post-colonial Gender/Nation Experiences

Perceiving the public/private divide as "central to classical western constructions of citizenship and nation/statehood," Saud Joseph (1997: 73) criticizes the tendency of Western feminists to universalize their preoccupation with it. In addition, she does not believe that opposing this divide typifies women's struggles everywhere. For example, nation-state building in Lebanon involved both kinship-based and patriarchal power relations, since kinship structures the government, the domestic sphere, and the non-governmental sphere of associations and the economy. Although a private/public divide is a central concept for a gendered understanding of modern nation-states in the West, Joseph believes the dichotomy between "kinship" and the "state" is much less relevant in many post-colonial countries. She theorizes that the private/public divide is about competing forms of power, which are segregated in the West. In Western, republican theory, state power in Western state theory is envisioned as abstract, secular, and neutral, legitimized by the national principle (and later by democracy) but with no basis in either kinship (dynasty) or religion. By contrast, pre-modern political power relations were legitimized by some combination of faith and (usually patriarchal) kinship. Joseph believes that for legitimization many post-colonial states continue to depend, in whole or in part, on some combination of kinship and religion(s) (often intertwined with ideology). In Lebanon, kinship remains "central to all spheres of social activity": because of the weakness of the state, "Lebanese citizens ... experience ... kin as the anchor of their security" (79).

If the state cannot or will not protect you or advance your interests, you must rely on kin or extended kin. Lebanese politicians use kinship ties to mobilize relatives or themselves into political office; and women holding office typically do so because of kinship ties. (Indeed, the continuing saliency of kinship or dynastic ties in many post-colonial countries helps explain why there are more women leaders in Asia, for example, than there are in the West.) Citizens in Lebanon expect their rights and access to resources to depend on kinship. Moreover, family law is the responsibility of eighteen recognized religious sects, which means that women's relationships to the state are mediated by kinship and monitored by religious authorities. In many post-colonial states, only some sectors of state activity in the original Western model are directly administered by the state. As in Lebanon, personal status issues, central to women's lives, are governed by religious and/or communal authorities, not by the state directly. In other cases, states elevate religious rules about personal status and women's dress and behaviour to public law, becoming the enforcing arm of religious authorities. Such states are often described by Western scholars as deficient or "soft" because non-state associations remain authoritative in some spheres of life, and state power to govern is incomplete.

The Western, modernist state model cannot explain women's relations with nation-states in all countries. Yet the model is considered universally valid. As Elisa P. Reis (2004: 252, emphasis added) observes, "The amalgamation of nation and state that originally took place in western Europe ... came to constitute the 'normal' way of organizing society ... Though nations and states are far older phenomena, it is only in the past two centuries that the fusion of the two *came to acquire the status of being the normal way of relating state and society* ..., a process that has meant that citizenship itself has come to be seen as the offspring of this marriage between authority and solidarity ... consolidating a politicized social identity along territorial lines." The modern nation-state model was spread from Europe through the international system. The actual marriage between authority and solidarity *within* each nation-state takes different forms, however; and the extent to which there is a private/public divide, as well as the form it takes, varies. The different models had different consequences for women. The original Western model incorporated early liberalism, conventional warfare, and bureaucracy. Whether a republican or a liberal model of citizenship was adopted, women's mothering and child-rearing roles were the basis of a passive form of citizenship, one with duties but without political, property, or most civil rights.[13] Even when these original nation-states were restructured and rights were granted to women, their family roles and exclusion from military power and state decision making limited the effectiveness of their citizenship (Walby, 1997). These original nation-states directly controlled sex/gender relations, limiting the role of kinship to the domestic sphere and substituting nationalism for religion as the main legitimizer of political rule. These powerful secular states exercised control over most personal status issues.

The national liberation movements in many decolonization struggles recruited women against colonial oppression. In the new post-colonial nation-states, women were usually granted citizenship along with men. In imitation of the Western model, modernizing elites often struggled to establish fully secular states and limit traditional authorities. But most national liberation movements also contained elements opposed to Western-style modernity and eager to revive or preserve tradition as well. Some post-colonial states combined modern state power over security and the economy, for example, with religiously sanctioned or dynastic power. As in Lebanon, they often excluded personal status issues from state control, or elevated the rules of religious codes to the status of public law.[14] However, the failure of many modern post-colonial states to deliver economic growth or security promoted more explicitly anti-modern nationalisms. Their fusion of faith and nationalism created new anti-Western movements in which the space for women to be citizens varied. But the established sex/gender regimes make women's dress and behaviour a matter of conflict between modernizing and anti-modern elites and religious authorities (Moghadam, 1994). Predominantly anti-modern post-colonial state nationalisms reject liberal rights, a secular state, and a private/public divide. Outside of the family, women are segregated or hidden from men and must conform to state/ religious norms. Although such states adopt some aspects of modern development (such as industrialization and technology), they valorize women's purity and subordinate them to national honour and patriarchal control.

Joseph's (1997) insight that nation-state founding involved competition between modernizing elites who were eager to establish modern secular states and traditional elites who were empowered by religion and/or kinship to oppose such secularization is useful here. Polities with strong modern-style states imposed secular rule by promoting a common national identity, subordinating divisive religious and kinship loyalties, and insulating the new "public sphere" from their influence. In this Western model, the public sphere is "the domain of the 'modernized,' homogenized, the universal, in which individualized citizens are [supposed to be] divested of particularistic status. It is the site ... in which national subjects have become standardized, interchangeable with one another, the industrial model of citizenship" (Joseph, 1997: 85). Initially, women were seen as differing from men and were relegated to the particularistic. They were not citizens, in part because they were not interchangeable with men. Joseph explains: "The domestic becomes the realm of the specific, of the sub national, racial, ethnic, religious, tribal, linguistic and familial differences ... the realm of diversity." That which particularizes women would gender citizenship. Women were to devote themselves to religious, kinship, and communal roles from within their families.

Many feminists see nations and nationalisms as purely masculine projects.[15] Indeed, official nationalisms created by states generally are. Yet women are involved in national movements to found and restructure nation-states in important ways. Nira Yuval-Davis (1997) believes gender is always "nationed," just as nations and nationalisms are always gendered. Regardless of which model of the state is in place, women's citizenship "is usually of a dual nature: ... they are included in the general body of citizens, [but] ... there are always rules and regulations and policies which are specific to them" (21). Laws and customs regulating marriage often construct women as inferior, dependent, and subject to men, even when legally they are equal citizens. In some national movements, women promote visions of the nation that include them as equal partners. But often, when the national project is won, they are forgotten and their goals are deferred or rejected (Moghadam, 1994). How can this variability be explained?

Theorizing Variability

Why do women have varied experiences with national projects? In core Western nation-states, women were simultaneously excluded from citizenship and alienated from national projects, but because of the successes of their nation-states, they gained materially with longer lifespans, increased literacy, and work opportunities beyond marriage. How did women's privatization contribute to the success of Western nation-states? Glenda Sluga (1998) argues that differentiation between men's and women's citizenship was *an essential feature* of European nationalisms and nation-states, a pattern I also found evident in many countries in the Americas. Why was this pattern not imitated in most anti- and post-colonial countries? Why women in much of the global South were mobilized by national projects has been little explored. When states such as Yugoslavia failed, and nationalism was blamed for rape camps and ethnic cleansing, this promoted the belief that nationalism is always bad for women. Feminists in post-imperial Western nation-states are especially hostile to nationalism. Led by Kumari Jayawardena (1986), however, many non-Western feminists argue that many Asian and some Middle Eastern women achieved legal rights, citizenship, and education by participating in *modernizing* anti-colonial national struggles. But Western scholars question whether the participants were "really feminist" and whether the results persisted after independence.[16]

Literature about national liberation struggles also challenges anti-nationalist views. Extrapolating from his (erroneous) predictions regarding how Algerians would come to terms with French-imposed "modernity," Franz Fanon

(1963, 1967) theorized that relationships between women and anti-colonial nation making went through three stages. Others believe *all* anti-colonial nationalisms and gender/nation relations combine elements of modernity and anti-modernity. Chatterjee (1986, 1989) argues exactly this regarding women's roles in India's anti-colonial struggles. Although they did gain citizenship and access to education and employment, at home women are still expected to be defenders of the traditions that nationalists believe embody India's spiritual superiority to the West. Valentine Moghadam (1994) suggests that changes in the nature of both nationalism and feminism, occurring since the period of the positive alliances described by Jayawardena, have reduced opportunities for further productive engagement. Disillusionment with modernization and with Western feminism's promotion of anti-natal, anti-family projects focused on sexual liberation weakened the link in the global South. Increasingly, anti-modern nationalisms focused on women's behaviour, dress, and bodies to express their hostility to Western modernity.[17]

Feminisms differ regarding whether

- gender conflict is the primary motor of women's politics;
- the family is an appropriate site for politics or solely one of oppression;
- women's maternal/nurturing roles should be a basis for politics;
- feminism is complete as a politics and as an emancipatory framework;
- women's agency can flourish in mixed-sex or male-led movements;
- male dominance and female power are a zero-sum game or can coexist.

Some versions of feminism, therefore, are more compatible than others with particular nationalisms. Nationalisms are multilayered and change over time, especially as the solidarity of anti-colonial struggles for independence fades and they become official and state produced. Organized women's relationships with national projects take at least ten different forms and change over time within each country (Vickers 2002, 2006a). Thus, there is *no single or essential relationship* between gender and nations, or between women and nationalism. Consequently, we need to understand how political and economic forces and ideas shape women's gender consciousness, their capacity for self-organization, and their relationships with national projects. Or, as Mary O'Brien (1981) has theorized, is there a separate dialectic of sex/gender changes related to reproductive consciousness and technologies?

There is growing evidence that transitions such as democratization, industrialization, and market liberalization; nation-state formation, partition, expansion, restructuring, and failure; colonialism, neo-colonialism, imperialism, and their demise; and militarization and war all affect sex/gender regimes. To theorize why gender/nation relationships vary, I draw on Walby's (1997) idea that "gender transformations" occur during the "rounds of restructuring" of nation-states that such transitions promote. This produces two main axes for variability: first, organized women's relationships with national phenomena may vary in a country over time; second, they may vary because of a country's location in the international political economy and colonial/neo-colonial or imperial power structures. Within any given country, minority national projects, including struggles for independence or more autonomy, may also involve gender/nation relations that differ from those of the country's dominant nation. Like Yuval-Davis, Anne McClintock (1993: 65) theorizes that a "woman's political relation to the nation was submerged as a social relation to a man through marriage ... so [her] citizenship ... was mediated by the marriage relationship within the family." In core Western nation-states, women's early passive citizenship was expressed only from within the domestic sphere. More recently, women experienced the conflict of being legally equal in one relationship but legally subordinate in another. This conflict is also manifested in women's participation in the making and restructuring of nation-states.

Women's mediations between modernity and the stability of the traditional, which anchors people to the past despite rapid change, may be a *common element* in the midst of much variability in gender/nation relations. If women didn't absorb the shocks and minimize the conflicts, modernization would be an even more disruptive process than it is, making changes in the nation-state form more destabilizing. Women's work as shock absorbers for modernization, however, involves high costs and disadvantages against which feminists have reacted. Western feminists also resisted gender scripts that justified the exclusion of women from the public sphere through a state-sustained public/private split and pro-natalist policies requiring them to have more children than they wished (Kaplan, 1997). Western feminists believe nationalisms and nation-states to be dangerous because they maintain male dominance, prosecute war, and further colonial and neo-colonial domination. Women who see feminism as universalistic and pacifist reject being implicated in such projects. But those who achieve emancipation as a result of being allied with national projects, both within the West and beyond, have other experiences – some involving violence – and different views.

Contexts Shape Gender/Nation Relationships

Anti-colonial writers note how imperialists targeted colonized women when they were consolidating imperial rule because women were important as reproducers of the language, faith, and collective identity, on which anti-colonial resistance could be based. Fanon (quoted in McClintock, 1996: 268) claimed that "to destroy the structure of Algerian society [and] its capacity for resistance," the colonizers recognized that they "must first ... conquer the women." Men of the dominated nation were displaced from the public sphere and replaced by male colonizers: *men and women experienced colonialism differently.* Although resistance was shared, women's roles in resistance were more complex than those of men. Colonial rule required control of women, who could reproduce indigenous languages, faiths, and identities; controlling women was key to disrupting or preserving national identities and the solidarities on which both modernization and resistance to colonialism were based. Colonized women were targeted for "liberation" from the oppression that colonizers attributed to indigenous cultures and faiths to disrupt resistance and prevent their reproduction. Some Western feminists among the colonizers joined the "liberation" project, although others rejected colonialism. Fanon observed that the French "rescued" Algerian women from "backward customs" by assimilating them into the modern European sector. But colonial rule also involved sexual domination of colonized women. Anti-colonial nationalists expected "their" women to support independence while also accepting the "traditional" identities some postcolonial elites would try to impose to restore cultural authenticity lost during colonial rule. In both cases, women were key to creating the solidarities needed to support political change. Creating stable nation-states, imposing colonial rule, or successfully struggling against it all required the mobilization of women, either in cooperation with male elites or controlled by them.

Nationhood and Women's Work of Mediation

Why are women so central to the processes of nation-state making, colonial domination, and successfully liberating a colonized country? Canovan (1996) observes that although nationalism is common, *nationhood* is quite rare. She believes that Western political theorists ignored nations and nationalism because they lived in countries where stable nationhood already existed before modern nation-states emerged, so they took them for granted. Countries with nationalist movements were those that had not developed nationhood before the nation-state system emerged. Those who built modern states on the basis of pre-existing nationhood had a strategic advantage, to which women contributed by mediating between modern and traditional values. Gendering the hyphen, then, may represent an advantage conferred by the sex/gender regime embedded in the Western nation-state model; it may help explain why the core Euro-American nation-states, which had the advantage of pre-existing nationhood, were so successful in modernization and especially in colonial ventures.

Canovan (1996) believes nationhood mediates between individual and universal, familial and political. Nairn (1977: 101) sees the nation as "the modern Janus," with one face looking back to timeless tradition, the other to the future. But the roles women play in mediating between tradition and modernity in their lives, and their families, are more complex than this image suggests. Writing about Turkey, Kandiyoti (1991: 431) sees nationalism in both anti- and post-colonial eras primarily *as a modern project that dissolves traditional identities and loyalties,* constructing new ones from a supposedly shared past. But in the case of Turkey, women are represented as traditional, embodying continuity with the past, in their bodies, lives, and values, whereas Turkish men represent all that is modern. Nonetheless, women must bridge the two worlds by abandoning traditional dress as dictated by law under Ataturk and becoming citizens along with men, even while still embodying continuity with the past. But this script was only for women of the dominant Turkish nation; Kurdish women (and men) were forced by law to abandon traditional dress and language. McClintock (1996) believes nationalism confers on women a timeless ahistorical nature, whereas men represent progress and change. In fact, much imperialist discourse portrayed *all* colonized people as stuck in timeless tradition, which was why Indian nationalists presented "their" women as modern to justify independence (Chatterjee, 1986). At the same time, Indian women were expected to perpetuate tradition and promote India's superior spiritual values in their homes. And though nationalists promoted education for women, most resisted changes in their own homes. Although what women are expected to represent differs, they are always expected to bridge modernity and tradition, despite the fact that what is perceived as traditional also changes. This is the theoretical essence of the hyphen.

Nations embody authority and community, which modern state-making elites appropriate to legitimize state power with the fiction of consent. The fiction that state elites ruled on behalf of the people preceded democratization. To capture the nation, state-making elites either appropriated a preexisting nation's cultural authority or created a new nationality by drawing on themes from the past of the dominant ethnic group. The legitimacy thus achieved was at risk, however, every time a nation-state was restructured, so successful states needed stable *nationhood,* the content of which, ironically, had to change over time, although the distinctive identity itself does not. Debates about nations always involve dichotomies: Is the nation a state? Or is it a community held together by language and culture? Is it constituted by birth? Or by choice? Is it a politicized version of ethnicity? Of individual or collective identity? Are nations natural or artificial? Are they ancient entities or the recent products of modernization? Canovan (1996: 69, 74) believes nationhood actually mediates, links, contains within itself, and holds together these apparent contradictions. She maintains that "a nation is a polity that feels like a community." It is "a contingent historic product that feels like part of ... nature." "It links individual and community, past and present," and "turns political institutions into a kind of extended family." The nation is both modern and timeless; it makes "a polity ... seem like the family inheritance of an entire population." Stable nationhood requires "mediation between state and community."

In the Western nation-state model, women's mediation was primarily between modern values and norms in the state and economy, and trad-itional (religious, kinship) values in the families and churches. Long after their legal enfranchisement, women still perform aspects of this mediation, which marginalizes them politically and economically. In nations without states (Guibernau, 1999) that are aspiring to autonomy or independence, women's roles in creating/re-creating and sustaining alternative collective identities are important. Women symbolize nations in their dress and be-haviour; but they also produce/reproduce nations in everyday life. Why does the gendered hyphen keep women's citizenship second-class and mar-ginal? A nation mediates among the people subject to a state, but how does it actually link them together? Most mainstream theorists stress the roles of media, intellectuals, and schools. But what women do at home, in their religious institutions, and in their face-to-face communities *as a minimum* reproduces identities originating in the public sphere. Sometimes women are merely conduits for transmitting state- or male-created values, but often they are agents (Vickers, 1994). This reproduction of "banal nationalism" is ignored by mainstream scholars (see Billig, 1995).

Gender scripts in the West used the trope of the patriarchal family to represent permissible relationships between women and authority. Women began as "citizen- or republican-mothers," then also moved outside the home, mediating between traditional and modern values in their "good works and social organizations" (Evans, 1999). Their agency began in per-forming maternal roles at home, which they developed into maternal femi-nism within their communities and eventually in civil society, trying to influence the public sphere. Canovan (1996: 74) believes that "part of the magic wrought by nationhood is to make the 'we' ... it constitutes seem as natural as a family group." Women naturalize nations, creating and re-creating collective identities by teaching children their mother tongue and generating the foods, customs, and rituals that make people feel related to co-nationals they have never met. Mainstream theorists ignore these ways of creating collective identity in everyday life because they fail to grasp women's agency in production and reproduction, or they ignore how women built nations because they see no importance in the domestic and commu-nal spheres in producing and reproducing nationhood. (Indeed, many West-ern feminists also ignore any positive or creative aspects of care work.) Yet nationhood is always created first at home through the words, smells, tastes, heroes and heroines, stories and songs of childhood that represent who we are, where we were raised, and with whom we share identity. What is little explored, however, is how nationalism's mobilization of women into pol-itics connects with their subsequent relations with state politics.

Fanon (quoted in McClintock, 1996: 265) considers gender to be a forma-tive dimension of nationalism, although he rejects the idea that *the* European family is normative. *He also rejects any logical isomorphism between family and nation.* He does believe that "militarization and the centralization of authority in a country automatically entail a resurgence of the authority of the father." Where militarism exists, he asserts, fathers, not mothers, are the agents in the nationalism created. Canovan (1996) also believes militarization, where central to nation-state formation, reinforces patriarchal authority. Therefore, the role of military struggle in the original formation of Western nation-states, and in many anti-colonial struggles, may explain why women's agency in shaping nation-state institutions has been limited. The path-dependent nature of political institutions generally means that, except in a few cases in which women managed to get in on the ground floor of political institutions, their ability to influence institutional design has been curtailed. It is primarily when women became allies in struggles against external domination that they have been mobilized politically by nationalism. Periods of restructuring, however, may also provide openings for similarly productive alliances.

Conclusion

Anthony D. Smith (1991: 132) asserts that "if any political phenomena are truly global, then it must be the nation and nationalism." What is not clear from Smith is why. Canovan (1996: 3) sees nationhood as a powerful battery "which can store power for future use without needing to be active all the time." Nationhood mediates between the familial and the political, but power structures in the two may differ: public democracy often coexists with authoritarian familes. Neither families nor nations are natural, but we experience an inevitability about them, because most of us grow up in them and so take them for granted. Nationhood stores up emotional power to weather crises of transition and restructuring, contradictions between the demands of the modern public sphere and the traditions reproduced by families, communities, and religious institutions. Legitimization of state power can also be achieved through religion or political ideology, but only nationhood "can attract so much support with so little by way of organization, doctrine and continuous mobilization." Legitimation depends on women's "labours of love" and their invisible work making nationahood an efficient and cheap shock absorber for this new political form.[18] Canovan believes stable nationhood is relatively rare, however, and attributes the conflict and violence associated with nationalist movements to its absence: if people don't share a common nationhood, violence may result from making them share a polity. Nationalist movements try to imitate "the magic wrought by nationhood ... to make the 'we' that it constitutes ... natural." "The most stable of modern states, those in which internal peace seems most assured, are precisely those that ... belong to a people" (138). Nationhood may be a "sticky cobweb of myths and mediations," but it can create internal peace and stability. Women helped constitute viable national communities in an unstable international system, but nation-state formation in most Western countries worked against women gaining authority. As Merry Weisner (2000: 295) puts it, "Rulers intent on increasing and centralizing their own authority supported legal and institutional changes that enhanced the power of men over the women and children in their own families." Women were sidelined, in part to contain traditional values. In the early modern period, "Christian virtues were privatized and feminized, no longer viewed as important in the public actions of rulers or political leaders, although ... private lives were still to give evidence of religious convictions" (296). The proper modern values for the public realm were rationality, efficiency, good judgment, and horizontal (male) comradeship. Enlightenment thinkers and Deists such as Voltaire expected wives, children, and servants to display Christian virtues. As capitalism restructured countries, the legitimization for women's political exclusion changed. But increased secularization in the public realm was still balanced by a sex/gender regime in which women preserved religious values (empathy, compassion) evicted from the modern state and economy. Nationhood mediated between the two. And although the kind of mediation that women were expected to perform and the content of "the traditional" differed in colonial and post-colonial contexts, there too women were to bridge contradictory values, absorb the shocks of rapid change, and represent continuity in their domestic and spiritual roles.

In most core Euro-American countries, the hyphen initially locked women out of the state, but not out of the nation.[19] Women filled it with their organizations committed to charity and the amelioration of poverty, slavery, exploitation, and oppression, and with their activism, on which they eventually based claims to citizenship and rights. Their work of mediation was as important as state-directed nation building in reproducing nationhood. In anti- and post-colonial national projects, women often became citizens when men did and in some cases were active in building nation-states in both public and private arenas. Where women were organized on their own behalf, nationalist projects often were potential sites for emancipation. But the expectation that they would still mediate between modernity and tradition limited the impact of their citizenship. In both contexts, women experienced contradictions between legal equality in citizenship and legal subordination in marriage. Only in some marginal cases did women use national mobilizations to make public institutions more women-friendly by getting in on the ground floor. In Quebec, where I began this text, women's relationship with the nation has varied over time: initially, it stressed their motherhood (while religion and an anti-modern nationalism constrained their agency); since 1960, a modern territorial nationalism developed that permitted a tenuous alliance between feminists and nationalists.

However unstable this alliance, it has drawn many francophone feminists into the ambit of Quebec politics to debate whether independence or more autonomy within Canada will produce greater gender justice for Franco-Quebec women. Nationalist governments wooed them, and feminists became incorporated into political parties, elected to the Assembly, and employed in the growing Quebec state. But that is another story.

2
Gender and Nation in the Soviet/Russian Transformation
Maya Eichler

Scholars of the post-communist transformation too often neglect the gendered nature of economic, political, and social change in the former Soviet bloc. They analyze the collapse of state socialism, the re-emergence of nationalism, and the liberal political and economic restructuring of former communist regimes without acknowledging their gendered underpinnings or gender-specific outcomes. This chapter introduces the reader to the vibrant feminist scholarship in the field of Soviet and post-Soviet studies by examining the Soviet/Russian transformation through an analysis of gender and nation, and the intersections between the two.

I draw on two key feminist insights. First, states shape and are shaped by dominant notions of masculinity and femininity and gendered relations of power. A state's "gender order" is crucial to the basic structuring and ideological legitimization of the social order (Matthews, 1984). Second, conceptions of the "nation," fundamental to the legitimacy of modern states and their policies, are almost always gendered (Yuval-Davis, 1997). This chapter argues that post-communist transformations can be seen as economic projects – creating new social relations of power in the economic sphere – that gain (or lose) legitimacy, in part, by being linked to notions of masculinity and femininity and constructions of the nation.

During the late 1960s and the 1970s, Soviet policy-makers, academics, and popular commentators began to question the appropriateness of the Soviet gender order, particularly regarding the tensions it created between women's dual roles as workers and mothers. Some participants in these debates drew attention to the negative effects of demographic developments on the Soviet nation. Reflecting these concerns, Soviet rhetoric and policies – though still maintaining the official goal of gender equality – shifted towards a greater emphasis on women's role as mothers. The transformation of the social order, which began during perestroika and was accelerated by Russia's economic reforms, drew partial legitimacy from the promise of a return to more "natural" gender roles and a definition of Russia as part of the West. The ideology of anti-communism and the free market was strengthened by the rejection of key elements of state socialism: the rhetoric of gender equality and a national identity defined in opposition to the capitalist West.

However, translating this new gender ideology and Western identity into practice proved difficult, which is evident in post-Soviet developments in the economic and military realms. Whereas the liberal transition promised the possibility for men's reassertion of their masculinity and women's return to the private sphere, in reality, neoliberal reforms increased women's double burden and aggravated the crisis of masculinity.[1] Neoliberal reforms impacted gender identities in class-specific ways, limiting the possibility of patriarchal gender relations and identification with the West to Russia's new capitalist class.[2] As the effects of "shock therapy" undermined the popularity of Yeltsin's reform agenda, the government adopted a more nationalist, anti-Western position, which was showcased domestically during the first Chechen war. However, as soldiers' mothers' protests and mass draft evasions attest, even in the military realm the prevailing gender ideology that relegates women to the private sphere and celebrates masculinity has found itself on shaky ground.

A gender analysis of the Soviet/Russian case is significant for the comparative study of former state socialist countries and for states undergoing neoliberal reforms more generally. The crisis and eventual collapse of the Soviet bloc coincided with the global spread of neoliberalism, which shaped the policy options available to post-communist countries (Pickel and True, 1999). The implementation of neoliberal reforms in the post-communist world has had similar gendered effects as witnessed in many Western countries (see Brodie, this volume), while coexisting with elements of the Soviet legacy (see Nikolic-Ristanovic, 2002; Molyneux, 1996; Teplova, 2003). At the same time, the comparative study of gender and post-communism highlights the similarities of communist gender orders and the differences emerging from the transformation that are important to the task of gendering the study of the nation-state (see Kuehnast and Nechemias, 2004; Gal and Kligman, 1997; Vickers, this volume).

The first section of this chapter discusses feminist insights into the relationship between gender, state, and nation. Second, I outline the Soviet gender order in relation to conceptions of the Soviet nation and debates challenging these since the late 1960s. The third section examines representations of gender and nation in the early post-communist period, as they appeared in the transition discourse and in its communist and nationalist critique. I analyze the gendered and class-specific effects of the economic transformation, and, finally, describe challenges to patriarchal notions of masculinity and femininity through the example of the Chechen wars.

Gender Orders and Nations

Feminist and gender scholarship has suggested that each society is, in part, constituted by its gender order: a particular set of gendered relations of power and dominant notions of masculinity and femininity (Matthews, 1984: 13-16; see Connell, 1987). Historically, gender orders have consisted of unequal relations that have subordinated women to men and assigned power to those institutions, practices, and activities associated with hegemonic masculinity. A gender order includes material, institutional, and ideological aspects, such as a gendered division of wealth and labour in the productive and reproductive spheres, legal norms and policy structures that shape gender relations, and normative understandings of masculinity and femininity.

The gender order informs, at the same time as it is reproduced by, the policies of the state, whether state socialist or capitalist, and the activities of other social actors and institutions. The state shapes gender relations and encourages particular notions of masculinity and femininity, but it also relies on the gender order for the ideological legitimation and day-to-day functioning of the larger social order. During times of crisis and transformation, people's actions, state policies, or existing material conditions may challenge common-sense notions of masculinity and femininity and lead to changes in the gender order. At the same time, popular dissatisfaction with the gender order can help propel broader societal change (Connell, 1990; Whitworth, 1994: 64-67).

The gender order intersects the construction of the nation at many levels. Conceptions of the nation lend legitimacy to the modern state and its policies by defining the relationship between state and subject in terms of citizenship, ethnicity, or socialist paternalism (Verdery, 1996: 63). Socialist paternalism was the key ingredient of "socialist nations" in the former Soviet bloc, as Verdery explains: "Instead of political rights or ethnocultural similarity, it [the socialist nation] posited a moral tie linking subjects with the state through their rights to a share in the redistributed social product" (63). All three types of state-subject relations are linked to specific notions of gender. The citizen has traditionally been imagined as male, giving rise to citizenship laws and political rights that have often applied differently to men and women. Ethnonationalist discourses usually construct women as symbols of the nation and target women's bodies, whereas socialist nations in the former Soviet bloc aimed at reducing differences between men and women by subordinating both to the "patriarchal" state (63-64).

Conceptions of the nation are also used to construct an understanding of "us" versus "them" in the realm of international relations. State elites significantly define their nation's identity in relation to other nations, thereby downplaying differences within the nation along class, gender, and ethnic lines. This construction of the "other" was a central component of Cold War rivalry, and at times drew on understandings about gender. For example, Susan Gal and Gail Kligman (2000: 9) point out that "communist theories and policies about families were framed in part as critiques and responses to the West." One of the Soviet state's claims of superiority vis-à-vis the capitalist West rested on assertions of gender equality in Soviet society.

Gender and Nation in the Soviet Union

As central ideological structures of the Soviet regime, gender and nation were used to legitimize communism as a superior mode of social organization. The Soviet leadership claimed that under communism – in contrast to capitalism – the "woman question" as well as the "national question" had been "resolved" (Verdery, 1996: 61). Women's high levels of integration into the workforce were cited as proof of their emancipation, and a spirit of internationalism and multi-ethnic brotherhood was to have replaced national and ethnic antagonisms. In reality, Soviet policies on gender and nation were ambivalent. The Soviet claim to have achieved gender equality through women's integration into the workforce coexisted with the notion of fundamentally different gender roles; in addition, the dominant status of Russians within the Union conflicted with the official concept of an emerging "Soviet people."

The state elite saw women as crucial to the production process as well as the reproduction of society, and expected them to fulfill the dual role of workers and mothers. State policies assisted women in their role as mothers through the provision of child care services and maternity benefits, and treated women as a special category of worker requiring protection from heavy and dangerous labour (although there were many exceptions to this). The numbers of women as part of the paid workforce increased from 25 percent in 1922 to 51 percent in 1970 (Lapidus, 1978: 166). Although the policy of integrating women into the paid labour force increased their autonomy, it did not fundamentally challenge the perpetuation of gender inequalities. For example, in the sphere of production, women were concentrated in "the least-prestigious and lowest-paying" sectors or jobs within male-dominated sectors (Sperling, 1999: 17). Women's increased labour participation was encouraged during times of labour shortages, such as during the Second World War and the early 1960s (Lapidus, 1978: 166-67), and discouraged when called for by economic and demographic conditions (such as after the Second World War and during the 1980s). The political sphere was similarly characterized by hierarchical gender structures. Suvi Salmenniemi (2003: 3) notes that "men dominated the Soviet political elite whereas women's political citizenship was practiced mainly through trade unions, official women's groups and local soviets." Furthermore, state policy did not tackle the transformation of unequal gender relations in the private sphere. Instead, it reinforced the notion of fundamental gender differences based on women as mothers and caregivers and men as primary breadwinners.

It has been argued that the state's valorization of motherhood, involvement in child rearing, and rhetoric of women's emancipation marginalized non-elite Soviet men and undermined their authority within the family (Kukhterin, 2000). According to Sergei Kukhterin (74), early Soviet legislation aimed at transforming the traditional family "reflected not so much the desire of the state to destroy the bourgeois family unit, but its desire to replace patriarchal authority with the authority of the state." Economically, men's wages were set at a level that excluded the possibility of a family wage model. Instead, the average Soviet family relied on the wages of husband and wife, and on state benefits linked to women's employment (Zhurzhenko, 2001: 86). Although various state policies weakened men's traditional position within the family, male dominance was deeply entrenched at the decision-making levels of the state and the top management positions in the economy.

The Soviet regime's leaders recognized that the construction of a Soviet identity rested on and could be deepened through particular notions of femininity and masculinity. Biological reproduction and motherhood were perceived as matters of state interest in regard to ensuring the health of future generations of workers and their ideological commitment to communism (Issoupova, 2000: 31). Thus, women in the role of biological and cultural reproducers were considered important allies in the building of communism. State policies challenged traditional notions of Muslim femininity in an attempt to undermine pre-Soviet cultural and kinship structures (Ashwin, 2000: 3-4). On the other hand, men were expected to fulfill the roles of worker and soldier, and thus of builder and defender of communism. The military, in particular, worked to foster a sense of Soviet patriotism across national and ethnic lines (Rakowska-Harmstone, 1990: 72).

During the Brezhnev period (1964-82), policy-makers and social scientists increasingly raised concerns about the proper place of women in Soviet society. The Soviet model relied on women's reproductive functions to renew the labour force and meet the need for workers, as well as on high levels of women's integration into the paid workforce (Zhurzhenko, 2001: 87). Women were choosing to have fewer children, and it was recognized that this could seriously undermine the future supply of workers. Birth rates had fallen from 42.8 births per 1,000 in 1913 to 15.2 births per 1,000 in 1970 (85). The population was still growing, but the rate of growth had slowed. Soviet scholars put forward two main explanations for what they regarded as a "demographic crisis." The first examined the impact of poor economic conditions on women's decisions about reproduction and considered the difficulties women faced in combining motherhood with full-time work. The second explanation posited the lack of "childbearing values" as the reason for shrinking family sizes (Rivkin-Fish, 2003: 291-92). Such arguments informed the increasingly popular view that Soviet notions of femininity required greater attention to women's role as mothers.

This reassessment of women's place in society coincided with the argument put forward by academics and journalists that Soviet policies had contributed to men's feminization and women's masculinization, thus producing unnatural gender roles. At the centre of this discourse stood the diagnosis of a crisis of masculinity, evident in the declining life expectancy and self-destructive behaviour of Soviet men. The crisis of masculinity was also associated with the lack of private property and economic opportunities for men, although this was not explicitly stated in the pre-perestroika period (Temkina and Zdravomyslova, 2001). Elena Gapova (2004: 93) points out that "the Soviet gender order made it difficult to confirm masculinity as constructed through access to 'money' (broadly understood)." This liberal critique of Soviet masculinity held on to the dominant notion of men as breadwinners, but argued that it could not be adequately realized under Soviet conditions.

In addition to questioning the Soviet gender order, debates about the demographic crisis highlighted a number of national anxieties. Soviet demographic debates conform to what Nira Yuval-Davis (1997: 26-38) terms the "people as power" discourse, which she identifies as one of the key discourses informing nationalist population policies. In it, the "national interest" is defined by stable or growing population sizes. As one Soviet demographer asserted, "A country's position in the world, all other things being equal, is determined by the size of the population" (quoted in Lapidus, 1978: 295). The ruling elite perceived the demographic decline as a threat to the USSR's military, economic, and political status as a superpower.

Demographic concerns revealed anxieties about the effects of declining birth rates among Slavic women, as compared to their Muslim counterparts, and the ethnic balance within the Union. Statistics from 1976 demonstrated that the population growth in the Central Asian and Transcaucasian republics was significantly higher than the Soviet average (up to three times as high in some Central Asian republics), whereas the Slavic (and Baltic) republics experienced below-average population increases (Lapidus, 1978: 296). The Central Asian and Transcaucasian republics were responsible for 30 percent of population growth in 1970, compared to 15 percent in 1959. These trends were of concern for the Russian-led, Slavic-dominated Soviet elite, who feared that the Soviet Union would eventually become a country where Muslims outnumbered Slavs, threatening the dominant position of Russians. Yuval-Davis (1997: 30) explains: "The 'demographic race' can take place not only where there is a national conflict on a contested territory but also where an ethnic majority is seen as crucial in order to retain the hegemony of the hegemonic collectivity." The Soviet Union was an example of the latter case, as Russians were "treated as the primary nation of the USSR" despite claims of multi-ethnic brotherhood (Service, 1997: 423). The notion of who constituted a desirable mother in this demographic race exposed the contradictions inherent in the Soviet gender order and in Soviet conceptions of the nation. Slavic women were "too" liberated and therefore choosing to have fewer children, whereas Muslim women's lower labour participation and higher fertility rates demonstrated the limitations of the official policy aimed at women's emancipation.

The growing focus on demographic changes also increased fears with regard to who could be considered a reliable soldier. Male military service played a fundamental part in the construction of a Soviet identity and highlighted the intersections between masculinity and nation. Teresa Rakowska-Harmstone (1990: 72) argues that "military service in the USSR is promoted as the 'School of the (Soviet) Nation' where young men of diverse ethnic origins and cultures are molded into model soldiers – and prototypes of the new 'Soviet man.'" Although the army was depicted as a tool of ethnic integration and Soviet socialization for men, it remained a Russian-dominated institution throughout the Soviet period, reflecting Russian and Slavic power in society more generally. The language of the Soviet army was Russian, and Russians, Ukrainians, and Belorussians were overrepresented in the officer corps. A survey of officers' surnames from 1976 to 1978 revealed that 92.75 percent of Soviet officers were Slavic, and 61.37 percent were of Russian ethnicity (Rakowska-Harmstone, 1990: 88).[3] It is therefore not surprising that anxieties about the emerging changes in the ethnic makeup of the Soviet population also found expression within the military. Anatol Lieven (1999: 191-92) explains: "From the early 1970s, Soviet generals were becoming increasingly concerned both by the growth in the number of Muslim conscripts relative to Slavic ones, and by the Muslims' supposed unreliability, low education and, above all, lack of knowledge of the Russian language." Projections estimated that the cohort of Slavic men reaching draft age would decrease from 79.6 percent in 1940-49 to 60.8 percent in 1988, and that the numbers of Muslim men reaching draft age would increase from 5.6 percent in 1940-49 to 20.0 percent in 1988 (Rakowska-Harmstone, 1990: 80). As the Soviet military became more reliant on non-Slavs to meet its manpower requirements, the contradictions in Soviet understandings of the nation became more apparent.

By the 1980s, the state elite's rhetoric and policies were encouraging women (and men) to define their identities in more patriarchal and less egalitarian terms. Various pro-natalist measures were introduced, emphasizing women's role as mothers rather than their integration into the workforce (see Bridger, Kay, and Pinnick, 1996; Buckley, 1989; Posadskaya, 1994). The policies of perestroika and glasnost both aggravated national/ethnic tensions and created new opportunities for their expression. Like the economic crisis, these developments were important in eroding the legitimacy of the Soviet regime, paving the way for its collapse and transformation.

The Post-Soviet Period: Neoliberal Reforms and Gender

The new Russian government under President Yeltsin embarked on the radical restructuring of the economy along neoliberal lines in 1991-92. The price liberalization, macroeconomic stabilization, and privatization entailed in "shock therapy" aimed at truncating the central role the state had played in Soviet society. The initial popularity of Yeltsin's reform government rested on the promise of improved social and economic conditions. The adoption of the neoliberal agenda was, among other things, legitimized by defining Russia as part of the Western capitalist world. Russia's economic reforms, it was hoped, would ensure Western financial support and entry into the club of leading capitalist countries (Maya Eichler, 2005: 74-81).

This liberal economic and "national" project invoked particular notions of masculinity. Some of Russia's reformers saw the "transition to capitalism" as an opportunity to overcome the perceived crisis of masculinity at the societal level, which was associated with men's supposedly subordinate status within the Soviet gender order. Ruslan Khasbulatov, a prominent Russian politician, captured this idea when he stated that the free market would allow men to reassert themselves as head of the family (quoted in Attwood, 1996: 258-59). The liberal transformation was thus in part legitimated by the idea that it would help overcome the unnaturalness of the Soviet gender order by enabling men to regain their status vis-à-vis women and the state, and for women to return to the private sphere. As this section will reveal, despite the prevalence of such a gender ideology (a continuation from the late Soviet period), post-Soviet developments in the economic and military realms have deepened the crisis of masculinity and not necessarily led to women's reprivatization.

Lynne Attwood (1996: 255) argues that market reforms have "been accompanied by a celebration of masculinity, both literally and metaphorically." Although this is true in terms of prevailing gender ideology, a more ambivalent picture emerges if we examine how non-elite men have been affected by the transformation. The crisis of masculinity has in fact been aggravated by the effects of marketization. Marina Kiblitskaya (2000) argues that men's superior status within the Soviet gender order hinged on their role as primary breadwinners, and that post-Soviet notions of masculinity are still informed by the breadwinner norm. She shows that male unemployment has seriously affected men's sense of status as "real men." This has further undermined men's position within the family, which depends on their ability to fulfill the breadwinner role. It is notable that both genders believe that men should fulfill the role of primary breadwinner, illustrating the continuity of Soviet ideas about appropriate gender roles (Ashwin and Lytkina, 2004: 192-95). The crisis in gender identity is especially pronounced among men who became economically dependent on an employed spouse during the transformation. In addition, working-class men's loss of economic (and social) status has been linked to "the declining status of old-style male professions," especially those in heavy industry, which were highly valued during Soviet times (Kiblitskaya, 2000: 101).

In contrast, research shows that men who belong to the group of so-called New Russians were more able to protect or regain their sense of masculine identity during the transformation period (Meshcherkina, 2000: 105). In interviews Elena Meshcherkina conducted with Russia's new capitalists, they often contrasted their liberated position today with their subordinate status vis-à-vis the Soviet state. Meshcherkina further explains that "such men are now embracing the values of risk, independence and individualism. This is part of a wider rehabilitation of entrepreneurialism in contemporary Russian society – a rehabilitation which links entrepreneurship with values which are being culturally defined as masculine" (109). Private business has developed as an almost exclusively male sphere of activity. It is important here to consider the class basis of masculinity, as dominant notions of masculinity are increasingly tied to capitalist values and the prototype of the New Russian (Gapova, 2004; Yurchak, 2002). However, due to inadequate employment or lack of capital, most men are not able to match either Soviet notions of masculinity (primary breadwinner) or newer notions of capitalist masculinity (entrepreneur). Thus, though the liberal transformation has been accompanied by a celebration of masculinity, it has also been characterized by an economic crisis that brings with it a crisis of gender identity for men.

On the other hand, the liberal agenda has been linked to a rejection of Soviet-era policies aimed at women's emancipation through employment. The general public, including many women, has come to see Soviet policies regarding women's emancipation as "unnatural," "oppressive," and "enforced," and women's double burden as workers and mothers as a manifestation of "over-emancipation" (Kay, 2002: 62; Voronina, 1994: 38). This gave rise in the late 1980s to the idea that women should have the freedom to choose between participation in the workforce and domestic labour. Some Soviet women, exhausted from their dual responsibilities at work and at home, considered the idea of a return to the private sphere as potentially liberating. At the same time, the media, social scientists, and policy-makers began more frequently to cite women's return to the home as a solution to existing social problems (such as drug abuse, crime, and rising divorce rates) and the expected advent of unemployment under perestroika (Bridger, Kay, and Pinnick, 1996: 24-26).

Women's economic position in post-Soviet Russia was undermined by the Soviet legacy of a gender-segregated labour force and welfare entitlements aimed at working mothers (Pascall and Manning, 2000: 248). It has been argued that women's "second-class" status within the Soviet labour force made them more "easily disposable" than male workers (Bridger, Kay, and Pinnick, 1996: 45). The late Soviet and post-Soviet gender ideology that constructed women primarily as mothers and housewives additionally justified their dismissal as workers. For example, in 1993 Labour Minister Gennadii Melikian commented, "Why should we employ women when men are unemployed? It is better that men work and women take care of children and do the housework. I don't want women to be offended, but I don't think women should work while men are doing nothing" (quoted in Kay, 2002: 57). Women, commonly the first to be laid off by state enterprises, made up over two-thirds of the registered unemployed by early 1994 (Sperling, 1999: 156, 150). The effects of neoliberal reforms and economic crisis such as rising unemployment, the erosion of welfare benefits, and the decline in real wages led to a further deterioration of women's economic status. Although gender-specific effects were particularly pronounced during the first years of reform, in Russia as in other post-communist countries, gender does not provide a straightforward indicator of the "winners" and "losers" of the economic transformation (see True, 2000: 21). For example, men's official unemployment (9.1 percent) was slightly higher than women's (8.3 percent) in 2002 (Ashwin, 2006: 2).

Although Russia's liberal transformation could draw legitimacy from the new common-sense notion that defined women primarily as reproducers, in practice neoliberal reforms did not lead to or allow for their return to the private sphere as it was not financially possible for most women to withdraw from the workforce (Kay, 2002: 61). Sarah Ashwin (2006: 3) argues that continuity with Soviet patterns has characterized the post-Soviet period, as men have "retained, or even increased, their relative advantage in the sphere of employment" and women have remained economically active. Women constituted over 47 percent of the workforce in 2000 (Ashwin and Lytkina, 2004: 193). However, the Soviet "contract" between state and working mother has been weakened by the fiscal crisis of the post-communist state, leading to a greater reliance on the family to fulfill the tasks of social reproduction previously provided by social services (Temkina and Rotkirch, 1997: 194-97). Although the "working mother" is still the norm, tensions between women's roles as mothers and workers have intensified in the context of Russia's economic crisis and the state's diminished role in the provision of welfare (Pascall and Manning, 2000: 250).

New notions of femininity have emerged during the transformation period. Anna Temkina and Anna Rotkirch (1997) argue that notions of femininity tied to women's involvement in the economic sphere, such as the Soviet notion of "working mother" or the newer one of "career woman," have limited appeal in post-Soviet Russia. Instead, popular images of the "housewife" and "sponsored woman" (a woman who lives on her own but is economically supported by a male lover) conform to the prevailing gender ideology of post-Soviet Russia (199-202). Women's ability to withdraw from the labour market is seen as dependent on male class location. The housewife and sponsored woman illustrate cases of women's economic dependence and are linked to the capitalist masculinity associated with the New Russians. These notions of femininity also intersect with ideas about the West. The image of housewife is tied to the ideal of the Western nuclear family; younger Russians in particular consider the sponsored woman to be a "normal" and "natural" phenomenon that exists "in other civilised countries" (202).[4]

Thus, the main features of the Soviet gender order have remained intact in terms of a dual-earner wage system and a traditional division of labour in the home. Late Soviet and post-Soviet notions of masculinity and femininity associated with the reprivatization of women and the resurgent masculinity of men under market conditions, and defined in opposition to the Soviet gender order, are not within reach for the great majority of the population.

Nationalism, Gender, and the Chechen Wars

The effects of shock therapy and the lack of substantial financial assistance from the West quickly eroded the popularity of Yeltsin's pro-Western reform agenda. This manifested itself in the 1993 elections, in which Yeltsin's communist and nationalist opponents won substantial support.[5] Sue Bridger, Rebecca Kay, and Kathryn Pinnick (1996: 72) explain the connection between economic crisis and nationalist reaction: "As the lights go dim on dreams of universal affluence and western agencies are seen to be not entirely committed to saving Russia's floundering economy, there has been an increasing general rejection of what is perceived as a cultural invasion from the West." The critique of neoliberalism emphasized an alternative view of Russia's identity: not as part of the West but as different – and currently under threat – from the West. The construction of this alternative conception of the nation has also relied on gender representations.

The nationalist and communist opposition used nationalism to legitimate its critique of government policies, arguing that neoliberal reforms are a threat to the Russian nation. In particular, it argued that neoliberal reforms had caused widespread poverty, reduced life expectancy, increased mortality, and decreased fertility rates; thus, the reforms were responsible for the deterioration of Russia's demographic situation.[6] In addition, some nationalists and communists linked reduced fertility rates to the decline in "family values" (Rivkin-Fish, 2003: 293). Others identified the demographic situation as a threat to the state's geopolitical interests, arguing that Russia's position within the post-Soviet space as well as in comparison to other great powers was diminishing due to depopulation (Zhurzhenko, 2004: 281-82).

Nationalists in particular emphasized the gendered nature of Russia's crisis in nationhood: they linked it to women's failure to fulfill their proper roles as wives and mothers. They conceptualized the Russian nation as feminine (Mother-Russia), and as fundamentally different from the West. Women, as "mothers of the nation," were represented as the repositories of culture and the guarantors of morality (Murav, 1995). Motherhood was defined not only "as a woman's natural destiny, but also as her national and patriotic duty" (Kay, 2000: 66). Russian nationalists depicted the country's turn towards capitalism and integration with Western institutions as "whoring" or "rape" and symbolically linked it to negative representations of femininity (Murav, 1995: 43).

State legitimacy has been undermined by the economic and social crisis unleashed by neoliberal restructuring. In response to the dwindling support for neoliberal reforms and the pro-Western definition of Russian identity, the Yeltsin government attempted to relegitimize its own position by taking a more nationalist, anti-Western stance. In 1993 Yeltsin began to play up Russia's unique Eurasian identity and adopted a "new assertiveness" that was showcased in the first Chechen war (1994-96) (Wagner, 2000: 58). This shift, which went hand in hand with an emphasis on strong statehood and order, was important to the Yeltsin government's ability to continue its domestic program of economic liberalization. Vladimir Putin, who won the presidential election in early 2000, put forward an agenda to strengthen the state and renew Russian patriotism, in which the second Chechen war (1999-present) was a central component.

Both Yeltsin and Putin used appeals to nationalism and patriotism to buttress their regimes' popularity. They adopted the nationalist and communist rhetoric regarding the demographic threat and the importance of the family. For example, in 2000 Putin (quoted in Herd, 2003: 41) stated that "population decline threatens the survival of the nation." However, in the context of capitalist transformation and a much-weakened welfare state, the Russian leadership has lacked the financial means to support a pronatalist demographic policy (Kay, 2000: 66-68). The translation of patriarchal gender ideology into practice has been limited in the economic as well as in the military realm. As the Chechen wars demonstrate, a significant number of men and women have challenged their patriotic, militarized roles as soldiers and mothers. Instead, the post-Soviet period has been characterized by a deepening crisis in militarized masculinity and some women's organizing against conscription and war.

As large-scale draft evasion (on average forty thousand per year) and desertion (estimates range from five to forty thousand per year) show, militarized masculinity is in disarray in post-communist Russia (Golts, 2004: 75; Weir, 2002). The weakened link between masculinity and the military is due to the systematic physical and psychological violence towards younger recruits *(dedovshchina)* and the lack of adequate food and medical care, both of which have become more pronounced during the economic transformation. On the other hand, Russia's young men are more attracted to the capitalist masculinity associated with the New Russians than to the militarized masculinity linked with obligatory military service (Lieven, 1999: 204). While militarized masculinity is rejected by many young men, capitalist masculinity is unattainable for most.

The weakening of militarized masculinity as well as challenges to notions of patriotic motherhood are evident in the activities of the Moscow-based Committee of Soldiers' Mothers, which serves as an umbrella organization for dozens of regional groups and the independent Soldiers' Mothers of St. Petersburg. Its members have criticized conscription policies and conditions during military service. They have supported draft evaders and deserters, and they have demanded recognition of human rights abuses and illegal conscription practices (Caiazza, 2002: 123-46). Soldiers' mothers were the most vocal opponents of military policy during the first Chechen war; their activities included pickets, demonstrations, petitions, and letters to the media and policy-makers (Eremitcheva and Zdravomyslova, 2001: 232; Pinnick, 1997: 144-45; Vakhnina, 2002). They have continued many of their activities during the second Chechen war, although under more difficult circumstances. These women have successfully used "motherhood" as a basis for their activism and a platform from which to voice their critique. While this strategy relies on a notion of femininity defined by motherhood, the soldiers' mothers defy the idea of women's redomestication and political passivity that informs post-Soviet gender ideology (Hinterhuber, 2001: 9).[7]

Disappointment with the economic situation increased popular support for the nationalist and communist opposition to Yeltsin's reform government. The nationalist discourse in particular drew on notions of femininity in its critique of Russia's liberal transition and westernization. On the other hand, Yeltsin and Putin's attempts to use nationalism and patriotism to rally Russia's men and women to their side met with difficulties. The Chechen wars illustrate the challenges posed to patriotic motherhood by soldiers' mothers activists and men's uneasiness about acting out their role as defenders of the nation-state.

Conclusion

This chapter has shown that an analysis of gender and nation improves our understanding of the Soviet/Russian transformation. It has outlined the main features of the Soviet gender order, such as women's emancipation through paid employment, the appeal to women as mothers, men's subordination to the state, and the perpetuation of a gendered division of labour in the private and public spheres. The creation of a Soviet identity relied on gender as, for example, women's emancipation and men's military service were aimed at reducing differences among men and women across national and ethnic lines. In such a context, late Soviet debates about the appropriateness of the gender order and anxieties about demographic developments contributed to an erosion of legitimacy for the Soviet regime.

Although the Soviet state officially espoused women's emancipation and anti-nationalism, the late Soviet period was characterized by a greater emphasis on women's reproductive roles and the re-emergence of nationalisms. This chapter has argued that Russia's post-communist transformation was legitimated by neoliberal ideology, the prospect of a more "natural" gender order, and a redefinition of Russia's identity as part of the West. Communist and nationalist critics depicted Russia's neoliberal turn and the economic and demographic crisis that ensued as threats to the nation. Russia's leadership under Yeltsin and Putin attempted to enhance its popularity by taking a more nationalist, anti-Western position, which in part expressed itself domestically in the waging of war against Chechnya. Using the Chechen wars as an example, I have argued that the patriarchal gender ideology that advocates women's return to the private sphere and celebrates masculinity has also not been readily translated into practice in the military realm. Instead, the leadership's use of nationalism and patriotism has been challenged by a crisis in militarized masculinity and the use of motherhood as a means of publicly critiquing the military.

The analysis of the Soviet/Russian transformation has demonstrated the significance of gender and nation in mediating and legitimating broader economic and social change. Struggles over the direction of change take place in the ideological as much as in the political and economic realms. Both neoliberal forces and their opposition have promoted forms of patriarchal gender ideology in post-Soviet Russia. However, as the analysis of the Russian case makes clear, we cannot assume that people's lived experiences match the prevailing gender ideology of the time.

3
Projecting Gender and Nation: Literature for Immigrants in Canada and Sweden
Shauna Wilton

> Becoming a citizen of Canada ... is also about identifying with the
> character of Canada ... Canadians work hard to nourish a peaceful
> society in which respect for cultural differences, equality, liberty
> and freedom of expression is a fundamental value.
>
> > – *A Look at Canada* (Citizenship and Immigration Canada,
> > 2001a: 1)

> Until just a decade or so ago, Sweden was a society that assumed
> all its residents were the same. They spoke the same language,
> shared the same history, religion and traditions, and had more
> or less the same ideas about what constitutes a good society. It is
> possible that the similarities seemed greater than they really were.
>
> > – *Sweden: A Pocket Guide* (Integrationsverket, 2001: 7)

Both of the passages above point to a consensus within Canadian and Swedish societies regarding their core values. In Canada, these fundamental values are presented as being "respect for cultural differences, equality, liberty and freedom of expression." The second quotation, from Sweden, implies a level of sameness among residents, while at the same time questioning their similarity. It refers to shared values, stating that Swedes had "more or less the same ideas about what constitutes a good society," but does not define the values themselves. These two passages come from literature created by the Canadian and Swedish governments for new arrivals in their respective societies. In general, these texts provide a guide for new members of the political community and fulfill a socialization role. In many ways, an analysis of texts created for new immigrants provides insight into the values that government agencies are attempting to promote and instill in the population.

This chapter explores the projection of gender roles within the literature produced for new arrivals by the Canadian and Swedish states. It asks two central questions: First, what can immigration policy and the literature for new immigrants tell us about the values surrounding gender and the nation? Second, what do the texts themselves reveal about gender roles and equality in Canada and Sweden? Both the Canadian and Swedish states have formal multicultural policies emphasizing the equality of all members. As well, both countries receive a significant number of immigrants and refugees each year, contributing to the challenge of constructing national identity and community. This chapter puts forward a state-centred analysis of how identity is defined and illuminates the primary values related to gender as advanced in these state documents. It begins by addressing the theoretical and practical import of immigration, nation building, and gender, and by drawing linkages between them. This is followed by an analysis of two Canadian texts and one Swedish text that the governments provided to new immigrants, focusing on the presentation of gender roles and equality within them. The chapter concludes by arguing that these texts reveal the underlying and ongoing assumptions about gender roles within each society, providing an implicit state endorsement of a specific organization of relations between gender, nation, and state that tends to privilege a Western, liberal understanding of equality in which the white male remains the norm. Both Canada and Sweden emphasize a liberal notion of formal equality, in which the primary guarantees of gender equality are the statements of legal equality in constitutional documents. Although the Swedish text does discuss the guarantees of equality that are provided through the welfare state, neither it nor the two Canadian works show how the value of equality in Swedish and Canadian society is translated across the difference represented by immigrant women.

Immigration and the Borders of the Nation:
Theoretical and Practical Significance

A significant body of literature investigates the relationship between gender, nations, and nationalism; it provides the theoretical basis for the analysis conducted here. The feminist work on nationalism and nation building reveals the obfuscation of gender roles within the literature, as well as demonstrating that women play central roles in reproductive and nation-building activities. Overall, this scholarship argues that mainstream theorizing is concerned with the public sphere and the activities of men, at the expense of women. Anne McClintock (1997: 89), for example, asserts that "nations have historically amounted to the sanctioned institutionalization of gender differences ... [Yet] male theorists have seldom felt moved to explore how nationalism is implicated in gender power." Floya Anthias and Nira Yuval-Davis (1989) provide one of the earliest challenges to the male-centred focus of the study of nations and nationalism. They argue that women are involved in ethnic and national collectivities in a variety of ways, including as biological reproducers, as reproducers of the boundaries of the group, as participants in ideological reproduction, as signifiers of national differences, and as active participants in national, economic, political, and military struggles (7). Overall, this literature tends to focus on the women who are already part of the nation or on women as a site of contestation in colonial struggles (e.g., Enloe, 1989; Stoler, 1997). The discussion of the role of women within nations and nation-building projects is further complicated when immigrant women are considered. However, this is rarely addressed in the literature on nationalism. The introduction of new members to the nation and the expectations placed on them reveal both the values of the nation and the potential tensions between multiculturalism and feminism.

Susan Moller Okin (1999: 17-22) argues that many minority cultures claiming group rights are more patriarchal than are mainstream cultures and that the advancement of minority cultural rights in the name of multiculturalism may exacerbate the oppression of women. In this manner, Okin posits that multiculturalism is not an ally for advocates of women's rights, but rather a potential threat. As Will Kymlicka (1999: 32) rightly points out, however, "both are making the same point about the inadequacy of the traditional liberal conception of individual rights." As well, both feminism and multiculturalism require different remedies in order to achieve substantive equality and dismantle the systemic discrimination that requires all to adapt to the white, male norm. Azizah Al-Hibri (1999) criticizes Okin's argument for employing stereotypical views of the "other" that are based on a limited understanding of different cultures and religious traditions. In the end, we cannot separate the struggle for gender equality from that for other forms of equality. Okin's assumption that such a separation is possible reflects her position as part of dominant Western culture and reveals a lack of understanding of the situations of other women and the interconnectedness of different types of identity and oppression.

The role played by women in nation building reflects their position in society, thus reinforcing the importance of a located approach that recognizes the interconnectedness of race, gender, ethnicity, and class. Floya Anthias (1991) holds that identities are intersectional. She bases her argument on the problems experienced by feminists and others in theorizing the interconnections between gender, race, and class, and she criticizes the idea that women are universally united by shared and essential feminine/feminist interests. Anthias states that "the notion of essential feminine interests failed to place women's interests concretely in historical social relation, assumed an essential opposition of interests between men and women and hegemonized the concerns of white often middle-class women" (34). Lois West (1997), for example, points to the positive connection between national goals and full equality for women in Quebec. Feminist theorizing on the intersections of identity reveals that studying one identity in isolation often leads to misunderstanding the role of identity in politics. Generally, the roles of majoritarian women in nation building will be very different from those of colonized or immigrant women. The ways in which they experience inequality will be structured by their relative positions within the gender, ethnic, and class hierarchies of their society. To assume that all women play the same role within a nation is to ignore the concrete differences that exist between them. Therefore, it is important not only to explore the construction of gender within state literature for new immigrants, but also to examine how gender issues are related to those of ethnicity, race, class, and nation.

Through immigration policy, state actors determine who may and may not enter the state and belong to the political community. Immigration policies reinforce national borders by providing a selection process and a set of criteria on which potential new members are evaluated. These policies are designed to choose the applicants that best meet the needs, goals, and values of a specific state. Through the literature produced by the state for its new members, the key characteristics and values of the nation are projected. This literature tells new immigrants what they need to know about their new home, what to expect, how to behave, what their rights and responsibilities are, and what part the state will play in their lives. In the end, this literature provides its readers with a key to understanding what it means to be "Canadian" or "Swedish" and, in doing so, relays certain expectations or assumptions about gender roles.

Historically, immigration policies have achieved two ends. First, basing their approach on societal values concerning the desirability (or otherwise) of certain ethnicities or a general fear of immigrants, they attempt to restrict who can enter. This can be seen in Canada with the colonial nationalism of the early twentieth century, which aimed to preserve the character of Canada in the face of large-scale immigration (Wilton, 2000). Eva Mackey (2002: 12) argues that this attitude represented a type of "strategic essentialism" that placed the "other" outside of Canada and created the image of a homogeneous, united population and a state innocent of policies that served to marginalize specific groups. This can also be seen recently in Sweden, where the entry of large numbers of Muslim immigrants is perceived as a threat to the values central to Swedish society and identity (Ålund and Schierup, 1991). In both cases, the perceived threat of the foreign "other" is mediated through immigration policies that aim to admit only those thought able to adapt, integrate, and contribute within the host society. The role of the "other" is often central to the construction of what it means to belong to a specific nation, as the characteristics of the nation itself are often defined in relation to the "other," or outsider. This relationship of "othering" commonly relies on maintaining the historical construction of ethnic or racial homogeneity within the nation. To this end, if outsiders are able to join a nation, they are expected to assimilate into it, not to change it. Policies of multiculturalism in Canada and Sweden, however, have challenged the idea that assimilation is good for the nation and state, instead promoting cultural tolerance and diversity as an alternative. In doing so, these policies provide new challenges to the ways in which nations are imagined and to the ability of states to construct national identity and community within their borders.

Second, immigration policies are designed to reflect the needs and demands (or lack thereof) of the economy and labour force. In this case, immigrants are often viewed as potential workers who can fulfill workforce needs and thereby contribute to the economic well-being of the society. This approach is reflected in the Canadian point system, which is used to assess individual applications for immigration. This "neutral" point-based system, introduced in the late 1960s, assessed immigrants on the basis of a number of factors such as proficiency in English or French, age, education, and job skills, and aimed to use immigration to fill certain labour force needs (Abu-Laban, 1998: 74-75). This is also evident in the post–Second World War immigration of workers to Sweden. Following the war, the Swedish economy was booming, resulting in a need for additional labour (Blanck and Tydén, 1994; Westin and Dingu-Kyrklund, 1997). During this period, and until 1985, the National Labour Board was in charge of immigrant reception and integration programs; it also oversaw the number of permits to stay in Sweden, reflecting the strong connection between immigration and Sweden's labour force demand (Westin and Dingu-Kyrklund, 1997: 9). Given this, the use of immigration as a mechanism for regulating the workforce is not new.

By establishing a set of criteria that defines the ideal characteristics of future members, immigration policies both reflect and reinforce the borders of the nation, as determined by state actors and institutions. The literature for new immigrants produced by state institutions and agencies, in this case Citizenship and Immigration Canada (CIC) and Integrationsverket in Sweden, provides new insights into these issues and our understanding of the relationship between immigration and societal values. Playing into the role of the state as an agent of socialization, these documents are intended to serve as key statements about the host society and the way in which immigrants are expected to integrate. They project an image of life in Canada or Sweden and set out what new arrivals need to do to belong and be "good" citizens.

Both of these goals and processes are gendered. The subject of the gendered implications of immigration policy has been addressed by various authors in the Canadian context, although little woman-centred analysis of immigration has been done in Sweden. In Canada, for example, Yasmeen Abu-Laban and Christina Gabriel (2002: 66) note the continuing failure of the point system, resting on the "skilled" and "unskilled" dichotomy, to recognize the value of women's work and activities. Rose Baaba Folson (2004) and Martha Donkor (2004) remark on the frequent dependency of migrant women, who have limited access to language schools or professional advancement programs, which are themselves designed around a male model. Folson (2004: 31) states that "this process is a sure path to the creation of a 'type' of woman who becomes part of an unskilled, cheap exploitable labour force." This body of work focuses on policy, programs, and outcomes, but gives little attention to the literature provided to new immigrants (either prior to or shortly after their arrival) and the projection of gender roles within it. Ultimately, however, such texts are worth considering, as they are concerned with nation building through the process of integrating and acculturating new members.

The Literature for Immigrants in Canada and Sweden

My analysis concentrates on three texts generated by the Canadian and Swedish states. *A Newcomer's Introduction to Canada* (2002) is published by Citizenship and Immigration Canada for new immigrants. *A Look at Canada* (2001a), also published by CIC, is intended for permanent residents preparing to take the citizenship examination. *Sweden: A Pocket Guide* (2001) is published by Integrationsverket (Swedish Integration Board) for all new arrivals. All three are primary texts, created for the purpose of introducing immigrants to their new home countries.

Both *A Newcomer's Introduction to Canada* and *A Look at Canada* are booklets available in English or French from immigration offices or over the Internet at the Citizenship and Immigration Canada website (http://www.cic.gc.ca). The former, thirty-eight pages in length, targets individuals and families who are preparing to move to Canada or who have recently arrived. The latter, thirty-nine pages long, provides the information necessary for permanent residents to pass the citizenship exam. That they are published solely in English and French can been seen as reflecting the assumption that new independent immigrants and family-class immigrants will have a working knowledge of one of the two official languages. As well, by the time residents prepare to write the citizenship exam, the expectation is that they will be fluent in either English or French. These assumptions have consequences for immigrant women, who, as mentioned above, typically have less access than their male counterparts to language-training programs (Folson, 2004: 31). This is often due to the gendered criteria for immigration (e.g., through the point system in Canada) and the assumption of the male as breadwinner, one that makes his access to programs a priority.

Sweden: A Pocket Guide offers a comprehensive guide to Swedish culture and life. The book is 280 pages long and is in colour. Although my analysis focused on the English-language version of the book, it is available in numerous other languages, including Arabic, French, Serbian, Bosnian, Croatian, Swedish, and "easy" Swedish, reflecting the primary linguistic groups of new arrivals in Sweden. The pocket guide is intended for all new arrivals, including family-class immigrants, individuals on work permits, and refugees, and reflects the understanding that many new arrivals will not have a working knowledge of Swedish. However, it does stress the importance for new immigrants of acquiring Swedish and emphasizes the relationship between the Swedish language and Swedish culture.

The following discussion of the texts consists of two parts. The first examines the images contained within them, analyzing them according to the numbers of women shown and the nature of their depiction. The second part focuses on the written text itself, in particular exploring how women, families, and gender equality are presented. Families are analyzed because of the traditional and ongoing gendering of family life and responsibilities, and in order to address the idea of women as biological and social reproducers of nations. The relationship between individuals and the state is also explored, reflecting the importance of women's relationship to the state in contemporary societies, as played out through the welfare state. Both sections consider issues regarding the intersections of gender, ethnicity, and class. Both begin with an explication of methodology.

Gendered Images

Michael Billig (1995) points to the role played by images of the nation in binding the nation together and reminding its members of the nation to which they belong. These images also provide new arrivals with an overall impression of the country and, in this case, of the role of women within it. They aid in the understanding of texts because they help readers interpret what they are reading. This section evaluates the overall pictorial representation of women, including the various roles in which they are presented, accounting for ethnic and class differences where possible. The conclusions outlined here are based on a catalogue of the images, which was created to describe each one and its content. Although determining a subject's sex was often fairly easy, the same cannot be said for ethnic diversity and class differences since these characteristics were not always obvious and often required the viewer to resort to stereotypes. In this analysis, I have tried to avoid guessing people's ethnicity and/or class, choosing instead to use specific identifiers, as discussed below. The images were first categorized by identifying the visible minority women depicted in them. The Government of Canada (1995) defines visible minorities as "persons, other than Aboriginal peoples, who are non-Caucasian in race or non-white in colour."

Obviously, not all immigrants or refugees are visible minorities; nor are all visible minorities new immigrants. As well, it is important to note that, though all women in these images are racialized, the racialization of white women (even in the Government of Canada definition) is "invisible." White women and men remain privileged, at the centre, the norm within both the Canadian and Swedish texts. Given this, it remains useful to identify both the raced and "non-raced" women in the images.

Women appear in about three-quarters (twenty-nine) of the thirty-eight images in *A Newcomer's Introduction to Canada* (Citizenship and Immigration Canada, 2002); of them, approximately half are non-white. As well, people of colour are represented in positions associated with prestige and power, including health care work, teaching, and business. Within this group, non-white women are also presented as obtaining positions of power in Canadian society; for example, some are depicted as doctors, teachers, and businesswomen. Images associated with the law and the state, however, all present white individuals; examples here include a female customs and immigration officer, female police officers, and a woman presiding at the taking of the oath at a citizenship ceremony. Although both white and visible minority women are presented in powerful positions and doing various kinds of work, that associated with the state is performed solely by white individuals; men and women are represented fairly equally. This suggests that a racialized power structure remains in Canadian society and reaffirms the idea of "white" as the privileged norm in Canada.

Gender equality and cultural diversity are very present in the images in *A Look at Canada* (Citizenship and Immigration Canada, 2001a). In terms of age, gender, and ethnicity, many of the group pictures of Canadians represent the diversity of the population. Only one image is restricted solely to visible minority people (two women of colour examining their new citizenship papers), which may suggest to readers that new Canadians will not be white (30). The presence of four images of Aboriginals may appear to contradict this "white" version of Canada. However, their representation as an additional "other" is strengthened by the fact that they wear traditional dress. This draws attention to their difference from the other individuals, who, with only a few exceptions (white Ukrainian dancers and a young white woman playing the bagpipes), appear in modern Western dress. Nonetheless, even these exceptions are clear indications of Canada's European heritage.

Overall, in both Canadian texts, the images display a conscious effort on the part of the state to represent Canada as diverse and welcoming of immigrants. Immigrants are seen as blending into the images of the nation, and women are presented as equal to men. This reflects the Canadian state's emphasis on multiculturalism, diversity, and tolerance. It also provides an interesting contrast to the representation of visible minority people in the Swedish text.

Sweden: A Pocket Guide (Integrationsverket, 2001) is much longer and contains many more images than its two Canadian counterparts. Also, captions accompanying some of the pictures state that they portray immigrants, even though they are not visible minorities. Of the 117 images in the guide, 3 are of immigrants (as defined by captions) and 17 show visible minority individuals. An additional 12 depict people whose ethnicity could not be identified. Together, these figures serve to portray Sweden as a very white country, despite the fact that many immigrants to Sweden in recent years have been visible minorities.

Women, well represented in the pocket guide, are included in slightly more than 50 percent of its pictures (59 of 117). They appear in all walks of life, including as health care workers, teachers, and students, and are shown engaged in political activities and cultural practices. However, they are overwhelmingly white. The guide contains only nine images of visible minority women, most of which feature women at home or young women studying. One, however, shows a group of hijab-clad women, along with their children, who are protesting outside the Iranian embassy in Stockholm (194). This image is interesting because it is the only depiction of Swedish political life that contains non-white individuals. The picture implies that mainstream political avenues remain closed to immigrants but suggests support for those political activities that reinforce democratic and Western values. This is similar to *A Newcomer's Introduction to Canada* (Citizenship and Immigration Canada, 2002), in which all individuals associated with the state were white. The pocket guide contains more images of people in their everyday lives than do its Canadian counterparts. Couples and families are overwhelmingly white and heterosexual, suggesting that this is the normal family unit. Women are not necessarily depicted as fulfilling their traditional roles; for example, men are sometimes shown caring for children, thus challenging the traditional gender roles within the family (Integrationsverket, 2001: 120, 129).

Overall, these depictions convey the impression that Sweden has a vertical mosaic in which the top of the social and economic pyramid is occupied primarily by white individuals (both men and women), and non-white individuals are not a part of mainstream Swedish society. Although the racial division in these images does reflect the reality of Swedish society (its political, economic, and social elites tend to be of Swedish ethnicity), an effort to include more images of immigrants and visible minorities, both men and women, would be proactive and would send a different message to new immigrants about what they can do. The pictures of women in the Canadian texts, on the other hand, reflect their cultural and ethnic diversity. At the same time, they focus almost exclusively on the public sphere, ignoring the private lives of male and female Canadians. As evidenced in the following sections, though the Swedish and Canadian books all stress the importance of equality, the image of equality put forward has serious limitations in both cases.

Writing about Gender

This section explores what the texts actually say about gender and, in some cases, what they omit. Its approach is loosely based on critical discourse analysis, which studies texts, their structures, and different linguistic, cultural, social, and political implications in order to determine how language constructs meaning. As Teun van Dijk states in *Racism and the Press* (1991: 6), the goal of critical discourse analysis is to explore *what* is being said and *how* it is said. Discourses are worthy of study because they convey social meanings that are politicized by the concepts of power embedded within them (Henry and Tator, 2002: 25). In *The Discursive Construction of National Identity* (1999: 8), Ruth Wodak et al. argue that a dialectical relationship exists between institutions and discourses. They state that "the situational, institutional and social contexts shape and affect discourse and, in turn, discourses influence social and political reality." The purpose of this section is to identify what is being said about women and gender equality, how it is being said, and what are the potential consequences of the message.

Thus, the texts were analyzed according to what was said, what was not addressed, and the order in which the information appeared. The latter can be seen as reflecting the relative importance of various types of information, as certain items are given primacy in the text or section of text (van Dijk, 1995). In this sense, information that appears at the beginning of a text is more likely to attract attention than that which is buried nearer the end. An analysis of where women appear in the Swedish and Canadian literature for new immigrants and what is said (or not said) about gender roles and equality reveals the emphasis within the respective texts.

This section demonstrates the stress laid by all three works on the formal equality rights of women and children. Such an emphasis may spring from the impression that certain immigrant cultures do not respect these rights. As well, the texts pay specific attention to reinforcing the legal equality of women. In the end, though the Canadian books do a better job of presenting women in all their diversity, they do not pay as much attention to women and gender equality as does the Swedish pocket guide. Nevertheless, though the two Canadian works fail to comment explicitly on gender, this omission still acts to project images of acceptable gender roles and norms.

In *A Newcomer's Introduction to Canada* (Citizenship and Immigration Canada, 2002), the family structures of the Canadian population are not examined until Chapter 7. In Chapter 6, the text discusses the people who make up Canada, presenting them in terms of language groups and regional distribution but not in terms of gender or ethnicity, suggesting that these are not the most important defining characteristics of the population. The fact that family structure and life do not appear until Chapter 7 speaks to the overall lack of emphasis placed on this subject. The chapter discusses gender equality in terms of equal gender roles within families, primarily through the sharing by men and women of responsibilities for housework and child care (31-32). The text also points out that most single-parent families in Canada are headed by women; however, it does not address the issue of the feminization of poverty related to this.

Gender equality arises again as an issue in the last chapter, Chapter 8, which discusses the rights and responsibilities of Canadian residents. This chapter again focuses on formal equality as the central measurement of women's place in Canadian society, stating that men and women are equal in all areas of Canadian life and that "violence against women is against the law" (36). Overall, this text is more focused on the concrete issues of moving to Canada than on the abstract transition of becoming a member of Canadian society. The process of adapting to the social and political values and norms of Canada receives more attention in the second text, *A Look at Canada*.

A Look at Canada (Citizenship and Immigration Canada, 2001a) is intended for permanent residents who have made the transition to Canadian life and now wish to become citizens. As such, it concentrates on Canadian values and the characteristics of a "good citizen" more than does *A Newcomer's Introduction to Canada*. This is apparent from its beginning: Page 1 outlines what is required and expected of citizens. A few pages later, the four key values underpinning Canadian citizenship appear: equality, tolerance, peace, and law and order (4). Equality in the Canadian context is described as follows: "We respect everyone's rights, including the right to speak out and express ideas that others might disagree with; governments have to treat everyone with equal dignity and respect, which are both fundamental to our form of democracy" (4). This definition does not mention specific types of discrimination or inequality within Canada, such as gender discrimination. The rights of women are not specifically addressed other than as an inclusion in the general principles of equality in society and under the law. In *A Look at Canada,* gender equality does not appear to be a societal issue. This suggests that it is either assumed or ignored by the Canadian state, neither of which bodes well for the situation of women in Canada or their interactions with the state.

The first line of *Sweden: A Pocket Guide* (Integrationsverket, 2001: 3) reads, "Welcome to Sweden. In our society, everyone is entitled to equal rights and opportunities. That includes you too." Enshrining such a statement at the beginning of the book clearly emphasizes the importance of equality in Swedish culture. The guide's first chapter, "The New Country," continues the commentary on equality. Its first line states that "until just a decade or so ago, Sweden was a society that assumed all its residents were the same ...

It is possible that the similarities seemed greater than they really were" (7). In this manner, the book emphasizes the importance of equality but attempts to differentiate this from previous ideas of sameness and assimilation. The first six chapters focus on Swedish history, culture, territory, and government. Gender equality is not discussed explicitly in any of them. The absence of women from the discussion of history and government (other than the occasional reference to a member of the royal family) effectively conveys the message that politics and governing remain part of the masculine domain, thus potentially perpetuating a gendered division of power in Swedish society.

The remaining chapters, which look at the more concrete aspects of living in Sweden, include a chapter on families that begins with a discussion of the changing role of women (126-28). These subjects are not raised until halfway through the book, suggesting that, in Sweden as in Canada, gender equality is not a top priority. However, the chapter on families does discuss the diversity of familial structures and relationships, as well as the equal opportunity of men and women to participate in family responsibilities and activities outside the home (126-29). The text states that gender equality is "considered such an important issue in Sweden that it is covered by special legislation" (128). It also outlines provisions for the care of children in society and notes that the Swedish state "has established a close-meshed safety net for them" (129). Further, it restates that one cannot be discriminated against because of sexual orientation (132).

Again, equality is offered as a central principle for the understanding of gender, but it remains unclear how this principle can overcome the challenges presented by immigrant women. However, the pocket guide does combine equality with a strong element of social justice and welfare, something that is missing in its Canadian counterparts. Its discussion of men, women, and children reinforces the role of the state in promoting and securing a level of equality for its members. Although the Canadian texts focus on legal rights to equality, there is little mention of programs aimed at ensuring equality or the role of the welfare state in its promotion. Gender equality remains defined in rather simple and formal terms. This is perhaps not surprising in either the Swedish or the Canadian cases. In Sweden, women's equality has long been measured against the opportunities enjoyed by men, particularly through workforce participation. In Canada, this omission can perhaps be attributed to concerns over the role of the state in individual lives or over differential treatment of certain groups.

As mentioned above, the differences between the two countries and their presentation of equality can also be seen in the relative importance accorded by the texts to social programs and the welfare state. The welfare state is grounded in a relationship of responsibility between individuals and states, and in the role the state plays in the lives of individual residents. It also represents the state's responsibility to care for its members, as well as the commitment of individuals to ensure that others are cared for by the state if necessary. This is of particular importance to women because of their unique relationship with the welfare state as both service providers and recipients of programs (Trimble, 2003: 143-45).

A Newcomer's Introduction to Canada (Citizenship and Immigration Canada, 2002) devotes limited space to the welfare state. Initially, it briefly outlines health care coverage and the role of the federal government in setting national standards (2). Towards the middle, one paragraph covers employment laws. A subsequent paragraph deals with discrimination and remarks that it is illegal but provides no information regarding what to do should one encounter it (21). This is followed by a section on taxation and the importance of paying income tax, as "this money helps pay the cost of government services" (21). Finally, the Canada Pension Plan and Employment Insurance are briefly addressed (21). Gender is not addressed as a specific issue; nor is the role of the state in the promotion of equality and social justice through the redistribution of wealth and the creation of social programs. For its part, *A Look at Canada* (Citizenship and Immigration Canada, 2001a) contains no mention of the welfare state or state-provided services that could establish a relationship between provider and receiver. The concept of social rights and mutual obligations is not introduced. Although equality is mentioned as a key value of Canadian society, no reference is made to how it is promoted or ensured, or to the role of the state in addressing the inequalities of Canadian society (4).

Overall, *A Newcomer's Introduction to Canada* (Citizenship and Immigration Canada, 2002) emphasizes the individual. In the sections on interacting with the government, state representatives are portrayed as holding their positions due to merit and as acting in a neutral and rule-bound manner (34). The idea of a strong relationship and high level of interaction between the state, its representatives, and the people does not appear. The only example of interaction is through the justice system and a very limited discussion of social programs, suggesting that interaction occurs primarily when the individual fails to uphold his or her responsibilities. This has consequences for women in Canadian society as the focus on the self-reliant, liberal individual suggests the reinforcement of the divide between the public and private spheres of life, the redrawing of boundaries between the issues that arise from these spheres, and the removal of the state as a key actor in the promotion of substantive equality in Canadian society.

In contrast, *Sweden: A Pocket Guide* (Integrationsverket, 2001) gives the impression of closer, stronger ties between the state and individuals, explicitly remarking that these are important components of Swedish state culture. Its historical section represents the twentieth-century history of Sweden as focusing on the building of the welfare state and the *folkhem* (People's

Home) (25). It comments that members of the social democratic government in 1928 put forward the idea of the *folkhem* to help those "who were
worst off. They spoke of creating a society that would be a home for the
People, folkhem, without great social and economic differences" (25). This
quotation suggests a number of things. First, it reiterates the importance of
equality in Sweden, in both economic and social terms. Second, it suggests
that the project of equality is driven by the state for the people and is "funded
by all residents of Sweden through taxes and fees"; this in turn reinforces
the relationship between individuals and the state, and stresses the collective nature of Swedish society (25-26). The welfare state, which plays an
important role in the pocket guide, appears in virtually every chapter, drawing linkages between the people and the state. Although gender issues are
not always made explicit, the focus on the welfare state as a key component
of the Swedish goal of promoting equality among citizens can be understood as benefiting women.

   Whereas the Canadian texts emphasize individuals and their responsibility to take care of themselves and their dependants, *Sweden: A Pocket Guide*
presents a better balance between individual rights and responsibilities and
the caring, sharing welfare society. In some ways, this reflects the immigration patterns of each country and the differing target audiences of the respective texts. In Canada, the majority of new arrivals are independent
immigrants (58.7 percent), followed by family-class immigrants (26.6 percent), all of whom are required by law to take care of themselves and not
depend on the state for assistance (Citizenship and Immigration Canada,
2001b). In Sweden, on the other hand, the majority of new arrivals are
family class (52.4 percent) or refugees (13.8 percent); all are entitled to state
benefits when they are granted residency (Migrationsverket, 2004). There is
a greater feeling of solidarity in the Swedish guide, in which more emphasis
is placed on the community through the welfare state, than in the Canadian publications, in which new arrivals are told from the beginning that
they must fend for themselves and that equality is something written into
law, but not guaranteed by the state.

Conclusion

In the end, issues of gender equality remain at the margins in both the
Canadian and Swedish texts, but specific gender roles and norms continue
to be projected and entrenched. Although the texts all put forward an idea
of individual equality early on, women's issues and gender equality tend to
be buried in the middle of them, indicating that they are considered less
important than other types of information and other forms of equality. Gender issues primarily arise in relation to discussions of family. By explicitly
identifying gender equality as a family issue, the books erroneously suggest
that the family remains the primary societal institution in which gender

still matters. This presentation of gender ignores ongoing issues relating to systemic discrimination against women in a range of institutions, continued income inequalities between men and women, and pervasive violence outside the home that women encounter daily. However, both *A Newcomer's Introduction to Canada* (Citizenship and Immigration Canada, 2002) and *Sweden: A Pocket Guide* (Integrationsverket, 2001) assert that gender roles have changed within families, perhaps suggesting that gender should not matter here either.

In the Canadian publications, men and women are presented as equal, but little information is given regarding how gender equality is promoted or the role of the state in ensuring it. Overall, the focus on individual equality is very shallow, as evidenced by the portrayal of men and women: it looks good on the surface, but little seems to lie behind it. Gender equality can be interpreted as one component of equality in Canada, but no more or less so than other forms of equality or the other key values promoted: tolerance, respect for diversity, liberty, and freedom. The Swedish guide, on the other hand, does a much better job of critically addressing issues of gender equality. Women's equality is mentioned repeatedly, and the role of the state in promoting and ensuring equality through social justice mechanisms is well documented. The vision of equality presented in Sweden, however, reinforces ethnic and class divisions within Swedish society.

These three documents reflect the vision of Canada and Sweden put forward by the Canadian and Swedish states through their actors and institutions. Directed at new members of the political community, they are intended to instruct them in the ways of Canadian and Swedish society. Given this, it would be naïve to presume that they would deliberately reflect the problems, divisions, and inequalities of each society. On the contrary, they aim to portray their respective societies in a positive manner. Even so, the issues surrounding gender could be presented in a proactive way that would encourage new arrivals to actively pursue positive gender models. For example, including images of non-white state actors would encourage immigrants to participate in political life. Also, discussing non-European cultural traditions and practices would suggest to the reader that they too are part of the nation. Adding images and text that challenge the gendered and racialized power structures of the society could promote change from within. This would also problematize the gender models and the understanding of equality presented in the books. The "average" white male Swede or Canadian who graces the pages of these works would be accompanied by certain "exceptions" to the norm, thus generating a greater impression that the "exceptions" are actually part of the norm.

Globalization, global migration, and transnationalism continue to provide challenges to the construction of the categories "citizen" and "nation" as new actors and factors enter into the discussion, as diversity increases, and as political units become larger and more complex. Therefore, it is essential to consider how the boundaries of the nation-state are defined and regulated, and to continue to challenge the role of gender within these constructions. The challenge to national identity posed by immigration requires careful analysis that must bring together the intersectional relationships of gender, ethnicity, and class in the construction of equality and democratic societies. The exclusion of immigrants and immigration from the literature on nations and nationalism must be remedied, for this is where the "other" is often articulated within modern Western societies. Linkages between the literatures on immigration, nationalism, and gender need to be explored. All three areas share much in common, revolving around questions of identity, inclusion and exclusion, and equality. Both the relationships between these areas and the reconciliation of the resultant tensions require further consideration. This chapter has explored one aspect of this, but more work is needed to problematize the role of gender within immigration and nations.

Part 2
Gender and State Processes

4

Assembling Women, Gendering Assemblies

Linda Trimble

To this day, women remain markedly under-represented in national and subnational legislatures. The goal of gender parity, achieving roughly equal proportions of men and women in elected representative institutions of government, remains rather remote in most parts of the world. Although some countries, notably the Nordic nations, approximate gender equality in their national assemblies, most reflect the sorts of trends that pull down the world average to a mere 17.4 percent of women (Inter-Parliamentary Union, 2007). Women's representation in the US Congress is just below the average. Western nations with Westminster-style parliaments feature slightly better representation for women, as they comprise 20 percent of the lower House in the UK, 25 percent in Australia, and 32 percent in New Zealand. In Canada, despite steady progress from the mid-1980s to the late 1990s, the feminist electoral project has stalled. As of May 2005, women held an average of only 20 percent of the seats in Canada's federal, provincial, and territorial legislatures.

The presence of more women "in politics" offers symbolic inclusion and disrupts the social construction of politics as a man's game. When the elected representatives are universally or predominantly white males, the gender order may remain invisible in debates, and thus the sex and race privilege enjoyed by white men largely uninterrogated. But there is more to the case for women's representation in formal politics than simply adding women for the sake of seeing them in places where they are not usually seen (or heard). Those who have spent considerable time and effort trying to answer the question of what difference it makes to elect women tend not to be satisfied with the argument that descriptive representation is good enough representation. Descriptive representation does not necessarily encompass the act of representing or guarantee the outcomes of the representative process. Although the "representative should not be thought of as a substitute for those he or she represents" (Iris Marion Young, 2000: 133), the representative *is* expected to represent something. Hannah Pitkin's (1967) distinction between descriptive/symbolic/passive representation and substantive/active representation remains persuasive. Thus, gender parity is advanced on the belief that female legislators are likely to engender political discourses and public policy outcomes by voicing women's policy concerns and supporting measures that improve the status of women. Numbers-based theories of women's political impact, including the critical mass theory, posit that when elected women exceed a numerical threshold, their presence can begin to make a difference for women. According to these theories, descriptive representation (standing *as* women) initiates substantive representation (standing *for* women). Assembling women in legislatures, therefore, is argued to constitute the most effective way of gendering legislative assemblies.

In this chapter I argue that the imputed link between descriptive representation and substantive representation needs to be interrogated, not least because it hinges on the problematic assumption that there is a set of coherent "women's interests" that can be identified, consolidated, and acted on. The idea that electing more women makes a substantive policy difference for women also implies that women are useful and valuable as legislators only when they are representing women's discrete and identifiable interests and opinions. This is dangerous as well, because it supposes that female legislators have sufficient autonomy and structural opportunities to engender policy discussions and shape legislative outcomes accordingly.

In what follows, I take a four-fold approach. First, I address the weaknesses of numbers-based theories of representation. Second, I discuss the complexity of representation. Since the nature of the legislative system is relevant to the quality of representation, I focus in the third section on the limits of parliamentary governance. I conclude with a call for greater attention to complexity and context in addressing representation. The study of "women in politics" needs to complicate how we think about what is being represented, the activities associated with representation, the various contexts within which the practices of representation occur, and the relationships between them.

Linking Descriptive and Substantive Representation: Numbers-Based Theories

Can legislative assemblies be "gendered" by assembling more women within them? Numbers-based theories suggest that they can. Karen Beckwith (2003: 2) puts forward that there are two types of sex-ratio theories – that is, two approaches to linking numbers of women legislators to legislative behaviour and outcomes: critical mass theory and proportions theory. Each will be discussed in turn.

Critical Mass Theory

The concept of a critical mass is borrowed from physics, where it refers to the minimum mass of a particular fissionable nuclide in a given volume required to sustain a nuclear chain reaction. Until that minimum mass is reached, nothing happens; once a certain proportion is attained, the results are explosive. Translated into the political realm, critical mass theory suggests that female legislators, like nuclear particles, are unlikely or unable to instigate changes until they have more than a token presence. As Beckwith (2003) explains, critical mass is an independent variable measured by women's presence in national or subnational legislatures. Group ratio, the percentage of women in legislatures, is believed to trigger policy change when it reaches a certain level.

Conceptual and practical problems with critical mass theory have been itemized by Donley Studlar and Ian McAllister (2002) and by Karen Beckwith (2003). The idea of a critical mass of women in politics is as yet undertheorized, as there is little rationale for the relationship between the independent variable (threshold number of women legislators) and dependent variables (behaviour and policy changes). It is simply assumed that once women reach the requisite threshold of 15 or 20 or 30 percent, they can begin to stimulate the chain reaction leading to more woman-friendly processes and outcomes. As well, a lack of consensus on the critical cut-off or threshold point makes critical mass theory difficult to operationalize. Although many scholars advocate a critical threshold range of 15 to 30 percent (Beckwith, 2003), the percentage needed to constitute a critical mass ranges from 10 to 35 percent or even higher (Childs, 2004a: 4; Trimble and Arscott, 2003: 126). Yet studies indicate that transformations can occur when women are represented at numbers below even the 15 percent threshold (Thomas, 1994; Trimble, 1993, 1997). Female legislators have been able to make modest changes to legislative style, discourse, and policy outcomes by engaging in "critical acts" even when they are not part of a critical mass (Dahlerup, 1988). Linda Trimble (1993, 1997) found this to be the case in the Alberta legislature, where the election of a handful of women to the opposition benches in the late 1980s had a limited but discernable effect on both the content and style of legislative discussions.

The sorts of effects thought to be activated by a critical mass of female legislators read like a wish-list of feminist political outcomes, including increased representation of women in legislatures, enhanced opportunities to enact policy, greater levels of discussion of women's issues in legislative debates, improved civility in legislative behaviour, feminization of public policy, and woman-friendly policy outcomes (Beckwith, 2003: 6). Why these consequences ought to be fostered by a specified proportion of women legislators rather than, say, a particular ideological or partisan configuration in the assembly remains unexplained. As well, the assumption that electing more women facilitates positive outcomes for women overlooks the possibility of a backlash or negative reaction to the increased proportion of women (Yoder, 1991). For instance, Lyn Kathlene (1994) found that in the United States the increased representation of women in state legislative committees prompted male committee members to become more verbally aggressive towards their female colleagues.

Although critical mass theory has enjoyed considerable intellectual currency, empirical evidence does not strongly support it (Studlar and McAllister, 2002: 234). Studies illustrate that even when women are elected in numbers within the posited critical mass threshold of 15 to 30 percent, their impact is considerably more gradual, indirect, and mediated than critical mass theory suggests (Childs, 2004a; Grey, 2002; Studlar and McAllister, 2002; Towns, 2003; Trimble, 1997, 1998). The strongest corroboration of the theory comes from the United States, where legislators do have considerable autonomy from partisan and executive strictures (see Swers, 2001: 173-75). Focusing on twelve American state legislatures, Sue Thomas (1991, 1994) examined the effects of increased numbers of women on legislative style and process as well as public policy outcomes. She found that electing more women did shape policy priorities and outcomes in areas related to family and children, but had little impact on legislative procedures. Yet Thomas argued that when women organize into separate caucuses and mobilize resources and strategies in their party, they can have an impact on public policy even when they form less than 15 to 20 percent of the legislators. Likewise, other studies of state legislatures in the United States found that a critical mass of elected women did not predict support for politics of concern to women or greater conformity in attitudes among elected women (see Studlar and McAllister, 2002: 237).

Female legislators in the United States have more autonomy than those in parliamentary systems because weaker parties and the separation of powers leave them less constrained by party discipline and executive control. Thus, it is unsurprising that tests of the critical mass theory in parliamentary regimes (with strong party discipline and the fusion of executive and legislative power) have proven less supportive of the notion of a critical numerical threshold. Sandra Burt and Elizabeth Lorenzin's (1997) study of Ontario legislative debates during the early 1990s, when women comprised 22 percent of the legislators, found that party was a better predictor of willingness to discuss women's issues, as there were instances when male legislators were as likely as their female counterparts to discuss daycare, employment equity, and abortion rights. Trimble's (1993, 1997, 1998) analysis of attention to women's perspectives and issues in Alberta legislative debates from 1972 to 1995 discovered that numbers matter less than party affiliation, ideological context, and legislative role. As Donley Studlar and Ian McAllister (2002: 238) summarize, several studies "have searched in vain for threshold or critical mass effects on agenda-setting, legislative voting, legislative behaviour and policy outcomes in various countries." Their own cross-national longitudinal study featured twenty countries and examined the period between 1950 and 2000 in an effort to test the hypothesis that electing a critical mass of women will accelerate increases in female representation in legislatures. According to Studlar and McAllister's analysis, the fact that women's increased electoral representation was incremental suggests it did not depend on a critical mass (247).

Proportions Theory

Proportions theory is more flexible than critical mass theory as it simply maintains that numbers do matter when a particular group, such as women, has minority status within an organization. Rosabeth Moss Kanter's (1977) work on proportionality and group dynamics indicated that the ratio of women in male-dominated business organizations has an effect on organizational and individual behaviours. When women are present in small numbers, they are tokenized, isolated, treated as anomalous. As the proportion of women increases, their isolation decreases, and their power and ability to organize based on their gender improves. Proportionality, or sex-ratio, arguments thus posit a relationship between numbers and outcomes, with larger numbers of women legislators generating at least the possibility of more representation of women's interests and better policy outcomes for women. Kanter found that when women were present in proportions below 15 percent, they faced pressures to conform by adapting and demonstrating loyalty to the organization. Scholars who have applied the proportionality argument to legislatures therefore look for change when women exceed the 15 percent threshold (see, for instance, Bystydzienski, 1995). However, this proportion is not assumed to be a magic number or particle accelerator; rather, it is seen as the minimum necessary for women to overcome the constraints outlined above.

Proportions theory allows for the possibility that the relationship between numbers and outcomes is neither linear nor unidirectional. Larger proportions of women can generate a backlash or negative reaction, especially when coupled with factors such as populist, anti-feminist rhetoric (Grey, 2006) or newness such as the sudden entry of a group of women elected for the first time (Beckwith, 2003: 14). For instance, the heightened media attention to and derisory treatment of "Blair's Babes," as the New Labour women elected to the British House of Commons in 1997 were labelled, arguably constrained their ability to rebel against the dictates of the party whip (Beckwith, 2003: 14; Childs, 2004b: 163). However, Sarah Childs (2006) found that the New Labour MPs freely engaged in a safer, less visible, legislative activity, that of signing Early Day Motions on matters of particular concern to women, such as the removal of the value-added tax on sanitary products.

Measuring the extent to which increasing percentages of women in parliaments affect women legislators' willingness and capacity to speak and/or vote for woman-friendly policies, even in defiance of the party line, to instigate policy changes that benefit women, or to organize gender-based alliances, requires cross-national and longitudinal analysis (Beckwith, 2003: 12). Such analysis needs to be complicated by consideration of intervening variables: the political opportunity structure, the nature of party competition and party ideology, institutional design, and even episodic factors such as the backlash against feminism come to mind here. Those who seek to test proportions theory should be wary of abstracting female representatives from the political and perhaps personal contexts within which they perform the act of representation. As Childs (2006: 162) argues, "An audit of the effect of particular women representatives ... will need to map the multiplicity of spaces within which women act, acknowledge the different roles that women representatives may have – as ordinary representatives, as members of a governing party or parliamentary actors – and contextualize them within the networks in which they operate, both within and outside Parliament."

For example, a particular opportunity structure fostered the "critical acts" supporting representation of (some) women's issues and opinions in Alberta from 1986 to 1993. The strong opposition presence posed a challenge to what was previously almost a one-party legislature; the women's movement in Alberta was active and vocal; the government was vulnerable to critique on a range of policy issues of particular concern to many women; and a handful of newly elected female Members of the Legislative Assembly (MLAs) identified with the policy goals of the Alberta women's movement (Trimble, 1993, 1997). In contrast, the election of the Klein Conservatives in 1993 instituted an entirely different legislative and ideological milieu. Record numbers of women were elected in the Klein years, exceeding 25 percent in 1997, but the Conservative government has pursued a neoliberal policy agenda, reducing funding and support for the women's movement, implementing deep cuts to welfare state programs, and obliterating the Alberta Advisory Council on the Status of Women (Dacks, Green, and Trimble, 1995). Because most of the female MLAs in Alberta were on the governing party benches, the increased numerical presence of women has been unable to prevent policy shifts harmful to many women, which supports Lise Gotell and Janine Brodie's (1991: 55) observation that "mainstream political parties can avoid hard programmatic commitments to the women's movement while being seen to be appealing to a women's constituency by recruiting highly visible and usually like-minded women to the parties' legislative ranks" (also see Sawer, 2000: 363, 367).

The Trouble with Numbers Theories

Critical mass theory is unsupported and largely unsupportable, but proportions theory holds more promise as an approach to gauging the effect of numbers on legislative behaviours and outcomes in a manner sensitive to partisan and ideological factors. However, there remain four significant methodological and theoretical problems with numbers-based theories, including proportions theory. The first lies with the measurement of the dependent variables. Greater proportions of women are thought to prompt more, and more effective, representation of "women's interests." Quantifying the impact of numbers either requires stripping women's diverse and sometimes conflicting experiences and policy demands down to a rather essentialist and exclusionary set of policy ideas or it means conflating women's interests with feminist policy demands. Second, even if women's interests could be reduced to something measurable, it is difficult to control for intervening variables. Ideological and institutional contextual factors, not least the male-dominated nature of parliamentary politics, provide overlapping and often simultaneous opportunities and constraints. This leads to the third problem with numbers-based theories. Linking numbers *of* women to outcomes *for* women places an undue and unfair representational burden on the shoulders of female legislators and suggests that male legislators need not concern themselves with representing fully half of the population. Finally, the measurement of substantive representation focuses on policy outcomes and activities that take place in legislatures, overlooking the rich possibilities in other modes and sites of representation and obscuring the relationships between constituents and legislators.

Representing Women

The theoretical and empirical research on the question of what, precisely, is being represented when we refer to the substantive representation of women indicates how difficult it is to define, let alone measure, the concept. The very category "women's interests" has been challenged for its homogenizing and essentialist underpinnings (Butler, 1990; Dobrowolsky, 2001: 244-45; Spelman, 1988; Iris Marion Young, 1990a, 1994). Iris Marion Young (2000: 136) presents a cogent argument "against the claim that structural social groups should be thought of in a substantial logic that would define them according to a set of common attributes all their members share and that constitute the identities of these members." Women share neither interests nor opinions. According to Young, interests are those matters that affect the life prospects of individuals. Because of their intersecting locations, individual women can bear multiple and even conflicting interests, and different women's interests most certainly diverge. Opinions are "the principles, values and priorities held by a person as these bear on and condition his or her judgement about what policies should be pursued and ends sought"

(135). Again, women's opinions are no less diverse than men's. Women's various and even inconsistent experiences, needs, and priorities cannot, therefore, be understood as a particular fixed set of identifiable political goals. Political interests are of course gendered, but the social construction of gender is constantly under renovation in ways that reflect class, ethnicity, sexuality, and bounded physical locations, among many other such factors (Towns, 2003: 5).

Attempts to identify women's interests as internally consistent shared political goals run up against the reality of women's diversity. For instance, Joni Lovenduski and Pippa Norris (2003: 88) accept the concept of women's interests as controversial but for the sake of measurement follow Lena Wängnerud (2000) in defining women's shared interests as lying in policies designed to increase women's autonomy. This definition of women's interests may obscure real political differences between women. There is no consensus within feminist thought or the women's movement about what constitutes women's autonomy, never mind the appropriate role of the state in promoting independence for differently situated women. Indeed, soul-searching internal debates about what is represented by and through the women's movement have exposed the partiality of feminist policy goals and organizing (Mandell, 1998; Yeatman, 1993: 228). For example, in Canada mainstream feminist organizations have been criticized for articulating an incomplete liberal-individualist perspective on women's autonomy, and for failing to recognize the perspectives of women from Asia, Africa, and the Caribbean (and, arguably, Aboriginal women) who look to the family and community as a source of strength and support (Agnew, 1996). There are undeniably some policy areas in which women's autonomy is clearly the centre of the issue, such as sexual assault, stalking, and domestic violence. Even if there is agreement on the gendered nature of these issues (and this is actually contested in Canada), solutions to the problem of violence against women differ based on the experiences of the women who are abused, the interests at stake, and the opinions of those seeking policy change (see Agnew, 1996: 54-55). As Iris Marion Young (2000: 122) observes, the "unifying process required by group representation tries to freeze fluid relations into a unified identity, which can re-create oppressive exclusions."

Another approach to operationalizing "women's interests" is to measure the differences between the attitudes and behaviours of women and men on the grounds that "women as legislators will only make a difference if women really are different from men" (Cowell-Meyers, 2001: 58). Lovenduski and Norris (2003: 89) assert that the politics of presence is measurable only if and when "women and men politicians differ in their underlying interests." It seems to me that defining substantive representation of women's interests as female legislators thinking and acting differently from men is untenably oppositional, as it overlooks the very important ways in which women and men share interests and opinions. For example, the political goals of Aboriginal women may reflect their gendered experiences within the context of a larger project of self-determination for First Nations (Green, 2001). In these and other circumstances, it may well be the case that when "men join forces with women to promote policies of sexual equality" (Phillips, 1995: 23), women's policy goals are more forcefully and effectively represented. Moreover, as Childs (2006) points out, the absence of sex differences in representatives' attitudes and behaviour may not mean that women are ineffective representatives of women's interests; it may actually signal convergence between the sexes and suggest that male legislators are learning from the ideas and policy goals of their female colleagues.

It seems plausible to bypass this conceptual and methodological conundrum by measuring the representation of *feminist* opinions and interests in legislative spaces. Even though many women do not choose to identify with feminism or share the policy goals of the women's movement (O'Neill, 2003), it can be argued that non-feminist women benefit from some of the substantive outcomes of feminist representation. It is useful to determine whether feminist values, opinions, and interests are manifested in the attitudes and behaviours of male and female legislators, but Manon Tremblay and Réjean Pelletier's (2000: 382) assertion that substantive representation of women is synonymous with feminist representation must be challenged on at least two grounds. First, representation of feminist opinions and interests can be carried out by men, so if this is the goal, there is no need to argue for gender parity in legislatures, or to test proportions theories. Men can articulate feminist ideas and push for the policy goals of the women's movement. In fact, Canadian studies have shown that party is often a better predictor of feminist consciousness than is the sex of the legislator (Tremblay, 1992; Tremblay and Boivin, 1990-91; Tremblay and Pelletier, 2000). If electing feminist men is "better" for women than electing non-feminist or anti-feminist women, then it is acceptable for women to be numerically under-represented in political office. The electoral project should, according to this view, shift focus from electing more women to electing more feminists, rendering the goal of gender parity beside the point. Indeed, non-feminist or anti-feminist women will not regard themselves as well served by legislators with feminist goals, be they male or female. In this way, women's various lived experiences, interests, and opinions demand representational diversity, including ideological diversity (Trimble and Arscott, 2003: 152).

Young has developed the concept of social perspective to avoid both essentialism and the trap of homogenizing women's interests. Social perspective reflects the collective "experience, history and social knowledge" derived from different social positioning (Iris Marion Young, 2000: 136). To use Young's words, from "a particular social perspective a representative asks certain questions, reports certain kinds of experience, recalls a particular line of narrative history, or expresses a certain way of regarding the positions of others" (140). Suzanne Dovi (2002) criticizes Young for abandoning the idea of group-based representation, asserting that it is important not to give up on the possibility that historically disadvantaged groups be represented by their own members. However, Young (2000, 137) does not in fact argue against this eventuality. Indeed, she maintains that people who share a social perspective may not always agree on interests or opinions, but they may find an affinity for the other person's way of describing his or her experiences and discover common starting points for discussion. There is evidence that female legislators do recognize their gendered social locations and their responsibility for representing their gender-based differences. In response to Tremblay's (1992, 2003) questions about their role, a majority of female MPs in the Quebec National Assembly and the Canadian House of Commons interviewed in the late 1980s and early 1990s said they had a special mandate to represent women. Women in the US Congress are inclined to see women as a unique part of the constituency and to believe they should represent women's interests in all aspects of legislative activity (Swers, 2001: 175). More than 80 percent of New Labour women MPs elected to Westminster in 1997 considered symbolic representation of women an important dimension of their legislative role (Childs, 2004b: 58). Research conducted in a wide variety of Western industrialized nations shows that most women politicians see their sex as posing unique representational responsibilities.

Contemporary feminist theory has contested the idea of gender as an individually situated identity (Weldon, 2002). In general, theoretical and empirical literature alike indicates that we cannot expect a few women, or even a "critical mass" of women, to stand for all women, given the complex, overlapping, sometimes contradictory, and often internally contested nature of their interests. So, though it is possible that elected women can and do represent their gendered positioning in their own ways, ways that may be neither observable nor quantifiable, the multiplicity and complexity of women's experiences and interests cannot be adequately represented by individual female legislators. After all, we do not expect male legislators to reflect a male gender consciousness in any identifiable or coherent way (though their gender identity tends to be taken for granted in male-dominated legislatures). That legislators share a social perspective because of their sex may lead them to see their representative role as gendered, but it does not infer that they will agree about opinions or policy goals. It is possible to look for representation of gender-based perspectives within the activities of representation. However, the articulation, and perhaps even the realization, of social perspective is both an ongoing process that cannot be captured in a single representative act and a collective endeavour that cannot be undertaken by an individual representative.

Bringing In the State: The Legislative Context

Since "political institutions are part of the construction of knowledge and meanings surrounding sex and thus help produce and reproduce gender," it is important to understand legislators as positioned within and influenced by the institutional context (Towns, 2003: 6). The formal and informal norms and assumptions embedded in legislatures assign different meanings to different actors and configure relationships between political actors. In short, political institutions are gendered. Gender cannot be disentangled from the act of representation itself or from the representational context, both of which play a role in constructing social and political understandings of gender, ethnicity, sexuality, and other identities. The relationship between representatives and their institutional environment must therefore be explored, since the organization of various branches of the state varies. In what follows I will concentrate on the constraints imposed by parliamentary systems.

Greater proportions of female legislators are thought to contain the possibility of more and more substantive discussion of women and their interests in legislative debates, and the feminization of public policy analysis and outcomes (Beckwith, 2003: 6). However, as noted, women in parliamentary systems arguably face more constraints than opportunities for discussing women's diverse interests and meeting their differential needs through policy decisions than do those in presidential systems. In Canada, for instance, parliamentary parties are strong and disciplined, and party whips exert tight control over everything from seating arrangements to speaking opportunities, committee assignments, and voting decisions. At the federal level, the New Democratic Party has on occasion allowed its members to take oppositional stands according to principle, and the Canadian Alliance Party was on record as permitting its representatives to break with the party when constituents' wishes clearly diverged from the official position. But these are exceptions to the rule; in general, in both federal and provincial legislatures, behaviour during debates and votes is focused on maintaining a cohesive party stance. Expecting women to break ranks or defy party whips by voting together on policy issues of concern to women is therefore unreasonable. The high-profile aspects of the job – committee work, debate, and question period – are similarly bound by the partisan straightjacket. The sorts of opportunities that do exist for legislators to escape from the tight confines of party discipline, such as private members' bills, private members' notices of motion, and MPs' statements, typically have little policy impact and negligible effects on the activities of the House (Tremblay, 1998:

442). Weekly caucus meetings offer the greatest opportunity for legislators to speak their minds because they are designed to air disagreements and resolve them so the party can present a united front in the House. However, unless the party style and ideology allow for articulation of diverse interests and opinions, female legislators will be constrained by their peers and/or their own ambitions. For example, Liberal MP Carolyn Bennett was chastised by Prime Minister Jean Chrétien in caucus for publicly criticizing the gender composition of a newly shuffled cabinet (Trimble and Arscott, 2003: 4-5).

Parliamentary systems such as Canada's, which feature executive dominance, concentrate policy-making power in the hands of the political executive. This means two things: first, cabinet ministers will dominate legislative speaking opportunities and, second, they will be overrepresented in debates (see Trimble, 1997). Backbench and opposition party women cannot speak at will, and in fact their opportunities for participation in debates, question period, and the like are controlled by party whips and House leaders. Expecting greater proportions of elected women to transform the content of legislative speeches is unrealistic under most circumstances. Trimble's (1997: 139) longitudinal content analysis of legislative debates in Alberta found that though the appearance of more opposition women MLAs increased the attention to gender-related public policy issues in the late 1980s and early 1990s, much of the discussion was led by cabinet ministers. Tremblay's (1998: 457) content analysis of debates conducted during the first session of the thirty-fifth Canadian parliament revealed that female parliamentarians spoke twice as often about women's issues as did their male counterparts, but this did not add up to very much discussion of women's policy concerns overall.

Additionally, women in cabinet may have their hands on the levers of policy, but backbenchers and opposition members cannot be expected to have much, if any, control over the policy agenda. Thus, expecting a large influx of women to make a difference to policy regardless of their legislative role is bound to be met with disappointment. Canadian women MPs, like their British counterparts, see parliamentary procedures and conventions as posing significant structural and attitudinal barriers to the substantive representation of gender-related issues (Tremblay, 2003: 228-29; Childs, 2004b: 187-90). This is not to say that female legislators have no say; in fact, there are some illuminating examples of women strategizing within and even across party lines to instigate policies to improve the status of women. In the British House of Commons, female Labour MPs and ministers worked together with women civil servants and activists to initiate and ensure the passage of the Sex Discrimination (Election Candidates) Act in 2001 (Childs, 2006). In Canada in the early 1990s, a subcommittee on the status of women featured cross-party cooperation between women from three political parties; its members were therefore able to advance a series of important policy initiatives, including greater firearms control, improvements to sexual assault legislation, and new breast cancer screening protocols (Lisa Young, 1997: 93-98).

Female legislators can learn the rules and can even strategize around them, for parliamentary procedure is transparent and knowable. Informal rules, performative norms, and behavioural conventions tend to be covert and the barriers they pose more difficult to overcome (Puwar, 2004). Canadian and British MPs cite the "old boys' network" as a problematic component of the informal parliamentary game (Tremblay, 2003; Childs, 2006). Canadian legislatures have been described as "men's clubs" that women enter at the risk of being ridiculed, harassed, mocked, and derided (see Sharpe, 1994: 34-52; Trimble and Arscott, 2003: 101). British Labour women MPs interviewed by Childs (2006) said that masculinist institutional norms and the dominant adversarial style of political debate made them feel uncomfortable in the House. Indeed, a magazine article called "Put Off by Parliament" referred to the blood sport of Canadian national politics as "Ottawa's macho game" (Delacourt, 2001).

The hierarchical and closed atmosphere of legislatures is poignantly illustrated by the following story. In the mid-1990s I was invited to give a presentation about my work on women in the Alberta legislature to a small group of former and sitting Alberta women politicians from three different political parties, on the condition of confidentiality about the group's members, name, and purpose. I was told that it had taken over a year of monthly meetings for these women to overcome partisan barriers and develop relationships of trust and support. The group invited me to join the meetings, which continued for another year, and whose discussions revealed a great deal about the institutional context for elected women. The clandestine nature of the group's name and meeting place illustrated how very dangerous it is for women to voice their perspectives in a manner that may be perceived as disruptive of political conventions and "normal" practices such as party loyalties. It also shows how deeply isolating, alienating, and damaging it can be for women to work in legislatures; as Nirmal Puwar (2004: 77) writes, the "costs of their existence, the assimilative pressure to conform to gendered 'fictions' and legitimate/imperial ways and means of parliament" take their toll on political intruders. Indeed, the Alberta group provided much-needed support and a safe place to reflect on personal and political matters. Not only did the sitting MLAs find understanding, advice, and encouragement, the retired politicians were also able to re-examine their experiences and in some cases recognize them as intensely gendered.

Given the extremely partisan, highly structured, and rule-bound nature of parliamentary politics, why would we expect the admission of a few more women into the legislative chamber to challenge long-established, deeply inscribed customs and practices? It is not clear exactly why the increasing proportion of women should have this sort of effect on parliamentary procedures (Grey, 2002: 19). Such change is unlikely without fundamental alterations to the institutions themselves (see Guttman, 2005; Warren, 2005). In the absence of democratic institutional reforms, expecting larger proportions of women legislators to represent women's diverse interests in an authentic, passionate, and effective manner is profoundly unfair to the women who are elected.

Rethinking Representation

Numbers-based theories reflect the expectation that female legislators must expand their rather arduous task of representing their party, constituency, country, and conscience to somehow speak for "all women" in a manner that brings obvious and measurable results. To suggest that more women ought to be elected *because* they will make certain changes and achieve certain goals is to assert that female legislators must accept a larger representational role than their male counterparts and must battle against all the factors that constrain the realization of this special role. As argued above, women cannot be regarded as a unified group with a common set of policy opinions and interests, and the institutional environment may work against the sorts of transformations that women are assumed able to implement. Insisting that the only valid representational acts *by* women, *for* women are those revealing, in a tangible way, women's discrete policy interests thus places an unreasonable burden on women, given the operating assumptions of parliaments, for example, which are structured to configure interests along partisan, regional, and/or ideological lines. The case for gender parity should not, therefore, be based on quantifiable outcomes. If women are elected in sizeable numbers and little or nothing happens by way of discernable policy changes "for women," they are seen as derelict in their duties when in fact the explanation may lie elsewhere.

Measuring the substantive representation of women as the expression of female legislators' attitudes, activities, and determination to challenge institutional norms on behalf of women requires female representatives to serve as delegates, acting according to the mandate of the diverse and arguably internally inconsistent female constituency they are expected to serve. This perspective does not burden male politicians with similar duties; rather, it frees them to act as trustees exercising independent judgment about the right thing to do under the particular circumstances. Moreover, linking descriptive representation of women to substantive representation for women removes men from a key part of the equation. It releases male legislators from the responsibility of ensuring that women's various experiences are taken into account, and that their policy needs are considered when making decisions. By placing the focus on women, numbers theories release men from their duty to represent half of their constituents. However, all politicians "must be held accountable for their contribution to improving gender equity" (Sawer, 2000: 376).

Suggesting that electing women matters only when female politicians change the style or business of politics not only creates unrealistic expectations for female politicians, it contracts the very meaning of representation. As Iris Marion Young (2000: 125) argues, we need to conceptualize representation outside a logic of identity, for such a logic requires the official to somehow "stand for" the entire will of the people she serves. The classic debates about representation reflect false polarizations, with the official as *either* a delegate *or* a trustee, *either* authorized to act as she wishes *or* held accountable to those she represents. Instead, as Young argues, representation is a complex and mediated series of relationships between members of a constituency, between the citizens and the representative, and between representatives in decision-making bodies (such as legislatures) (128-33). These are interrelated, linked through space and time and history: "Representation is a cycle of anticipation and recollection between constituents and representative, in which discourse and action to each moment ought to bear traces of the others" (129). The official is, or ought to be, authorized by constituents through processes of nomination, constituency and party-level discussions about policy, and elections. Ideally, these processes are participatory and inclusively deliberative (see Dobrowolsky, 2001: 243). In legislatures, representatives should not merely express a mandate, such as a party platform, but participate in meaningful discussions and debates with their peers. At the same time, an elected official should, while deliberating, recall the discussions involved in the processes of authorization, not least because she will need to relate and justify them to the constituents in the processes of accountability. Practices of accountability, presently very weak, typically centre on the blunt instrument of re-election, but Iris Marion Young (2000: 133) feels these should be strengthened by representative activities "where constituents call representatives to account over and above re-authorizing them" and "through which citizens discuss with one another and with representatives their evaluation of policies representatives have supported."

Young's notion of representation as a plural process intrinsic to strong democracy offers two key points for this evaluation of numbers-based theories. First, it shows that representation cannot be reduced to particular attitudes or acts by elected officials. Instead, it is a series of interrelated activities and relationships. Knowing what a politician said about or how she voted on a particular issue may tell us very little about the nature and quality of the representational work she is doing. Second, the activities of representation are much more extensive than the words uttered and deeds enacted in legislatures. I have attempted to capture Young's theory of representation

Figure 4.1

Iris Marion Young's concept of representation as a relationship

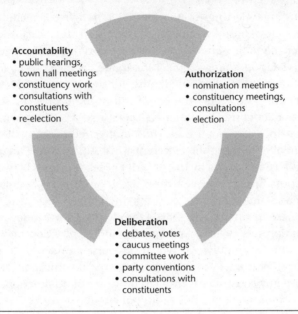

in Figure 4.1. It indicates that there are multiple sites, many of them private and inaccessible to the academic researcher, where the gendered nature of the relationships can be realized. It also shows that in measuring the strength and effectiveness of representation, it is not necessary to abandon the plurality of the represented, or of the representatives themselves, for that matter; rather, we can see these multiplicities as properly expressed within the relationships between constituents and legislators.

Conclusion

It is fair to argue that descriptive representation in and of itself is a shallow and insufficient vision of gender-based representation. Representation is an activity, a process, a job, a performance. Saying "she doesn't represent me" conveys something meaningful about the ideas and actions of both representative and represented, as well as regarding the relationships between them. That group-based identities, standpoints, and affiliations have the potential to shape legislative deliberations is undeniable. Without representation of the needs and perspectives of oppressed and disadvantaged groups in legislatures, "deliberations and outcomes will most likely reflect the goals of the dominant groups" (Young, 1990b: 184). Ideas cannot be detached from the bodies that conceive, utter, and act on them. However, numbers-based theories need to be complicated by consideration of women's diversity, institutional norms and processes, ideological and social movement contexts, and the multi-varied nature of political representation itself. As Judith Squires (1999: 185) notes, no "single form of representation will be sophisticated enough to represent complex subjects in all their aspects."

Even though numbers-based theories can be challenged on both conceptual and empirical grounds, it remains possible to make a strong case for assembling women in representative institutions and including them in all manner of representative practices. Arguments for enhancing the descriptive representation of women with a goal of gender parity should centre on the need to speak for women *as* women (Mansbridge, 1999; Williams, 1998). Jane Arscott and Linda Trimble (1997: 4) distinguish between representation *by* women and that *for* women, arguing that though men can participate in the latter, they "cannot claim power for women and they cannot hold power in women's stead." Those who do not count themselves among the elected decision-makers are political minors, subjected to the rule of others, infantilized as subjects rather than included as full citizens in democratic deliberations (Phillips, 1995: 39). The entry into elected political institutions of those who have been excluded or marginalized is a crucial gesture of recognition, "a public acknowledgement of equal value" and of the capacity for self-government (Phillips, 1995: 40). For all of these reasons, and arguably many others based on justice and democratic legitimacy, women ought to be represented in numbers roughly proportionate to their presence in the population, regardless of how they conduct themselves as public officials or what interests they serve. The goal of gender parity in legislative assemblies need not be linked to specific outcomes such as more civility in legislatures, progressive policies, or institutional redesign.

Iris Marion Young (2000: 128) suggests that rather than construing "the normative meaning of representation as properly standing for the constituents, we should evaluate the process of representation according to the character of the relationship between the representative and the constituents." This view, echoed strongly by Alexandra Dobrowolsky's (2001: 243) call for "democratic expansionism," suggests fruitful avenues for future research. Connections between representatives and constituents are facilitated by constituency work, especially in non-proportional electoral systems. Childs' (2001: 178-80) interviews with Labour MPs revealed the symbolic and experiential links between constituents and their female representatives. Research on the substantive representation of women should therefore examine the collective practices that might allow politically marginalized social perspectives to be voiced and debated both inside and outside parliamentary spaces. As well, Young's relational view of representation prompts expansion of the research question. In wondering how women can be both corporeally and substantively represented in legislatures, we should also ask how democratic political institutions themselves can be reshaped to become more consultative and inclusive in their processes, more thoughtful and thorough in their deliberations, and more considerate of a diversity of perspectives in their outcomes.

5

Feminist Ideals versus Bureaucratic Norms: The Case of Feminist Researchers and the Royal Commission on New Reproductive Technologies

Francesca Scala

Reproductive technologies have become one of the most contentious issues facing governments in Europe and North America. Infertility treatments such as in vitro fertilization, assisted insemination, and surrogacy challenge prevailing values and practices surrounding reproduction, parenthood, and the family. Much media attention and public debate has also focused on the ethical and moral issues raised by the use of embryonic stem cells in scientific-medical research. In Canada, the most vocal critics of these technologies have been feminist researchers and organizations. In the 1980s, several feminist academics and activists formed the Canadian Citizens' Coalition for a Royal Commission on New Reproductive Technologies to lobby the federal government to appoint an inquiry into the social and ethical implications of these technologies for Canadian society and for woman in particular. In 1989, Ottawa appointed the Royal Commission on New Reproductive Technologies. The commission recruited several self-described feminists to participate in its research program as contract researchers and staff employees.

This chapter examines feminists' engagement with the Canadian state in the production of policy-relevant knowledge on the issue of reproductive technologies. It explores the challenges feminist researchers faced in reconciling their role as advocates for women's health with the bureaucratic demands for "neutrality" and "impartial" policy advice. Drawing from feminist research on the bureaucracy and interviews conducted with feminist researchers, staff members, and several commissioners, the chapter argues that a number of normative and institutional factors undermined attempts by feminist researchers to bring a gendered perspective to the commission's official debate on reproductive technologies. It explores how feminists who wanted to forge an open and democratic debate on the issue were hampered by the commission's strict adherence to classical bureaucratic norms of secrecy, centralized authority, and a hierarchical chain of command. The bureaucratic notion of neutrality was also a source of conflict. Whereas individual feminist researchers saw themselves as conducting objective empirical research on issues relevant to women, commissioners and top senior officials regarded them as advocates for special-interest groups. Moreover, the adoption of evidence-based medicine as a guiding principle for the commission's work led upper management to regard certain disciplines, such as science and medicine, as providing more accurate, "hard" evidence than the qualitative studies conducted by feminist researchers hired by the commission. Finally, the bureaucratic and intellectual separation of research from policy analysis meant that feminist researchers employed by the commission would be excluded from participating in the development of policy recommendations, an exercise commissioners viewed as their exclusive domain.

The next section of this chapter overviews two broad perspectives regarding the relationship between feminists and the bureaucracy: the first, a critical position, asserts that bureaucratic organizations are antithetical to feminist ideals; the second regards the bureaucracy as an important site for feminist activism. Both highlight institutional and normative factors that can either enhance or impede the ability of feminists to act as advocates for women within the state. The chapter then explores the research-oriented work of the Royal Commission on New Reproductive Technologies. It examines the structure of the research program as well as the organizational norms and practices of the commission, which would ultimately undermine the influence of feminist policy research on the issue of reproductive technologies.

Feminists and the Bureaucracy: Friend or Foe?

Feminist research offers a diversity of views on the bureaucracy. In general, however, two broad perspectives have emerged on the relationship between gender and the bureaucracy as well as on the usefulness of the bureaucracy as an instrument for women's empowerment. The first perspective, best exemplified by the work of Kathy E. Ferguson (1984), regards the bureaucracy as antithetical to the feminist goal of women's emancipation and empowerment. Ferguson contends that feminism is fundamentally incompatible with the bureaucracy, given that its organizational practices and norms exclude feminist ideals of "care-taking, nurturance, empathy and connectedness" (25). The classical Weberian model of the bureaucracy, which is governed by the principles of political neutrality, hierarchical control, impersonal rules, and technical rationality, stands in sharp contrast to the feminist ideals of democratic participation, consensual decision making, and decentralized authority. Consequently, the bureaucracy can act only as an instrument of women's domination. Ferguson warns that feminists seeking to engage the bureaucracy in an attempt to address women's concerns have little hope of bringing about real change within a bureaucratic organization. Instead, women must reject the bureaucratic institution in favour of organizations that are small and decentralized, and that emphasize democratic practices and a vertical rather than hierarchical division of labour. It is also important for Ferguson that feminist institutions remain independent from the state by having an independent source of revenue.

The second feminist perspective on the bureaucracy, though cognizant of the challenges it presents to feminist principles, is more receptive to women's engagement with the state. As a source of policy expertise, the bureaucracy provides an opportunity for feminist activists to bring a gendered perspective on the government's policy agenda as insiders rather than outsiders. This view is encapsulated by the concepts of state feminism and the femocrat phenomenon, which regard the bureaucracy as "an additional, alternative site for activism" (Chappell, 2002: 85). The concept of "state feminism" refers to the "activities of government structures that are formally charged with furthering women's status and rights" (Stetson and Mazur, 1995: 1-2). These agencies, and the feminist advisors who occupy positions within them, act as vehicles for addressing issues central to women and providing important linkages between government and the women's movement. In Canada, Status of Women Canada and the Canadian Advisory Council on the Status of Women are examples of such agencies. The ability of femocrats to influence government policy is not guaranteed; rather, it is contingent on a number of factors, including the institutionalized position of feminists within the bureaucracy and the pervasiveness of classical bureaucratic norms, such as political neutrality. Louise Chappell's (2002) study of femocrats in Canada, the United States, and Australia found that Australian femocrats were much more successful than their Canadian or American counterparts in pursuing a feminist agenda because women's agencies were strategically placed within the bureaucracy. In Australia, the Office of the Status of Women is located in the Department of the Prime Minister and Cabinet; other women's agencies are found in key line departments. This institutional positioning was key for femocrats in Australia. As Chappell explains, "Having a core coordinating body located in a central agency has meant that femocrats have also been able to enjoy the privilege (and exploit the political advantage) of the imprimatur of the Prime Minister or Premier of the day" (87). Feminist activists in Canada, on the other hand, do not enjoy the same prominent institutional positions.

The case under investigation in this chapter draws on a number of insights from the two contending feminist approaches to the bureaucracy. The collectivist-democratic perspective advanced by Ferguson and others critical of the bureaucracy highlights the normative and institutional differences between a feminist organization and a bureaucratic one. Whereas the classical bureaucratic organization adheres to principles of neutrality, technical expertise, hierarchical control, and secrecy, the ideal feminist organization is more open and egalitarian, with a power structure characterized by decentralized authority and consensual decision making. Feminists accustomed to these organizational practices will have a challenging time adjusting to a highly bureaucratic agency while acting as advocates for the women's movement. Conversely, feminist activists within the bureaucracy will be perceived as representing special interests within the public service (Chappell, 2002: 86). The femocrat and state feminism literature suggests that it is possible to reconcile the bureaucracy with feminist goals. The success or failure to do so depends on the institutional position of feminist activists within the bureaucracy as well as on the relative strength of bureaucratic norms, such as political neutrality.

These factors played a defining role in the failure of feminist researchers and activists in advancing a feminist agenda within the Royal Commission on New Reproductive Technologies. Adopting the standpoint of both expert and activist, feminist researchers typically seek to advance both social scientific knowledge and social change. Roberta Spalter-Roth and Heidi Hartmann (1999) conceptualize this phenomenon as the dual vision of feminist policy research, whereby researchers seek to satisfy both the standards of social scientific research and the feminist goals of ending various forms of women's oppression. Feminist researchers therefore use academic research to "raise public consciousness, advance public recognition of social problems, mobilize political support to change public agendas and encourage structural reform" (333).

The challenge emerges when feminist researchers engage with the administrative structures of the state. The state has certain expectations regarding the content and goals of policy research, especially as they relate to the principle of objectivity and the distinction between analysis and advocacy. Feminist policy research implies a dual role for the researcher – that of social scientist and advocate for women's issues. By definition, feminist research not only advances knowledge on a particular issue but is also a political project. This dual vision contradicts bureaucratic notions of political neutrality, which stands in sharp contrast to the advocacy work of feminist researchers. As the next sections reveal, these competing values and principles are even more problematic when deliberation involves subjects that have not been traditionally defined as "women's issues" per se, such as science and technology policy.

Engaging the State: Feminist Demands for a Public Inquiry

The lack of public attention given to the moral and social implications of reproductive technologies prompted the 1987 formation of the Canadian Citizens' Coalition for a Royal Commission on New Reproductive Technologies. Of great concern were the potential health risks associated with infertility treatments and medication for women, and the commercialization of human gametes and embryos. Initiated by feminist organizations, researchers, and health groups, the coalition argued that discussions on reproductive technologies were being adjudicated without the input of civil society. The coalition was especially concerned with the lack of attention conferred to the broader implications of these technologies for women. It regarded a royal commission as an effective vehicle to voice these concerns and to produce original research on the viability of these so-called miracle treatments.

In 1987, the coalition launched a large-scale and intensive lobbying effort that involved a number of different activities, including a rally on Parliament Hill, one-on-one meetings with individual politicians and ministers, and a general and well-publicized meeting on Parliament Hill with representatives of all political parties. The main objectives of the group were to increase public awareness on the issue and make the case for the need for a royal commission (Margrit Eichler, 1995). The coalition viewed a royal commission as a powerful vehicle for politicizing issues traditionally regarded as private matters (author interview with Margrit Eichler, 1999). Canadian governments have regularly appointed royal commissions to investigate acts of government misconduct or broad policy issues. Although commissions have had varying levels of influence on actual government policy, they have nonetheless mobilized the intellectual resources of academics and researchers, and have shed light on pressing matters facing Canadian society.

Not all feminist researchers and activists were in favour of pressuring the government for a public inquiry. For example, Varda Burstyn, an activist in women's reproductive health, doubted that a royal commission would address the pressing concerns of reproductive technologies for women (author interview with Varda Burstyn, 2004). Echoing some of the issues raised by Ferguson's perspective on the bureaucracy, Burstyn was concerned that a royal commission would allow the state to co-opt feminist rhetoric while proposing policies that could be detrimental to women. Moreover, she was skeptical that a royal commission would lead to real policy changes in the field of reproductive technologies, given the lack of influence exerted on government policy by past royal commissions (author interview with Varda Burstyn, 2004). However, most activists and researchers in the area believed that the commission would galvanize a public debate and shed critical light on the social and ethical implications of these technologies, especially as they pertained to women. The desire for a government-appointed inquiry was very much influenced by the experience and legacy of the 1967 Bird Commission on the Status of Women. Several members of the coalition wanted to emulate the Bird Commission's success in raising awareness and consciousness nationally about women's issues.

In 1989, responding to the lobbying efforts of the coalition, the federal government announced the appointment of the Royal Commission on New Reproductive Technologies (also called the Baird Commission, after its chairperson Patricia Baird). It was asked to identify national policy needs and develop policy recommendations on various reproductive technologies, including assisted insemination, in vitro fertilization, embryo research, prenatal diagnosis techniques, and surrogacy. The commission was to inquire into the medical and legal issues involving these technologies; their implications for women's reproductive health and well-being; their social and legal arrangements, such as surrogacy; and "ownership" rights and economic and commercial considerations, such as research funding and marketing regulations (Royal Commission on New Reproductive Technologies, 1993).

As is the case with most federally appointed royal commissions, the commission's membership reflected Canada's regional and linguistic diversity. Moreover, the multidisciplinary nature of the commission's mandate and future work was reflected in the diverse academic and professional backgrounds of the seven individuals appointed as commissioners. These commissioners represented different fields of expertise, including medicine, genetics, law, theology, sociology, and anthropology. For example, Chairperson Patricia Baird was a professor of medical genetics at the University of British Columbia and a member of the Science Council of Canada Study Committee on Genetic Predisposition. Other commissioners, including Maureen McTeer, a lawyer, and Louise Vandelac, a sociologist, were outspoken critics of reproductive technologies.

Soon after the commission's appointment, thirty experts were invited to participate in a "search conference" intended to help the commission identify themes and issues relevant to its mandate. Among the invitees were feminist activists and researchers who had been working in the area of reproductive technologies.[1] Four workshops were organized to investigate specific topics. Their purpose was twofold: First, they would serve as vehicles for the commission to inform experts of its research agenda and keep them abreast of the commission's thinking on certain issues. Second, the workshops would provide a forum for experts from different disciplines to discuss and debate issues surrounding reproductive technologies (minutes of 31 July 1990 meeting of commissioners, Vancouver).

Of these thirty participants, over a third came from medical or scientific backgrounds, with a particular emphasis on reproductive medicine and genetics. The second- and third-largest groups represented in the search conference were lawyers and representatives of women's advocacy groups.[2] A few participants were recruited from the fields of religion, philosophy, and sociology. Two came from the biomedical/pharmaceutical industry, and two represented infertility awareness associations (Royal Commission on New Reproductive Technologies, 1993).

The background of experts who participated in the search conference suggests that the commission regarded medical-scientific knowledge as more relevant to its work than other types of expertise. Several participants at the conference, in particular feminist researchers and academics, felt that the medical framing of the issues marginalized alternative perspectives during discussions (confidential interviews, 1999 and 2001). Moreover, though the conference was supposed to bring together the combined expertise of law, medicine, sociology, and philosophy to identify gaps in current research, a number of conference participants were left with the impression that the chairperson had already decided on the research areas and the approach the commission would adopt (Margrit Eichler, 1993). Although several critics attributed the failure of the conference to Chairperson Baird, one participant blamed the "incompetence" of the private consulting firm hired to organize it. A feminist academic who had attended the conference argued that the firm had little knowledge of the issue of reproductive technologies. Its main area of expertise was in facilitating meetings in a "very technical, professional way" (confidential interview, 2001). The conference was organized into small workshops with specific and narrowly defined topics. Participants were assigned to workshops by the consultants and were not permitted to stray from their designated tasks. One recalled that facilitators assigned to each workshop would block any effort to reframe the debate or to question the relevance of the predetermined topics: "They were the professionals ... They came with a list of the right way to address these questions" (confidential interview, 2001). This approach stifled people who, for example, wanted to talk about women's health issues or the impact of reproductive technologies on persons with disability. Whereas the search conference organizers were concerned with the operational needs of the commission, such as timeliness of decisions, feminist participants favoured a more open, deliberate discussion of the technologies that would incorporate the needs of their constituents.

Many of the participants soon became frustrated with the whole process. Shortly after the conference ended, feminist researchers met to discuss their concerns about the commission's work and to reconsider their role in the entire process: "About seven or eight of us like-minded folks got together to discuss what went wrong and to ask ourselves 'What are we doing here? Are we [as feminists] being co-opted?'" (confidential interview, 2001).

Their dissatisfaction was shared by Commissioners Maureen McTeer, Louise Vandelac, Maurice Hebert, and Bruce Hatfield. By some accounts, the lack of trust plaguing the Baird Commission throughout its term, especially among the four commissioners themselves, can be traced to the mishandling of this search conference by the consulting firm. As a conference participant explained, "This was actually the time the original mutiny occurred ... The four [commissioners] couldn't stand what was going on" (confidential interview, 2001). This mistrust would continue to characterize the working relationship between the four commissioners and the chairperson.

Deciding on the Research Program: Marginalizing Feminist Commissioners and Feminist Concerns

Although public hearings were set up soon after the appointment of the commission, the development of the research program proceeded at a much slower pace. A number of factors impeded its advancement. First, the position of research director was not permanently filled until July 1990. Second, the development of the research program was regarded as a more difficult undertaking, given that most participants in the public hearings already possessed clear and well-established positions. As one staff member explained, "It was easier to organize public hearings. A lot of groups had positions they wanted to advance. They had specific claims, specific opinions they wanted to be made public. It was a no-brainer. It wasn't too hard to set up public hearings as opposed to the research program that had to be thought out and had to complement the information commissioners were hearing unsolicited" (confidential interview, 2001). By the time the permanent research director, Sylvia Gold, was hired, the research program had already been established by the chair and the executive director of the commission, John Sinclair.

The research program and the issue of governance would be major points of contention among the commissioners themselves. From the beginning, the working relationship between certain commissioners was tense and conflict-ridden. Four of the original commissioners – McTeer, Vandelac, Hebert, and Hatfield – publicly criticized the technological and scientific bias of the research program as well as what they perceived to be Chairperson Baird's autocratic management style. By the summer of 1990, the conflict between the dissenting commissioners and the chair had rapidly escalated. The four commissioners began boycotting meetings in protest of the chair's management style. They had a meeting with the clerk of the privy council in August 1990 to discuss the commission's Order-in-Council, specifically whether decision-making authority rested with the chair or was to be shared among all seven commissioners. The dissenting commissioners argued that part 1 of the Inquiries Act's reference to "commissioners" in the plural meant that all seven commissioners were required to share decision-making authority over the commission's work.

The Prime Minister's Office responded by issuing a second Order-in-Council and bringing on board two new commissioners, Bartha Knoppers, a professor of comparative law at the University of Montreal, and Susan McCutcheon, former chairperson of the Women's College Hospital board of directors. The two new commissioners helped solidify Baird's leadership by effectively transforming the four dissenting commissioners into a minority group. Moreover, the language of the second Order-in-Council formally assigned all decision-making authority to the chair. It essentially "revoked crucial provisions of the original Order-in-Council and which had the effect of stripping the Commissioners of all of their responsibilities (save for delivering a Final Report) and transferring these responsibilities to the Chairperson exclusively" (Statement of Claim, 6 December 1991, paragraph 23).

Several of the commissioners went to the press with their complaints regarding Baird's dictatorial style and their mistrust of the commission's research program and public hearings. This led to more friction among the commissioners. In an unprecedented move, the four dissenting commissioners filed a suit against Baird and the federal government under the Inquiries Act, arguing that the second Order-in-Council constituted a legal violation and therefore should be overturned. In the statement of claim, the four dissenting commissioners asserted that they had been prevented from participating in any meaningful way in several areas of the commission's work, including financial decisions, management activities, and the public hearings process. The commissioners also felt that their expertise was not being used in the commission's work, thereby undermining its original commitment to multidisciplinary research. They argued that responsibility for these problems lay squarely with Chairperson Baird and her management style (Statement of Claim, 6 December 1991, paragraph 13).

In the end, the Prime Minister's Office responded by firing the dissident commissioners. This was the first time in the history of royal commissions that commissioners had been fired. Some argued that the move was an attempt to avoid a public scandal, which would undermine the legitimacy of the commission. Others, however, argued that the Prime Minister's Office had no choice but to fire the four commissioners, given that they had launched a lawsuit against the government (confidential interview, 2001).

Other commissioners, including Suzanne Scorsone, felt that the chair was open to all suggestions and had made an effort to reach a consensus on the research program. However, she argued that certain commissioners had a sense of ownership of the issue of reproductive technologies and came into the process with preconceived notions about the technologies. Some commissioners came in with a very clear idea about how the research program was going to be organized and which researchers to enlist. She stated, "One group wanted to call the shots. Some commissioners knew what we should do, who should be brought in as researchers ... The rest of us did not want the process hijacked by a particular view" (author interview with Suzanne Scorsone, 1999). Each camp appeared to fear that the research program was in danger of being dominated by one of two perspectives: the medical model associated with Baird or the feminist social deconstructionist perspective espoused by Vandelac.

Although they recognized management style and the research agenda as contentious issues, others argued that much of the conflict among commissioners resulted from the Privy Council decision to appoint individuals not on the basis of their expertise but for the constituencies they represented. Problems arose when certain commissioners could not set aside their personal beliefs and the interests of their constituents while working for the commission. According to one senior official, this prevented an open and dynamic dialogue among commissioners (confidential interview, 2001). Some people were named to represent certain constituencies and had very little experience on reproductive technologies: "People were picked to represent constituency angles, political angles, religious angles. That's a recipe for disaster. Different viewpoints are okay, but when you're representing certain constituencies, then you have people you have to answer to. Then you're not free to engage in an open, flexible dialogue" (confidential interview, 2001). Due to their external connections with the women's movement and feminist organizations, Vandelac and McTeer were viewed as representing sectional interests – women's interests – rather than those of the general public. Their feminist stance and their links to a network of feminist scholars and activists critical of reproductive technologies were perceived as obstacles to an "objective" analysis of the issue.

In the end, the Baird Commission's research program would be structured in four general categories of medical practices and technologies. These were, first, the prevalence, risk factors, and prevention of infertility; second, methods of assisted human reproduction; third, prenatal diagnosis techniques and genetics; and fourth, research involving human zygotes, embryos, and foetal tissue (Royal Commission on New Reproductive Technologies, 1993). Each group was assigned a deputy director and several research coordinators, who were responsible for identifying the experts in their respective fields and for contracting research projects. The ways in which these technologies were altering prevailing notions of motherhood, reproduction, and the family were not afforded their own research category. Moreover, a research team was not organized around issues pertaining to women, such as the potential exploitation of poor women in surrogacy arrangements and the increased medicalization of reproduction entailed by these technologies. Instead, concerns relevant to women were dispersed among the four research teams.

The decision to structure the research program according to these technologies would have a significant impact on the type of experts recruited by the commission and consequently the terms of reference that would be used to evaluate the technologies. Although the Research Branch recruited experts from a variety of disciplines ranging from law and biomedicine to sociology and ethics, the vast majority of experts came from scientific, medical, or legal backgrounds (confidential interviews, 2001). Several staff members recalled that the commission's overall research program reflected a general bias in favour of scientific and medical expertise over that of other disciplines. Early on, several staff members and commissioners believed that a hierarchical order of importance that privileged medicine and science developed among the expertise solicited by the commission (confidential interviews, 2001).

The importance assigned to medical and scientific experts is most apparent in the commission's work on embryo research. Studies were conducted predominately by scientists or medical experts recruited from scientific "institutes of excellence." Not surprisingly, this would lead to the recruitment of medical-scientific experts who shared the same worldview on the issue of embryo research. For example, two of the researchers hired by the commission, Bernard Dickens and Michelle Mullen, were professors in the Faculty of Medicine at the University of Toronto. Both examined the issue from a medical-scientific perspective, advocating regulation rather than criminalization of embryo research and foetal tissue transplantation. Keith Betteridge and Don Rieger, leading researchers in animal embryology, were also recruited to write a study on the scientific merits of embryo transfer and related technologies in domestic animals. Once the permanent director was hired to manage the embryo research team, his legal background led to the commissioning of research projects with a legalistic focus. The social sciences, however, were absent in this research area. As a consequence, debates surrounding the moral and social status of embryos took a back seat.

The research team on prenatal diagnosis and genetic technologies also drew experts from the medical-scientific community. Indeed, the deputy director assigned to this research was F.C. Fraser, a geneticist, who was a close colleague of Chairperson Baird. Although a few social scientists were recruited to explore the impact of these technologies on pregnant women and the disabled, medical and scientific experts in the field carried out the majority of the studies. Most of the social scientific research focused on the availability and quality of the delivery of prenatal services, including genetic counselling, a current preoccupation in human genetics (confidential interviews, 2001). The two other research teams – those dealing with the prevalence and prevention of infertility, and human-assisted reproduction – drew from a wider spectrum of expertise. Both deputy directors were health policy specialists, with academic backgrounds in the social sciences. They, in turn, recruited several social scientists who represented diverse areas of specialization, including history, family studies, and philosophy. However, even in these groups, the medical-scientific model for evaluating the technologies would shape the research direction. An important factor that would contribute to the marginalization of non-scientific perspectives was the adoption of evidence-based research as a guiding principle in the commission's work.

Evidence-Based Research and the Privileging of the Quantitative Method

One of the reasons for the scientific orientation of the research was the emphasis placed on evidence-based research and meta-analysis by the commission, two approaches borrowed from the field of medicine. Evidence-based medicine (EBM) utilizes quantitative methods, such as meta-analysis, decision analysis, and cost-effectiveness analysis, to synthesize evidence needed to make clinical decisions and formulate public policy in health care.[3] It has become a popular approach to clinical problem solving, here and abroad. According to the American Medical Association (1992: 2422, emphasis added), EBM constitutes a new paradigm for medical practice that "de-emphasizes intuition, unsystematic clinical experience, and patho-physiologic rationale as sufficient grounds for clinical decision-making, and stresses the examination of evidence from clinical research. Evidence-Based Medicine requires new skills of the physician, including efficient literature-searching, and the application of *formal rules of evidence* in evaluating the clinical literature."

Evidence-based medicine, though not displacing traditional methods of history taking, physical examination, and diagnostic strategies, emphasizes the importance of formal scientific investigation. Medical practitioners are encouraged to record their observations systematically and to apply the rules of evidence in examining the results of studies. Moreover, EBM establishes a pyramid of evidence, with randomized controlled studies viewed as the most reliable method of data collection.

At the time of the commission's deliberations, EBM was fast becoming a popular tool among decision-makers in the health care system. It was and is regarded as an effective tool for setting priorities in health care and for determining the cost-effectiveness of treatments and services (American Medical Association, 1992). The commission adopted evidence-based research practices to evaluate the cost-effectiveness of fertility treatments in the context of Canada's health care system. The commission regarded EBM as a "rational" approach to determining the most effective use of finite resources: "Decisions about which services are publicly supported through provincial health insurance coverage have been influenced historically not by evaluation results but by lobbying, media coverage, and emotional appeals ... Not surprisingly, this situation is of great concern to governments, which now want to be able to make empirical, evidence-based decisions about how much of which technologies or procedures should be provided" (Royal Commission on New Reproductive Technologies, 1993: 89). Declining economic growth, rising health care costs, and the expanding definition of health services made the cost-effectiveness of new reproductive technologies an important area of study, for both government and the commission. The issue of health care funding of reproductive technologies, as well as their effectiveness and safety as medical treatments, would become a central theme in the commission's work.

The adoption of evidence-based research as the guiding principle in the commission's work would inevitably privilege research that could produce "hard" facts through the scientific method. A commission staff member specializing in the area of women's reproductive health stated that researchers using qualitative research methods had a difficult time grappling with the evidence-based approach and its rules of evidence. They were repeatedly asked by senior staff members and the chair to substantiate their positions with hard data. "Where is the data?" was a recurring question posed to social scientists by the chair and her staff. As the staff member explained, "Every time we tried to broaden the view of infertility [from a narrowly focused medical condition], we were asked to be responsible and to provide hard data on how many people are infertile. There was no database in Canada with this information" (confidential interview, 2001). Indeed, the commission's preference for the quantitative mode of inquiry led to a shift in focus from prevention and alternatives to reproductive technologies to determining the rate of infertility in Canadian society and the effectiveness of several treatments (confidential interview, 2001).

Research proposals that did not conform to the technological categories of the program and the methodological requirements of evidence-based research were often seen as obstructing the work of the commission. For example, a researcher active in the women's health movement wanted to conduct a study on the prevention of infertility, but the proposal was rejected outright because it did not conform to the narrow interpretation of the research agenda, which emphasized access to treatments and their safety. All other research was seen as "muddying the waters," and researchers who tried to challenge the dominant discourse were regarded with suspicion by top-level managers and the chair (confidential interviews, 2001). As a staff member explained, "Researchers were viewed [by Patricia Baird] as an impediment to the drafting of the Final Report. It seems researchers were constantly irritating Dr. Baird by pointing out 'minor' problems, such as major gaps in the research" (quoted in Margrit Eichler, 1993: 217).

Other researchers also felt that the commission regarded quantitative methods as the best tools for producing policy-relevant knowledge. A commission staff member recalled that quantitative data were valued over qualitative approaches because they were considered more neutral. The staff member argued that the role of researchers in the commission's work was to "collect and coalesce up-to-date information. The social aspect or qualitative dimension of the research was to be dealt with elsewhere, in the public hearings organized by the commission's Consultation and Communications Branch" (confidential interview, 2001). The perception among upper management and some of the staff was that the Research Branch would be responsible for producing "objective" policy expertise, whereas the Consultation and Communications Branch would provide qualitative analysis of what was heard during the public hearings.

Two external researchers who were hired to conduct qualitative studies also recalled the clear preference for quantitative research. One feminist researcher remembered receiving negative comments on her research proposal due to its qualitative methodology. Although her proposal was eventually accepted, she felt it was important to justify the qualitative approach in her study and its methodological rigour and reliability (confidential interviews, 2001).

The adoption of evidence-based research and quantitative methods meant that feminist researchers working in the social sciences were often called upon to be more objective in their approach. During the review process, several researchers were frequently asked to offer a more balanced analysis of their subject matter and to use neutral language. One feminist researcher recalled being asked to avoid using certain terms, including "patriarchy" and "eugenics," when analyzing the issue of surrogacy. The researcher, who found such requests extremely heavy-handed and difficult to deal with, remarked, "I couldn't understand how we could have a discussion on surrogacy without mentioning patriarchy" (confidential interview, 2001). Another interviewee cited a case in which one researcher was asked to replace the term "judicial interference" with "judicial intervention" in her study of women's reproductive rights because the latter was viewed as being more neutral. A staff member who oversaw some of the research projects argued that wording changes were sometimes necessary in order to avoid any semblance of "bias" in the research: "With judicial interference, you don't have to read any further. You've already telegraphed your conclusion ... If you decide a certain practice is negative, you better put forward data to support your conclusion" (confidential interview, 2001).

Researchers themselves were divided on which sets of values should govern their work. This would lead to different interpretations of several issues, including who should be determining the commission's research agenda and program, as well as the level of control exercised by the chairperson on research matters. For example, though some resented the lack of autonomy afforded them by Chairperson Baird, others had no problems with her control of the research program. As one interviewee explained, "My feeling is this: The chair is appointed by an Order-in-Council. The prime minister asks Patricia Baird basically to design the research and *we were the arms of that decision-maker*. He [the prime minister] didn't ask me ... Ultimately, the success or failure lies with that decision-maker" (confidential interview, 1999).

The willingness of researchers to accept requests for changes to their studies varied according to how they interpreted their role in the commission's activities. A staff member employed in the Research Branch noted that non-academic researchers or consultants hired by the commission were more likely to accept such revisions than their university-based counterparts (confidential interview, 2001). Non-university researchers were said to be more accommodating than were academics, who resisted any changes to their work. The positions taken by researchers on the review process depended on whether they saw themselves primarily as policy analysts and consultants or as independent academics governed by the principles of discipline-oriented research and academic freedom. Several researchers, working both inside and outside the commission, saw themselves as consultants hired to meet the needs of their client (confidential interview, 2001). The client, in this case, was the commissioners. Many of these researchers had prior experience with consulting for government agencies and were familiar with this type of review process. Some of the researchers inside the commission also viewed their role as producing knowledge that the commissioners needed to inform their decisions. As one staff member explained, "The royal commission ... had a mandate. It had very specific objectives. It had to write a report. And, as such, it needed very particular elements of research to build this edifice of knowledge" (confidential interview, 2001).

Conversely, academic researchers, including several feminist researchers, believed that the commission exercised too much control. Several of them felt that they were being asked to make substantive changes to their work (confidential interviews, 2001). Several senior managers and commissioners held that these revisions were necessary to ensure "balance" and "objectivity" in the research program. Since research studies are public documents, commissioners should have maintained a light editorial hand in the review process to ensure balance. As one interviewee put it, "An author has the freedom to say that certain practices could be considered eugenics or in some countries there were eugenic laws, like sterilization laws. It depends on how these technologies are used. But with that kind of inflammatory language, you want the research to read in a way that brings forth knowledge not coloured by bias" (confidential interview, 1999).

The review process put in place by the commission was also criticized by some staff members and researchers for not conforming to academic norms and standards. For the most part, proposals and studies were reviewed not by academic peers but by the research director, the executive director, and the chairperson. Although this practice is not unique to the Baird Commission, it was not employed in other policy-oriented commissions – most notably the 1982 Macdonald Commission on Canada's Economic Prospects – that had adopted an academic peer review process. Chairperson Baird was especially prolific, offering detailed comments and suggestions on almost every proposal and study received by the commission. Both her supporters and detractors characterized Baird as a hard worker, taking an active interest in every aspect of the commission's activities. However, though her supporters described her feedback as providing "firm direction," her critics regarded it as pushing the research into a different direction.

Feminists Pushed Aside: The Policy Research of the Baird Commission

Ultimately, evidence-based research, and the quantitative methods it uses, influenced the direction of the commission's research. For example, a large segment of the research conducted in the four research areas outlined above relied heavily on empirical-analytical methods, causal explanations, and technical expertise. The combined studies on infertility were basically an extensive review of existing scientific literature on the underlying causes of infertility. Cost-benefit analysis and meta-analysis were two methods used to evaluate the effectiveness of treatments and the actual and potential risks for the user. The commission relied heavily on the expertise of researchers affiliated with two health technology assessment centres: the University of British Columbia's Office of Health Technology Assessment and the Manitoba Centre for Health Policy and Evaluation at the University of Manitoba. These centres were two of several research institutes established by provincial governments in the late 1980s and early 1990s to evaluate the effectiveness and efficiency of medical technologies and services. Other researchers were also recruited from McMaster University's Centre of Clinical Epidemiology and Biostatistics. Ron Goeree and Roberta Labelle of McMaster were specialists in EBM and had published extensively on the economic evaluation of medical treatments and practices. The research found that funding decisions in the area of reproductive technologies had been made in an ad hoc and fragmented manner, without reference to available evidence on treatment effectiveness and safety. Much of this research focused on establishing, in scientific terms, whether technologies such as in vitro fertilization should be regarded as experimental treatments or routine procedures to be covered by Medicare. In contrast, there was little discussion in the research regarding whether delivering a child to whom one is genetically related is a privilege or a right that should be protected by the state via the availability of state-subsidized fertility treatments.

The legal research generated by the commission reflected the traditional concerns of legal analysis of policy issues, such as constitutionality, consistency with statutes, human rights, and questions about jurisdiction (Pal, 1997). Some of the research studies analyzed the implications of reproductive technologies on the legal status of children and parents. Questions that were addressed included "Who can claim the children produced from a donated ovum or embryo?" and "Who is the legal parent in the cases of surrogacy?" However, the majority of the studies produced by legal experts focused on the implications of reproductive technologies for Canada's current legal system and their impact on Canadian laws governing commercial interests and the medical community. As a result, some commissioners and staff members felt that too much of the legal research concentrated on issues surrounding the informed consent of patients undergoing infertility treatments. As Louise Vandelac (1993: 272) remarked, "There seems to be a growing tendency to use the notion of consent as a modality for transferring responsibility for experimentation from the researcher to the individual object of experimentation. This is obviously the logic that underlies the Baird Commission giving so many research contracts to examining the issue of informed consent."

In contrast, little research was conducted on the legal rights of women or couples vis-à-vis the medical community or the biomedical industry, such as women's rights to free and safe contraceptives. The only legal research that examined women's issues was a study on judicial intervention in pregnancy and childbirth, and a legal-ethical analysis of surrogate motherhood.

A few studies were commissioned on the social and ethical dimensions of both infertility and reproductive technologies. These drew attention to a number of issues, including the commercial or scientific exploitation of embryos and genetic engineering, and the implications of reproductive technologies for women and ethnocultural communities. For example, studies were conducted on the impact of prenatal diagnosis on attitudes regarding the disabled as well as on women's experiences with technology during pregnancy. Background papers were also commissioned on the global and political-economic contexts of reproductive technologies. However, the scientific and legal studies far outnumbered those examining the commercial dimension of reproductive technologies. Furthermore, most of these were considered supplemental parts of the larger scientific or legal research projects (confidential interviews, 2001).

Questions surrounding the impact of reproductive technologies on certain segments of society, including women, minority communities, and the disabled were not afforded their own research area. They were raised during the commission's hearings by several women's organizations and disability rights groups, which argued that many of these technologies were detrimental to the most vulnerable women in society. For example, groups such as the National Action Committee on the Status of Women asserted that prenatal diagnostic testing contributed to the widespread discrimination against people with disabilities because it reinforced the notion of the "perfect baby." Poor women could also be compelled to enter into a surrogacy arrangement due to their circumstances. These concerns would be dispersed among the four scientific research areas. Moreover, the volume of studies on society-related issues was narrow in scope and analysis. Two studies were essentially descriptions of current social values and attitudes of Canadians towards reproductive technologies. Indeed, their author was Decima Research, a survey firm whose findings were derived from focus groups and a nation-wide survey. The purpose of the two studies was to take a "snapshot" of current public opinion on reproductive technologies rather than to provide an analysis of their origins or social implications.

The decision to organize the research program according to technological categories and the adoption of evidence-based research as a guiding principle in the commission's work helped advance the medical-scientific framing of reproductive technologies. It reaffirmed the status of medical-scientific experts in the policy debate on the issue and marginalized research areas that could not be evaluated through scientific rules of evidence. Qualitative researchers interested in uncovering the social and moral implications of these technologies were asked to provide hard data to substantiate their claims. These findings accord with Richard Simeon's (1987) argument that royal commissions tend to privilege academic disciplines that provide a consistent and unified approach to understanding a particular issue. For the Macdonald Commission, the neo-classical model of economics provided commissioners with a clear framework for devising economic policy in Canada. The medical-scientific model did the same for the Baird Commission.

Separating Facts from Values: The Bureaucratic and Intellectual Division of Research from Policy Analysis

An important organizational feature of the royal commission was its bureaucratic separation of the research work from policy analysis. The Policy Analysis Unit was located in the Consultation and Communications Branch. The unit had a number of functions to perform in the commission's work, including preparing commissioners for public hearings, conducting environmental overviews of existing policy on reproductive technologies, reviewing international reports, and analyzing what was said during the public hearings and consultations for the commissioners (confidential interview, 2001). Whereas the Research Branch was responsible for generating empirical evidence, the Policy Analysis Unit focused on "non-research" inputs, such as the existing literature and the public hearings (confidential interviews, 2001).

When the commission was first created, the rationale for distinguishing research from analysis was discussed. Some staff members from both sides questioned how one could conduct research without engaging in analysis. Some recalled minor tensions among staff members, particularly in the beginning, when it was not at all clear what the relationship would be between the two components (confidential interviews, 2001). Early on in the commission, an attempt was made to bring together members of each unit into small groups in order to facilitate communication and interaction among the different spheres of inquiry. Eventually, however, considerations such as limited office space, time constraints, and work tasks made this option impractical.

The commission's decision to organize research and analysis in different functional specialties was based on the view that the Research Branch's primary task was to produce technical, "value-neutral" studies that provided scientific evidence without taking a normative position on the issue of reproductive technologies (confidential interviews, 2001). The Policy Analysis Unit, on the other hand, would provide commissioners with information on the political and social context of reproductive technologies – fundamentally, "non-scientific" or subjective knowledge. The unit was essentially responsible for uncovering "the bigger picture" and investigating the political, social, and economic elements of the debate as a whole. As one staff member explained, "The research was always a little bit further away from what drives things at the political level. Policy analysis was that much closer" (confidential interview, 2001).

The bureaucratic separation of research and policy analysis was premised on the view that researchers should not engage in the policy debate on reproductive technologies but rather produce observable, reliable data that would aid commissioners in developing their recommendations. As one interviewee explained, "The Research Branch is there to generate empirical information – to gather information and to generate new information. It is not their [the researchers'] role to propose policy. Mind you, in the course of the research, researchers do bring forth policy ideas. One of our tasks was to marshal the feelings of researchers – private researchers but primarily academic researchers. The political work, that is, policy development, lay elsewhere, with the commissioners" (confidential interview, 2001).

Given the bureaucratic and functional distinction between research and policy analysis, there was little lateral communication between the Research Branch and the Policy Analysis Unit. Thus, no mechanism existed to channel information gathered from the public hearings and consultations to the research staff. Due to the nature of their work, Policy Analysis Unit staff attended several of the public hearings and consultations set up by the commission and had access to the transcripts. Moreover, they received copies of all intervenor submissions or briefings to be used for their analysis of issues raised by community groups and individual citizens. This information, which called attention to the implications of reproductive technologies for different communities and individuals, was not relayed to the research staff. It could have helped identify gaps in the research and push for more community-based research and qualitative analysis in the commission's work. However, the division of research and analysis into two separate functional units limited the communication of ideas between the two groups and therefore kept intact the pre-eminence of the medical-scientific orientation of the research projects. As one interviewee remarked, "There was no community-based research [on the issue of infertility]. The assumption was that they [community perspectives] were being heard in the public consultations" (confidential interview, 2001).

Equally, employees in the Policy Analysis Unit were not kept apprised of the studies being commissioned by the Research Branch. Analysts were not given access to research findings, and some argued that barriers were deliberately set up to minimize the sharing of information between the two groups, especially during the last year of the commission's work. A staff member recalled, "I was doing some analysis on a topic and heard there were some research findings in on it but was told I couldn't have access to them. To me this was highly unreasonable ... My experience is that, generally speaking, if you work in the same organization, and you need to know something you can access it ... There wasn't a lot of sharing of information in the commission" (confidential interview, 2001). Some staff members felt that a rigid chain of command put in place by upper management and the chairperson undermined an open flow of communication between organizational units. Several also felt that upper management controlled vertical communication between themselves and the commissioners. As one commented, "Nothing would go directly to commissioners. Staff-commissioner interaction was not encouraged. If we ran into a commissioner who wanted something, we had to give the request to the director; then he or she would give it to the deputy director. Upper management controlled information that was coming from staff" (confidential interview, 2001).

Senior managers were said to control information they felt did not conform to what the commissioners wanted to hear. This was especially the case during the commission's last two years when it was in the process of developing the framework for the final report. This conflict is typical of what Alan Cairns (1990) views as the tension between academic and bureaucratic values inherent in royal commissions. Although researchers and analysts wanted to engage in an open debate and introduce new areas of inquiry, upper management, including the commissioners, was more concerned with administrative issues, including respecting hierarchical organization of authority, the specialization of duties, and the maximization of technical and organizational efficiency (Margrit Eichler, 1993).

The bureaucratic distinction between research and policy analysis would make the writing of the final report a contested issue. Considerable debate occurred within the commission concerning which unit would write it. This decision would have a number of important consequences: First, it determined which staff members would be let go in the last year of the commission's work. Second, it affected how the research would be used and interpreted in the final report. As one staff member explained, "There is always going to be tension about communicating your messages and the research that supports that message. And there is going to be disagreement in terms of who does the research, what the research says, and then how you interpret" (confidential interview, 2001).

Chairperson Baird and Executive Director John Sinclair decided to assign the task of writing the report to the Policy Analysis Branch. Researchers were asked to produce studies that were value-neutral and objective, devoid of any normative statement on the issue of reproductive technologies. The Policy Analysis Unit, under the firm direction of the chairperson and the other commissioners, would then decipher the policy implications of the research for the final report. Several researchers, including feminist researchers, resented relinquishing ownership of their work to the Policy Analysis Unit, fearing that it would not be interpreted in an appropriate manner (confidential interviews, 2001). Towards the end of the commission's deliberations, when the final report was being written, many of the researchers were let go. Some asserted that they had been fired because of their critical stance against certain reproductive technologies. Senior officials offered a different interpretation of the event, arguing that after the studies were submitted and the commission began writing the report, the need for in-house researchers declined. As the commission's activities wound down, so did the size of the staff. Maintaining the same number of employees the commission initially had would have been an expensive proposition (confidential interview, 1999). Discontent that arose during this time sprang from the ownership that certain researchers felt regarding their studies and their wish to be involved in writing the report. According to several senior officials, this exercise was the exclusive domain of commissioners (confidential interview, 1999).

Conclusion

The 1989 appointment of the Baird Commission provided an opportunity to expand the boundaries of the debate on reproductive technologies beyond the scientific-medical realm. Several feminist researchers and activists were optimistic that the commission would encourage multidisciplinary collaboration in its research program. Over time, however, it became clear that certain types of research were regarded as more relevant for policy analysis than others. In particular, researchers using a feminist lens or qualitative methods were perceived as advocates for women's issues rather than as impartial, objective analysts. A number of factors contributed to this situation. First, the decision to structure the research program along scientific and technological lines contributed to the privileging of medical-scientific expertise over that of other disciplines. The establishment of four research groups studying the technologies themselves led to the recruitment and privileging of medical-scientific experts as opposed to sociologists, philosophers, or feminists. With a few exceptions, the studies produced by the commission focused on the cost-effectiveness and safety of the technologies rather than analyzing their current and future impact on specific communities and society as a whole.

Another factor contributing to this disciplinary hierarchy was the adoption of evidence-based research as a guiding principle. This approach, rooted in the medical-scientific community, specifies certain methods of collecting and analyzing data that are not easily transferable to other disciplines, especially feminist studies working with the qualitative method. Evidence-based research sought to generate the "hard facts" about the various technologies through biostatistical techniques. Therefore, quantitative methods rather than qualitative analysis were the preferred mode of inquiry in the commission's research. The influence of research that could not meet the rules of evidence set out by evidence-based research was muted.

The bureaucratic division of policy analysis and policy advice within the commission represented the organizational manifestation of the fact-value dichotomy that informs mainstream policy analysis. Researchers were expected to provide objective data without offering any advice on policy recommendations. This exercise was supposed to be left to the commissioners, who were to interpret the data and decide on policy recommendations. Advocacy on the part of feminist researchers was discouraged on the basis that community views and perspectives would be relayed by the representatives of the communities themselves during the commission's public hearings. Feminist researchers who had hoped to broaden the debate on reproductive technologies to include their repercussions for women and the disabled found themselves functioning within a hostile environment. Ultimately, the inherent bias in the commission for quantitative research and the intellectual and bureaucratic division of policy analysis and policy advice proved incompatible with the dual vision of feminist policy research.

The challenges encountered by feminists working for the commission are not unique. Within the Canadian federal bureaucracy, connections between feminist bureaucrats and grassroots organizations have generally been viewed with skepticism. Chappell's (2002) study of feminist bureaucrats in Canada and Australia reveals a lack of tolerance within the Canadian bureaucracy for advocacy of sectional interests. Bureaucratic norms of neutrality and impartiality make it very difficult for internal feminist activists to lobby on behalf of women's issues. This was definitely the case in the Baird Commission.

The marginalization of feminist researchers, however, was not inevitable. The experience of other commissions, such as the Royal Commission on the Status of Women and the Royal Commission on Aboriginal Peoples, reveals that advocacy and analysis are not always regarded as separate or conflicting research activities. In fact, both of these commissions hired researchers with strong connections to grassroots organizations, believing that they would best capture the concerns and realities facing women and Aboriginals in Canadian society. The role of researchers in setting the research agenda and writing the report also varies with each commission. Although the chair and senior management were responsible for the direction and orientation of the Baird Commission research program, other commissions seek greater involvement on the part of researchers. This was the case with the Macdonald Commission, for which the research director, not the commissioners, determined the research agenda and oversaw the writing of the final report. Here, academic standards rather than the views of commissioners informed the commission's research work. Use of this model in the Baird Commission would perhaps have allowed for greater recognition and appreciation of methodological diversity among researchers.

Finally, the internal governance regimes vary from commission to commission. In the Baird Commission, bureaucratic principles, such as secrecy and the hierarchical chain of command, effectively quashed open deliberation on substantive issues among commissioners and staff. Other commissions, such as the 1963 Royal Commission on Bilingualism and Biculturalism and the more recent Royal Commission on Aboriginal Peoples, represent the potential of commissions to foster open and ongoing dialogue among commissioners and researchers. A commitment to open deliberation among researchers, staff, and commissioners may have provided feminist activists and academics with a more receptive forum for their policy research on reproductive technologies.

6
Framing Feminists: Market Populism and Its Impact on Public Policy in Australia and Canada
Marian Sawer

Populism and populist name-calling has a long history in English-speaking democracies; the arrival of representative democracy was accompanied by repeated claims that politicians and political elites were betraying the interests of the people. The message of populism was that despite doctrines of popular sovereignty, politics had actually escaped popular control (Canovan, 2002: 27). Populist politicians called for the reassertion of popular control through devices of direct democracy, such as referenda.

There have been many different kinds of populism, including right-wing and left-wing forms, but all are characterized by both anti-elitism and the exaltation of and appeal to the people (Canovan, 1981: 294). The structure of populist discourse is based on drawing a political dividing line between, on one side, an untrustworthy and parasitic elite and, on the other, the virtuous and long-suffering people. Or, more briefly, between us and them. Populist leaders offer to defend the interests of the people, constructed as a homogeneous group free of gender, race, or class divides, from the depredations of the elite and their ancillaries. This is the grammar of populism.

The grammar of populism also involves another element. If political emotion is to be effectively mobilized along the us versus them divide, elites should be shown to feel contempt for ordinary people and their values. This attribution of contempt is central to current populist strategies in countries such as Australia and Canada. It is an aspect of populist discourse that has often been overlooked in the classical analyses of populism, such as that by Margaret Canovan (1981), but can be seen again and again in contemporary political speech.

It may be that the attribution of contempt becomes particularly important in the context of what Thomas Frank (2002) has nicely termed "market populism," to distinguish it from the kind of populisms currently found in Europe, which combine xenophobia with economic nationalism. Market populism, which normalizes self-seeking behaviour and aspirations to wealth, displaces the old "Mr. Fat" characterizations of elites. If self-seeking is normal, showing that elites are self-seeking will not be sufficient – they must also be typified by their contempt for mainstream values. This move is part of the "culture wars" that distract attention from the distributional consequences of market populist agendas.

Although populist leaders historically galvanized hostility against big-city financial elites whose loyalties were cosmopolitan, the market populism of today has quite a different target. This new populist discourse constructs a divide between a welfare state elite and associated special interests, on one side, and ordinary people or mainstream taxpayers, on the other. The elites are no longer bankers, corrupt politicians, and international financiers but rather "the bleeding hearts, the politically correct, who control everything we do" (letter to the *Australian*, 9 September 2004: 12). They are still city-based, but are predominantly humanities, arts, and social science graduates rather than bankers or financiers. They are teachers and social workers, and, at the expense of business and taxpayers, they are responsible for the growth of welfare state regulation and redistribution. Current anti-elitist discourse has little in common with the academic study of elites, in which elites are made up of those who exercise political, economic, and perhaps symbolic power. It is symbolic power alone that is the focus of current anti-elitist discourse.

Elites are held responsible, first, for imposing political correctness and then for disputing the people's verdict at elections and continuing to complain about issues such as human rights and social justice or the environment. A federal minister in Australia decried the need to pander to "people who spend time sitting in cafés sipping lattes" when deciding such issues.[1] Although, according to the theorists of deliberative democracy, talk about public issues may be the defining element of democracy, populist discourse is dismissive of those who engage in public debate and who embrace diversity and difference in perspectives.

Situated as they are within the new class elite that does well out of equality and has contempt for mainstream values, feminists turn up on the wrong side of the us versus them divide. In public choice terms, they are classical rent seekers, meaning that they aim to achieve better returns through the state than they can achieve through the market. Public choice theory, as developed by American economists James Buchanan and Gordon Tullock (1962), stems from rational actor premises, whereby both individual and collective actors are motivated by the desire to maximize returns rather than by broader notions of the public interest. The attribution of contempt to teachers and social workers may seem odd, but it helps to delegitimize feminist and other equality projects and values.

This chapter draws on evidence from both Australia and anglophone Canada of the reshaping of public discourse under the impact of market populism.[2] It begins by providing a genealogy of key components of market populist discourse, the concepts of new class/welfare state elites and special interests. These concepts distinguish market populism from older forms of populism while retaining the basic semantic grammar of the latter.

The chapter then examines the effects of market populism in delegitimizing social justice and equal opportunity agendas. In particular, it sheds light on how feminists and other equality seekers have been framed as rent seekers, lacking any moral authenticity. It analyzes the populist rejection of the accommodation of group difference and the revival of ideas of equal treatment as same treatment. It notes that men's rights groups and anti-feminist women's groups in the two countries play similar roles in promoting the idea that equal opportunity programs discriminate against men and the women who choose to be economically dependent on them. The discussion concludes by analyzing the impact of market populism in delegitimizing the role of intermediary institutions in policy debate, or at least those that provide voice for women and other groups that look to state intervention to achieve equality.

Introducing the "New Class"

The significant populist upsurge in Western democracies is often attributed to the insecurities fostered by globalization and to the pace of social, economic, and cultural change. It was marked by the emergence of parties such as Reform in Canada and Pauline Hanson's One Nation in Australia. Although parties of this kind have drawn on traditional wellsprings of popular discontent, they are also influenced by new international discourses emanating largely from the United States. In Australia one of these discourses has been the concept of the "new class," as reworked in the 1970s by American neo-conservatives, many of whom had been influenced by Marxism in their youth (Dymond, 2004). New class discourse had its origins in the Trotskyist critique of state socialist societies: a new class based on ownership of cultural capital had usurped power and was maximizing redistribution from the workers to further its own agendas.

The new class identified by American neo-conservatives consists of university-educated intellectuals radicalized by the social movements of the 1960s. This class has a vested interest in expanding the public sector, in which it will play a leading role thanks to its cultural capital. This new class speaks a language of public interest and equal opportunity, masking its own self-seeking and indifference to ordinary people. Economists Milton and Rose Friedman helped popularize the concept in their bestselling *Free to Choose* (1980: 142, 301), which depicts the new class as acquiring high incomes for itself through preaching equality and promoting and administering the resulting legislation.

The neo-conservatives associated the new class with values such as environmentalism, feminism, multiculturalism, and minority rights more generally. These values were not regarded as having any authentic ethical content: rather, they were seen as elite fashions that received the collective label "political correctness." In the influential essays of Christopher Lasch (1995), the new class elite was characterized not only by cosmopolitanism and political correctness but also by contempt for unfashionable Middle American values. The idea that the new class is contemptuous of ordinary people's values, or just of ordinary people themselves, becomes very important in mobilizing political emotion around this new discursive divide. American new class discourse was soon imported into Australia through neo-conservative organs such as *Quadrant,* the journal of the Association for Cultural Freedom.

Both new class and traditional populist themes were presented in *Pauline Hanson–The Truth,* a book published in 1997 to mark the launch of Pauline Hanson's One Nation. It devoted a chapter to attacking new class or "cognitive" elites and their "betrayal" of Australia (Hanson, 1997: 56-108). However, Hanson was too entrenched in the tradition of the old populism to omit xenophobic and economic nationalist attacks on "Asianisation" and the internationalization of the economy. Her attacks on free trade and competition policy guaranteed less than sympathetic treatment by the main vehicles of market populism; after initial electoral success, the party quickly disintegrated.

The most elaborate presentation of new class concepts in Australia has been that of sociologist Katharine Betts in her popular book *The Great Divide* (1999). This book positions the author on the right side of the "great divide" between the world of ordinary people and the cosmopolitan world of the elite or new class. It reproduces the full grammar of populism, with the new class being contemptuous of the materialism and parochialism of the working class and lecturing it to accept asylum seekers (81ff). This view of a new class elite lecturing the electorate to accept asylum seekers and wincing at "basic Australian values" has been taken up with enthusiasm in free-market journals and in the Murdoch press.

In Canada, as will be discussed below, anti-elite discourse has exhibited many of the features of new class discourse, but without the explicit use of a Marxist framework linking ownership of cultural capital to class and class exploitation. For example, David Frum, a *National Post* columnist from 1998, made regular attacks on the social engineers who promote bilingualism, cultural diversity, indigenous sovereignty, and welfare dependency in Canada.

Although new class discourse rarely made it explicit, the core members of this supposedly privileged new class, defined by concern over issues such as the environment and human rights, were the well-educated but underpaid members of feminized professions such as social work, teaching, and librarianship. One of the key characteristics of the new class is, in fact, its female identity.

Unmasking "Special Interests"

The public choice concept of "special interests" has formed another element in recent populist discourse. As we have seen, public choice theory debunks the idea that the motivations of groups who purport to pursue the public interest differ in any way from the motivation of others. The term "special interests" is particularly applied by public choice theorists to groups such as environmentalists or equality seekers who invoke state interference with the market.

Friedrich A. Hayek (1976), who inspired much of this new discourse, said in his major philosophical manifesto against the welfare state that the idea of social justice was a mirage. It was a licence for interfering with the mechanisms of the free market and an intrusion on the liberty expressed through market choices. Market outcomes should not be the subject of moral disapprobation or material reparation, because they were the result of an impersonal but beneficent process rather than being "willed." In denying the legitimacy of redistribution, Hayek attacked the rationale of the welfare state at its heart (99).

Public provision to ensure equal opportunity was alien to Hayek's view of the world. Those who advocated such provision could not represent the mythical public interest, but must be "special interests" that fed off the state. Such groups, he believed, falsely promoted the moral superiority of the non-profit sector over the for-profit private sector and championed the myth that the public and community sectors were without vested interests. In contrast, public choice analyses seek to show that the activity of public interest groups, whether seeking to protect workers, consumers, or the environment, or to promote equal opportunity, will invariably be of greatest benefit to the new class. This class thrives on the growth of state intervention in the private sector.

Public choice theory has been very successfully popularized in the English-speaking democracies, both through think-tanks created for this purpose and through means such as the *Yes, Minister* BBC television series devised by a Friedman disciple, Tony Jay. The think-tanks took up Milton Friedman's challenge to "sell ideas like soap" – that is, by dint of constant restatement, re-endorsement, and repackaging. The model was the UK Institute of Economic Affairs, founded in 1955. In Canada the Fraser Institute (founded in 1974) and in Australia the Centre for Independent Studies (1976) and the older (1943) Institute of Public Affairs, which became Hayekian in the 1980s, were to wield similar influence. Hayek, Friedman, and Buchanan served as advisers to these think-tanks. The special-interest discourse they disseminated became part of the governing discourse of Britain's Thatcher regime and of other English-speaking democracies.

The think-tanks operate at a number of levels. They have enjoyed exceptional access to the mainstream media, particularly to papers once owned by Conrad Black in Canada and still owned by Rupert Murdoch in Australia. For example, a study of Murdoch's flagship paper the *Australian* found that from 2003 to 2004, authors from free-market think-tanks were eighteen times as likely to be represented on its Opinion page as those from "progressive" think-tanks.[3]

The publications of the think-tanks themselves, such as the *Fraser Forum* in Canada and *Policy* and the *IPA Review* in Australia, specialize in exposing the cosy conspiracy between rent-seeking special interests and bureaucrats wishing to maximize their budgets. One example of a rent-seeking special interest consists of single mothers who have calculated that they can obtain a better "rent" through the state than they can through the market or marriage (Swan and Bernstam, 1987). Women's units within the state, or femocrats, to use an Australian term, are deemed to promote the organization and interests of sole parents while at the same time ensuring good jobs for themselves. The activities of feminist policy-makers supposedly exemplify the way in which special interests construct sections of the population as victims in order to justify intervention and public expenditure.

Institutionalizing victim status means discouraging personal responsibility for health, safety, and financial security, and encouraging dependence on the nanny state. Elsewhere (Sawer, 2003), I have explored the way in which female metaphors such as "nanny state" or "weaning off the breast" are used to reinforce the neoliberal attack on the welfare state by associating the latter with loss of masculine values such as self-reliance and independence. Women social reformers of the first wave of the women's movement were deeply implicated in the transformation of the "nightwatchman state" of classical liberalism into the public caring associated with the welfare state. This maternalizing of the state is now denounced as resulting in a loss of masculinity, through both overprotection and usurpation of male provider roles.

Public choice repositioned equality seeking as the rent seeking of special interests rather than an authentic public value (see also Brodie, this volume). Whereas social liberalism had emphasized the responsibility of the state to provide all citizens with the opportunity to develop potential, the new emphasis was on choice, something that only markets could provide. If the term "equal opportunity" was used at all, it was the "thin" version, meaning absence of legal restraints on competing for unequal rewards, not opportunity for development of potential. Any defence of the welfare state could be reframed as resistance by minority and special-interest groups to the economic reform required for global competitiveness and the tax cuts desired by ordinary people.

The New Populism in Australia

In 1996 the discursive reframing of welfare state and equality projects in Australia was given increased impetus by the election of a Coalition government at the federal level, with Liberal leader John Howard as prime minister. In a "headland" lecture outlining his philosophy before winning government, Howard (1995) claimed that under Labor a bureaucracy of the new class had taken over. Moreover, "mainstream" Australians felt powerless to compete with the noisy vested-interest groups that had come to dominate decision making. His goal was to reverse this trend and institute government for the mainstream.

Howard (1994: 22) also depicted human rights and equal opportunity issues as purely elite concerns, referring to race, gender, and sexual preference as the "designer forms of discrimination in the 1990s." As we have already seen, it is a common feature of new class discourse to denigrate such concerns as elite fashions. Like the US Republicans, Howard was trying to reach blue-collar workers believed to be hostile to such fashions and resentful of their own role in funding the welfare state. When the Liberals won the election, many interpreted their victory in Howard's terms, as a defeat for the "special interests" such as feminists, multiculturalists, and Aboriginal advocates (Sawer, 1997).

Although Howard was already taking the newly elected Coalition government in a populist direction, his approach differed from that of the more overtly populist Pauline Hanson's One Nation. The Howard government deprecated One Nation's naïve views on economic globalization but adopted elements of its social policy, including an increasingly punitive regime for asylum seekers and onshore refugees, as well as a men's rights agenda in relation to custody and child support.

Both One Nation and the new Coalition government (like Reform in Canada) played up populist themes of the need to strengthen border security and defend sovereignty. They suggested that new class elites, the courts, and international tribunals were in league to overturn the measures (such as mandatory detention) taken to discourage asylum seekers from arriving on Australian shores. John Howard (1994: 25) deplored the way in which the domestic affairs of Australia had been influenced by the fine print of international treaties and the deliberations of "foreign" (that is, United Nations) committees: "There is an overwhelming view in this country that Australian law should be governed and determined by Australia alone."

As framed by market populism, liberal elites are always prone to selling out the national interest. When they are unable to secure an electoral majority for their agenda, they turn to the international arena and to "like-minded self-proclaimed champions of social justice sitting in Geneva, Brussels or New York" (Albrechtsen, 2002: 30). Or, as the Howard government's chair of the Australian Broadcasting Authority put it, "if the people will not accept your agenda, the elite guardians can have it adopted through the back door by a consensus among the international elites" (Flint, 2003:

162). However, the same kind of censure is not applied to free-trade agreements that will constrain the ability of governments to implement popular mandates or will enable corporations to take popularly elected governments before international tribunals.

The public choice view is that human rights advocates who try to work through multilateral bodies are serving the interests of their agencies and staff more than the interests of human rights. The Howard government demonstratively turned its back on such interference from United Nations human rights bodies and was applauded by the free-market think-tanks: "By refusing to participate in UN shame games, the Howard government – along with its Canadian and US counterparts – is starting to bring an end to the whole advocacy charade" (Nahan, 2000: 2).

In taking up such themes, Prime Minister John Howard appealed to a mainstream Australia, in particular to the fears, resentments, and insecurities of this mainstream. Howard relied heavily on promoting an us/them division around which such resentments could flourish. Elites appealing to international human rights norms or writing "black-armband history" (mourning the treatment of indigenous peoples) were showing contempt for and sneering at the national pride felt by ordinary Australians. Feminists promoting equal opportunity were expressing contempt for the values of ordinary women. Howard (1998) talked of the "stridency of the ultra-feminist groups in the community" who sneer at and look down on women choosing to provide full-time care for their children.

The attribution to feminists of contempt for ordinary women was a necessary part of the functioning of anti-elite discourse. It did not require evidence. In fact, in both Australia and Canada, it was feminists who campaigned for national time-use surveys to measure the incidence and distribution of unpaid work and to calculate its value to the national economy. Nonetheless, the idea of contempt was extremely useful in delegitimizing the work of feminist bureaucrats, particularly where such work involved redistribution or regulation.

The demonizing of equality seekers was reinforced by inflaming resentment regarding visible minorities. Pauline Hanson (1996: 1) appealed on behalf of mainstream Australians against those controlling the "taxpayer-funded industries servicing Aboriginals, multiculturalists and a host of other minority groups." Hanson (1998) also agreed with the public choice analysis of single motherhood, another industry she said One Nation would put a stop to. Increasingly, the welfare state was characterized as benefiting "do-gooders" and their constituencies at the expense of the mainstream who paid for it. A volume of essays put out at this time by a Liberal Party think-tank suggested mainstream Australia was fed up with an inner-city "café society" social justice agenda that got in the way of its mortgage payments (Goldsmith, 1998).

As we have seen, this new divisive discourse had emerged from a number of directions: traditional populism, with its paranoia about cosmopolitan elites, the neo-conservative theory of the new class, the public choice notion of special interests, free-market think-tanks desiring to discredit welfare state redistribution, and political exploitation of resentments within the community for short-term electoral purposes. What was paradoxical was that this discourse, aimed at least in part at weakening the left, was energetically taken up by some prominent figures within the Australian Labor Party (ALP). They agreed that the villain was the "new class elite" and blamed special interests such as "the Greens, gays, feminists, ethnics and disabled" for alienating the electorate (Johns, 1996). This ALP susceptibility to market populism was in distinct contrast to the relative immunity of the comparable union-based Canadian party, the New Democratic Party (NDP).

Australian Labor leader Mark Latham (2003-05) was one of those who adopted a combination of special-interest and new class discourse. He identified a "symbolic class" that spoke a language of rights and entitlements and supported redistribution at the expense of working-class taxpayers (Latham, 2001b). The symbolic class included groups such as Women's Electoral Lobby that promoted abstract rights through constructing women as victims (Latham, 2001a). The equal opportunity project of identifying and addressing sources of institutional bias became labelled, in the new discourse, as special treatment for special interests.

Once market populist frames are accepted, the central conflict is no longer a class struggle between capital and labour, but one between blue-collar workers and middle-class elites. Big business and the interests of multinational corporations are rendered invisible when the target shifts to special interests (Johnson, 2001: 142-43). The real enemy is the new class, including women whose public sector jobs are allegedly at the expense of working-class taxpayers. One site of conflict between feminists and Labor concerned the latter's retreat from centralized wage fixing, which had enabled much greater progress on gender equity in wages than was possible under decentralized systems such as that of Canada. In the 1990s some labour leaders began to portray redistribution as the domain of special interests who were holding up economic reform. Equality seekers were framed as part of the latte-drinking new class elite, whereas blue-collar workers were depicted as "aspirational voters" interested in self-advancement rather than equality.

The New Populism in Canada
In Canada populism enjoyed an electoral surge in 1993. The populist Reform Party had been the only party to oppose what was depicted as the elite-driven Charlottetown Accord on constitutional reform. What followed at the federal level was the electoral collapse of the Progressive Conservative Party and the rise in its place of Reform, renamed Canadian Alliance in

2000. In 2003 the Canadian Alliance and the Progressive Conservative Party merged in the new Conservative Party, of which Stephen Harper became leader. It won (minority) government in 2006, using discourse much like that of John Howard ten years previously, promising to govern for mainstream Canadians and accusing other parties of putting special-interest demands ahead of the needs of ordinary working families for tax cuts.[4]

Reform, the populist heart of the new Conservative Party, dates from 1987 but drew on a much older political tradition of populism in Western Canada. Populism had long been a vehicle for expressing strong regional sentiment and distrust of the political elites of Central Canada. Reform was able to capitalize on Western resentment of official bilingualism and of the proposed constitutional recognition of Quebec as a distinct society. It countered major party proposals for the accommodation of difference with its own platform of "equality of citizens and provinces" (discussed below).

Reform broke the consensus on official bilingualism; like its Australian counterparts, it also ruptured party consensus on multiculturalism and immigration (Kirkham, 1998). Regarding asylum seekers, it emphasized border security and draconian action against "illegal entrants." In relation to immigration more generally, it called for limitations on reuniting families and for the closer alignment of immigration with Canada's economic needs – that is, the prioritizing of immigrants with labour-market and linguistic skills that minimized the need for settlement services or recognition of cultural diversity. Indeed, as in Australia, multiculturalism was framed as state-fostered special-interest politics that encouraged ghettoization or the maintenance of distinct communities outside the mainstream. The disruption of party consensus and the consequent shift in public discourse brought in its train policy shifts in both Canada and Australia.

Like its Australian equivalents, Reform also took up the discourse of special interests, labelling as a special-interest group any organization that promoted state intervention to redistribute market-generated incomes (Barney and Laycock, 1999). Thus, feminist groups, First Nations associations, multicultural and minority ethnic bodies, official language minorities, and unions all became special-interest groups. As Reform complained in a 1992 pamphlet, "In Ottawa, every special interest group counts except one, Canadians" (quoted in Laycock, 2002: 61).

Reform became the major political vehicle in Canada for discourse targeted at state-assisted elites who promoted equality agendas and public intervention in the distribution of social and economic goods. Unlike the earlier populism of Social Credit, that of Reform did not attack business or banking elites; indeed, the party won considerable corporate and media backing in English-speaking Canada. This and its support for free trade distinguished it from Pauline Hanson's One Nation and made it more similar to the Howard-led Liberal Party in Australia.

For much of the period after the Second World War, social justice and social equity had been seen as legitimate goals, and groups pursuing such goals had been regarded as part of the political mainstream (Jenson and Phillips, 1996: 119). The discursive shifts encouraged by Reform meant that doubt was cast on the authenticity of such goals and on the interests and motives of their proponents. Equality seeking was labelled as an elite agenda inconsistent with majority political values. Feminist organizations, such as the National Action Committee on the Status of Women (NAC), the umbrella body for the anglophone women's movement, came under increasing attack. They were no longer regarded as having an authentic democratic role in crystallizing and representing women's views but rather were depicted as self-interested and unrepresentative special interests (Dobrowolsky, 1998: 719).

An intriguing development in Canada, without a direct parallel in Australia, was the emergence of the self-styled Calgary School of political scientists, who played a significant role in populist politics as well as in free-market think-tanks such as the Fraser Institute. In Australia a number of economists have taken a prominent role in promoting public choice frames of analysis, but this has largely been via think-tanks rather than direct involvement in party politics.

In Canada, the Calgary School includes Tom Flanagan, originally an adviser to Reform founder Preston Manning and later the national campaign director for Conservative Party leader Stephen Harper in 2004 and senior campaign adviser in 2006. Flanagan has been credited with Reform's original breakthrough into national politics, via his advice to come out against the "elite-driven" Charlottetown Accord in the early 1990s. He has been an outspoken critic of political correctness and "Aboriginal orthodoxy." His *First Nations? Second Thoughts* (2000), funded by the Donner Canadian Foundation (also a generous donor to the Fraser Institute), was comparable to the books being produced in Australia as part of the history wars and indeed was taken up by Gary Johns of the Institute of Public Affairs. Flanagan preferred to describe First Nations as "first immigrants" and argued that special treatment related to indigenous status, including land rights, benefited only the interests of a small elite of activists, politicians, and administrators. Aboriginal peoples would be better served by policies of assimilation and same treatment. Flanagan continued to provide much of the intellectual underpinning of Stephen Harper's leadership (McDonald, 2004).

Two other members of the Calgary School, Ted Morton and Rainer Knopff, have been responsible for a sustained attack on the way the Canadian Charter of Rights and Freedoms has allegedly undermined Canadian democracy. Their book *The Charter Revolution and the Court Party* (2000) details how special-interest groups have used Charter litigation to pursue policy demands rejected by elected governments. Hostility to the Supreme Court and "unelected judges" has been common among Reform politicians but was kept in check during the Conservative Party's bid for government. It resurfaced in May 2006 when a Conservative Party MP and long-time critic of judicial activism, Maurice Vellacott, attacked the Supreme Court chief justice Beverley McLachlin for assuming god-like powers. She had stated in a speech to New Zealand university students that the rule of law required judges to uphold unwritten constitutional norms, such as the right not to be punished without a trial, even in the face of clearly enacted laws or hostile public opinion. Following pressure from opposition parties over his remarks, Vellacott resigned his position as chair of the House of Commons Aboriginal Affairs Committee.

Like other members of the Calgary School, Morton and Knopff reproduce the main features of US anti-elite discourse – much of it taken directly from Christopher Lasch – including the distinction between elite fashions and mainstream traditional values, and the tyranny of political correctness. Morton and Knopff (2000: 82-83) suggest that, unlike farmers or homemakers, those who belong to the postmaterialist knowledge class, such as feminists, are "fatally removed from the physical side of life," which accounts for their social-engineering ambitions. Apparently, feminists, as distinct from "homemakers," do not have caring responsibilities for children, elderly parents, partners, or siblings, and apparently the women's movement did not emerge from the lived experience of such responsibilities. According to Ted Morton (1998: 5), the coalition of self-styled equality seekers – "feminists, anti-poverty groups, the gay-rights movement, natives and other ethnic and racial minorities" – both demand and depend on state funding and state intervention, at the expense of taxpayers, gun owners, and those with traditional family values.

As in Australia, the market populism of Reform and its successors was not just significant in itself but also in its more general influence on political discourse and public policy, including the downgrading of state agencies associated with multicultural and women's advocacy. Impact on approaches to equal opportunity and processes of policy consultation are further discussed below.

In terms of the media, the Reform agenda received generous coverage in the newspapers and magazines owned by Conrad Black and by the Byfield family in Western Canada. Conrad Black's *National Post,* one of Canada's two national English-language newspapers, supported the Reform agenda from the time it was established in 1998. Black was praised by Stephen Harper and Tom Flanagan (1996/97: 34) for the conservative voices he brought to papers that were previously "monolithically liberal and feminist." Conrad Black and Rupert Murdoch have played similar roles in promoting market populism and giving access to think-tanks such as the Fraser Institute.

A different kind of body, with no equivalent in Australia, is the National Citizens' Coalition (NCC), founded in 1967. The NCC (National Citizens Coalition, 2007) describes itself as a watchdog on government, animated by its belief in "more freedom through less government." It takes pride that it neither lobbies government nor accepts money from it, choosing instead to speak directly to fellow citizens through targeted advertising campaigns, using newspaper ads, radio commercials, TV spots, billboards and direct mail. Stephen Harper was NCC president from 1998 to 2001, during a period out of parliament before he became leader of the Canadian Alliance and then the Conservative Party. The NCC has been one of the players in the shift in public discourse in Canada. The implications of such discursive shifts for equal opportunity agendas are discussed in the following section.

The Implications of Special-Interest Discourse for Equal Opportunity Agendas

Special-interest discourses have been vigorously promoted in Australia and Canada by free-market think-tanks and subsequently by the mass media and politicians. What are the implications for the equal opportunity agendas developed in the 1970s and 1980s? In those decades, feminists and other equality seekers helped achieve an equal opportunity jurisprudence that accommodated group difference. In part this was attained through incorporating concepts of indirect discrimination. This meant recognizing that apparently neutral requirements might discriminate against those with particular group characteristics. For example, continuity of service as a condition for job promotion might discriminate against women because they are typically the primary carers of children and more likely than men to have broken careers. Other seemingly neutral requirements might compound collective disadvantage experienced in the past or present.

Since the 1990s, market populism has effectively pushed back equal opportunity understandings and promoted a return to those of equal treatment as "same treatment," regardless of effects on those who differ from the norm. It rejects the "sophisticated jurisprudential theories of disparate impact and systemic discrimination that invite judicial revision of legislative decision-making" (Morton and Knopff, 2000: 68).

Reform was committed to an idea of equality that meant government would treat people identically, regardless of their differences. Any accommodation of group difference or policy of affirmative action could lead only to a politics of privilege and special status at the expense of ordinary Canadians. Stephen Harper expressed the Reform position on equality as rejecting proactive approaches by government: equality for people, provinces, or groups could be achieved only by identical treatment, not through "different sets of rules or standards" (quoted in Kirkham, 1998: 259).

The Saskatchewan Party, a populist party founded in 1997, similarly pro-claimed its commitment to "equality for all, special privileges for no-one" (quoted in Wishlow, 2001: 191) in a way very reminiscent of Pauline Hanson's First Speech (1996). Like its federal Reform associates, the Saskatchewan Party opposes any deviation from the principle of same treatment, whether affirmative action for the socially and economically disadvantaged or rec-ognition of indigenous land claims or of the distinct society status of Que-bec. Both Reform leader Preston Manning and Pauline Hanson rejected state-supported multicultural and other policies that promote equality by recognizing and accommodating group differences and linguistic diversity. Reform opposed the inclusion of sexual orientation among the prohibited grounds of discrimination in the Canadian Human Rights Act, arguing that protection should be available not on the basis of personal characteristics or group membership but on that of equality before the law. Organizations advocating human rights protection on the basis of sexual orientation were described as special-interest groups "hijacking the status of the disadvan-taged," (*House of Commons Debates*, 30 April 1996: 2115) despite the specific harms that their status in fact attracted.

The public choice assumption of the self-interested nature of all welfare state intervention has also served to delegitimize social justice agendas and mobilize opposition to equality seekers. Equal opportunity for development of potential has been a core value in the social-liberal traditions of both countries (Sawer, 2003). Its current displacement proceeds at a number of levels.

First, concern with equal opportunity is portrayed as unauthentic, a mask for the rent seeking of the new class that will do well out of equality. Con-cern over equal educational opportunity, for example, is regarded as pro-moting the interests of teachers and academics, at the expense of taxpayers. As an Australian Labor minister for finance said, you can be sure that any group "which calls itself a 'public interest' group is up to its eyeballs in self-interest" (Walsh, 1990).

Second, if concern with equal opportunity is not a form of rent seeking, then it is an elite fashion, which serves the function of social closure and helps distinguish the new class from ordinary people. The expression of "moral" views is the equivalent of wearing a designer label or some other form of distinguishing dress, according to the Murdoch-owned *Australian* newspaper. It has editorialized (29 December 2003: 10) on how "the moral middle class has discovered in asylum-seekers a new mascot through which it can demonstrate its innate superiority over common folk."

Third, the negative attributes of new class elites (self-interest, insincerity, superiority) are given a more active relational character. As we have seen, welfare state elites sneer at, despise, look down on, or wince at the values of ordinary people; feminists sneer at other women.

Women outside the paid workforce become the alleged victims of elite contempt, but they are also seen as heroes because they are assumed to make few demands on the state, to be content to be economically dependent on husbands, and to provide community services on an unpaid basis rather than demanding equal pay. Groups such as REAL Women (Realistic, Equal, Active for Life) in Canada and Women Who Want to Be Women in Australia (now Endeavour Forum) highlighted through their names an implied contrast with equality seekers, who were not real women. Although the initial impetus for the formation of such groups was opposition to abortion, they have taken up a much broader range of issues, opposing feminist influence on government and promoting "family values." They have been welcomed within free-market circles because their claims are seen as compatible with cheap government in a way that those of feminist equality seekers, wanting paid community services, are not.

REAL Women has opposed pay equity on the grounds that comparable worth evaluations would require "a huge bureaucracy at taxpayers' expense"; it also rejected the concept of "universally-available, government-subsidized day care" (REAL Women of Canada, 2003). Increasingly, any measures to provide equal opportunity to women in the paid workforce, such as paid maternity leave, subsidized child care, or re-entry allowances and training programs, are framed as a form of discrimination against women who have chosen to be homemakers, in addition to being wasteful public expenditure. The retention of the individual as the unit of account in the tax system is also seen as discriminating against single-income families; as a result, groups such as REAL Women favour family unit taxation, which would impose high rates of tax on second earners. Anti-discrimination legislation is opposed on the ground that private employers, with the incentive of the profit motive, will make wiser choices than "equal opportunity bureaucrats whose salaries are paid by taxpayers" (Francis, 1994).

Such groups not only decry the self-seeking and contempt that typify equality seekers, they also appropriate their language. They claim that, in fact, ordinary Australians or Canadians are being discriminated against by the special treatment of minorities or women. All that is needed is for everybody to be treated "the same." In both Australia and Canada, this has been by far the most important discursive strategy used against affirmative action programs, indigenous land and fishing rights, ethnic-specific services, and multicultural programs. It has also been employed by the men's rights movement, which constitutes another element in the anti-elitist discourse coalition.

In both Australia and Canada, men's rights groups proliferated in the 1990s. In the view of Dads against Discrimination (Australia, Canada, and the US), the Men's Rights Agency (Australia), and Men's Equalization Inc.

(Canada), feminists have captured state power and are responsible for policies and legislation that victimize men (Kaye and Tolmie, 1998). According
to these groups, policies that recognize the effect of caring work on earning
capacity, as in child-support formulae, result in preferential treatment for
women. They see legislation requiring the identification and removal of
barriers to equal opportunity for women and specified groups in a similar
light. Programs dealing with domestic violence are discriminating against
men by regarding them as always the perpetrators. Alternatively, such programs fail to recognize that men's violence is a consequence of their power-
lessness in the face of a feminist-dominated system. Small steps towards
greater gender equity in public policy are vastly exaggerated in the eyes of
those who believe they are the new victims of feminist elites and gender
bias in the state.

In Canada the judicial interpretation of the Charter of Rights and Freedoms, and the ability of the women's movement to bring Charter challenges, has been depicted as part of an elite conspiracy against the people.
Through the lens of market populism, equality means formal equality of
individuals only, not special treatment of groups in order to achieve more
substantive equality of opportunity.

Delegitimizing NGO Advocacy

In the 1970s and 1980s, equality seekers and their organizations fitted easily into dominant discourses of equal opportunity and social citizenship. In
Canada Prime Minister Pierre Trudeau had been promoting an agenda of
more inclusive citizenship, one aimed at encouraging political participation by cultural minorities and disadvantaged groups and funding "political voice" for them (Pal, 1993). Non-government organizations (NGOs) were
seen as having a central and legitimate role to play in promoting more
inclusive and active citizenship. Indeed, there was "a boom in state support
for intermediary organizations which might represent citizens to and in the
state" (Jenson and Phillips, 1996: 118). In Australia such programs were
couched less in terms of citizenship and more in those of equitable access to
government, but the outcome was similar. In both countries, it became policy
to provide public funding for advocacy in order to strengthen weak voices
that would otherwise not be heard in the policy process.

Impetus for wider forms of consultation came from the new social movements, such as the women's movement, the environment movement, and
the movement for indigenous and multicultural rights and recognition. The
demand for consultation in policy development became normal at all levels
of government and was particularly strong in Canada following the failure
of top-down constitutional reform efforts. But in order for it to occur, governments needed bona fide and representative organizations with which to

consult. In some cases this involved fostering the creation of associations that could perform the role of community representative at the table. New peak bodies funded by government eventually enabled groups marginalized in public decision making, such as immigrant women, or stigmatized groups, such as sex workers, to be represented in ways not possible through the majoritarian institutions of representative democracy. For the first time, women with disabilities, lesbian women, or homeless women had their own advocacy organizations through which they could develop and voice their perspectives on the national policy process. Such groups of women had previously found their views overlooked by male-dominated NGOs in, for example, immigrant, visible minority, and disability sectors; they also felt overlooked by women's peak bodies such as the National Action Committee on the Status of Women (NAC) in Canada (Vickers, Rankin, and Appelle, 1993).

In Australia the official rationale for funding such bodies was that it enabled disadvantaged groups to be represented in the formulation and implementation of policy and to balance the input of organized private interests. A parliamentary report strongly endorsed the view that "an integral part of the consultative and lobbying role of these organisations is to disagree with Government policy where this is necessary in order to represent the interests of their constituencies" (House of Representatives, 1991: 16-17).

The subsequent discursive shifts that cast doubt on equality seeking rendered such an approach to extra-parliamentary representation increasingly vulnerable. As we have seen, both Reform and its successors in Canada and the Howard government in Australia were attempting to reposition equality-seeking groups as special-interest groups, inimical to the interests and values of the mainstream. If public-interest groups were really special-interest groups, then governments were entitled to subject them to much greater control. Peak bodies critical of government were defunded or had their funding sharply reduced, as happened with NAC in Canada and the Women's Electoral Lobby in Australia. Peak associations were increasingly provided with project rather than core funding and with contracts that restricted their capacity to engage in advocacy critical of government policy.

Free-market think-tanks stepped up their attacks on NGOs after the successful international mobilization to defeat the Multilateral Agreement on Investment. The defunding and reduced access to government of community-based peak bodies performing advocacy and representational work particularly affected groups that spoke for disadvantaged sections of the community, those who were most in need of the social programs being cut by government (Sawer, 2002; Laycock, 2002: 37-40; Jenson and Phillips, 1996: 119).

The legitimacy of peak organizations was undermined through suggestions that they did not represent their supposed constituencies and that they distorted grassroots opinion. There was a new privileging of non-deliberative and unmediated opinion as reflected, for example, through opinion polling, in preference to representation through intermediary groups. The gap between elite and non-elite opinion was regarded as proving the case that self-appointed representatives distorted the views of their constituents. Little credence was given to the deliberative democracy argument that the views emerging from deliberation within NGOs and out of engagement with the policy process will differ from the non-deliberative responses of individual citizens to a pollster or market researcher. The public choice view was that the self and its interests were pre-political, rather than developing within a context of active citizenship.

The distrust of intermediary institutions is consistent with the populist preference for forms of direct democracy, such as citizen-initiated referenda, as a source of public policy. This fairly raw populism at the political level was underpinned by public choice arguments suggesting that to involve relevant groups in policy design led invariably to agency capture. In order to avoid this, and the consequent growth of public expenditure, government had to distance itself from demands for participation in the policy process while talking up citizen engagement and partnerships with civil society.

Conclusion

In the 1970s and 1980s, new social movements, including a renewed women's movement, were able to take advantage of strong equal opportunity or social citizenship discourses in Australia and Canada to make policy gains. Today such discourses have been dislodged, or at least powerfully shaken, by the new market populism. Equality seekers are now located on the wrong side of an us and them divide, among the liberal elites who are contemptuous of the values of ordinary people but anxious to spend their tax dollars. Feminists are as guilty of rent seeking as all those who invoke the public sector, and, like the rest of the new class, they create dependence among those whom they purport to help.

This is a brave new world, where projects promoting the equality of women have become special-interest projects, and the only gender equity initiatives likely to get a hearing are those directed to the scholastic under-performance of boys, not the gender gap in wages or the feminization of poverty. Although affirmative action to recruit male teachers to mentor boys is seen as legitimate, the same is not the case for policies to redesign paid work to accommodate family responsibilities. Workers with such responsibilities are now expected to receive "same treatment" in workplaces designed for those who are not primary carers, or else to negotiate a better deal for themselves without government interference.

The shift in what can now be heard in terms of public policy is a tribute to the power of discourse in reshaping the world. The same us versus them frame that makes feminists part of the elite renders invisible the real gender, class, and race inequalities that continue to be important. Indeed, we might argue that the attack on spurious elites usefully distracts attention from the actuality of increased inequalities. It conjures up a world in which corporate capitalism sides with the people, offering them the market choices that the social engineers seek to deny them – every choice, that is, except for the public sector options on which women have disproportionately relied.

7
Women's Rights and Religious Opposition: The Politics of Gender at the International Criminal Court
Louise Chappell

Despite the rhetoric of a borderless globalized world and talk of the end of state sovereignty, states remain the fundamental unit of international relations and retain extensive authority within their defined territory. As the other chapters in this book demonstrate, this authority extends to shaping gender relations within these defined spaces. Yet it is also the case that institutions of global governance exert an important influence on the behaviour of states. These institutions help set the broader decision-making context in which nation-states operate; like the states themselves, they are not gender-neutral. As a relatively new institution, the International Criminal Court (ICC) has been alert to gender issues and seeks to further the principles of gender justice through its capacity to influence developments in criminal justice at both the international and domestic levels. The court promises to reflect and extend norms that recognize women's experiences of war and conflict, and in doing so, to establish a jurisprudence that can filter down to the level of the state to influence national legislation in areas including rape, sexual discrimination, and women's claim to refugee status.

The ICC was created in 1998 at the United Nations Conference of Plenipotentiaries on the Establishment of an International Criminal Court (the Rome Conference). The conference generated the Rome Statute of the International Criminal Court, the treaty that defines the court's jurisdiction. Given the potential of the ICC to shape global and state-level responses to gender justice, it is not surprising that the institution has been an important site for transnational feminist activism. At the Rome Conference itself and the preparatory committees predating it, transnational organizations such as the Women's Caucus for Gender Justice (WCGJ) successfully advocated for the inclusion in the Rome Statute of gender-justice principles. As a result of such feminist lobbying, the Rome Statute formally recognizes that women's experiences of war and conflict differ from those of men, that women experience certain crimes precisely because they are women, and that international law should treat these crimes with the gravity that it accords to others. Not only are these developments internationally significant, but they also establish important new laws and norms relating to women's rights that can potentially be used by feminist activists to challenge gender inequities at the level of the nation-state. Although state parties to the ICC retain their sovereignty under the Rome Statute, it is expected that the legislation and legal arguments at the domestic level will come to reflect the advances in gender justice arising from this new institution of global governance.

Although impressive, the international advances in gender justice secured through the Rome Statute were not won without a struggle. Women's activists have had to contend with a so-called unholy alliance composed of Vatican representatives, political elites of certain Catholic and Islamic states, and North American "pro-life" organizations that have attempted to hinder their work. When others are arguing about the "clash of civilizations" between the West and Islam, it appears that they miss an important synergy between these purported rivals – that is, their mutual desire to maintain a form of patriarchal control over women's lives and bodies. In the context of the ICC, this synergy was made apparent in relation to three specific aspects of the women's rights agenda: the development of an international definition of gender, the inclusion of a new crime of forced pregnancy under international law, and the efforts to address sexual violence in the private realm.

The first aim of this chapter is to outline the politics of gender in the development of the ICC, with a particular focus on these three areas of contention. This focus may augment the growing feminist literature on UN conferences and the nature and operation of the "unholy alliance." Examining the ICC forums and the conference's outcome document, the *Rome Statute of the International Criminal Court* (1998), is especially useful because they produce the basis for new norms that will contribute directly to interpretations of "hard" international law. Some members of the influential WCGJ, a key player in these forums, have already written of their experiences (see Bedont, 1999; Copelon, 2000; Facio, 2004; Spees, 2003). As yet, however, no work has concentrated specifically on the conflict between women's rights advocates and religious contenders in this arena.

The chapter's second objective is to consider how the actions of feminists, state actors representing conservative religious views, and religious forces fit within the existing literature on transnational activism. It also assesses the extent to which this literature needs to be expanded to better explain the developments at the ICC (and other international conferences that deal with women's rights more generally). Building on the discussion in this volume's introduction about how well attuned feminists are to the notion of boundaries, this chapter will highlight the importance for domestically based gender equality activists to look across national boundaries to the transnational arena, first, to learn new strategies for combating conservative forces at home, and second, to assist in diffusing new international gender norms to the state level. The evidence used to develop these arguments is based on the available documents of the Rome Conference and preparatory committee meetings as well as the submissions, press releases, and commentaries of the activists involved. The chapter also relies on secondary material related to women's and religious transnational activism.

The discussion begins by locating this study within the literature on feminist activism in the international arena and transnational activism more generally. It then sketches the features of the newly established ICC in order to better understand the ground over which the politics of gender has been fought. It outlines the perspectives of the key players in the contest – official state and religious representatives with conservative views, and feminist activists. The analysis then turns to the central areas of conflict between these two groupings and considers how their competing visions of women were ultimately reflected in the final text of the Rome Statute of the International Criminal Court and associated legal documents. The next section considers how developments around gender and international law affect activists seeking to address gender inequality at the level of the nation-state and assesses the challenges women's activists might confront when trying to import these new international norms into domestic law. The chapter concludes by considering how well the gender politics at the ICC can be explained in the literature on transnational activism and what this study contributes to it.

Transnational Activism and Women's Rights

In recent years, feminist scholars have turned their attention to the importance of the transnational arena as a site for gender equality activism (Moghadam, 2005, 2005; Buss and Herman, 2003; Friedman, 2003; Joachim, 2003). As much of this scholarship demonstrates, the point of this activism is not to avoid engaging in politics at the level of the nation-state. Instead, it seeks to extend it in ways that will make state-level debates matter in the global context while simultaneously bringing a broader international and comparative perspective to bear on local concerns. But as scholars of social movements such as Sidney Tarrow (2001) and Doris Buss and Didi Herman (2003) have pointed out, the socially progressive movements are not alone in setting their sights on the transnational realm. Increasingly, conservative movements, especially religious-based organizations, have followed equality seekers into transnational arenas, including the United Nations, to advance an array of counter-claims (see Buss and Herman, 2003; Chappell,

2006). The views of these forces regarding the nature of women and their rights differ markedly from those advanced by feminists. The focus of the feminist literature has been on the "unholy alliance," a growing religious coalition or network that includes state and non-state actors. The former are the official representatives of certain countries with majority Catholic or Muslim populations. Representatives of the United States, increasingly willing to advance arguments that reflect a conservative evangelical/Protestant discourse on women's rights (a trend that has continued since the 2004 reelection of George W. Bush), are numbered here as well. The non-state actors include the Vatican, through its diplomatic mission at the UN – the Holy See – and NGOs including anti-abortion groups, many of which are based in North America.

One feminist exploration of the alliance is Palena R. Neale's (1998) article on the role played by the Catholic Church, in concert with some Islamic states, in influencing the outcome document at the 1994 Cairo International Conference on Population and Development (ICPD). Neale illustrates how these religious and state forces successfully blocked moves to expand reproductive rights to women in the final text of the *Cairo Program of Action*. Another excellent account of the influence of the religious alliance is provided by Doris Buss (1998), who focuses on the 1995 Fourth World Conference on Women (FWCW) in Beijing. Her work considers the extent to which the alliance was able to stop any advancement on developing a consensus around the concept of gender, among other things, in the *Beijing Platform for Action*. Dianne Otto (1996) also provides an account of the FWCW and notes the limitations that religious forces placed on furthering sexuality rights in its outcome document. Sabina Lauber (2001) demonstrates how the religious-based opposition to a sexuality rights agenda was successfully reinforced at the Beijing Plus 5 Conference. Held in New York in 2000 as a follow-up to the FWCW, this conference was intended to assess state responses to the Beijing Platform for Action throughout the previous five years and to pressure governments to renew their commitment to key aspects of the platform. Due to the presence of oppositional forces at this conference, and their efforts to wind back some of the more progressive text of the Beijing document, it was dubbed by some women's NGOs as "Beijing minus 5" (see Frostfeldt, 2000).

Neither the present study nor those mentioned above suggest that all religious groups, or states with a large religious base, support a conservative position on women's rights. Indeed, some countries with large Islamic or Catholic populations, such as Indonesia and Italy, have not featured in the ICC debates at all. Nonetheless, official state representatives from countries with a strong religious tradition who intervened at the ICC to block women's rights issues – such as those from Egypt, Iran, Libya, the United Arab Emirates, Argentina, Guatemala, Ireland, and Poland – also have a history of intervening in other international forums on issues related to limiting women's sexuality and reproductive capacity. It must also be remembered that these representatives have usually been men voicing patriarchal beliefs. Clearly, however, they do not express the views of all the citizens of their countries. Women's activists with opposing views exist in all these states, often working within the same religious tradition as the representatives themselves. If not directly involved in the transnational women's rights movement, they nonetheless support the positions it advances (see, for example, Tohidi, 2003 on feminist critiques within Islam; and Feijoo, 1998 on the Argentine women's movement opposition to the official state position at Beijing).

Similarly, a range of views on women's rights exists within the Catholic Church and the broader global religious community. The Catholic Church, officially represented by the Vatican, includes the papal offices in Rome as well as the Holy See, which has observer status at the United Nations and acts as the pope's representative in international affairs. The Vatican is a conservative body in the sense that it seeks to maintain the status quo in connection with church doctrine and teaching. This conservatism was a feature of Pope John Paul II's period as head of the church, particularly in relation to matters concerning the family and sexual issues (see Finkle and Mcintosh, 1994: 23). At the international conferences referred to above, the Vatican's position was clear: it advanced a view of women as different from men and as nurturers who were firmly rooted in traditional heterosexual family relationships.

However, within the church, an array of individuals and groups promote readings of doctrine and the Bible that differ from those championed by the Vatican (see Buss, 1998: 341). Of relevance here are two US-based feminist Catholic organizations: the first, Catholics for a Free Choice, advocates for a woman's right to control her sexual and reproductive capacities; the second, the Women-Church Convergence, describes itself as a coalition of women "rooted in the Catholic tradition and feminist in commitment" (Women-Church Convergence, n.d). The existence of a broader alliance of religious groups with a more sympathetic position on women's rights was made obvious previous to the Cairo ICPD when, anticipating the force of the anti-abortion lobby, progressive religious thinkers met in Belgium to prepare a religious response to the lobby's arguments (Keck and Sikkink, 1998: 190).

While acknowledging these nuances in the community of international state and non-state religious actors, this study focuses specifically on the relationship between those of conservative orientation and women's rights activists in relation to the ICC. Such a focus affords a unique opportunity to re-examine the general literature on transnational activism. In particular, it can test the important ideas advanced in the work of Margaret Keck and

Kathryn Sikkink (1998) on transnational advocacy networks. In explaining the operation of transnational actors, Keck and Sikkink use the language of a network, rather than a coalition or alliance, because in their view it best captures the "fluid and open relations among committed and knowledge-able actors working in specialized issue areas" (8). According to their defini-tion, such transnational advocacy networks (TANs) are "networks of activists, distinguished largely by the centrality of principled *ideas* or *values* in moti-vating their formation" (1, emphasis added). TANs are identified by various other features, including operating at the international level, sharing a com-mon discourse, believing that individuals can make a difference, using in-formation creatively, and employing sophisticated political strategies (2). In order to influence change at the international level, TANs rely heavily on symbolic politics; in doing so, they carefully frame issues in ways that will attract attention. Dealing in the realm of ideas and values, they often frame their demands in a symbolic as opposed to a strictly rationalist way, employ-ing simple terms that suggest there are right and wrong answers to complex moral and political questions. Using moral leverage, TANs seek to persuade powerful actors at both the domestic and international level that a problem exists that needs attending to, that certain parties are responsible for it, and that the TANs themselves can provide credible solutions to it (19).

In relation to the themes of this book regarding the importance of the nation-state, a crucial point is that though the central aim of TANs is to influence state behaviour, they seek to achieve this through working at the international level. In what they call the "boomerang effect," Keck and Sikkink (1998: 13-14) describe how actors who are unable to effect change at the domestic level establish links with like-minded activists in the inter-national realm and work through international forums to encourage (or shame) domestic governments to change their policies and practices. Ac-cording to Keck and Sikkink, TANs have most success when they seek to influence issues involving bodily harm to vulnerable individuals or those concerned with legal equality of opportunity. This is because, in their view, these issues transcend a specific cultural or political context (204). The ques-tion of how relevant their framework is for understanding the nature, strat-egies, and levels of success of feminist activists and the conservative religious forces operating in the ICC forums will be addressed in what follows.

The Site of Contestation: The Establishment of the International Criminal Court

Although an international criminal court had been mooted since 1937, the proposal that led to its actual conception was not given serious attention until the early 1990s. The process of devising and ratifying the Rome Stat-ute was facilitated by the ending of the Cold War – which enabled greater consensus within the United Nations, including the Security Council – as well as growing international pressure from a range of NGOs to bring an end to immunity for perpetrators of international criminal law (Dieng, 2002: 690-93). The creation in the early 1990s of two UN ad hoc tribunals to prosecute war criminals from the conflicts in the former Yugoslavia and Rwanda also led to demands for the development of a permanent international body to uphold international criminal law.

After the idea for the ICC re-emerged in the post–Cold War era, the institution developed relatively quickly. In 1993 a proposal to establish the ICC was put on the agenda of the General Assembly of the UN. In 1995, preparatory committee meetings (known as prepcoms) commenced, and in June-July 1998 the Rome Conference was held. The conference was attended by 148 states, 120 of which voted in support of the final outcome document the *Rome Statute of the International Criminal Court* (1998). The statute and two subsidiary documents, the *Elements of Crime Annex* (EOC) and *Rules of Procedure and Evidence* (RPE), devised at later prepcoms, combined to form important additions to "hard" international humanitarian law. The ICC came into being in July 2002 after it was ratified by sixty states. Those states that obstructed the addition of a gender focus to the ICC have had a mixed record in ratifying the statute. Moreover, the US, which participated in the Rome Conference and demonstrated a degree of support for the court (under the Clinton administration) has since refused to ratify the treaty.[1]

The court agreed to in Rome is a unique institution, one differing from other international legal bodies such as the International Court of Justice (ICJ) as well as previous and existing ad hoc international criminal law tribunals. One of its key features, which differentiates it from the ICJ, is its ability to hold *individuals* (not simply states alone) accountable for criminal acts under international law. Unlike the ad hoc tribunals, the court is a permanent treaty-based organization. It has jurisdiction over crimes committed within the territory of a ratifying state or by a national of a ratifying state who operates in another country.[2] The statute also gives the UN Security Council the ability, under certain circumstances, to refer a crime to the court that involves a non-state national or occurs on the territory of a non-signatory state.

At the heart of the ICC is an attempt to balance the central dilemma of international politics in a globalized world: the desire for states to maintain sovereignty at the same time as facing an increased pressure/desire to cooperate to address supranational problems – in this case, grave breaches of human rights and human security. The Rome Statute recognizes that state sovereignty remains a fundamental principle of international law and politics. The most obvious way it does this is through the notion of *complementarity,* which dictates that national courts should be the first choice for handling a breach of the Rome Statute. As is outlined in Articles 17 to 19 of the statute, the ICC can intervene to prosecute an alleged criminal only when a state has demonstrated its *inability* or *unwillingness* to carry out an investigation (see Robertson, 2000: 350). Moreover, the Rome Statute upholds the principle of double jeopardy, which means that once a national court has heard a case, so long as the proceedings are legitimate, it cannot be reheard by the ICC.

Although it upholds the sovereignty principle, the court also recognizes that to address the transborder issues related to human security, the sanctity of sovereignty must be balanced against its own jurisdictional capacity to reach across state boundaries. First, it attempts to do this by recognizing that it is *individuals,* not disembodied states (the traditional subjects of international law), who must be tried for actions that breach international humanitarian and human rights norms. In doing so, the Rome Statute raises the prospect that the ICC could intervene, at least when states are unable or unwilling to take action, to bring to justice individuals who contravene international law. The second way in which the court attempts to balance sovereignty with justice is through a more subtle and long-term process: the diffusion of new norms arising from ICC jurisprudence into the laws of nation-states. Indeed, for some commentators (see, for example, Warbrick and McGoldrick, 2001: 428), the ability of the ICC to bring perpetrators to justice is less important than the obligation of signatory states to bring their laws into line with the Rome Statute or the "importation" of ICC jurisprudence into their domestic judicial and legislative arenas.

The ICC has jurisdiction over four main categories of offences: genocide, crimes against humanity, war crimes, and aggression.[3] Some of these crimes have previously been codified under international law such as in the Convention on Genocide, the Geneva Conventions and Protocols, and the Convention against Torture.[4] However, these instruments have been difficult to enforce, allowing violators to escape justice. The ICC therefore provides the first permanent court with the capacity to enforce penalties for these execrable crimes. Also, under the Rome Statute and the ICC's two subsidiary documents, these crimes have been restated to give them greater currency (Lee, 2002: 751). At least in relation to the first three categories of crime, the Rome Statute also reflects important recent developments in international criminal jurisprudence, especially those arising from the International Criminal Tribunal on the Former Yugoslavia (ICTY) and the International Criminal Tribunal on Rwanda (ICTR). As will be discussed below, the elaboration of these categories of crimes in the ad hoc tribunals and their codification in the Rome Statute have provided an important opportunity structure for feminist activists wanting to reconfigure gender norms under international law.

Identifying the Contenders: Religious and Feminist Activists at the ICC

The Rome Conference and the ICC prepcoms were the result of much preparation and planning. Extensive negotiation occurred prior to and during each meeting between the participants, which included states, non-state actors such as the Vatican, and NGOs. In terms of the politics of gender, the most important actors at the ICC were elites of certain states with large Catholic or Muslim populations, the Vatican, and NGOs. The most prominent Catholic-oriented states were Ireland and Guatemala; the Muslim states included Syria, the United Arab Emirates, Qatar, and Nigeria. Two key sets of NGOs were involved: the first, most of whom came from the US or Canada, took a pro-life/anti-abortion position; the second consisted of women's groups, in particular the transnational WCGJ. The WCGJ was instigated by feminist lawyers in New York but came to encompass women's activists from across the globe including those from India, the Philippines, and South American and African states.

Official Religious Contenders

During the formation of the ICC, religious forces were key contenders in the battle concerning gender politics. Although no single multi-denominational organization operated in ICC forums to voice shared traditional values, it was nevertheless clear that a network of religious actors advanced a consistent and complementary conservative position on gender issues. A central player here was the Holy See, whose special status at all UN meetings extended to the ICC forums. Ireland and Guatemala worked alongside the Holy See to push a conservative agenda. More controversially, given the historic and current tension between the West and Islam over other issues, the Holy See and some Catholic-oriented states aligned themselves with certain Muslim counterparts, including Syria, the United Arab Emirates, Qatar, and Nigeria, whose points of view on a range of gender-related issues resembled those of the Vatican.

No one should have been surprised by the intervention of these religious representatives at the ICC. By the time of the Rome Conference in 1998, the link between the Catholic Church and particular Islamic states around gender issues in the international area had become increasingly apparent. The international UN conferences held throughout the 1990s provided a new opportunity not only for human rights advocates but also for those more skeptical about the advancement of an international human rights agenda – especially the extension of women's rights – to meet, converse, and lobby around rights issues. At the 1994 Cairo ICPD, the international press noted as remarkable and controversial the pre-conference caucusing and lobbying that occurred between the Vatican and certain Muslim-populated states including Egypt and Libya to block the extension of women's reproductive rights (Singh, 1998; Neale, 1998). The following year, at the Beijing Fourth World Conference on Women (FWCW), lobbying by this "bloc," which included the Holy See, Iran, Egypt, and Libya, had expanded into all areas of women's rights: reproduction, health, marriage, sexuality, and the definition of gender (Otto, 1996).

In these other UN forums, the Holy See and some Muslim state elites worked together to frame women in a particular way. They conceived of women in terms of their "special" attributes and reinforced the notion that they differed from men. Women's autonomy was couched in moralistic terms, especially in connection with women's rights to control their sexual and reproductive lives. Moreover, these actors shared the view that giving women sexual freedom would promote homosexuality among them and allow for sex outside conjugal relations. Should women take up the opportunity to live in non-traditional relationships, the family – the realm in which they "naturally" exist – would be directly challenged. Moreover, giving women the right to control their child-bearing capacity would not only conflict with important religious and moral reasoning on the right to life but could result in sexual promiscuity also an outcome that could only accelerate the demise of the traditional family (for a full discussion of this framing in other UN contexts, see Chappell, 2004). As the following discussion illustrates, these "frames," used so successfully in other UN venues, were also employed by religious forces in ICC debates.

NGO Contenders

Through their participation in ICC forums, NGOs of varying philosophies also played an important role in shaping the Rome Statute and its subsidiary documents. Purportedly pursuing a "pro-life" agenda, Christian-based NGOs operated alongside and largely in support of the "official" religious forces. However, as indicated below, they also became involved in issues related to the definition of gender and questions of national sovereignty versus international human rights. These groups, based primarily in the US and Canada, included Focus on the Family, Catholic Family and Human Rights Institute, Campaign Life Coalition, and REAL Women of Canada. Nor was this the first time they had agitated around gender-related issues at the international level. Many had attended the 1993 Vienna Conference on Human Rights, the Cairo ICPD, and the Beijing FWCW. At these venues, their opposition to the expansion of a women's rights agenda was almost identical to that voiced by the more formal religious groups.

Standing in contrast to these NGOs in the ICC forums was the WCGJ, a feminist-oriented coalition. Drawing on their experience at other UN meetings, including the Vienna, Cairo, and Beijing conferences, a number of New York–based feminist activists set about forming a permanent organization to lobby for the inclusion of a gender perspective in the Rome Statute (Facio, 2004). Created in 1997, the WCGJ, which came to include over three hundred women's organizations and five hundred individuals from across the world, was an independent member of the broader NGO Coalition for an International Criminal Court. The WCGJ operated with three primary goals in mind: first, to ensure a worldwide participation of women's human rights advocates in the ICC treaty negotiations and to lobby for an effective and independent court; second, to educate government delegations and mainstream human rights NGOs on their commitments to women and the need to integrate a gender perspective into the UN; and third, to raise the public awareness of the horrific nature of crimes committed against women (Facio, 2004: 315).

Although religious and conservative groups attempted to discredit the WCGJ by constantly referring to its members as "radical" feminists (see Lifesite, 1999, 2000; REAL Women, 1998; Mallon, 2000), this was not its orientation. Indeed, its willingness to engage with the UN and become involved in pursuing a women's rights approach to gender justice prompted criticism from some feminist activists of a more radical persuasion (for a critique, see Charlesworth and Chinkin, 2000). The WCGJ was clearly located within the broader liberal human rights movement that works through existing and new *institutions* to advocate for *individual* human rights for all. It used an individualistic human rights lens to frame its arguments around women's rights, which was suggestive of its strong liberal feminist bent.

The Politics of Gender at the ICC

The WCGJ had a strong influence on the outcome documents of the ICC forums. In relation to the Rome Statute, it had an effect on those articles concerned with the categories of crimes, court structure, and court procedures. Frustrating the efforts of the feminist-inspired coalition were conservative religious forces that clashed with the WCGJ over three specific gender-related issues: the development of an international definition of gender, the inclusion of new crimes related to women's experience of war and conflict, and the efforts to recognize gender-based violence in the private realm. This section will outline the major advances made by feminist activists at the ICC before turning to those three areas of contestation.

Feminist Advances in International Humanitarian Law

The WCGJ and other like-minded activists had some success in influencing the Rome Statute as well as the EOC and RPE documents in terms of the nature of crimes. Due in part to their efforts, Article 7, relating to crimes against humanity, and Article 8, concerning war crimes, referred to sexual violence as acts constituting such crimes. In the Geneva Conventions, sexual offences had been imbued with a moral element, one that linked them to "honour" and the lesser crimes of "humiliating and degrading treatment." Articles 7 and 8 of the Rome Statute removed the moral aspect and placed the crimes in the category of "grave breaches" of international law. Further, to emphasize the gravity of sexually based crimes against humanity, feminist activists successfully lobbied to have them enumerated in a separate sub-paragraph (Moshan, 1998: 177).

Feminist activists also succeeded in securing a broad-based definition of the types of sexual violence that constituted crimes against humanity and war crimes. Included under the Article 7(1)(g) category of the former were "rape, sexual slavery, enforced prostitution, forced pregnancy, enforced sterilization, or any other form of sexual violence of comparable gravity." Similar offences were enumerated under the Article 8(2)(b)(xxii) category of war crimes. For the first time, the offences of sexual slavery and forced pregnancy were codified as an element of crimes against humanity and war crimes (discussed in detail below), a significant shift towards international law better reflecting women's experience in situations of armed conflict.

Feminist activists also influenced the structural aspects of the court. After much lobbying from the WCGJ, some effort was made to ensure that ICC staff represented women and gender interests more broadly. Article 36(8)(a)(iii) of the Rome Statute stated that the court should consist of a "fair representation of female and male judges." Article 36(8)(b) noted that in nominating judges, state parties "shall also take into account the need to include judges with legal expertise on specific issues including ... violence against women or children." Elections for the first bench of the ICC were held between 3 and 7 February 2003. At the conclusion to a drawn-out election procedure, seven women and eleven men were elected as judges. When the second bench was elected in 2006, the balance was even closer, with eight female and ten male judges. Most of the female judges had extensive experience in dealing with issues related to violence against women (International Criminal Court, 2002; Women's Initiatives for Gender Justice, 2006).

Feminist concerns regarding procedural matters were also reflected in the Rome Statute. Drawing on (mostly negative) experiences at the UN ad hoc tribunals, the WCGJ pushed to ensure that ICC prosecutors were obligated to address gender issues. As a result, under Article 54(1)(b), prosecutors were charged with investigating and prosecuting crimes in a way that "respect[s] the interests and personal circumstances of victims and witnesses, including ... gender." They were also required to "take into account the nature of the crime, in particular where it involves sexual violence, gender violence or violence against children." Article 68 of the statute, which gave the court the authority to protect victims and witnesses, specified the need to accord due attention to victims of sexual violence, which may include the use of in camera evidence to shield them from confronting their aggressors in the courtroom.

Contesting the Definition of Gender

Feminist activists also succeeded in having the term "gender" mainstreamed in sections of the statute. For instance, Article 7(1)(h) includes gender as a ground for persecution actionable under international law (alongside political, racial, religious, and other such categories). Similarly, Article 21, prohibiting discrimination based on gender in the application and interpretation of the statute, reflects an attempt to integrate gender concerns within the ICC. Gender activists hoped that this article would be applied in cases in which state parties prove "unwilling or unable" to investigate and prosecute gender-based crimes.

However, these positive developments belie the contentious politics surrounding gender justice issues at the ICC in general and the definition of gender in the statute in particular. The question of defining gender had been a long-standing area of dispute between progressive and conservative transnational actors. It had been hotly debated at other UN conferences, including the Beijing FWCW, held three years before the Rome Conference. At Beijing, due to irreconcilable differences on the issue between feminist and conservative proponents, the term had been left undefined. However, the Rome Conference could not follow suit. As a justiciable document under international law, the statute could not make reference to gender without defining it.

When gender was first debated at the preparatory meetings for the ICC, the Holy See and a group of Arab League countries including Syria, the United Arab Emirates, and Qatar contested the inclusion of the notion of gender-based (rather than sex-based) crimes (Copelon, 2000: 236; Bedont, 19994). Their particular fear was that the inclusion of these crimes could provide the grounds for homosexuals to claim rights under the statute. Later in Rome, gender again became a focus of dispute. According to Alda Facio (2004: 327), WCGJ director at the time, hostility to inclusion of gender in the statute "was gradual and spread throughout a number of working groups, particularly those having to do with definition of crimes, composition and general principles." The issue came to a head when the Guatemalan delegation, representing a strongly Catholic state, formally proposed that the term "gender" be deleted from the statute (327). After much debate, the word remained in place: Article 7(3) of the statute notes that "the term 'gender' refers to the two sexes, male and female, within the context of society. The term 'gender' does not indicate any meaning different from the above."

This definition is a confused statement, one that reflects the differing positions used by both sets of contenders to frame the term. On one hand, by mentioning the "context of society," the definition underscores the feminist understanding of gender as a social concept and therefore allows for the possibility that an individual's gender status might change. On the other, the mention of "two sexes" and the additional rider about disallowing other interpretations reflect the arguments of conservative religious and state-based actors that gender must be understood as a *biological* fact and not as *socially* constructed. This latter approach to gender treats it as if it were somehow natural and immutable. The biological approach to gender supports the view that men and women differ in essential ways, thus enabling the justification of their different roles in society. This also disallows any degree of fluidity in a person's gender/sexual identity, thereby foreclosing the possibility of recognition of homosexual or transgender identities (Copelon, 2000: 236).

Feminists were clearly disappointed with the final definition of gender under the ICC (see Copelon, 2000). Nevertheless, many of them were keen to put the best gloss on the outcome. Shortly after the Rome Conference, WCGJ director Alda Facio (1999) stated, "Although this definition may be considered imperfect by some, having the term in a legal or 'hard' document like the ICC Statute as opposed to a policy or 'soft' document such as the Vienna, Cairo and Beijing Platforms, is a definite stride in the right direction toward real justice for women." Facio went on to encourage feminists to remain active in connection with the issue and to seek to have the term more clearly defined in future UN forums and through intervention in domestic-level legal cases. Meanwhile, religious conservatives expressed some relief about their "victory" but also cautioned supporters about the need for continuing vigilance on the issue. After the Rome Conference, an editorial on Lifesite (1998), a Canadian pro-Christian and anti-abortion website managed by the Campaign Life Coalition, referred to the definition of gender in the statute and noted that "the words 'within the context of society' could be used by western activist judges to undermine the traditional values intent of the entire definition of gender."

Contesting New Gender-Based Crimes

As noted above, the WCGJ successfully lobbied to have sexually based crimes included in the Rome Statute under the categories of war crimes and crimes against humanity. Again, this was neither a smooth nor straightforward process. Tensions were especially apparent after religious forces were antagonized by the elaboration of the newly recognized crime of (en)forced pregnancy. Why did this issue become so contentious, whereas other equally significant developments, such as the inclusion of sexual slavery and enforced prostitution, did not?

In the crime of enforced pregnancy, which typically occurs during armed conflicts between ethnic groups, the soldiers of one group rape women from the opposing group until they are impregnated. To prevent their access to abortion, the women are confined until they give birth. The intent of this crime is to produce children whose ethnicity will differ from that of the mother and her community. Shaming both mother and child, it will sever their community connection; its ultimate goal is to destroy the rival ethnic group. As witnesses had testified to both the ICTY and the ICTR, enforced pregnancy has become a commonly used weapon of war (see Boon, 2001: 656-67). With these testimonies fresh in mind, WCGJ members became determined to see this crime codified in international law through the Rome Statute. However, they encountered strong opposition from the Holy See. The Vatican argued that the term was ambiguous and that actions related to the confinement of a woman for the purposes of keeping her pregnant should be prosecuted under existing international law related to rape, enforced prostitution, and genocide, among others (Holy See, 1998: 2). It also asserted that the term "enforced pregnancy" could be interpreted to mean denial to terminate a pregnancy (2). In other words, it feared that, were forced pregnancy included in the statute, the failure to provide abortion on demand could become a crime. This concerned the Holy See not only for moral reasons but also for more practical ones, given the role of the Catholic Church in providing hospital services throughout the world.

The Holy See, which took the lead on the issue of enforced pregnancy, was joined by pro-life lobbyists as well as a number of states including Ireland, Nigeria, and various Gulf Arab countries who opposed the provision. Ireland and the pro-life NGOs shared the Vatican's concern that the inclusion of enforced pregnancy in the statute could lead to the "right" of abortion on demand (see, for example, Lifesite, 1998; REAL Women, 1998). However, this was not the primary concern of their Muslim allies. They feared that it could open the door to international intervention in domestic laws more generally ("Who's Obstructionist?" 1998). This position was consistent with the strong objection put by Muslim states such as Kuwait, the United Arab Emirates, Syria, Jordan, Egypt, and Yemen to any international efforts to develop women's rights that could interfere with the practise of Shari'a law (see "Who's Obstructionist?" 1998; Tohidi, 2003; Organization of Islamic Conference, 2000). The Vatican was sympathetic to the position of these delegates, arguing that states should have the right to make their own laws without external interference. In its view, forced pregnancy raised "the ironic prospect of making the enforcement of legitimate state and conventional law [against abortion] a 'war crime'" (Holy See, 1998).

From the viewpoint of feminist activists, the objections voiced by these religious contenders were spurious. They dismissed the Vatican's argument that enforced pregnancy was an "ambiguous construction," developed in the jurisprudence of the ICTY and ICTR. As the activists pointed out, some of the other crimes the Vatican had thought appropriate to prosecute had themselves only recently been developed through the same tribunals. But also, the WCGJ argued, the debate was simply an excuse to introduce the politics of abortion into the ICC agenda. As it (Women's Caucus for Gender Justice, 1998) noted at the time, "It is difficult to understand how the debate about the crime of enforced pregnancy has become a debate about abortion. National laws which criminalize the termination of pregnancy are not violations under international law and thus would not come within the ICC's jurisdiction." What is clear is that once the topic of abortion was opened for debate, it became one of the most contentious and drawn-out issues at the Rome Conference (see Bedont, 1999; Copelon, 2000). Whether or not its introduction was a deliberate tactic on the part of religious and anti-abortion groups, it considerably slowed proceedings.

Eventually, the crime of forced pregnancy was included in the Rome Statute. Article 7(2)(f) defines it as "the unlawful confinement of a women forcibly made pregnant, with the intent of affecting the ethnic composition of any population or carrying out other grave violations of international law." However, as with the definition of gender, an important rider was added to the statute: "This definition shall not in any way be interpreted as affecting national laws related to pregnancy." In relation to this crime, feminists could claim a qualified success: they had achieved their main goal of codifying forced pregnancy under the statute but were obliged to compromise in connection with its wording. The WCGJ dropped its preference for "enforced" over "forced" pregnancy and allowed for the inclusion of the interpretive clause, which it viewed as redundant. In doing so, it had come to the realization that it was "painfully unrealistic to expect" that its broader objective would be met, namely, to ensure that withholding abortion from raped women would be considered a war crime and a crime against humanity under the ICC (Facio, 1999). In accepting the limited definition, the WCGJ convinced its opponents that upholding existing criminal abortion laws would not be considered a crime under the jurisdiction of the ICC (Facio, 1999).

Contesting Gender-Based Violence in the Private Realm

A third area of contention between feminists and religious forces related to criminalizing domestic violence under the crime against humanity (CAH) provisions of the Rome Statute. In taking up this issue, the WCGJ hoped to advance a long-term priority of the broader transnational feminist activist community: the international recognition of and punishment for gender-based violence. The issue of domestic violence did not receive a great deal of attention at the Rome Conference itself but came to a head in November 1999 at an EOC prepcom meeting when eleven Arab League countries introduced a petition to "exclude crimes of sexual or gender violence when committed in the family or as a matter of religious or cultural concern" from the CAH category (Women's Caucus for Gender Justice, 2000: 2).[5] In addition to concerns about the definition of sexual violence in the private sphere, these states also feared that the statute's Article 7(2)(c) definition of "enslavement" could apply to women who worked at home. Although there is no available record of an official Vatican response to the issue of enslavement, the Catholic Family and Human Rights Institute (1999), a UN-focused Catholic lobby group, did enter the debate, supporting the Arab League proposal because it feared that attacks on family traditions, including that of women staying at home, could come from interpretations of sexually based crimes against humanity.

The WCGJ strongly objected to the exclusion of "private" acts of violence from the CAH provisions. In its view, "Precluding family situations from the definitions of crimes of sexual violence completely undermines the essence of these crimes and would prevent many situations of severe sexual and gender violence from ever being prosecuted" (Women's Caucus for Gender Justice, 1999). Moreover, the WCGJ argued that, given the anti-gender-discrimination provisions of the statute, these states should not have been allowed to have this matter considered at the Rome Conference. In their view, these provisions ruled out the possibility of introducing discriminatory matters. The caucus also criticized delegations such as that of the US for negotiating on the issue with certain Arab League states in order to win concessions on other matters, specifically raising the threshold for all crimes against humanity (10). In its view, "these discussions have created a situation where elements of sexual violence crimes are being used as a bargaining point to raise the threshold for crimes against humanity when in fact the 11 Arab countries' proposal on sexual violence crimes had no basis to be considered in the first place" (10).

Eventually, WCGJ lobbying helped ensure that sexually based crimes remained in the Rome Statute's CAH category without allowing any derogations based on cultural specificity. However, it lost the important battle regarding the threshold test for CAH. Once other delegates had agreed that the threshold be increased, the oppositionist states abandoned their attempts to have sexually based crimes removed from CAH. As a result, under Article 7(1) of the Rome Statute, crimes against humanity must be demonstrated to be part of a "widespread and systematic" attack, and state and non-state actors must be seen to "actively promote or encourage" the commission of such crimes. As the WCGJ and other commentators subsequently pointed out, this threshold test creates potential problems for addressing women's experiences of armed conflict. Often, attacks on women are isolated events, and, at least in the case of forced pregnancy, a perpetrator can use a defence of not knowing that he had impregnated the victim (Moshan, 1998: 183).

As the above discussion has illustrated, issues related to gender justice were highly contentious in the establishment of the ICC. Feminist activists, represented by the WCGJ, advanced a particular view of women and their rights, framing them as autonomous individuals with the right to have recognized under international law those crimes specifically directed at them due to their gender. Religious forces, which included the Holy See, elites officiating in some Catholic and Muslim countries, and pro-life groups, were challenged by this view of women and advanced an alternative and more conservative point of view. Their arguments presented women as biologically determined, heterosexual, and unable to fully control their reproductive lives. Underlying these frames was a traditional view of women, as wives and mothers who exist within the private realm of the family.

In terms of outcomes, although women's rights activists were able to shape the final Rome Statute, the EOC, and the RPE in significant ways, their attempts to fully integrate gender into these documents were blocked. Feminists had to compromise in a number of areas including the definition of gender and enforced pregnancy, and the threshold test for CAH. Each of these compromises was forced by the combined lobbying of religious groups and particular states with a strong religious orientation. Thus, religious concerns played a highly significant role in the establishment of the ICC.

The Rome Statute and the Nation-State: The Shifting Battleground of Gender Politics

The establishment of the ICC meant that, for the first time, victims who could not prosecute domestically were provided with an international venue through which to do so. However, its impact reaches further than this. The Rome Statute, as well as the jurisprudence stemming from future ICC decisions, will not only affect parties to ICC disputes but may also be taken up in the prosecution and judgment of relevant cases within state jurisdictions. As noted earlier, under the court's complementarity provisions, the onus for bringing war criminals to justice remains with domestic-level legal institutions. It is expected that in hearing cases related to war crimes and crimes against humanity, these institutions will apply the latest international legal norms and jurisprudence (Warbrick and McGoldrick, 2001: 428), and through this process will import or diffuse new international humanitarian legal norms to the national level. As a result, it is likely that the focal point of gender politics will shift, or in some cases revert back, to the legal arena in nation-states.

Women's rights activists, alert to the importance of the spillover effects of the ICC, have already begun to think strategically about which of the legal norms could be relevant to women seeking gender justice at the national level. One potential area concerns the inclusion of gender discrimination as a form of persecution prohibited under the Rome Statute. This provision could be applied by domestic-level women's rights activists in advocating for the expansion of women's claims to refugee status that in most jurisdictions does not include gender-specific forms of persecution (Charlesworth and Chinkin, 2000: 320).[6] Another area to be developed concerns the application of the expanded definition of rape accepted in recent international jurisprudence and in part by the ICC. The evolving definition emphasizes the violation from the point of view of the victim rather than that of the perpetrator and could be instrumental in challenging common consent-based rape laws that are seen to discriminate against (mostly) female victims. The enumeration of the crimes of sexual slavery and enforced prostitution has also been identified as strengthening the foundation for the prosecution of traffickers of women and children at the state level.

Like their feminist counterparts, conservative religious groups who lobbied at the ICC also understand that the court provides potential opportunities for the expansion of women's rights at the national level. They too have begun to contemplate tactics, but theirs are focused on stopping any advancement of this agenda at the state level. As noted above, at the time of the Rome Conference, several US-based Christian organizations expressed fears about the influence that Western judges could have in extending the definition of gender in the ICC. The Christian, anti-abortion Lifesite (2000) also warned its readers of a post–Rome Conference "radical feminist" agenda, citing the view of WCGJ member Rhonda Copelon "that the Court can be used to change domestic laws." It suggested that pro-lifers should be alert to "the influence of feminists and the homosexual lobby at the international level and their potential to influence to implement their agenda at the highest level of [domestic] judicial appeal." The Catholic Family and Human Rights Institute joined Lifesite in expressing apprehension about the extent to which the ICC will allow extension of women's rights in general and abortion in particular. The institute (Mallon, 2000) sounded the following warning: "Make no Mistake: The constant repetition of new 'rights' is the premeditated attempt to establish customary international law for exactly the purpose of enforcing them. The subtext of the mantra that women's rights are human rights is to place these rights on a par with the universally recognized right to life and with the universally recognized rights guaranteed by the 1948 Universal Declaration of Human Rights. As the camel comes into the tent, something else will have to exit to make room for him."

Like the Christian and anti-abortion groups, a number of states with predominantly Muslim populations fear that the new international gender norms will filter down to the domestic level. Their long-time concern regarding this eventuality is reflected in a resolution passed by the Organization of Islamic Conference (2000), which condemned the use of the "universality of human rights as a pretext to interfere in ... states' international affairs and impair their national sovereignty." The extension of women's rights is a particular concern of many of these states, which, according to Lisa Hajjar (2004: 15), perceive it as part of a cultural onslaught emanating from "else-where." As a result, in a conservative Muslim culture, "the disadvantages that women experience *as women* can be justified and defended – even glorified – as an aspect of that particular culture."

Evidence that certain Muslim states resist the extension of women's rights appears in the many reservations made by Organization of Islamic Conference states, such as Egypt, Syria, Iran, the United Arab Emirates, and Kuwait, to a range of UN documents relating to the topic. These included the *Beijing Platform for Action* and the *Cairo Program of Action* (see Buss, 1998; Neale, 1998; Chappell, 2006). In almost all cases, the reservations state that local law, including Shari'a law, which is used to various degrees to govern family and private relations, takes precedence over any international commitments. Many of these countries voiced similar concerns in the context of the ICC, as illustrated in the earlier discussion of the sexually based CAH provisions. Given that for many Muslim countries state sovereignty takes precedence over international rights, it is likely that they too will challenge any attempts by local NGOs to use the Rome Statute to extend gender justice where it conflicts with local laws.

Transnational Activism at the ICC: Some Conclusions

At this point, it is important to consider how the instance of transnational activism at the ICC fits with theoretical accounts of the process. The following discussion assesses how well Keck and Sikkink's (1998) explanatory framework concerning transnational advocacy networks (TANs) applies to activism around the ICC and outlines some ways in which this framework might be extended for future analyses of international rights issues activism. Finally, it addresses the importance of ongoing feminist religious analysis that can provide a tool in combating challenges to women's rights internationally.

The first conclusion to make, in support of Keck and Sikkink's thesis, is to reiterate the importance of framing in relation to advancing claims in the international arena. In the battle over gender at the ICC, both sides paid careful attention to framing their arguments in moralistic black-and-white terms and used them to put forward distinct and contrasting views about women and their legal rights. The WCGJ tended to rely on liberal feminist arguments that emphasized the individual rights of women and the need for the Rome Statute to recognize and provide for their particular experiences of war and conflict. Religious groups, despite coming from various traditions, championed a conservative view of women's rights, arguing for the need to limit their reproductive rights and sexuality, and to re-emphasize their position in the private sphere.

The experience of activism at the ICC also reinforces the argument of Keck and Sikkink that transnational advocates achieve most success on issues involving bodily harm to vulnerable individuals and the legal equality of opportunity, as these issues transcend political and cultural divides. Interestingly, it can be suggested that the contenders on both sides of the gender politics divide at the ICC used arguments related to these two areas. Both enjoyed some degree of success. Religious representatives from vastly different spiritual traditions were able to find common ground on abortion, other reproductive issues, and questions of equality. Feminists also employed arguments regarding women's bodily integrity and equality to gain support from moderate states for their proposals that gender be mainstreamed throughout the Rome Statute and that limitations on sexually based crimes be resisted. The fact that the statute now contains compromise positions on gender, enforced pregnancy, and sexually based CAH, all of which involve bodily integrity or equality, suggest that Keck and Sikkink are correct in highlighting these issues as central to successful advocacy in international forums.

This study also points to some ways in which the work of Keck and Sikkink could be developed. Their analysis focused on the activities of NGOs, a field of vision that could be expanded to include the actions of *official* state delegations that also pursue normative agendas at the international level. Further, for those pursuing women's rights claims, it is important to remember that such delegations, which tend to consist of men who hold conservative views about women, do not necessarily represent all the citizens of their state. Obviously, NGOs such as the WCGJ and pro-life groups played a key role in the gender politics of the ICC. However, equally important were the stances taken by states in connection with religious and moral issues. The Vatican, officially a non-state observer but operating through the Holy See very much like a state actor, sat at mid-position here. More clear-cut were the roles played by Catholic states such as Ireland and Guatemala in supporting a broader Christian anti-abortion position and those of a number of Muslim states such as Oman, the United Arab Emirates, and Nigeria. The latter pursued their own goals in relation to gender politics at the ICC but, where their interests coincided with those of their Catholic counterparts, also provided crucial support to the Holy See and Catholic states on particular issues. Due to their experience at other UN forums, feminists at the ICC were not surprised to find that these state delegations generally aligned themselves at points where issues of women's rights were at stake. Given the growing use of religious and moral arguments by states internationally, including the US, future analyses of transnational activism must be more alert to, and think more conceptually about, exactly where state-based players fit into the schema of transnational activism.

The role played by states and non-state actors pursuing normative agendas at ICC forums also presents another challenge to the literature. It is difficult to prove that the Vatican and certain states, such as those from the Arab League, actually did operate as a network in the sense defined by Keck and Sikkink. The public record is silent regarding whether these groups met to caucus or strategize about how best to approach gender-justice issues. However, in rebutting feminist positions, they usually put forward complementary, if not identical, arguments, though whether this sprang from coincidence or something more deliberate is unknown. In-depth interviews with participants on both sides of the gender divide might throw light on the question, but given that activists commonly prefer not to reveal their strategies, ascertaining the full extent of the linkages could prove impossible. Although it might be misleading to call these religious forces a network, they nevertheless exerted a great deal of influence at the ICC (as at other UN forums; see Chappell, 2006). Finding a way to define and describe the linkages between these protagonists in international gender politics is a challenge that needs to be taken up in future accounts of their activities.

A final distinguishing factor between this study and the work of Keck and Sikkink concerns the application of the "boomerang effect." The WCGJ and its role in the ICC forums fit neatly within the TAN framework. Identifying impediments to the pursuit of women's legal rights in the domestic arena, members of the caucus worked cooperatively through the international arena to develop new gender-justice norms, and did so in the hope that domestic-level feminist actors would be able to import these norms back into legal arguments and judgments. However, this boomerang effect does not encapsulate the orientation of religious contenders at the ICC. Their participation in the international realm was not grounded in a desire to overcome obstructions to reform at the state level. Rather, they sought to protect the status quo at that level by attempting to stymie the emergence of progressive women's rights norms and to frustrate, where possible, any new norms filtering down to the domestic level. The shared objective of the religious forces was to ensure that the boomerang did not fly. Given this, their success needs to be reconceptualized. Their achievements cannot be judged in terms of changes at the international and domestic levels but in other, negative terms. That is, in examining their victories in shaping the texts of international documents, one must also consider the negatives, what their successes blocked from inclusion. Thinking through these negative measures of success is also a task for future analyses.

Finally, this study also points to important developments in the wider field of women and religion. While official state representatives attempt to limit women's rights at home and abroad, many women are working to redefine the major religious conceptions of women's rights and gender equality. Feminist scholars and activists have revealed the extent to which many spiritual teachings are based on cultural patriarchal assumptions that have little or no foundation in the key religious texts (for Catholicism, see Neale, 1998; and Buss, 1998; for Islam, see Al-Hibri, 1999; Hajjar, 2004; Tohidi, 2003). As these critics explain, spiritual leaders have too often distorted scripture, making rules to uphold the cultural practices that maintain their own authority. The developments at the ICC and in other UN contexts demonstrate that this distortion is also being played out internationally. Thus, feminist efforts in the future should encompass two crucial points: first, feminists within these faiths should keep up their efforts to separate the cultural and political from the spiritual teachings and to reveal the egalitarian tendencies in these religions; second, the transnational feminist community should ensure that these powerful countervailing voices are included in its broader struggle to achieve gender justice.

Feminist actors had some success in influencing the outcome of the Rome Statute of the ICC. As a result of their efforts, international law now better reflects women's experiences of war and conflict. Through the application of the statute and the development of jurisprudence by the ICC and domestic-level courts, women's legal rights may be further extended. However, in their effort to shape the ICC process, feminists had to battle against the alternative view of women and their rights presented by religious groups. These groups, both state- and non-state-based, were also able to mould the outcome of the ICC, not only in terms of what the statute included but also in what it excluded. Both sides achieved some degree of success through the careful framing of their arguments and by focusing on issues related to bodily integrity and legal equality. To this extent, the case of transnational activism around the ICC fits with existing explanations of the process. However, it also raises important new issues, in particular how best to understand the roles of state actors who, though they may not work as a network per se, nevertheless have an important (negative) influence on the outcome of international debates. Given the increasing influence of religious forces in the contemporary international arena, these pressing concerns need to be taken up in future research on transnational activism.

Part 3
Gender and Citizenship

8

Putting Gender Back In: Women and Social Policy Reform in Canada

Janine Brodie

Since the late 1980s, Canada has witnessed profound shifts in both the prominence afforded to women in political debate and the ways in which gender roles and gender inequalities are addressed in public policies. Over these years, the politics of gender has moved in contradictory and often unanticipated directions. In the 1970s, feminist researchers and activists began the task of making gender visible in the politics and policies of the post-war welfare state. They demonstrated how this governing regime rested on a post-war gender order in which some women were offered what was, at best, second-class citizenship, whereas other women – those marginalized by race, sexuality, and class – were accorded ongoing poverty, insecurity, and exclusion. Later, during the early 1980s, feminists saw many of their issues – among them, legal equality, political representation, reproductive freedom, and protection from domestic violence – recognized as legitimate citizenship claims, which in turn were partially integrated into the mainstream policy agenda. Since then, however, the issue of gender equality has been progressively erased from official policy discourses and practices. This disappearance of gender coincides with the implementation of neoliberal governing practices in Canada and most advanced liberal democracies. Although the scope and degree of neoliberal policy reform vary widely among these states, neoliberalism has greatly influenced the framing of citizenship claims as well as relationships between the state and both the private sector (the economy and civil society) and the private sphere (the individual and the family) (Brodie, 1997; Clarke, 2004b). In the process, we have been submerged in a politics that seeks to reform and transform the irredeemably gendered subjects of the post-war welfare state into genderless and self-sufficient market actors.

This chapter explores the gendered underpinnings of this transformation through the lens of social policy reform in Canada. Although all Western democracies have been engaged in social policy reform in recent years, the substance of these reforms, especially with respect to gender, varies widely from one jurisdiction to the next. Many European countries, for example, have implemented social policies that are designed to help women reconcile the multiple and often conflicting demands of paid work, child care, and domestic labour. In Canada, in contrast, there has been a sustained, if not laboured, erasure of gender as a relevant factor in the design of a new social policy regime. As this chapter explains, although cast in the language of gender-neutrality, the family, and individualism, contemporary social policy reform projects are gendered differently from those of the post-war era but are nonetheless decidedly gendered in their impacts. This chapter examines the ways in which gender and gender orders historically have been written into social policy regimes as well as how the post-war gender order has been disrupted by neoliberal governing practices. It then discusses how the gendered subject of the post-war welfare state has been progressively erased through the complementary processes of invisibilization and individualization.

Social Policy Regimes and Gender Orders
Gøsta Esping-Andersen (2002: 1-2) argues that the history of welfare states can be viewed as the combination of brief pivotal moments of epochal change and long periods of politics as usual. In fact, paradigmatic changes in the logic and institutions of modern welfarism occurred only twice before this current era of transformative developments – in the late decades of the nineteenth century and in the years surrounding the Second World War. Both moments were marked, first, by intense ideological debates about rival visions of "the good society," then by consensus-building around a particular model of social governance, and finally, by long periods of consolidation when new governing logics and social goals were translated into policy instruments. In this latter period, the social imaginaries that informed social policy changes are embedded in the way citizens think about themselves, others, and their relationship with the state.

Esping-Andersen might have added that these rare moments of epochal redefinition also had pronounced gendered underpinnings that reflected and enforced both a new gender order and a new equilibrium between the prevailing demands of economic production and social reproduction – that is, between the requirements of "varieties of capitalism" and the daily creation and maintenance of persons and communities (Hall and Soskice, 2001; Bakker and Gill, 2003). Feminists have long recognized that social policy regimes, whether implicitly or explicitly, envision and enforce a particular model of gender relations or gender order, which defines "normal" gender identities, behaviours, and roles as well as "natural" family forms. These gendering strategies are institutionally embedded in the assumptions informing the design and goals of social policies, in the categories specifying eligibility for programs, in the penalties, both formal and informal, exacted for non-conformity, and in the identification and targeting of subpopulations for remedial interventions. Both groups and individuals generally have to fit with the dominant cultural and regulatory constructions of gender in order to benefit from legal protection and government social programs. These constructions, in turn, reinforce in the public imagination common-sense understandings of normal and aberrant as well as deserving and undeserving.

However, the fit between prescribed and enforced gender orders and social policy regimes is neither total nor static. Dominant constructions of the gender order may not correspond to the lived experiences of significant subpopulations, and individuals and social movements may rebel – in the name of freedom or equality – against dominant cultural expectations and sanctions related to "appropriate" gendered behaviours. As well, during periods of transformative economic and social change, gender orders are often destabilized, lose their coherence, and eventually unravel. During such periods, social policy reforms are deeply implicated in the regendering of social formations and in the production of structures, practices, symbols, and norms that give personal and political meaning to gender (Orloff, 2003). Social policies can embody any number of representations of an appropriate gender order. For example, policies may assume and enforce male authority and agency (patriarchalization), or the primary role of families in ensuring individual well-being (familialization), or they may altogether disregard the importance of gender and the gendered division of labour (invisibilization and individualization).

The different models of social governance associated with the nineteenth-century laissez-faire state and the twentieth-century welfare state are illustrative of the correspondence between gender order and gendering strategies. The laissez-faire state, for example, enforced a rigid distinction between the public and private spheres, and assigned primary responsibility to the family for attending to those members who, whether through disability or misfortune, were unable to care for themselves. This model of social governance also enforced an equally rigid gender order, which confined women to the private sphere and assigned them sole responsibility for care and the maintenance of the home and family. They birthed and cared for children, as well as attending to the sick, the disabled, and dying people of all ages. This gender order rested on the cultural claim that it was both normal and natural for women to be excluded from the public sphere of politics and the world of business, and that they submit to patriarchal rule in the home and community. Yet, this social imaginary was also underwritten and enforced by a series of gendering strategies, embedded in public policy, which, among other things, denied women most civil and political rights, blocked their paths to financial and legal independence, and provided social protections only to those who conformed to the prevailing construction of the "good woman." Indeed, it was this construction of women as the selfless, nurturing, and moral mothers of race and nation that eventually provided the political currency for women's claims to citizenship rights in the early twentieth century.

The development of the post-war welfare state is generally portrayed as a settlement between capital and labour that promised improved security to societies that had been shattered by the ravages of depression, war, and genocide. However, if welfare state policies emerged partly in response to market failures, they also addressed what Nancy Folbre (2001) calls "family failures" – in effect, crises in care – where networks of family and kin, church and community proved incapable of underwriting the social reproduction of mass industrial societies. This post-war model of social governance largely revolved around the iconic figure of the male breadwinner. This model fortified a working- or middle-class nuclear family, supported by a male wage earner, a dependent female caregiver, and several children. The state, in turn, ensured an adequate family wage with income supports and limited collective provision for, among other things, unemployment, disability, illness, and old age. Moreover, in many countries, Canada among them, the state provided an allowance to mothers to assist with the costs of raising their children. A woman's paid labour, according to this formula, was deemed unnecessary or, failing that, secondary to that of her husband. Across liberal democracies, the post-war contract was thus built on the expectation that women would marry and "withdraw into housewifery" (Esping-Andersen, 2002: 20). As in the earlier regime, however, this social imaginary was explicitly enforced through gendering strategies embedded in public policies that discriminated against women workers or entrepreneurs, restricted their avenues to financial independence, prohibited contraception, and, in various ways, sanctioned pronounced power imbalances in intimate relationships, not excluding domestic violence and marital rape.

Although the post-war social policy regime was embroidered with discourses of universality, unconditionality, and citizen equality, it was also gender-biased. Social citizenship rights were largely premised on full-time employment. This definition of citizen-worker, combined with the post-war construction of the appropriate gender order as male breadwinner/ dependent wife, meant that men gained entitlements to social citizenship. Women, in contrast, were cast as dependent citizens – dependent either on individual men or on state-funded and state-delivered social welfare programs that often involved surveillance, conditionality, social stigma, and low levels of compensation. Feminist scholars have also demonstrated that this particular articulation of the gender order excluded the experiences of many poor, unmarried, and minority women who did not fit into the prototypical model of the nuclear family. This model of gender relations was actively cultivated in popular culture and enforced, sometimes aggressively, through public policy and state institutions. Indeed, during these years, many welfare regimes regularly enforced the "man in the house rule." According to this practice, women on state assistance were cut off from benefits if welfare workers found evidence of cohabitation with a man.

However, this popular assessment of the gendered underpinning of the welfare state does not tell the whole story. The welfare state's promotion of the idea of universal citizenship equality also provided individual women and a nascent women's movement with discursive space to pronounce themselves as something different from and more than dependants, wives, and mothers. Women were encouraged and, indeed, empowered by the state to make political claims as citizens who had been actively denied the promise of equality, although all too frequently it was white middle-class women who had the loudest voice. The welfare state, in other words, promoted its own style of politics, identity formation, and mobilization among disadvantaged groups (Brodie, 1997). This politics, as Carol Smart (1995: 107) points out, was "dependent upon the identification of an interest group with a shared identity" that could be shown to have been "denied their full and proper legal and/or human rights." This kind of politics presumed the existence of a welfare state because it assumed immutable linkages among social rights, social equality, and social progress. The welfare state held out the promise that structural and systemic disadvantages, rooted in the postwar social and economic order, could be tempered through collective intervention and public policy (Brodie, 2002: 94).

Gender Dis-orders

The logic of the post-war welfare state and the gender order that underpinned it progressively unravelled in the latter decades of the twentieth century. Governments, regardless of partisan stripe, increasingly lost their capacity to insulate national economies from the liberalization of the international political economy, energy shocks, and intense competition from newly industrializing countries. Rising unemployment, inflation, and burgeoning government deficits convinced policy networks and governing elites that post-war social programs and the idea of the family wage were not affordable, posing a competitive disadvantage in the international market. Thus, throughout the 1980s and beyond, the welfare states of most advanced capitalist countries and the politics they inspired were systematically eroded by retrenchment and restructuring.

The assault on the logics and institutions of the post-war welfare state was most intense in liberal welfare regimes that embraced the imperatives of neoliberal governance as an alternative to post-war welfare liberalism. Neoliberalism is both a theory of economic growth, adapted from classical liberal economics, and an experiment in contemporary governance. Stripped to its bare essentials, this governing philosophy prioritizes economic growth and market logics over all other goals and instruments of public policy. Primary among its arsenal of governing strategies are privatization, deregulation, marketization, decentralization, and fiscal austerity, especially with respect to social expenditures. Proponents of neoliberal governance have consistently indicted the welfare state for weighing down and crowding out markets, which are assumed to be more efficient, adaptive, and innovative than the public sector, and for creating a culture of dependency among recipients of social welfare programs. Neoliberals consider the market to be the primary source of individual well-being and choice; as a consequence, they advocate a withdrawal of the state from the provision of social services and supports. The role of the state, according to this formula, should be confined to enhancing markets for social goods and services and to increasing self-sufficiency and labour force participation among those "addicted" to government assistance.

These and other uncompromising critiques of the welfare state have generated varying degrees of support among Western democracies, finding less fertile ground in continental Europe than in the Anglo-American world. Almost everywhere, however, neoliberalism's influence on social policy reform has been subtle, influencing prevailing thinking about the objectives of social policy as well as shifting the weight of responsibility for social provision and social reproduction away from the state to the family, the market, and communities. In effect, as John Clarke (2004a: 62) explains, the neoliberal governing project aspires to the "economization of the social" – that is, to reduce social life to economic phenomena and to subject society to, rather than protect it from, the uncertainties and inequalities associated with market logics and processes.

These critical shifts in thinking about social governance have had decided impacts on the politics of gender and social reproduction. Although neoliberalism is largely silent on the gender question, feminist scholars and activists, in Canada and around the world, anticipated many of the gendered implications of the shift from the post-war breadwinner model to the market logics of neoliberalism. In a challenging essay written in the early 1990s, for example, Donna Haraway (1991: 166) predicted that the current era would be marked by the simultaneous erosion and intensification of gender, both literally and metaphorically. Indeed, these contradictory tendencies are embedded in the neoliberal worldview. It erodes the political and social relevance of gender in daily life and in policy making by constructing both men and women as genderless individuals and, optimally, as self-sufficient market actors in pursuit of self-interest, freedom, and choice. Of course, neither men nor women live their daily lives in gender-neutral ways. Neoliberals, however, tend to bracket out women's reproductive labour, unpaid domestic work, and caring activities as having no market value or, at best, as existing as an externality – that is, as an activity located outside of the productive economy (B. Young, 2003). Neoliberal fundamentalism assumes that "there exists and will always exist a pool of private labour" to attend to social reproductive needs (Hankivsky, 2004: 107). In the process, the lived realities of an ongoing and deeply entrenched gendered division of social reproductive labour are simply erased from governing equations.

Predictably, this erasure has been accompanied by an intensification of the experience of gender in the daily lives of most women, especially the poor and the marginalized. This can be observed on many terrains, not least in the feminization of poverty, both domestically and globally. Drastic cuts to Canadian social welfare programs, for example, have increased the incidence and depth of poverty among single mothers who, lacking the option of affordable child care or flexible employment policies, often have no choice but to accept social assistance until their children reach school age. Once in the labour force, the majority of women workers continue to be locked into stereotypical female job ghettos that are marked by low wages, few benefits, part-time work, and precarious employment. In addition, the disappearance of the family wage has meant that the female partner in most families must work part- or full-time, while still maintaining primary responsibility for unpaid care and domestic labour in the home. This is especially the case for less affluent women who can purchase neither caring services nor domestic labour, tasks undertaken almost exclusively by other women. The commodification of caring work, in turn, has aggravated racial and class disparities among women themselves, enabling some women to buy and exploit the domestic services of other women, a social reality that has increasingly taken on global proportions.

Pressures on social reproduction have intensified as neoliberal governments divert ever more caring responsibilities from the public sphere to the private sphere. Because of decreased public support for those with special needs, the elderly, and the convalescing, women have been forced to pick up the slack (Bakker, 2003). Many Canadian women now find themselves primarily responsible for both child care and elder care, prompting Statistics Canada to label them as "the sandwich generation." Yet, there is little reason to believe that the difficulty in reconciling work and life expectations is a generational effect. Rather, it is embedded in a governing philosophy that fails to appreciate that a major role of modern social policy is to negotiate a sustainable balance between the demands of economic production and social reproduction. The supposedly genderless individualism exercised in the paid labour force, in other words, is not reflected in the private sphere, where a gendered division of unpaid housework and caring labour remains intact. Issues of time, health, and the quality of intimate relationships are rapidly becoming the new feminine mystique for contemporary women – in Betty Friedan's (1963) terms, "the problem with no name."

These and other factors have contributed to other unanticipated social trends such as increased divorce rates, multiple family forms, postponed family formation, declining fertility, and pronounced stress levels among working women.

Contemporary Social Policy Reform

Across Western democracies, these and related social trends have prompted policy-makers to revisit the question of gender and the fit between production and social reproduction in contemporary formulae for social governance. In the process, as Sylvia Walby (2004) explains, these countries are incorporating a reconfigured gender order into social policy reform. Unlike their post-war counterparts, however, "the gender problem" and its attendant policy prescriptions are now framed in uneven, often contradictory, and inconsistent ways. A comparison of the dominant strains of thinking behind social policy reform in the United States and Europe, for example, demonstrates, in stark relief, the different ways in which gender is being rewritten into public policy. In the United States, both political rhetoric and public policy have concentrated on reviving a patriarchal gender order and on rebuilding self-sufficient families comprised of sole or dual earners. *The Great Disruption* (2000), by the prolific American social conservative Francis Fukuyama, provides the Coles Notes on the thinking that underlies American social policy reform. Assigning almost sole responsibility for America's crumbling social order to shifting gender roles, Fukuyama argues that the "most dramatic shifts in social norms that constitute the great disruption concern those related to reproduction, the family, and relations between the sexes" (36).

Fukuyama asserts that the only way to reverse the erosion of the American social fabric is to rebuild male-headed nuclear families and responsible communities, an approach that is consistent with the central threads of American social conservatism. This social imaginary underlies the 1996 Personal Responsibility and Work Opportunity Reconciliation Act (PRWORA), which represents the most significant change in American social policy since the 1930s. The PRWORA is commonly associated with workfare programs, but it also identifies marriage as the foundation of society. Under its provisions, a growing envelope of federal funds has been allocated to reducing out-of-wedlock births and promoting marriage, especially among welfare recipients. As well, programs, often designed by faith groups, have been developed to help women find a "good man" and to teach inner-city youth how to be such men, which typically involves getting a job and taking financial responsibility for partners and children. Of course, this social imaginary of the American family is a myth, but it is a myth with discursive and legal force, which reasserts that social reproductive work is a private responsibility, primarily of women. There is little concern here regarding whether women perform these functions themselves or contract out domestic and caring work to others, usually low-paid women of colour and recent immigrants, who in turn must find private solutions to their own caring needs.

Writing from a geopolitical and discursive space that differs markedly from Fukuyama's America, European social progressive Esping-Andersen (2002) nonetheless makes a similar diagnosis of the "problem" but offers very different policy prescriptions. He suggests that Western democracies are now in the "midst of a revolution in demographic and family behaviour, spearheaded by women's embrace of personal independence and lifelong careers" (2). Pointing to a transformed economic and demographic policy environment, Esping-Andersen argues that contemporary labour markets and households can no longer support the foundational goals and programs of the post-war welfare state. These social changes, he underlines, do not release the state from providing social protection for its citizens – a strategy reflected in neoliberal social policy reform. Instead, Esping-Andersen's vision of a new welfare state involves the negotiation of a "new gender contract" that would better enable women to strike a sustainable balance between the growing necessity of workforce participation and the multiple and gendered demands of social reproduction (68-95). In some cases, this new gender contract also involves exercises in social engineering, inviting men to share in domestic labour, usually through targeted inducements such as parental or father leave. However, there is little empirical evidence to suggest that these policy "carrots" have had an appreciable impact on the gendered division of domestic work.

Esping-Andersen argues that gender equity has become "the lynchpin of any positive postindustrial equilibrium between households and the economy" (69), but he also asserts that gender equity policies should not be regarded as simply a concession to women's claims. His reasoning is far more instrumental (Lister, 2004: 18). According to this, as well as to many other contemporary social policy analyses, governments need to enact social policies that enable women to reconcile the demands of paid work and family responsibilities because contemporary economic and political realities *require* women's productive *and* social reproductive labour. As already noted, many families now need one-and-a-half wage earners, if not two, to sustain them. As well, it is argued that the postindustrial labour force needs women workers to fill growing labour shortages, which are exaggerated by fertility declines, to increase the ratio of working to non-working populations in order to sustain social programs, especially retirement benefits for an ageing baby boom, and to reduce child poverty (Esping-Andersen, 2002: 9). This need for women workers, it is argued, demands a new gender contract, through which "improving the welfare of women means improving the collective welfare of society at large" (20).

Although European countries differ with respect to both the scope and design of this new gender contract, the pervasive trend is towards enhanced work-life reconciliation policies that enable families, and especially women, to better balance the demands of paid labour with child birth, child rearing, and domestic responsibilities. This gendering strategy, also referred to as "women-friendly" or "defamilialization" policy, involves, among other things, provisions for public and affordable child care and early childhood education, paid maternity and parental leave, flexible hours and employment guarantees, and short leave provisions for family caring duties. In effect, as Mary Daly (2002: 254) notes, European welfare states are increasingly compensating families for the costs, both in time and money, involved in caring for children.

This apparent convergence around work-life reconciliation policies reflects domestic path dependencies as well as the consensus of a series of European Union summits (such as Lisbon 2000, Barcelona 2002) that have set targets to increase both the participation of women in the labour force and the provision of child care (Bettio and Plantenga, 2004). For many feminists, however, this particular operationalization of the concept of defamilialization is both necessary and inadequate. For one thing, it does not address persistent gendered inequalities in the labour market – indeed, flexible work practices may reinforce gendered disparities in income and deny women advancement in their careers or places of employment. For another, work-life reconciliation policies may exacerbate the deeply entrenched and uneven gendered division of labour in the household insomuch as they assume the ongoing feminization of domestic work. In contrast to those of the post-war gender order, these policies tend to promote a construction of the "normal" woman as being both a full-time worker and a domestic caregiver.

Social Policy Reform in Canada
Since the 1990s, Canada too has enacted a series of social policy reforms that focus on social reproduction processes and the gender order that underlies them. In the so-called post-deficit era (1997 and beyond), the federal government introduced the much applauded National Child Benefit (NCB, 1997), the Caregiver Credit (1998), extended maternity and parental leave (2000), the Child Disability Benefit (2003), the Compassionate Care Benefit (2004), the now defunct Early Childhood Development and Education Initiative (2004), and the Universal Child Care Benefit (2006). Some commentators, moreover, have praised these initiatives as evidence of the passing of the dark days of neoliberal social policy retrenchment and the tentative coming out of a post-neoliberal state form – the social investment state (SIS).

This term was first coined by Anthony Giddens to describe and promote New Labour's "Third Way," which was introduced in the United Kingdom in the mid-1990s. The election of the Blair government brought a shift in social governance from Thatcherism's punitive social retrenchment and privatization policies to active welfarism, which promised to invest in individual skills and capacities, giving the marginalized a hand up rather than a handout. As the Policy Research Initiative (PRI) (2005: 14), a policy research arm of the federal government, explains, the SIS "seeks to target social expenditures, as investing in the human capital of its citizens, to ensure that people are equipped with the skills and resources to negotiate life's challenges." In recent years, the federal government has also frequently deployed the language of social investment, especially with respect to child-centred social policy (Dobrowolsky, 2004).

After almost a decade of post-deficit spending, however, there is little evidence to support the idea that Canada has entered a new era of social investment. The introduction of the Canada Health and Social Transfer in the 1995 federal budget downloaded responsibility for the development of social welfare policy to the provinces. Since then, the provincial governments have consistently cut benefits and tightened eligibility for welfare programs while channelling few new funds to social capacity building, save perhaps for health care. As for the federal government, its flagship initiative, the National Child Benefit, as well as other new initiatives, represents only a fraction of new federal spending. By most indicators, then, Canada's contemporary policy regime is better characterized as social divestment rather than social investment. This said, it is also the case that the federal social policy initiatives of the past decade advance a model of gender relations that differs markedly from either its post-war equivalent or the work-life reconciliation policies currently being pursued in the EU. As I argue in the next section of this chapter, federal social policy reform reflects two gendering strategies – invisibilization and individualization – that complement and reinforce neoliberal governing practices. In particular, the National Child Benefit is discussed as an example of invisibilization. The chapter then turns to the research on social exclusion and poverty published by the Policy Research Initiative to demonstrate the logics of individualization.

Invisibilization and the Disappearing Gendered Subject

From the mid-1980s, Ottawa increasingly berated feminist groups for being unrepresentative of the interests of the silent majority of Canadian women, and the issue of gender equality was progressively displaced from the political agenda (see Brodie, 2007). However, the disappearance of the gendered subject of social policy is perhaps mostly clearly tracked through federal policy discourses and initiatives, which effectively cast the child as the focal point of post-deficit social spending in the late 1990s and beyond. As Wendy McKeen (2004) documents, the ascendancy of the child as the iconic subject of social policy reaches back to the late 1980s when Ottawa, following a growing international trend, pledged to end child poverty by the turn of the millennium. After the ratification of the UN's Convention on the Rights of the Child in 1991, the Mulroney government embarked on what it termed its "child's agenda," concentrating its energies particularly on "children at risk" (94).

Ottawa's almost singular concern with the child and children's poverty intensified during the Chrétien years, especially after the introduction of the National Child Benefit (NCB) in 1997. Comprising a tax credit (Canadian Child Tax Benefit, CCTB), which is given to families with incomes below a generous cut-off, and a supplement for poor families (National Child Benefit Supplement, NCBS), this initiative was welcomed as the most significant federal social policy innovation in a generation. It was designed to prevent and decrease child poverty by providing additional income directly to poor working families and to create additional fiscal space for the provinces to provide programs and services for the poor (Paterson, Levasseur, and Teplova, 2004). Since its introduction, the CCTB has been significantly enhanced to include a larger proportion of Canadian families, and Ottawa's total expenditures on its child agenda increased by 60 percent in the 1997-2007 period (Battle, Torjman, and Mendelson, 2003: 2). This flagship program nevertheless represented only 10 percent of the total tax expenditures introduced by the federal government in the 1997-2004 period (Yalnizyan, 2005).

The goal of eliminating child poverty in Canada was both overdue and necessary, but in many ways the elevation of the abstract "poor child" as the focus of social policy reform incorrectly specifies the policy problem. As poverty groups have stressed, the effect is to set up an opposition between the child and other disadvantaged groups – as a dichotomy between the deserving and undeserving poor as well as between child and parent. Moreover, these policy discourses depict the poor child as a homogeneous category, veiling over considerations of how all children are themselves differently configured by, among other things, gender, race, ethnicity, sexuality, and national origin. As Ruth Lister (2004) observes, the ascendancy of the homogenized and decontextualized category of "child" effectively sidesteps structural social divisions that consistently correlate with official definitions and lived experiences of poverty. Among these correlates, Lister adds, "gender constitutes the most profound differentiating division" (54). Canada's child-centred social policy agenda, however, has effectively excised women and gender concerns from the official stories of poverty (McKeen, 2004: 102).

The inadequacy of the children's agenda extends beyond these political implications, for it fails to acknowledge the inescapable fact that in the vast majority of cases, poor children live with poor women who experience poverty in many different ways. Studies demonstrate, for example, that within poor families, women often endure hidden poverty because they usually have less disposable income than do men, sacrifice for other family members, and devote inordinate time to the task of managing their family's poverty. They are also more likely than their male counterparts to fall deeper into poverty if there is a marriage breakdown (Lister, 2004: 56). Other examples of the gendered face of poverty are more easily tracked. National poverty statistics remind us that single mothers (and thus their children) are among the poorest of the poor in Canada – a trend that has changed little since implementation of the child-centred social policy. The National Council of Welfare's 2004 Report Card on Child and Family Poverty indicates that slightly over half of single mothers live below the poverty line, as compared to 10 percent of couples with children. Among the million-plus poor children in Canada (approximately 16 percent of all Canadian children), 57 percent live in two-parent families, 36 percent with single mothers, and 3 percent with single fathers (National Council of Welfare, 2004: 110). Moreover, child poverty among Aboriginal, immigrant, and visible minorities is now twice the national average (Muhtadie, 2004).

Clearly, gender (and race) is a critical factor in the child poverty story. Although women may be erased from the analysis, as Linda Brush (2002: 175) reminds us, most mothers, whether single or not, continue to pay a child penalty, and single mothers often bear the weight of both a child and marriage penalty. It is commonly understood that women's disproportionate share of domestic work and child-caring tasks (child penalty) correlates with labour-market discrimination, subsequent inequalities in pay and the quality of jobs, and career mobility (Stratigaki, 2004: 31). Inadequate provisions for social care mean that many single mothers must fashion their labour force participation to accommodate their caring responsibilities (marriage penalty), often working part-time in precarious "feminized" sectors that offer few or no benefits and minimum wages. Others have little alternative but to rely on the minimal income provided by provincial and territorial social assistance programs, at least until their children reach school age. Although these programs generally provide drug and other benefits not available to part-time workers, most mothers on social assistance have seen little appreciable increase in their incomes since the introduction of the NCBS. Under its terms, the provinces are allowed to lower their social assistance payments by the amount of the NCBS and use these savings to support other programs and services for low-income families. Yet, there are no mechanisms to ensure that the provinces do, in fact, redirect these savings to the poor, especially single mothers with children. Although some provinces no longer claw back the supplement, many women with children who are on social assistance continue to be denied this federal benefit.

In sum, then, the structure of gender (and race) weaves through both the incidence and the experience of child poverty. However, the erasure of systemic considerations from social policy analysis does not diminish their persistent effects. As Lister (2004: 55) underlines, "A gender analysis of poverty reveals not simply its unequal incidence but also that both cause and effect are deeply gendered. The conceptual and methodological implications go well beyond "adding women in." In the absence of policies and programs addressing the structural basis of women's poverty, a child-centred agenda is unlikely to meet the objective of reducing child poverty (Paterson, Levasseur, and Teplova, 2004).

Individualization and the Politics of Renaming
The final section of this chapter shifts our analytical eye from federal policies to research conducted by the PRI to demonstrate how individualization, as a (de)gendering strategy, renames gender-based and other group differences as the discrete characteristics of genderless individuals. The PRI was established within the Privy Council Office in 1996 to provide research on emerging horizontal policy issues – that is, issues that cut across the policy terrains of traditional line departments – and to integrate its research findings into government policy. With the reorganization of the Privy Council Office under the new Harper Conservative government in 2006, the PRI has been placed under the broad umbrella of a new mega-department, Human Resources and Social Development. However, since its inception, the PRI research agenda has consistently focused on questions of social governance, taking on the task of replacing the remnants of equality-based social citizenship thinking with neoliberal assumptions and policy frames. Our focus will be the PRI's work on poverty and social exclusion, and the individualization agenda that underlies it.

Individualization is a dominant undercurrent in contemporary social policy reform. Since the 1990s, social policy regimes in virtually all Western democracies have turned from a rights-based and redistributive model of social governance towards so-called active welfare policies, which place priority on the development of human capital, individual self-sufficiency, and labour force participation. This shift in thinking minimizes, if not explicitly rejects, two critical assumptions that informed the development of the post-war welfare state: first, social structures systematically advantage some groups and disadvantage others; and second, public policy appropriately corrects for systemic barriers and inequalities. Individualization, as we will see, masks systemic inequalities such as gender and race in determining vulnerabilities to poverty as well as capacities to achieve self-sufficiency.

Ulrich Beck and Elisabeth Beck-Gernsheim (2002) characterize individualization as part of a broader contemporary compulsion "to live a life of one's own." As they explain, the meaning of individualization differs from that of individualism, which is generally understood as either self-actualizing or self-seeking behaviour. Individualization, in contrast, places steeply rising demands on people to find personal causes and responses to what are, in effect, collective social problems. In the view of Beck and Beck-Gernsheim, we are all now compelled to find biographic solutions to systemic contradictions (xxii). This new governing formula demands that individuals imagine themselves separately from group identities and claims, and that they conduct their own lives without recourse to group-based claims on the state. Responsibility, for both social crises that find their genesis in such macro processes as structural unemployment and structural disadvantages related to the gendered division of labour or racism, is shifted onto the shoulders of individuals. Living your own life thus includes taking personal responsibility for your own failures, especially dependency on social assistance. As a result of this discursive manoeuvre, structurally disadvantaged groups are collectively individualized, both in popular cultural representations and in public policy (23-27).

Individualization redefines poverty as arising from personal deficits with respect to, among other things, skills development, moral direction, social capital, and self-discipline. Contemporary social policy reform thus aspires to correct the apparent deficiencies of poor people through discipline, coercion, skills enhancement, and certain technologies of self-help. The specific kinds of state intervention vary widely across different kinds of welfare regimes, from the punitive workfare programs associated with American welfare reform to the various training and labour-market strategies associated with many European welfare regimes. In Canada, individualization has not figured prominently in federal social policy discourses until recently, although clearly, provincial workfare policies adopted in, for example, Ontario, British Columbia, and Alberta enforce the logic of individualization.

The PRI's 2003 research theme on poverty and social exclusion thus stands out as a concerted and often laboured attempt to refract the experience of poverty in Canada through the lens of individualization. This research initiative is firmly cast within a neoliberal policy frame, beginning with four tenets of neoliberal fundamentalism:

- Poverty is natural and inevitable. "Poverty and exclusion will remain a fact of all societies rich and poor" (Kunz and Frank, 2004: 8).
- Poverty is not solely about income. "Our thinking about poverty should no longer be confined to a narrow conceptualization related to point in time income" (Voyer, 2004: 1-2).
- Poverty alleviation is dependent on the integration of the poor into existing social structures and relations. "Poverty is the cause and consequence of social exclusion" (Kunz and Frank, 2004: 4).

- Poverty reduction is not an exclusive mandate of governments. "Responsibility for reducing poverty and exclusion does not rest solely with governments" (Voyer, 2004: 2).

Reflecting these claims, the PRI further argues that cohort data, gathered from Canadians during the past decade, have provided the empirical grounding for a conceptual breakthrough in social policy research. Poverty, it is argued, is best understood as something that happens over an individual's life course – the result of missed opportunities, bad decisions, or unfortunate events – rather than as a reflection of either structural inequalities or life-cycle effects. According to this analysis, for the vast majority, poverty is a "fluid and temporary" experience: entry and exit from low income is associated with events and transitions that occur over the course of one's life such as changes in family or employment status (Kunz and Frank, 2004: 4-5). Again, reflecting its neoliberal orientation, the PRI next asserts that individuals normally have (or should have) the resources to ride out these temporary experiences of "being poor." PRI researchers contend that "individuals" "usually have a set of resources at their disposal including personal characteristics, social relations, human and financial resources, and government support. If these buffers are not strong enough to overcome life's calamities ... individuals risk being at the margins of society" (5).

Having untied both the experience of and responses to poverty from their structural moorings, the PRI does concede that there are identifiable subgroups in the general population – approximately 8 percent of working-age Canadians in 1996 – for whom poverty is neither temporary nor fluid. Canada's "persistently poor" are largely confined to five groups – lone-parent families, persons with work-limiting disabilities, recent immigrants, Aboriginals living off reserves, and unattached older individuals (forty-five to sixty-four years). These groups are five to nine times more likely to experience long-term poverty than other Canadians (Hatfield, 2004: 19, 22). Although they are conceptually distinct, "these groups," according to the PRI (Kunz and Frank, 2004: 5), "share a number of things in common. Each group carries an identity marker defined by an event occurring over the course of life, ranging from a change in family status or lack thereof, a change in health status, or a change in place of residence." "Departure from some of these characteristics," the researchers add, "reduces the risks of long-term poverty."

Table 8.1 shows that approximately one-quarter of the working-age population of each group experienced persistent low incomes between 1996 and 2001 (Hatfield, 2004: 19, 23). Perhaps a more striking observation to be drawn from these data, however, is that these are largely structural markers from which the poor cannot realistically depart. Persons with work-limiting disabilities, for example, generally cannot simply chose to transcend the

Table 8.1

Poverty rates among the persistently poor

	% of group in poverty 1996-2001	% women in poverty in 2001 (before tax)
Lone parents	22	38*
Disabled	26	26
Recent immigrants	26	35
Aboriginals off-reserve	16	36
Unattached (45-64)	26	41**

* After tax
** Low income cut-off
Sources: For 1996-2001, Hatfield, 2004: 23. For women in 2001, Townson, 2005: 2-3;
National Council of Welfare, 2004: 101.

physical, social, and institutional constraints associated with disability. Neither can Aboriginal people, on or off reserves, depart easily from a historical legacy of social and institutional racism. Relatedly, the term "recent immigrant" masks the fact that the vast majority of recent immigrants in Canada are people of colour. Thus, race, rather than length of residency, may be the critical marker underlying the growing incidence of poverty among this group of Canadians. Indeed, only two of the five groups – lone parents and unattached individuals – appear to be able to depart from their marker, most obviously through marriage.

Disregarding these palpable contradictions, the PRI offers the following advice for "avoiding low income for members of all high risk groups" (Hatfield, 2004: 22). The most important factor identified is *attachment to paid work* accompanied by the following individualized strategies:

- exit from high-risk group
- draw on spouse for support
- belong to only one high-risk group
- graduate from high school
- live in a region with a high employment rate (22-23).

The PRI's conceptual breakthrough is a quintessential example of neoliberal individualization. Although it identifies Canada's poor by group-based markers, its proposed strategies for poverty alleviation are framed in terms of individual choices and private solutions. In effect, Canada's persistently poor are advised to get a job, get married, or move to a wealthy province such as Alberta. Clearly, this policy advice simultaneously downloads all responsibility for structural inequalities and risk management onto individuals (Brush, 2002: 168) and validates the market as the primary mechanism whereby individuals secure personal security and well-being (Clarke,

2004a: 90-91). Indeed, this naturalization of the market as the primary source of human welfare is a familiar theme in the contemporary social reform literature. Although neo-classical economics similarly conflates human welfare, in all its complexities, with market income, this measure does not account for, let alone recognize, the many contributions to human well-being that are generated outside the market through unpaid care, kinship, social citizenship, solidarity, and political equality.

Individualization purports to transcend "old" political debates about systemic inequalities, but the traces of gender cannot be erased, either empirically or conceptually, from this script of social policy reform. Available gender-disaggregated poverty statistics demonstrate that most of the PRI's five categories of the persistently poor are themselves internally skewed by gender (see Table 8.1). National Council of Welfare (2004), for example, shows that female single parents are twice as likely than male single parents to be poor, and that unattached women, whether seniors or of working age, are significantly more likely than their male counterparts to have low incomes.

These data on cross-cutting gender disparities are neither new nor surprising. Among other things, they reflect a deeply entrenched gendered division of labour that assigns to women the weight of unpaid social reproductive work, low pay in feminized job ghettos, restricted access to unemployment benefits, precarious part-time work that affords few benefits or other forms of income security in later life, and few governmental supports either for child and elder care or for training programs and skills upgrading. Renaming women as well as members of other socially disadvantaged groups as individuals does not erase the spaces that they occupy in the economy or the household. We do indeed live our own lives, but we do so within broadly entrenched and often inequitable social contexts.

Zygmunt Bauman (2002: 68-69) questions whether it is actually possible for the marginalized poor to find a biographic solution to systemic contradictions: "In fact, a 'biographical solution to systemic contradictions' is an oxymoron; it may be sought, but it cannot be found ... The subjects of contemporary states are individuals by fate: the factors that constitute their individuality – confinement to individual resources and individual responsibility for the results of life choices – are not themselves matters of choice."

This said, the PRI's advice to the persistently poor to get a job or depend on a spouse must be read with considerable skepticism. Although the market is represented as the most important source of human welfare, it is not a neutral mechanism. Markets have proved themselves time and again to be notorious places of discrimination, exploitation, harassment, stress, and exclusion. Thus, it is far from axiomatic that paid work is a passport to social inclusion, especially in an increasingly polarized labour market. Bad jobs may provide only what Amartya Sen identifies as unfavourable or disempowering inclusion (cited in Lister, 2004: 79). Individualization invites women to embrace the stereotypical "male biography" (Esping-Andersen, 1999: 70) of worker-breadwinner, but few women are able to draw on the reservoir of unpaid domestic and caring work on which this role has traditionally depended. The PRI allows that the persistently poor can also escape low income by depending on a spouse and presumably taking up this unpaid work. Neither model, however, speaks to the lived realities of most working women, who struggle on a daily basis to balance the simultaneous demands of paid work and unpaid caring responsibilities.

The PRI's research on social exclusion envisions society as comprised of insiders and outsiders, with labour force participation being the principal delineating factor between the two. According to this view, the primary challenges for policy-makers are twofold: identify the deficiencies of those outside the paid labour force and devise strategies to draw them into either paid work or intimate dependent relationships such as marriage. Once inside, these groups are no longer considered to be a policy problem as their fate is determined by neutral market forces or private relationships. This formulation stands in stark contrast to feminist analyses of inclusion/exclusion, which emphasize not only the "absence, marginalization, and exclusion of women in different situations but women's position with respect to power relations in the public, private, and symbolic domains" (Daly and Saraceno, 2002: 84). Moreover, feminists stress the interdependence of power relations across these domains. Although contemporary social policy reform encourages (re)forming those at the margins, the source of marginalization often rests at the centre, especially in the prevailing gender order that mediates the interface between production and social reproduction (100).

Conclusion

A series of indicators suggests that Canada, like other advanced liberal democracies, is poised at the edge of a crisis in social reproduction. To name a few such indicators, fertility rates are declining, the population is ageing, income gaps between rich and poor are growing, intergenerational mobility has ground to a halt, numbers of lone-parent families are growing while two incomes are increasingly necessary to support a family, the demand for child care and elder care is not being met – and the list goes on. As already noted, some countries have responded to these social trends with defamilialization policies aimed at easing the competing demands of paid work and caring responsibilities for both men and women. The gendering strategies discussed in this chapter, in contrast, largely ignore the interface between production and social reproduction, as well as the unstable gender order underlying it. Invisibilization tactics embodied in the federal government's child agenda assume that the persistent problem of child poverty can be resolved by marginally increasing family income, especially for the working poor. This strategy disregards the question of how income is distributed within the family and has not drawn a significant proportion of families headed by women across the poverty line.

Individualization fails to appreciate the effects of social structures in which individuals are variously and differently embedded. If over two decades of feminist policy analysis tell us anything, however, it is that these structures are always already fraught with gendered identities and inequalities. The federal policy documents examined in this chapter reflect a profound and laboured resistance to incorporating gender, let alone feminist insights, into their policy frame. But to the extent that the new roadmaps to social policy (re)form fail to factor in gender, they contribute to rather than provide solutions for a growing crisis in social reproduction. Thus, as the complex and uncertain politics of reforming Canada's social architecture advances, it is imperative that feminists devote ever closer scrutiny to the foundational assumptions of competing models of social provision and insist that both gender and the state be brought back in.

9
Citizenship in the Era of "New Social Risks": What Happened to Gender Inequalities?
Jane Jenson

There is a familiar story about the links between citizenship regimes and the social and political conflicts of the 1930s through the 1960s. Social citizenship is described as being built for and by a male-dominated industrial working class and its allies. Women's place and roles are rarely highlighted in the narrative, except when attention turns to home and hearth, kith and kin. And then the story becomes one of change and modernization. From the 1960s through the 1980s, movements mobilized to contest the status that post-1945 citizenship regimes assigned to women and the structured gender equalities they reinforced. Claims-making was in the name of equality. It was demanded first for "women." Then mobilization in the name of more nuanced "racial," ethnic, and class categories shattered the univocal discourse but maintained the claims for equality. These were addressed to the state in the name of full citizenship. As Sandra Burt (1995: 92) described the women's movements in Canada in the 1990s, "This call by feminist advocacy groups for equal rights is primarily a call for government action, in the form of either social programs or funding of women's groups."

The social dimensions of these citizenship regimes are now being redesigned. Policy communities prescribe a shift from supposedly passive spending on social protection to investments that will generate an "active society" and an "active citizenship." At the same time there is a shift in thinking about the role of the state and, therefore, the very portion of well-being that will be subject to the principles of citizenship. In addition, whereas the post-1945 representational forms in citizenship regimes depended on parties, unions, and other intermediary associations as the major routes to representation, governance practices are now changing. Policy communities inside the state as well as outside advocate a greater involvement of the community sector and more direct citizen engagement as well as a larger space for market principles in the distribution of well-being.

Neoliberalism in the 1980s and 1990s clearly had significant negative effects on the capacity of women's movements and other progressive forces to make equality claims (Jenson and Phillips, 1996; Brodie, this volume). Policy preferences for market-based choices, for example, generated back-tracking on earlier commitments to public services such as child care, access to which is key if women are to achieve some measure of economic autonomy (Jenson and Sineau, 2001). Disdain among populists and neoliberals for group-based claims sidelined women's movements in many places (Sawer, this volume; Dobrowolsky and Jenson, 2004; Bashevkin, 1998).

This chapter nonetheless argues that the story is no longer a straightforward one of neoliberalism triumphant. Neither social policy reforms nor new governance in its contemporary manifestation is *simply* neoliberal dogma. The situation is more complicated. Recent developments in policy perspectives and practices have led some analysts to postulate that we can describe the current era as that "after neo-liberalism" (Larner and Craig, 2005; Lister, 2003). Others, however, casting their analysis at a structural level and analyzing discourse more than policy practices, continue to claim that, as Jamie Peck and Adam Tickell (2002: 380) put it, "neoliberalism seems to be everywhere" (see Larner, 2003 for a useful comment on this position). Relying on historical institutionalism and its concern with interests and institutions as well as ideas/discourse, this chapter is aligned with the first perspective.

Since the late 1990s and certainly in the current decade, a number of countries in Europe as well as the English-speaking world are stepping away from the cuts and constraints of neoliberalism towards a "social investment perspective," helping counter the "new social risks" by making "social investments." However, long-standing and new forms of gender inequality are rarely considered from within the social investment perspective popular in Canada.[1] Whereas citizenship regimes in the 1960s and 1970s accommodated an equality discourse that provided some space for women and women's movements to make claims for services and supports as well as for expanded access to representation, equality claims for adults are now difficult to sustain. When governments in the mid-1990s began to consider the possibility of "investing" again after years of cutbacks and downsizing, the spending and program redesign de-emphasized class, gender, and other structures of inequality among adults. This chapter documents these changes – small and large – with particular attention to social citizenship and governance. It examines their consequences for gender relations.

The Concept of Citizenship Regime: Historical Institutionalism with Another Story

The notion of citizenship regime owes a good deal to the historical institutionalist tradition in political science and sociology.[2] Yet, it does not share some of the basic assumptions that originally founded that analytic perspective.

Historical Institutionalism and the Issue of Change

It is ironic that many historical institutionalists, despite their focus on time, have concluded that little change occurs through time, except in rare moments when equilibrium is punctuated by large historical events. Theirs is not a story of change: rather, it is one of continuity and reinforcement, often described as path dependency. As recent overviews by Paul Pierson and Theda Skocpol (2002) and Kathleen Thelen (2003) emphasize, a key argument of much historical institutionalism is that the longer institutions exist, the more their patterns of politics, including interest intermediation, are reinforced. Because interests and their defenders are increasingly entrenched, policy reform becomes harder; it is difficult to dislodge organized interests once they have widespread and even institutionalized support in civil society and the state.

However, such a conceptual approach makes it difficult to understand major changes in the patterns of interest intermediation in Canada. One such change is the sidelining and silencing in a very few short years of the major movements representing women at both the pan-Canadian and Quebec levels. Beginning in the 1960s, Canadian women's movements had been building strength, with support from the state as well as in civil society. Indeed, they were sometimes described as among the strongest in the world.[3] But by the mid- to late 1990s, the movements had lost virtually all influence in the public policy process; civil society groups, such as unions, anti-poverty movements, child care advocates, and other progressive forces, once their strongest allies, now framed their claims in ways that were almost silent about gender equality (Dobrowolsky and Jenson, 2004: 168; Dufour and Giraud, 2004).

Although the concept of citizenship regime is rooted in historical institutionalism, it rests on another notion of time than that of path dependency; it depends on the idea that a variety of processes may make significant change and it shares the premise of recent analyses (for example, in Streeck and Thelen, 2005) that change can and does happen.[4] Therefore, the goal of this chapter is to document the move away from a citizenship regime that had incorporated and institutionalized the principles of gender equality in social policies (such as pay equity) and institutions that had opened routes to women's representation towards one that downplays gender equality as a political goal and principle of social justice, and has dismantled many of the institutions of interest intermediation. Long-standing and emerging forms of gender inequalities are hidden from view by the social policies and representational arrangements of the current citizenship regime.

Citizenship Regime: The Concept

By the concept of "citizenship regime," we mean the institutional arrangements, rules, and understandings that guide and shape concurrent policy decisions and expenditures of states, problem definitions by states and citizens, and claims-making by citizens.

There are four elements of a citizenship regime, and each contributes to setting its boundaries and giving content to the institutions that sustain it:

- Citizenship involves the expression of basic values about the *responsibility mix,* defining the boundaries of state responsibilities and differentiating them from those of markets, families, and communities in the four-faceted "welfare diamond" of state/market/family/community.[5] The result is a definition of "how we wish to produce welfare," whether via purchased welfare, via the reciprocity of kin, via collective support in communities, or via collective and public solidarity – that is, via state provision and according to the principle of equality among citizens.
- Through formal recognition of particular *rights and duties* (civic, political, social, cultural, and individual and collective), a citizenship regime establishes the boundaries of inclusion and exclusion of a political community. In doing so, it identifies those entitled to full citizenship status and those who, in effect, hold second-class status only. Identities of "bearers of rights" and the "excluded" take on meaning according to these patterns.
- A citizenship regime also prescribes the democratic rules of the game for a polity. Among these rules, we include the institutional mechanisms giving *access* to the state, the modes of participation in civic life and public debates, and the legitimacy of specific types of interest intermediation. Claims-making may turn to demands for better access and inclusion, via more open routes to representation.
- A citizenship regime contributes to the definitions of political identity, in both the narrow passport-holding sense of nationality and the more complicated notion of national, subnational, or other political identities. It thereby establishes the boundaries of *belonging.*

The next section describes shifts on all of the dimensions of the citizenship regime from the beginning of the 1990s through the middle of the next decade. Each dimension has been altered. Although under neoliberalism the goal of pushing aside the claims of women and their movements (especially the latter) was quite explicit, in the last decade the now deafening silence about gender equality resulted from the fact that civil society actors as well as the state had been seduced by the ideational frames of the social investment perspective and its emphasis on the future, innovation, investment rather than consumption, fiscal prudence, and new governance.[6]

Shifting the Citizenship Regime: From Risks Faced by Adults to Investing in Children

This section tells the story of the citizenship regime that has unfolded in three steps since 1945. The initial period focused on building a regime that combined both a universal and a residualist policy logic to protect adults, one that included state support for intermediary bodies representing groups at risk of less than full inclusion. The second phase saw a neo-liberal narrowing of the state's roles and therefore of the space for citizenship in the responsibility mix of the welfare diamond, both in terms of spending and ensuring full access. The third period featured a redesign to address "new social risks" and to promote new practices of governance from within a social investment perspective.

From the 1940s through the 1980s: Protecting Adults from Life's Risks

Through the 1970s, the Canadian government designed social citizenship using notions of social risk and equality derived from social liberalism (Mahon and Phillips, 2002: 195). A key assumption about the responsibility mix in the welfare diamond was that the labour market would pay sufficiently high wages to allow almost all families to provide for their own needs. The norm was self-sufficiency, and individuals' responsibility was to contribute to the general well-being by paying taxes as well as supporting themselves and their family. In most cases, it was assumed, a single salary would suffice and family allowances were therefore set very low. Social risks followed from the breakdown of these norms, when the main earner was unemployed, retired, still in education, and so on. Expectations about gender relations were originally derived from traditional views of the family, but by the 1970s they were being shifted towards a greater stress on gender equality. Thus, families might "choose" to have two earners.

The state's share of the welfare diamond implied provision of social rights and other benefits to protect against inequalities and inequities associated with life-cycle risks faced by adults. Core programs were Unemployment Insurance and Family Allowances, followed in the 1960s by the Canada Assistance Plan (CAP), Canada and Quebec Pension Plans, universal health care, and so on. In addition, the state had a responsibility to ensure well-functioning intermediary institutions. As Bernard Ostry, a former assistant under-secretary of state, said of the goal of the Citizenship Branch in the 1970s, it was to "develop and strengthen a sense of Canadian citizenship, chiefly through programs that would aid participation and assuage feelings of social injustice" (quoted in Pal, 1993: 109).

Social programs followed three policy logics. First, an insurance model underpinned unemployment insurance and the Canada and Quebec Pension Plans. Benefits received depended on contributions made. Second, health care, old-age security, schooling, and family allowances, available to all Canadians as a right of citizenship, were based on the policy logic of universalism. They were designed to smooth over the unequal and widely experienced risks and costs of sickness, old age, or child rearing. Third, and here the CAP is the classic example, some programs were designed to provide a minimal level of support to those who had fallen out of the structures that were supposed to maintain their autonomy and income security, such as the labour market or the family (Guest, 1985: 116) or even the other social programs themselves. For example, social assistance was intended for lone parents who had "fallen out" of the protection of marriage or for the long-term unemployed who had "fallen out" of unemployment insurance, and so on.[7] These programs expressed a residualist logic, designed as benefits of last resort to protect against market and family failures to provide sufficient income.[8]

According to all three logics, however, the ideal-typical citizen represented in this regime was the adult and often the worker; other statuses were defined in relationship to this figure. Many social citizenship rights depended on being an unemployed worker, a retired worker, a school-aged "worker in training," and so on. Thus, in the 1970s when it finally became clear to policymakers – under pressure from the women's movement – that women's labour force participation was rising, a set of new social rights was invented. Equality rights and anti-discrimination protections were reinforced. Pay equity was created as a new tool to overcome systemic discrimination in the workplace, and new institutions and representational quotas of various kinds were developed to promote women's access to citizen participation.

The family sector of the welfare diamond was reinforced without, however, changing the basic principle that parents had almost exclusive responsibility for their children's well-being (Jenson, 2004b). In this post-war citizenship regime, parents were supposedly free to choose between employment or child rearing, as well as between parental or non-parental and formal or informal child care. The state was relatively neutral about mothers' decisions to participate in the labour force. In 1971 maternity leaves (later called parental leaves) were grafted onto the Unemployment Insurance system, and the tax code was modified to provide a Child Care Expense Deduction (CCED). But significant tax deductions for non-earning spouses also recognized that some couples might choose full-time parenting by one of them. Social assistance rules also allowed mothers heading lone-parent families to hew to the societal norm of full-time parenting.

Parents also had full responsibility for ensuring that their preschool children were thriving and prepared to enter school. The major risks in early childhood were related to safety. In most provinces the government issued regulations about health and safety in daycare settings, but it took very little interest in the educational quality of care. Parents who needed it were free to choose informal child care – indeed, they were encouraged to do so by the rate at which the CCED deduction was set – and thereby retain all responsibility for monitoring health and safety risks themselves. The state's primary interest, expressed through the rules governing the CCED, was in ensuring that payments were duly receipted by babysitters and other caregivers, and therefore taxable.

A universal logic was also embedded in ideas and actions about the access dimension of the citizenship regime. This resulted in significant involvement by the state in ensuring that the community sector would have sufficient resources to play its role in ensuring that groups gained representation. Here, the state was heavily involved in endowing the community sector with sufficient resources for the latter to aid various groups in their efforts to gain representation. Women's full access to political participation was considered important enough to merit state funding from the first years of the 1970s, once the 1970 report of the Royal Commission on the Status of Women recommended supporting (and indeed creating) a range of organizations that would function as advocates for women. The National Action Committee on the Status of Women (NAC) was one such group. Founded in 1972, it immediately received a substantial level of core funding from the federal government, as did a number of other women's groups (Burt, 1995: 87; Jenson and Phillips, 1996: 121).

The Neoliberal Moment: Reducing Access and Retracting Rights

Neoliberalism swept through Canadian policy circles in the 1980s and first half of the 1990s. A casualty of this process was the idea that providing support to women's groups is legitimate because they act as intermediary associations to help women achieve full economic, social, and political citizenship. Indeed, the solidification of right-wing populist discourse about forms of access and representation was one of the first signs that the citizenship regime was being altered by the forces of neoliberalism, which became entrenched in the party system with the rise of the Reform Party. Retraction of social rights, however, was less visible because it was carried out "by stealth" (Battle, 1993). Non-transparent manoeuvres included greater reliance on the tax system as a social policy mechanism and increasingly restrictive targeting of programs, rather than eliminating them or even making major reforms, both strategies that provoked public outcry when attempted.

The focus on institutions of representation and the reliance on stealth as a policy device can be traced to the reality that throughout the late 1980s Canadian politics was in turmoil, and opposition to state programs, policies, and strategic directions for social citizenship was both lively and directly linked to wrenching debates about North American free trade and constitutional reform. The key battles through these years brought NAC, the most visible representative of women's citizenship claims, into coalition with other movements and groups (Bashevkin, 1998: 88; Macdonald, 2003: 50).

The self-named Popular Sector mobilized to oppose the Free Trade Agreement (FTA) between Canada and the United States, as advanced by the Mulroney Conservative government. In the name of its definition of Canadian nationalism, the Popular Sector pledged to protect social programs and autonomy from the United States, and was therefore intervening around the belonging dimension of the citizenship regime. For example, in the free-trade debates, NAC positioned itself as a defender of Canadian national identity defined in terms of social citizenship, represented by the health care system. It acted in concert with almost all the progressive forces in the country, which had formed a wide-ranging grouping in the Action Canada Network. The FTA was achieved in 1988 only after a heated debate in many arenas, including an election campaign, in which NAC was a key player in the coalition of opposition.

A second issue directly touching on the belonging dimension of the citizenship regime arose when the Popular Sector rejected both the Meech Lake and Charlottetown constitutional accords. Between 1987 and 1990, NAC and other anglophone feminist groups rose in opposition to the Meech Lake Accord; subsequently, they renewed their efforts in connection with the Charlottetown referendum campaign in 1992. Through these two initiatives, the political class hoped to bring Quebec into the constitutional fold by meeting some of its historical demands for constitutional recognition; therefore, the very definition of "Canada" itself lay at stake. Ultimately, Meech and Charlottetown failed, and NAC was vociferously in the front line of opposition.[9]

Before these debates had unfurled, however, explicit opposition to a progressive vision of feminism had already appeared in the mid-1980s, represented by groups such as REAL Women.[10] By 1987, REAL Women was contesting the rules used by the Secretary of State's Women's Program for distributing funds to women's groups. The right-wing populist Reform Party targeted NAC as nothing but a "special interest" and an elitist one at that.[11] Having lost the support of the media and the state, NAC and other organizations entered into a period of invisibility, greeted by hostility whenever they did get any attention (Rebick and Roach, 1996). Thus, even when a Liberal government replaced the Conservatives in 1993, it failed to return to earlier positions. Its 1995 dismantling of the "women's state" provoked little opposition (Jenson and Phillips, 1996: 122).

Social rights were also being retracted, albeit in the least visible way possible. The story of the Family Allowance program, a flagship post-1945 universal program, provides an instructive example, similar to those regarding other initiatives in fields such as pensions.[12] As early as 1972, a federal government proposal sought to replace universal family allowances with a Family Income Security Plan, which would have directed higher benefits to the lowest-income families. However, opposition to the reform, dissatisfied with its lack of universality, succeeded in stopping it (Guest, 1985: 175-76). Over the next fifteen years, family allowances were allowed to wither by being only partially indexed to inflation. Then, in 1989, they were clawed back at tax time, so many families gained nothing from them. Finally, in 1993, family allowances were eliminated altogether. At the same time, Ottawa was developing two other instruments. In 1993 existing tax credits and the family allowance were rolled together to form an income-tested Child Tax Credit and a Working Income Supplement, the latter going to families with both children and earned income (Guest, 1985).

From 1972 until 1993, the direction of these changes was clear and consistent. First, child benefits were being directed towards low-income families, whether they were on social assistance or earning wages. As the family's income rose, the full benefit was gradually reduced until it disappeared completely. Second, the Child Tax Credit firmly and irrevocably linked delivery to the tax system, basing it on the income tax return (including the necessity of filing one). This characteristic both minimized visibility of the program by hiding it in the arcane world of taxes and shifted policy influence towards ministries of finance. Such reforms were part of a steady move towards targeting and the use of "negative income tax" or "guaranteed income" policy instruments for a wide range of social policies, including those for seniors (Myles and Pierson, 1997). In the two decades after 1975, targeted benefits rose from one-fifth to more than one-half of the benefits provided by governments in Canada (Banting, 1997).

Another change was also under way in the domain of social citizenship. Throughout the 1980s, the tendency grew to speak of "the child," and policy discourse tended to substitute "children" for "families." The name of the Child Tax Credit indicates this representational shift as the family-centred focus implied in "family allowance" was discarded. But this was only one of many representational shifts initiated by the state to indicate its new interest in children. The House of Commons voted unanimously in 1989 "to seek to achieve the goal of eliminating poverty among Canadian children by the year 2000" (Dobrowolsky and Jenson, 2004: 167). Prime Minister Mulroney then co-hosted the 1990 World Summit for Children at the United Nations, and Canada ratified the UN Convention on the Rights of the Child in 1991. In 1992 the federal government instituted two new community development programs, making a direct representational connection between interventions for young children and community well-being, and calling on "partners" in the community to deliver them.[13] This design was part of the new governance style popular in the emerging citizenship regime. It emphasized partnerships and shared responsibility across the state and community sectors of the welfare diamond, with the public sector financing services and the community sector delivering them (Timpson, 2001: 170; Jenson, 2004b).

Nor was the state alone in moving in this direction. The strategy of child-care advocacy groups, for example, was changing from one focused on the child care needs of employed women to "a broader approach to policies for children that emphasize[d] early child development and support for parents. This approach promotes high quality child care as one means by which to provide support for children and parents" (L. White, 2001: 98). A wide range of social policy advocates became active in campaigns directed against "child poverty," thereby contributing towards shifting the discourse about poverty from one that deployed categories such as "women and poverty" and the "feminization of poverty" to one that focused on "child poverty" (McKeen, 2001; Wiegers, 2002). Campaign 2000, for example, at first tried to retain the language of the post-war citizenship regime by arguing that universal family benefits were the best way to fight poverty.[14] It appeared before parliament and in other forums to call for a return to principles of horizontal equity and support for all families. However, this stance was difficult to maintain, while also claiming that "poverty" was the problem. The complicated message was hard to communicate (Mahon and Phillips, 2002: 202, 214n37). The coalition increasingly found itself drawn into detailed assessments of how to target benefits and to what ends.[15]

Paul Martin's infamous federal budget of 1995 marked the zenith of Canadian neoliberalism. It unilaterally abolished CAP, the shared-cost program that had shaped income security since the 1960s. In its place Ottawa launched the Canada Health and Social Transfer (CHST) as the mechanism for transferring funds to the provinces. Recounting all the financing details is not necessary here; suffice it to say that Ottawa's new measure presented the provincial governments with a trade-off: in exchange for a reduction of several billion dollars of transfers, they would exercise more independence in their spending decisions.[16]

Almost immediately, Ottawa realized that by dramatically reducing its role in social-spending transfer payments allocated to the provinces, it had almost "given away the store" where intergovernmental relations were concerned. In order to recover lost ground and again intervene in the area of income security, it availed itself of a new set of instruments and a new discourse that had become increasingly popular in civil society and the state. Both the instruments and the discursive framing became building blocks for a general redesign of social programs, one that particularly targeted women heading lone-parent families and low-income couples with children under eighteen.

"Reinvesting" in the Social after 1995

It is ironic that the social investment moment began with one of the most draconian experiences of budgetary reduction and federal unilateralism. The trade-off offered to the provinces, which did not please them, resulted in years of dispute about the model for intergovernmental relations (Boismenu and Jenson, 1998).[17] They were forced to meet their ongoing spending commitments with significantly reduced revenues. When the premiers met in the summers of 1995 and 1996 to craft their demands to Ottawa about federalism and social policy, they put social assistance reform on the agenda. The National Child Benefit (NCB) was the eventual result of the process, and it became a model for the intergovernmental relations inscribed in the Social Union Framework Agreement, which was signed by the federal government and all provinces but Quebec in 1999. The NCB was a strategy to redesign income transfers to families, including those on social assistance, and to promote labour force participation.[18] It resulted in the removal of children from social assistance by locating benefits elsewhere in the income security system. Once this was in place, social assistance could be further delegitimized and the benefits of less "worthy" groups – those not responsible for raising children – could be cut.

The official goals of the NCB (in effect since July 1998) are to reduce the depth of child poverty and to promote parents' attachment to the workforce. Income supplements, provided by the federal and provincial governments to families whose income is low or moderate, constitute the major component of the NCB. These supplements reflect Ottawa's desire to maintain a visible presence in the lives of individual Canadian families. Such attention to the belonging dimension of the citizenship regime was especially necessary after 1995; as the provinces were left to their own resources and any pan-Canadian role for the federal government was held hostage to deficit reduction, this period was characterized by the clear sense that reasons for keeping the country together were being whittled away.

The second component of the NCB is provincial "reinvestments" in services. Such new spending was intended to create a more stable situation for low-income families who faced frequent job changes or who moved on and off social assistance, by lessening the negative consequences of taking a low-wage job.[19] Provinces would provide a series of transitional benefits; for example, social assistance recipients who had recently taken a low-paid job could temporarily retain some of the health, dental, child care, and other benefits not provided by their new employers. In some instances, the provinces would even provide full health and dental insurance to all children whose parents' employment did not include such benefits.

A second major social policy development was also emerging. In 1971 the Royal Commission on the Status of Women had asserted that universally accessible child care was indispensable to achieving women's equality of opportunity. The Royal Commission on Equality of Employment (the Abella Commission) followed suit in 1984, as did the 1986 Task Force on Child Care headed by Katie Cook (Mahon, 2004: 4). By the 1990s, however, this argument was no longer heard. Instead, calls for a pan-Canadian ("national") child care program were framed almost exclusively in terms of the needs of the child, and activists against child poverty joined a wide spectrum of groups to argue that good child outcomes depended on high-quality child care.[20] Thus, the child care agreements finally signed between Ottawa and several provinces in 2005 reflect a major shift in ideas regarding why spending in this area is important. The following statement from the Agreement-in-Principle between Canada and Nova Scotia (Canada-Nova Scotia, 2005: 1) (signed on 16 May 2005) is typical of all these agreements: "The early years of life are critically important for the development and future well-being of children. Research demonstrates that high quality early learning and child care (ELCC) can play an important role in promoting social, emotional and cognitive development of young children. Promotion of learning and development in early childhood supports the participation of parents in employment and education, and supports parents in their primary responsibility for the care and nurturing of their children by improving early learning and child care for families with young children." These agreements are anchored in the four principles of QUAD (meaning high quality, universally inclusive, accessible, and developmental) (3-4). The principles were developed after long exchanges between child care advocates and state bureaucrats.

Here we see a summary of what had come to be a shared understanding as to why a pan-Canadian child care system was necessary. It would meet the needs of children, was based on research findings, and would enable parents to work or attend school. This shared discourse took a number of years to develop (Mahon and Phillips, 2002). It was firmly in place, promoted by the federal government and agreed to by a majority of the provinces, until the 2006 election brought the Conservative Party to power. The new government immediately introduced its Universal Child Care Benefit, which actually marks a return to taxable family allowances. However, such was the power of the child care discourse that the Conservatives were obliged to present their new measure as providing "choice in child care," even though their true intent was to supplement the income of single-earner two-parent families (Battle, 2006).

What are the consequences of this major overhaul of social citizenship, one that alters the very principles regarding who "deserves" state support and why they deserve it? These reforms all present a new equilibrium within the welfare diamond. The market sector determines the distribution of welfare to virtually all adults via the wage-relation. There is now a clear assumption that every adult is employable. Adults no longer have a "choice" about whether to participate in the labour force, unless the family is wealthy enough to live on one income. Other than a tax deduction for a non-earning spouse and the $1,200 Universal Child Care Allowance, there is little financial support for full-time parenting. For their part, low-income parents have incentives in the form of income supplements to take a job, schooling, or training.

This reliance on market outcomes to determine the distribution of welfare has brought increased income gaps. Whereas through the 1980s market inequalities in income were significantly narrowed by the redistributive effects of taxes and transfers, this effect was significantly moderated by the later 1990s. As Ken Battle (2001: 190) points out, "In 1989, families in the top quintile had 4.9 times the share of after-tax income of those in the bottom quintile, but by 1998 that ratio had increased to 5.5 times." Now, when the market "fails" and earned income still leaves workers poor, governments step in to provide income supplements and other benefits "to make work pay." These latter include several projects explicitly targeted at women who head lone-parent families. Thus, the goal is poverty reduction rather than equality or equity in employment.

Alongside this acceptance of market-directed outcomes for adults, a reconfiguration of the division of responsibility between state and family appears in several policy areas. Increasingly, governments are claiming that they *share* responsibility for children's well-being with parents. In the post-1945 citizenship regime, family responsibility for decisions about children and for intergenerational outcomes was, as we noted above, virtually unchallenged. Currently, several Canadian governments (albeit not the remaining neoliberal ones) vaunt their willingness to share some of the burden and more actively shape the lives and life chances of children (Jenson, 2004b). In the neoliberal period, talk about "the child" was rarely accompanied by new spending. Throughout the 1980s and until 1999, spending levels remained "more or less flat" as the same level of spending was redistributed differently. Since 1999, however, new money has been put into the pot, and child benefits have recently been a major area of increased spending (Battle, 2001: 187).[21] Spending on child care has also been increased.

Why the Silence on Gender Inequality?

How can we understand the fact that the citizenship regime emerging after the neoliberal moment is silent about gender equality and women? When neoliberalism held sway, the discourse was both highly critical of public spending and unambiguously skeptical of state involvement in the institutions designed to ensure women's access to full citizenship. Therefore, it is not surprising that the years of neoliberal predominance saw assaults on the legitimacy of intermediary institutions such as NAC and other equality seekers. But why did the silence about gender inequalities persist after 1995, even after several Canadian governments became willing to spend again, and even when a well-developed discourse of "the social" was concretized in programs such as the NCB and the Early Childhood Development Initiatives, both of which involved new social spending? Indeed, this silence was particularly jarring before 2006, when Canada finally seemed to be installing the pan-Canadian child care system that, as early as 1965, feminists had identified as an essential pillar of women's equality.[22]

Several explanations have arisen, of course. Some people argue that neoliberalism simply continues as an example of a major shift, one that makes use of long-standing elements such as patriarchy to move away from the citizenship and other practices of the post-1945 years (for example, Mishra, 1999; Brodie, 2002, and this volume). It is of course impossible to *disprove* that the current period is not simply neoliberal. If the patterns of new spending are taken as evidence of such a structural change and attributed to the structural necessities of neoliberal global capitalism, then we are, by definition, still in neoliberal times. Such large-scale and sweeping structuralist narratives cannot account, however, for the coincidence of social-spending patterns that differ from those of the neoliberal moment *and* the lack of any attention to gender inequalities. All the factors that made structuralist accounts less than fully pleasing in the past plague these ones as well. Particularly problematic is the absence of attention to differences across time as well as space (Jenson, 1986).

Others have attributed the absence of attention to gender inequalities to ideas, the rise of a child poverty discourse, and the silencing of institutions representing women (for example, McKeen, 2001; Wiegers, 2002). Although these narratives are descriptively accurate, they are too limited. We still need to account for the power of the child poverty frame itself and the restructuring of social policies around it.

Our claim in this chapter is that the discourse of "child poverty" does not exist alone, but is deeply rooted in a major reinterpretation of social risks and understandings of the sources of welfare. Social policy has always been about managing social risk. Social citizenship, therefore, involves adopting positions regarding which sector of the welfare diamond is responsible for ensuring welfare, including which social risks will be pooled by collective choice mechanisms (that is, by the state) and which will be left to the market, family, or community sectors. In recent years, understandings of social risks have changed substantially. Child poverty, indeed, poverty in general, is only one social risk in this reinterpretation, albeit an important one. In a similar way, the emphasis on activation and work for everyone is only one prescription in this reinterpretation, one that includes a full menu of spending on preschool education and wage supplements.

The social dimensions of many citizenship regimes are now being redesigned, not only in Canada but in Europe and elsewhere, in reaction to an increasingly popular understanding of "new social risks" (Pearson and Scherer, 1997: 6; Bonoli, 2005; Jenson, 2004a; Taylor-Gooby, 2004). The new social risks can be summarized as the income and service gaps generated by the transition to postindustrial labour markets and societies, in which there is a decline of well-paid and traditionally male industrial jobs, an increase in low-paid and often precarious service jobs, and a rise of the female employment rate overall. The challenges generated by women's labour force participation (and their concomitant lack of availability for full-time caring) as well as by changes in family forms (especially the rise of lone-parent families) also create new income and service gaps. Therefore, women's employment as a social necessity (no longer a "choice") is at the heart of the analysis, as is attention to the situation of lone-parent families.

Policy may attempt to increase the employment rate so as to ensure the future of expensive social programs that protect against "old" social risks. Other common policy responses include mechanisms, like income supplements "to make work pay," that address the income insecurity associated with low-paid employment. These instruments generally target the working poor with young children in order to reduce the long-term risks associated with poverty during childhood, as revealed by longitudinal research analyses.[23] The instruments for supplementing low earnings and ensuring higher labour force participation rates – especially by women – have been accompanied by new spending and attention to skills acquisition, as well as other forms of investment in human capital for the groups considered most vulnerable. These include women who head lone-parent families, young workers, and the long-term unemployed. Such developments constitute more than mere talk. Attention to new social risks has resulted in significant new public spending on services, especially for child care and elder care, as well as on wage supplements.[24]

Moreover, the attention to new social risks is wrapped in a paradigm shift, one that replaces notions of "social protection" with the ideas and practices of the "social investment" perspective. Currently, a number of countries in Europe and the English-speaking world are addressing the new social risks by designing responses framed as social investments. The core beliefs of the social investment perspective, promoted by international actors such as the Organisation for Economic Cooperation and Development (OECD), Third Way politicians such as Tony Blair, and influential policy experts (for example, Gøsta Esping-Andersen et al., 2002), can be summarized as follows:

- Good social policy must be oriented towards the future.
- Social spending is productive, and because social inequities may undermine economic innovation, good economic outcomes depend on good social policy.

- Good social policy depends less on how much is spent than on where investments are made.
- Fiscal prudence is a value in itself.
- Investments in both social inclusion and human capital are necessary, in order to ensure that flexibility and innovation are maximized.
- Governance matters are expressed in public-private partnerships and revamped public administrations (this summary is from Dobrowolsky and Jenson, 2005).[25]

The elaboration of the ideas of social investment has had an unanticipated outcome: "the child" and children now provide a much more important frame for social and economic policy analysis than they did in post-war citizenship regimes (Jenson, 2001). Improving the life chances of children is sometimes the key metaphor that justifies and legitimates new spending on services and benefits. Such ideas cast government spending in a very different light than in the post-1945 years. Framing that presents income transfers and credits as devices to "end child poverty," to "give every child the best start in life," and to "make work pay" differs markedly from a discourse of "welfare" and equality in the here and now. In this new discourse, unemployment benefits and social assistance levels can legitimately be reduced, while increased spending on preschool education, developmental health, child benefits, and income supplements paid to families raising children can be justified. In analytic terms, "the child" matters to the social investment perspective because human capital formation is at its core (Myles and Quadagno, 2000: 161).

The child poverty focus that has preoccupied analysts who wish to explain the lack of concern for gender inequalities is, then, but one trope in a broader analysis of new social risks and the social investment perspective. At the same time, given such a paradigm shift, it may appear strange that attention to the new social risks focuses on women's circumstances, especially as heads of lone-parent families and employees of choice for low-paid work, but policies do not always advance an equality agenda for adults.

The explanation for this conundrum lies in the risk analysis that underpins the social investment perspective. First, according to this perspective, lack of labour force participation is a danger in itself. Policy-makers cite research findings to demonstrate that, in and of themselves, low incomes, whether from social assistance or poorly paid work, are a risk factor jeopardizing good child outcomes (Dobrowolsky and Jenson, 2005). However, as long as families in liberal welfare regimes remain on social assistance, they will be poor. This is because the assistance rates are deliberately kept low so as to minimize the "moral hazard" – the temptation for recipients to stay on assistance rather than take a low-paying job. Therefore, the only way to reduce their poverty is to move the parents into the labour force, and then, as needed, supplement their low wages. Even in continental and social democratic regimes, where social benefits are more generous, policy experts point to the significant risk of the intergenerational transmission of poverty and note that lone-parent families (most of which are headed by women) are much more likely than couple families to be poor, in part because of lack of access to child care services but also because many jobs in the postindustrial labour market involve low-paying service-sector work (Esping-Andersen, 2002: 36; Taylor-Gooby, 2004: 3). Second, when policy discourse situates the achievement of equality in the future rather than the present, it is already too late for today's adults (Jenson and Saint-Martin, 2003: 83-84). The most that can be done is to ensure that their circumstances do not undermine their children's future.

The policy challenges are clear. The problem is how to proceed when the market sector fails to do its job. The working poor exist. Therefore, the policy prescription is for the state to supplement market outcomes (earnings) and to move more people over the poverty line. But as noted above, a low income is a risk in and of itself. Therefore, the social investment perspective *also* prescribes early learning and child care services. The developmental benefits of stimulation and education in quality child care are meant, in part, to counter the inadequacies associated with life in a low-income family or in a family stressed by a labour market demanding long hours of work.[26] For those committed to the social investment perspective, our future cannot be left to individual parenting practices. Whereas the post-1945 social citizenship regime valued lone parents' full-time child care more than their earnings, the current citizenship regime is skeptical of their capacity to give their children the "start they need," and prescribes parenting courses.

This shift of the policy lens also affects the way that other forms of care, in particular for the dependent elderly, are addressed from within the citizenship regime. Here, too, concern with gender inequality has been dropped in favour of providing some care for those who are no longer a "good investment." Families and communities have been called on to fill the gaps in the homecare and health services that are needed by the growing numbers of elderly Canadians. Although men and women are almost equally involved in caring for seniors with health problems, the consequences for women are significantly larger in terms of effects on their own health and future income prospects (Jenson, 2004a: 14-16). Threats to women's pensions and other income are rarely taken into account when policy encourages – if not compels – prime working-age women to leave their jobs in order to care for their elderly relatives. Why? Again, this is because in the social investment perspective investing in adults is less of a priority than investing in young people.

Conclusion

With this analysis we have documented that the Canadian citizenship regime is changing, and that, in this social investment moment, even the move towards greater spending and more focus on the state's responsibility for social justice has not returned attention to gender inequalities. This silence has several immediate consequences. A citizenship regime in which rights are recognized primarily as situations of "good investments" is one that fails to address the needs of huge numbers of citizens, both men and women, but especially women. They are still targeted for low-paid and precarious jobs, and they still provide most of the informal care within families. A citizenship regime that ignores the continuing blockages to full access to participation, whether they arise because of women's lack of time or because structured gender inequalities are not recognized, is one that does not provide full citizenship. Indeed, a child-centred definition of equality is one that obfuscates the need for collective action by citizens who are mobilized to make claims and thereby to use the state against all forms of unequal power, particularly the power of market forces (Jenson, 2001).

Although inequalities may be less visible, they are not inevitable. Because a citizenship regime is a political construction, it can be constructed differently. The narrative of "new social risks" and the social investment perspective provide space for claims-making. Indeed, in many ways, the invisibility of gender inequalities in the current moment is similar to that of the post-1945 years. Taking them out of the shadows will require, as it did then, a significant mobilization by everyone concerned with reaffirming an equality agenda. Now, more than ever, there is still a need for access to quality jobs and a just distribution. The impediments to their achievement must be identified. The limits of the child-centred social investment perspective must be revealed. To get there, women and their allies must reclaim access to full citizenship participation as well as social rights.

10

Care*fair:* Gendering Citizenship "Neoliberal" Style

Paul Kershaw

Literature about gendering citizenship challenges the tendency for scholarship to focus on the circumstances of the male breadwinner or soldier by changing the subject in order to examine explicitly the contributions and needs of the battered wife or working mother (see, for example, Brush, 2002). This change in subject resists the androcentrism of mainstream literature by demanding that the citizenship expectations, practices, and constraints experienced by diverse groups of women become integrated into social policy and the redefinition of political norms. One implication of this change in subject is the observation that gendering citizenship requires reformation of male citizenship practices in light of women's experiences (Kershaw, Pulkingham, and Fuller, forthcoming). Social institutions must be reorganized to induce more men to forgo and condemn male violence, and also to model their behaviour on that of most women today, who shoulder daily primary care work of young children, the sick, and the elderly in addition to other citizenry obligations and ambitions. Nancy Fraser (1994) championed the latter social reform with her influential discussion of the universal caregiver model. In this chapter I explore further the policy logics available to the state and others to oblige men to take on a fair share of primary care, especially in affluent anglophone democracies.

Primary care refers to time allocated specifically to activities that address the personal needs of dependants: these include dressing, feeding, washing, and medical care; providing intellectual or social stimulation; and, in the case of children, supervision, instruction, or discipline. In Canada, as in many other countries, women typically retain most responsibility for primary caregiving, including care for young children, on which I focus below. Ninety-four percent of stay-at-home parents are women (Statistics Canada, 2000: 110). Women between the ages of twenty-five and forty-four who work part-time are fifteen times more likely than men of the same age to report that child care responsibilities preclude them from pursuing full-time positions (125). Women who are employed full-time consistently provide more unpaid caregiving than do their male equivalents (Silver, 2000).

Some social democratic countries already take seriously the need to reform patriarchal citizenship patterns by encouraging men to care more. In an effort to redistribute the care of young children between men and women, Norway and Sweden have experimented with parental leave policy by reserving one month of benefits exclusively for fathers. By most accounts, the policy has had only modest success, since a significant share of fathers continue to take no or very little parental leave (Hojgaard, 1997; Olson, 2002: 390). The slow pace of male reform prompted Sweden to increase the economic incentive for men to assume early child-rearing responsibilities: it added a second month of parental leave benefits to its national system, for which fathers alone are eligible.

The modest response demonstrated by Scandinavian fathers to the daddy month(s) underscores that changing men's behaviour is no small task. The challenge lies in large part with what Kevin Olson (2002: 393) terms "a circular relation between choice and cultural background norms." The actions, attitudes, and decisions of citizens in any democratic welfare state "will be inextricably entangled with its cultural, economic, and social milieu." Before men will choose en masse to care more, norms about masculinity, fatherhood, mothering, and employment must evolve to endorse male caregiving as a valuable practice on par with other citizenry pursuits that enjoy more social status for men. But before such norms will become solidly woven into the cultural fabric, men must start to care more, irrespective of the patriarchal values and patterns that pervade their cultural context. The circular relation thus underscores a classic chicken-and-egg scenario. Which change must come first?

The most target-efficient way to resolve this circularity is to employ public policy to influence men's choices directly so that they will resist patriarchal routines in favour of more gender-progressive decisions. I will defend this strategy below, in part by proposing for Canada a more aggressive version of the daddy leave policy that has become the norm in Scandinavia.

The focus on Canada is useful because the country has a well-entrenched system of maternity and parental leave, in contrast to the United States. But like the United States, Canada falls within the liberal welfare regime cluster that is more culturally predisposed to exude greater caution about interventionist government policy than are social democratic countries. This cultural characteristic is evident in the gender-neutrality that rhetorically defines Canadian parental leave legislation: the state is ostensibly neutral about which parent takes the benefits and for how long. However, I will show that, in practice, the leave policy intersects with the patriarchal division of labour and the gender earnings gap to reinforce a very gendered distribution of care responsibilities.

An aggressive daddy leave proposal is bound to invoke considerable resistance from some. A recommendation to utilize the state's coercive power for the purpose of altering citizenry decisions sits in considerable tension with the value placed on freedom of choice in a democratic political system. Representing this resistance, Olson (2002: 387) is sensitive to the fundamental place that choice enjoys in welfare theory. He states that, "In a general sense, democrats see the state as a choice-promoting institution, one that opens up a wide variety of life options for its citizens rather than dictating particular forms of life to them. Any [broadly democratic] state would have to countenance a certain amount of choice in the benefits people receive. For instance, universal caregiver would presumably permit people to choose their own mix of caregiving labour, other forms of labour and leisure."

Accordingly, Olson rejects any proposal to "radicalize the daddy month." He concedes that this reform may promote sharing of infant care more equally between women and men "by subsidizing [this activity] to the fullest extent only when it is evenly divided" (394). But it would also "introduce[e] a substantial amount of paternalism into welfare, stipulating social relations in a way that welfare theorists find quite problematic in other contexts."

The anti-paternalism that Olson professes, however, mischaracterizes contemporary debates about welfare policy. Paternalistic use of state power to privilege some social choices over others has become a (perhaps even the) dominant view among welfare theorists in respect of the primary subject of debate – that is, unemployment and income assistance. Mainstream welfare scholarship is replete with favourable discussions of welfare contractualism and "workfare," which impose a work test or job search obligation as a condition for receipt of social benefits (Giddens, 1999; Mead, 1997; Stuart White, 2000). This scholarly development tracks a burgeoning policy and electoral trend in liberal welfare regimes in which politicians and citizens increasingly focus on work obligations to counterbalance the alleged excessive emphasis on social rights that emerged in the first decades after the Second World War.

It is precisely this level of cultural support for enforcing social obligations through paternalist policy that I argue should become the model for a universal caregiver policy blueprint. Just as many governments employ workfare or other active labour-market policies to encourage or compel citizens to discharge their paid work obligations, so we also need what I have referred to elsewhere as a "care*fair*" policy commitment (Kershaw, 2005), one that will encourage or compel citizens who neglect informal care activities to discharge citizenship duties in the domestic domain.

Strategically, a principal virtue of this argument is that it draws on policy logic that is pervasive in the liberal regime cluster. Whereas an aggressive daddy leave system would borrow from the Scandinavian model, the proposal I recommend does not entail implanting policy that works in one cultural context into another milieu where its logic does not resonate. To the contrary, a radical parental leave policy that more insistently urges fathers to discharge some of their care responsibilities turns for its justification in Canada and other liberal states to two arguments that currently defend workfare successfully in these countries: what I term below the moral hazard argument and the new paternalist "competence" argument.

The chapter develops by summarizing these arguments as they are typically articulated in defence of active labour policies. Their logic is then applied directly to patriarchy and the persistent sexual division of care. The care*fair* concept is first carved out by applying the moral hazard argument to the question of parental leave in Canada and investigating the policy reform it would require. The chapter continues by identifying a second justification for the proposed leave reforms that adapts a version of the new paternalist competence argument.

Duty Discourses and Active Labour Policy
In recent decades, duty discourses have emerged across disparate political camps within the liberal regime cluster, including among care ethic feminists (Gilligan, 1982), communitarians (Etzioni, 1996), and social conservatives (Popenoe, 1996). However, debate focused specifically on paid work responsibilities has been concentrated among neoliberals and proponents of the Third Way. The moral hazard logic is evident in both circles. The competence argument is specific to neoliberals.

The Moral Hazard Argument for Employment Duties
The moral hazard concept is common in economics discourse with respect to insurance systems. It reminds us that policy may provide individuals and firms that are insured against loss with incentives to behave in socially non-optimal ways by taking less care to prevent that loss than they would were they not insured. In welfare debates, morally hazardous dynamics are linked to incentives institutionalized by income assistance that allegedly invite "transfer dependency." Commenting on the United States, Lawrence M. Mead (1986: 3) suggests that "government programs have given [the message] that hard work in available jobs is no longer required of Americans." If employment conditions are disagreeable or remuneration too low, passive employment insurance and welfare programs institutionalize morally hazardous dynamics by relieving citizens of the responsibility to work for pay. The generosity of income assistance, coupled with the failure to obligate benefit recipients, does the disadvantaged a disservice, Mead maintains, by "undercutting" incentives to acquire "the competencies [they] need to achieve status" and social belonging (12). The result, he concludes, is a population of social assistance recipients who are permitted to remain dependent on

the largesse of the public sphere rather than striving for self-sufficiency and the accompanying self-respect.

As a result, active labour policy has become a key plank in postindustrial welfare platforms for both neoliberals such as Mead and Third Way proponents such as Anthony Giddens. Giddens (1999: 114-15) argues that even critics of neoliberalism must countenance the possibility that "benefits meant to counter unemployment ... can actually produce unemployment if they are actively used as a shelter from the labour market." Unemployment benefits should therefore "carry the obligation to look actively for work, and it is up to governments to ensure that welfare systems do not discourage active search" (117).

Many versions of the moral hazard argument are careful to divert blame from transfer dependency away from welfare recipients and towards policymakers. The driving assumption is that passive income assistance and unemployment insurance institutionalize counterproductive economic incentives to which reasonable people respond. "It isn't so much that some forms of welfare provision create dependency cultures," Giddens states, as it is "that people take rational advantage of opportunities offered" (114-15). The welfare trap, in this view, ultimately reflects a "system dysfunction," to borrow a phrase from Thomas J. Courchene (1994: 29-30), and is "not in any way related to the character of individuals that may get caught in these transfer-dependency syndromes." Rather, for Courchene, the essence of the welfare trap is that the post-war welfare regime institutionalized incentives that have for decades interrupted the adjustment processes of the national economy, including interregional migration among the un(der)employed. This interference "was bound to serve to entrench and, in many cases, exacerbate the pre-existing degree of disparity [between citizens]," since, "by and large, [benefit claimants] have acted *entirely rationally* in the face of a wholly inappropriate set of incentives" (29, 30, emphasis in original).

The New Paternalist Competence Argument for Employment Duties

Like Courchene and Giddens, Mead acknowledges the system dysfunction inherent in passive benefit policies. However, he does not agree that blame for transfer dependency should be diverted away from the poor. Rather, anticipating critics, Mead (1986: 10) embraces the charge that welfare contractualism is "nothing more than an elaborate way of 'blaming the victim'" but denies that this reproach is punitive. The charge is misguided, he argues, since accepting personal responsibility is a necessary condition for social inclusion. As he puts it, "True acceptance in ... society requires" that citizens fulfill social requirements, "such as work" (4). So long as welfare policy is structured around passive benefits, recipients will be "defined by their need and weakness, not their competence" (9). Policy must therefore "require work as well as offer support ... if the recipients [are] to be integrated and not just subsidized" (14). From his perspective, then, workfare is not so much a measure by which the state blames those who deviate from societal expectations as it is a means to "persuade them to *blame themselves*" (10, emphasis in original).

Accordingly, Mead supplements the theme of moral hazard with more politically controversial questions about the actual competence of long-term welfare recipients. Competence, in this context, connotes an individual's ability to behave in a manner that promotes her or his self-interest. In Mead's view, this competence cannot be assumed to exist among the poor; we cannot take for granted that it is simply social barriers or dysfunctional policy incentives that impede individuals from acting in their own self-interest. The assumption of competence is suspect, Mead (1997: 24) argues, because in the absence of legislated work obligations, "the effect of welfare incentives and disincentives on how many recipients work is remarkably small. This is hardly surprising, since not working and bearing children out of wedlock, the behaviours that do the most to precipitate the poverty of the working-aged, are themselves contrary to self-interest as most people understand it. They cause poverty or make it worse. If self-interest were a sufficient motivation, living in poverty and being on welfare should themselves motivate people to avoid or leave those conditions."

Implicit in this analysis is Mead's opposition to the assumption typical of economists such as Courchene that all individuals, including the poor, "are rational maximizers who act to advance their own self-interest if not society's" (28). No social science, he suggests, "that assumes an invariant, optimizing mentality can deal well with the self-defeating aspects of the poverty lifestyle. Understanding dysfunction requires positing a more complex psychology, where people fail to do what they themselves desire and thus fail to exhaust the potential of their environment." In response, the purpose of enforcing employment obligations is to close the gap between intention and action that some long-term poor suffer in regards to paid work.

Duty Discourses and the Distribution of Care

These two arguments for workfare offer feminists who aim to gender liberal welfare states with culturally successful schematics to follow when making the case that some level of care (*not* reproductive) activities should be institutionalized as *duties* of citizenship. It is a failure to treat care as one such duty that underpins Olson's (2002) charge that aggressive daddy leave policies are too paternalistic. Rather than recognize some care activity as a social responsibility that binds all citizens, he posits that feminist visions of citizenship must ultimately leave care commitments as a matter of choice. As Olson puts it, a universal caregiver citizenship model would "permit people to decide the extent to which their informal, unwaged labour involves caring for friends and relatives, to what extent it involves voluntary community activities, and to what extent it pursues *completely different ends*, such as education or job training" (387, emphasis added).

But as Annette Baier (1987: 49) and other feminists have long observed, an adequate theory of citizenship cannot posit caring as one life plan among many, as opposed to a moral requirement that constrains all life course patterns. Whether one has a taste for caregiving is often beside the point in familial relationships in which care obligations arise. Although reproduction should always be a matter of choice, the obligations to nurture a vulnerable child emerge upon birth and persist for what has become a socially sanctioned period of roughly eighteen years in North America. During this time, society does not tolerate neglect of a dependent child, even if the relationship is one that a parent or guardian wishes to terminate as it evolves. Conversely, although children do not choose their families, receipt of adequate nurturing during their period of dependence sets in motion social dynamics of reciprocation: as their parents age and become potentially vulnerable, the children may legitimately be obliged to care for them in return.

The cultural permission Olson would grant for some, but not all, to cultivate a nurturing disposition has also historically disadvantaged women who perform unpaid care work in their own familial contexts, as well as the domestic workers and child care employees who supplement familial care. There is no reason to expect this enculturation to produce different results in the future. Although some public policies recognize that familial caregiving is vital work from which the public benefits, the value of this caregiving does not lend itself well to computation through market exchange. Specialization in care thus marginalizes individuals from the primary nexus of wealth creation in society. Even if we imagine a society in which familial care specialists are well compensated monetarily for their socially valuable labour, along the lines of Fraser's (1994) caregiver parity model, the specialists will nonetheless be marginalized from other important areas of social life that offer opportunities for personal fulfillment, social inclusion, and the cultivation of power. Hence, adequate theories of citizenship cannot regard socially vital care labour "as an optional charity left for those with a taste for it," to invoke a phrase from Baier (1987: 53). If society aims to sustain itself, it must formally countenance, accommodate, and enforce the participation of all its citizens in the care work necessary to provide for its own continuers, "not just take out a loan on a carefully encouraged maternal instinct" (53).[1]

If provision of socially valuable care for children, the infirm, or the aged is not an optional charity, the latitude permitted by Olson – in which citizens can choose between care and other activities – may sanction a free ride for some: while others perform the care work, they may garner more opportunities for economic security and status through market participation. The only way to defend against this risk is to embrace a vision of citizenship in which some care activities are seen as a civic duty that binds men as much as women and that are enforced on par with emergent employment obligations, as well as taxation. This intention is captured by the concept of care*fair*.

The objective of care*fair* is that which informs Fraser's (1994) universal caregiver model: to provoke far more men to reorganize their behaviour so that they more closely resemble the many women today who perform primary care in addition to fulfilling employment and other citizenry ambitions and responsibilities. The concept serves as a cultural analogue to workfare. Through workfare, governments employ the power of public policy to compel citizens to fulfill their employment duties as a condition of receipt of social assistance. The care*fair* idea implores governments to demonstrate a comparable concern to use policy to address the gendered division of care. The aim is to redesign policy to change the system of societal incentives in which men decide how much time to allocate between employment and caregiving. Under care*fair*, the incentive structure would be reorganized to urge men to assume a more equitable share of the informal care work that is just as essential, if not more important, to social (re)production as market participation.

As an analogue to workfare, care*fair* does not lend intellectual support to any specific active labour-market policy that exists cross-nationally. Nor does it deny the punitive character of workfare in some North American jurisdictions (see, for example, Klein and Long, 2003). Instead, the concept affirms that social rights imply an unconditional entitlement of reasonable access to some social good, while granting that reasonable access may include the performance of select social duties. (For a development of this theme, see Stuart White, 2000.) This understanding of entitlement allows us to retain the enormous value of social rights to which the Marshallian tradition points (T.H. Marshall, 1964), while compensating for any risks to civic-mindedness that this tradition permits because it focuses principally on the issue of individual entitlements.

The Moral Hazard Argument for Care*fair*

Care*fair* maintains that the habits of free riding on female care permitted to half the population constitute a much more significant case of moral hazard than those of the relatively small percentage of citizens for whom social assistance or unemployment benefits may erode the motivation to engage in paid work. The legacy of patriarchy includes cultural, political, and economic incentives that encourage men to behave in socially non-optimal ways by performing less caregiving than they could in the absence of the gendered division of care. As Peter Taylor-Gooby (1991: 202-3) observes, many state welfare systems "act as a transmission mechanism" for these inequalities. Whenever social policy does not explicitly challenge the gendered division of labour, it risks becoming implicated in and contributing to the pattern of incentives that induces many men to evade care work. In such instances, the welfare state emerges as "an apparatus of moral hazard" in respect of numerous informal systems of domestic care provision. Maternity and parental leave benefits in Canada illustrate the point.

Research confirms that the birth of a child sets in motion a series of normative expectations and economic incentives that propel many heterosexual couples to approximate patriarchal patterns. Upon the onset of parenthood, couples become more traditional in their care, housework, and employment decisions, with the most significant changes occurring in women's routines. In particular, the total amount of work that new mothers perform increases disproportionately compared to that of new fathers, although relatively little of this extra work is in paid employment (Sanchez and Thomson, 1997).

Parenthood often crystallizes the gendered division of labour because the person who limits attachment to the paid workforce, typically the mother, becomes especially skilled in rearing the child due to her regular caring experiences. In contrast, reduced female earnings often motivate a male spouse to increase his employment hours to compensate for the loss of household income, which limits his time to acquire expertise in caring for young children. The result, Deborah Lupton and Lesley Barclay (1997: 148) report, is that "it is all too easy for men to lag behind their female partner in developing the skills of caring for their children, even when the men may strongly wish to do so, and it can be difficult for them to make up for the lost ground."

Maternity and parental leave policies in Canada exacerbate this dynamic, despite recent improvements to the system. In 2001 the federal government extended the leave benefit period available through Employment Insurance (EI) from roughly six months to fifty weeks. Fifteen weeks of this are maternity leave for which only biological mothers are eligible. The remaining thirty-five weeks are parental leave, and may be taken by the mother or father (biological or adoptive), or divided between the two. The benefit value is income contingent, calculated at a rate of 55 percent of earnings up to $39,000. Access to employer-sponsored supplementary compensation is rare in Canada. Just one in five mothers on leave in 2001 reported benefits other than what is provided through EI (Katherine Marshall, 2003: 6).

The value of Canadian leave benefits deters male participation in the program. The system generates incentives for the lower earner within a couple to take leave since couples maximize household income when the higher earner avoids the minimum 45 percent reduction in pay. The persistent gender earnings gap makes it much more likely that the lower earner in heterosexual couples will be the mother, as employed women earn on average 64 percent of average male earnings (Statistics Canada, 2000: 141). This policy incentive, combined with the gender earnings differential, helps explain why just 11 percent of benefit recipients are fathers, and why men stay on parental leave for a much shorter period than do women. The median claim for men in 2001-02 was just fifteen weeks, compared to thirty weeks for women (Canada Employment Insurance Commission, 2003: 18).

To remedy this morally hazardous EI dynamic, it is necessary to reorder the economic incentives generated by leave benefits. Numerous changes are required, including the following three reforms, which are illustrative but not exhaustive:

- For those earning annual incomes of up to $60,000, benefits should be calculated as 80 percent of previous income, as is the case in Sweden, much like the measures institutionalized by the Quebec government in January 2006.
- A substantial portion of the benefits should be reserved exclusively for fathers, with appropriate exceptions for single, divorced, and lesbian parents.
- Take-up of leave should be linked with the Canada and Quebec Pension Plans (CPP/QPP), so that every month on leave reduces the total amount of employment time one must bank before becoming eligible to receive a full CPP/QPP.

The first recommendation responds to research showing that the point at which a father involves himself in primary child care has long-term consequences for his participation in child rearing. Scott Coltrane (1996: 82-83) reports that heterosexual couples who generally share most responsibility for care tend to involve the father in routine child rearing from early infancy. This finding provides reason to revamp maternity/parental leave entitlements in Canada to counter the structural barrier posed to male use of leave opportunities by limited benefit rates in combination with the gender earnings gap. The more policy reduces the financial loss incurred by families when the higher earner withdraws from the labour force, the more the structural barrier will be minimized. A leave system that remunerates 80 rather than 55 percent of previous earnings up to a maximum annual salary of $60,000, rather than $39,000, would represent significant progress on this front, while still remaining attentive to the demands of political feasibility. This care*fair* proposal, for instance, is only modestly more generous than the parental leave legislation implemented by the Province of Quebec starting in 2006.

Mitigating the legacy of patriarchy will require more than increased benefit rates, however. The countries that stand out in terms of male parental leave usage are Norway and Sweden. Norway is especially exceptional, since roughly 70 percent of fathers take some leave (Katherine Marshall, 2003:

10). Both countries reserve leave time exclusively for new fathers. In 1993 Norway led the way on this front by reserving four weeks of benefits. If a father does not make use of this time, it cannot be transferred to the mother and is deducted from the overall benefit (EIRR, 2001a: 18). The Swedish government followed suit in 1995, also reserving thirty days of leave for fathers (EIRR, 2001b: 14-15).

The results of the Swedish experience suggest the importance of being aggressive with daddy leave. The 1995 introduction of one daddy month saw the share of male leave recipients in Sweden rise 2.6 percentage points (from 28.5 to 31.1 percent) by 1996, an increase that surpassed that of the previous four years combined. The accelerated pace of male participation continued throughout the rest of the decade so that, as of 2000, 37.7 percent of benefit recipients were fathers. However, Swedish men still use only 12.4 percent of the days for which a parental allowance is paid by the state, up from 9.2 percent in 1995.[2] In response to the increased (albeit still small) share of days that fathers take, the Swedish government extended the period of leave reserved exclusively for them to two months. No data are yet available documenting the impact of this policy change.

Building on the Swedish experience, a commitment to care*fair* would see the Canadian federal government reserve at least two, and ideally four, months of the leave period for fathers. If the value of leave benefits is enriched to 80 percent of previous earnings, the four-month requirement would constitute a significant incentive for men to involve themselves early in primary child care. Any policy reform should also promote shared caregiving among lesbian couples, while exempting lone parents from the care*fair* requirement so that the state does not impose a spousal structure on parents who severed their legal attachment or did not establish it in the first place.

Although reservation of benefits exclusively for fathers will be important, the limited share of leave taken by Swedish men provides reason to remain skeptical that this change will trigger an immediate refashioning of the gender order in Canada. Scholars who examine the Swedish system point to the significance of gender symbolism in explaining the modest response to daddy months by men. Lis Hojgaard (1997: 258), for instance, argues that a father's decision to care actively for (not just about) his newborn "challenges a very basic symbolic meaning of masculinity as it involves work performance." The resulting symbolic discord, she argues, is a major "reason that men do not take full advantage of the possibilities of ameliorating the contradictions between work and family that are, albeit ambiguously, offered by the work place culture and by welfare state policies."

This line of analysis confirms Olson's (2002) point that a universal caregiver strategy must reconstruct the symbolic meaning of fatherhood (without conceding that changes to financial incentives are inappropriately paternalistic). In response, I recommend linking participation in maternity and parental leave programs with public pension systems. In the Canadian context, every month of leave that someone takes should reduce by four months the total amount of (self-)employment that he or she must perform to qualify without penalty for CPP/QPP benefits. Under such a system, parents who take six months of leave would receive CPP/QPP payments two years earlier than they would had they not taken the leave, at age sixty-three rather than sixty-five.

Pensions represent the social citizenship benefit that is most definitively linked to extensive paid work performance. Retirement, when non-work becomes socially sanctioned in recognition of a successful history of productive contribution, is a unique point in the adult life course. By linking public pension entitlement to participation in parental leave programs, the care*fair* concept would make explicit that informal care is a social responsibility just as much as employment. When the public determines eligibility for its paramount social citizenship benefit, such a linking would overtly signal that caregiving counts as civic work alongside labour force participation. A connection between leave and pensions would thus advance at the level of symbolic politics the idea that caregiving should count for masculine (not just feminine) ideals of work performance. The one-to-four ratio in CPP/QPP eligibility contributes aggressively to this symbolic message, signalling that the state privileges specialization in infant care over employment during certain life course stages, and implores employers to accommodate more male participation in this mode of social (re)production. Although the appropriateness of the one-to-four ratio is open to debate, the need for further scrutiny is part of its utility. The proposed weighting is sufficiently counter-cultural that it is bound to spark a level of public dialogue that will create opportunities for symbolic reform.

Linking maternity/parental leave to pension eligibility is by no means neutral about the choices that men make; nor are the other leave benefit reforms that I propose. Rather, the recommendations presume that caregiving is a social responsibility akin to employment or taxes, and they publicly strive to entice men to perform an equitable share of caregiving.

By designing public policy to oblige citizens, the proposed leave reforms invoke a now well-accepted Weberian analysis of the state. As Taylor-Gooby (1991: 208) notes, "Many definitions of the state do not pay much attention to the meeting of citizens' needs, but all put the 'monopoly on the legitimate use of violence within a given territory', in Weber's terminology, at their heart. Welfare states are not simply about doing good to individuals by meeting their needs, they are about sanctioning, controlling and directing people's behaviour as well."

Sanctions and controls are vital to the state, even in the liberal tradition, because the state functions as a guarantor of individual liberty and equality. Should a citizen's activity encroach on the liberty of others or otherwise inflict injury, a government may rightfully exercise its power to limit that activity, even when it does so against the citizen's will. This insight is the foundation of John Stuart Mill's (1975: 10-11) famous harm principle, which argues that "the only purpose for which power can be rightfully exercised over any member of a civilized community, against his will, is to prevent harm to others."

The harm principle illuminates one linchpin in the case for invoking the authority of the welfare state to address the gendered division of labour. The perverse incentives that perpetuate male free riding on care by diverse groups of women undermine equality of opportunity and place women at risk of economic insecurity and marginalization from important social areas. The solution to this moral hazard demands a vision of citizenship that institutionalizes sanctions as much as benefits, just as the harm principle prescribes use of state power to shield individual liberty. As Taylor-Gooby (1991: 208) observes, we must recognize that "equal enjoyment of rights requires that some people should be prevented from infringing the human need for freedom of others by not participating in the paid and unpaid work that is necessary to the continuance of society."

The New Paternalist Competence Argument for Care*fair*

A second linchpin in the care*fair* argument can be adapted from current workfare debates by drawing on new paternalist discussions of competence. Recall that "competence" connotes an individual's ability to behave in a manner that promotes her or his self-interest. Rejecting the assumption that individuals are rational maximizers who optimize their self-interest wherever possible, the competence question favours a more complex psychology that explains the self-defeating dynamics that occur in contexts of dependence in which people may fail to act on their desires.

Following this pattern, the second argument for care*fair* raises questions about dysfunction. But this care*fair* argument departs from the right-of-centre tendency to question the competence of the poor alone by raising questions about men's competence more generally as it plays out in respect to the patriarchal culture of male dependence on female care.

The competence argument explicitly resists the assumption that men's neglect of some care activities is entirely in their self-interest. Many men benefit financially from the less encumbered status they enjoy, as compared to women, since men are not culturally, politically, or economically expected to perform a fair share of care work. But the appropriate response to this patriarchal dividend is *not* to align care with what Jean Bethke Elshtain (1981: 333) terms the "shitwork," which risks implying that citizens should minimize the contribution they make to the social product through caregiving. Rather, the literature inspired by Carol Gilligan (1987: 32) acknowledges an "essential ambivalence" to human connection that recognizes care as both a site of immense satisfaction and frequent discrimination for many women. Care is not just instrumentally valuable for social reproduction: it is also intrinsically valuable as a source of protection, identity affirmation, group membership, and fulfillment.

The latter themes are evident in work by scholars, especially Patricia Hill Collins (1991, 1994), who push the experiences of women of colour to the centre of feminist theorizing. Collins (1994: 50) explains that caring often represents "mothers [of colour] fighting for the physical survival both of their own biological children and those of the larger ... community." Care is "a form of resistance" for some minority mothers whose care labour on behalf of their own family and ethnic group defies the expectation of servitude to whites (Collins, 1991: 140).

This line of analysis is significant because it reminds us that domesticity can be a site of solace where individuals may cultivate the kinds of intimate relationships that are constitutive of social belonging. Family and cherished friends not only furnish material assistance in difficult times but may also provide emotional support by affirming the personal values and self-definitions that individuals need in order to flourish. Because members of minority ethnic and faith-based groups, as well as gay and lesbian communities, may not encounter this recognition in public domains, the positive recognition of their self-definition that can be found in domestic spaces grows in significance. In this instance, domesticity assumes the status of an essential sphere of social inclusion where the nurturing of their identity helps individuals to resist externally imposed denigrating images, while fostering the collective identities of the ethnocultural, religious, and sexual orientation groups in which they belong (for a more thorough discussion of this theme, see Kershaw, 2005: Chapter 6). The web of relations in which citizens provide and receive care thus becomes a location where, as Collins (1991: 118) reports, members of marginalized social groups "express and learn the power of self-definition, the importance of valuing and respecting [them]selves, the necessity of self-reliance and independence, and a belief in [their] empowerment."

The role that caring plays in self- and community definition remains muted in theorizing that reflects dominant ethnocultural and other group perspectives in which the collective identity is not at risk. But relative silence does not mean that time for care is any less critical to the development of identity among members of the dominant culture. Domestic care is an activity that facilitates individuals, regardless of their privilege, to explore their place in a family and community lineage as well as the values and life pursuits that this social location affirms. Thus, although the Collins literature illuminates the importance of domestic care as a form of resistance among some minority socio-cultural groups, it also underscores the broader point that informal caregiving is integral to identity formation among all citizens irrespective of the security of their ethnocultural background. Private time for care is an issue of identity politics that commands attention from us all.

One shortcoming of the Collins literature is that her discourse focuses almost entirely on mothering. There is no reason, however, to believe that her treatment of care as a potential source of affirmation and social belonging reveals social dynamics that are exclusive to women. To hold this view would be to embrace an essentialism that much contemporary feminist scholarship rejects (Spelman, 1988). Accordingly, a significant implication of the finding that domestic care fosters identity and belonging is that many successful male breadwinners may be marginalized from an important sphere of social membership. Care ambitions that go unfulfilled or even undiscovered may undermine some men's full participation in this key domain of affectivity.

There are data to support the view that some men suffer this under-theorized source of social exclusion. For instance, David J. Eggebeen and Chris Knoester (2001: 389) find that, for fathers, their "level of involvement with their children made a substantial difference" to activities well beyond child rearing. "The more these men were engaged in activities with their children, the more satisfied they were with their lives, the more socializing they did, the more involved they were in their communities, [and] the more connected they were to their families."

Lesley Barclay and Deborah Lupton (1999: 1019) add that many new and expecting fathers wish to be more involved in child rearing than were their own fathers. There is a gap, however, between their intentions and actions: "Nearly all our participants found fatherhood, in the beginning at least, to be disappointing and frustrating. Most of the group expected to be more involved than they actually were ... The emotional rewards for new fathers appeared to be in proportion to the amount of time and energy they expended in intimate contact with the child. Only a minority of participants did not want to provide this care, but most men found it difficult to find the time away from paid employment to develop the skills they required to do so adequately."

If, as these studies suggest, caring for young children is something that many new fathers wish to do and is also an activity that yields spillover benefits for their social networks and life satisfaction, then the patriarchal division of labour raises serious questions about men's competence, in the new paternalist sense of the term. This research indicates that neglecting caregiving in favour of additional breadwinning or leisure is out of step with some interests to which men subscribe. One could therefore reasonably posit that the acquiescence of some (many?) men to a rather strict gendered division of care reflects their failure "to do what they themselves desire and thus to exhaust the potential of their environment," just as Mead indicts the long-term unemployed (1997: 28).

As a counterpoint to some men's stated care aspirations, the pervasiveness of primary care provision by women reveals in part the degree to which male (and female) behaviour is not fully strategic but bounded by patriarchal enculturation. Without denying that human behaviour is rational, men turn to established routines to attain their purposes. As part of this process, the institution of patriarchy provides moral and cognitive templates for interpretation and action. Men are embedded in a world of institutions constituted by the vestiges of patriarchal symbols that provide filters for interpretation of situation and self. Subject to a legacy of male free riding on female care, men from diverse socioeconomic and cultural groups risk internalizing a pathology of patriarchal dependence that obstructs their interest-satisfaction vis-à-vis their (potential) network of care relations. In response, directive social policy such as the aggressive daddy leave proposed above is necessary to close the gap between men's care intentions and their actions, just as Mead proposes workfare to assist the economically marginalized in closing the gap between their employment interests and their dearth of paid work.

Conclusion

A care*fair* analogue to workfare would address the circular relation between individual choices and prescriptive patriarchal norms by employing public policy levers to nudge men economically and symbolically to make more socially responsible choices about caregiving. The nudge remains relatively gentle, since under care*fair* men would not be forced to care more. They could still choose to continue current care patterns; but there would be new consequences, such as postponed eligibility for a full public pension and the loss of leave benefits. Thus, care*fair* would not so much compel care activity as it would change the system of incentives within which men make choices between market and domestic activities. In this regard, the analogue is dramatically less coercive than, say, conscription, which was historically a badge of male citizenship.

The level of suasion characteristic of care*fair* also stands in contrast to the much stronger coercion that Mead advocates in his paternalist vision of workfare. Reforms that redesign policy incentives to encourage paid work do not figure in his preferred category of workfare policies. Mead (1997: 47) discounts tinkering with policy incentives because such reform "leave[s] work as a choice." Because Mead rejects the assumption of competence, he is leery of the idea that individuals will respond to policy-induced economic incentives, even those incentives in which paid work is clearly in their own self-interest. He therefore concludes that reordering policy incentives will never be enough: if it is to be effective, a workfare scheme must also employ direct supervision to coerce citizens to work.

Although the reforms I propose are informed by Scandinavian experience, care*fair* does not presume that policy suitable for social democratic regimes in Europe is culturally appropriate for their liberal cousins, such as Canada. Policy innovation stands a greater chance of success if it embraces one or more key norms common in the cultural context in which it is to be tried. Antonio Gramsci (1971) reminds us that a paradigm is hegemonic only because it resonates (at least in part) with much of the citizenry, including those who are ultimately disadvantaged by the paradigm. The path to replacing a dominant paradigm thus does not lie so much in negating it as in refashioning critical elements that have broad appeal in order to reprioritize values that are missing and exhaust problematic features that are prominent.

Here lies the unique opportunity that duty discourses in liberal regimes present for local proponents of gender equality. Belying the assertion that use of state power to privilege some social choices introduces a level of paternalism about which theorists and the public are skeptical, citizens in these states regularly (re-)elect policy-makers who employ the authoritative power of government to compel citizens to discharge social duties in respect of paid work. Exercising the same state authority to impose citizenry care obligations can therefore be presented as a logical next step in this cultural milieu. Although the punitive character of some workfare policies appropriately draws critique (Klein and Long, 2003), it turns out that renewed commitment to enforce civic work obligations represents a solid cornerstone for developing a gender equality framework premised on the universal caregiver model. For just as moral hazard and paternalist arguments defend workfare, they also have potential to champion a policy regime that demands that men discharge civic care duties.

The appropriation of these arguments is not without irony. Who would have thought that the likes of Mead could prove to be a closet force for a feminist vision of citizenship that aims to equalize care responsibilities between men and women?

11

Republican Liberty, Naming Laws, and the Role of Patronymy in Constituting Women's Citizenship in Canada and Québec

Jackie F. Steele

> Naming – having a word for it – is an important part of the process of evolving consciousness. Naming a person isolates and defines one soul, one individual, one unit in the stream of the whole.
>
> – Lucille Hoerr Charles (quoted in Alford, 1988: 1)

The idea that a woman and her offspring are the property of the male "head of the household" is not only obsolete, but it smacks of an ideological familialism that is counterintuitive to the liberal-individualistic notions of citizenship underpinning modern democracies of the Anglo-American tradition. Nonetheless, remnants of this patriarchal gender system continue to find expression within the naming laws of most Canadian provinces. Susan Moller Okin (1991: 181) defines the "gender system" as the "deeply entrenched social institutionalization of sexual difference." The following inquiry is grounded in the assumption that cultural/gendered systems of naming are imbued with the symbolic meaning of an individual's location, loyalty, and connection to family, the political community, and the larger web of communities within which she or he circulates. It likewise assumes that naming is a *political activity*, wherein "to give a name is to give power *to*, or gain power *over*, the named" (Alia, 1985: 34, emphasis in original). Its aim is to explore what Anna Yeatman (1994: 31) has called a "politics of representation," in order to uncover the material effects of the discursive power of naming. Feminist insight into the role of language and naming/labelling as constitutive of the identity and value of oneself and/or one's cultural group likewise forms the backdrop of this inquiry into the genealogy of patronymic naming (renaming of wives after their husbands) and its contemporary expression in Canada.[1]

As the first symbolic/linguistic means by which infants come to understand themselves as unique and distinct individuals, the personal name is arguably one of the most important markers of selfhood and sexual difference. Nonetheless, it must be added that sexual difference as power/institution is a convenient fiction; indeed, as Rosi Braidotti (1992: 185) notes, "there can be no subjectivity outside sexuation, or language, that is to say, the subject is always gendered: it is a 'she-I' or a 'he-I.'" Highlighting the performativity of gender, Judith Butler (2004: 1) observes that we are "always 'doing' [gender] with or for another even if the other is only imaginary." Passive/non-reflexive, as well as chosen/conscious participation in the symbolic gender system(s) constitutive of the dominant cultural backdrop can work to both expand and/or limit the diversity of our own individual subjectivities.

In what follows, I will argue that the ongoing legal and social tolerance of patronymy reinforces a monovocal notion of womanhood, thereby striking at the heart of women's right to liberty and unique personality. Moreover, patronymy persists as a twenty-first-century simulacrum of the legal inferiority of women vis-à-vis their male spouses and of a juridico-political culture that denied women's personhood. Employing the republican concept of liberty as non-domination to critique neoliberal attempts to privatize responsibility for patronymy, I will demonstrate that the passive legal tolerance of such symbolic practices, which sustain an obsolete gender hierarchy based on male supremacy, has important consequences for Canadian women's status within the political community. I will argue in favour of the adoption of laws, such as those of Québec, that take women's liberty seriously and that constitute sexual difference through relations of mutual non-domination.

Naming Intersecting Systems of Oppressions

The current discussion will focus on the naming of wives, as distinct from the patriarchal naming of children (patrilineality). As regards liberty, the issue of adult women being coerced to rename themselves upon marriage differs qualitatively from that of daughters being named after their fathers: their brothers will be similarly named. Socialization into patronymy affects the value accorded/invested in daughters' names (as compared to those of sons), given that they are expected to adopt their future husband's (more important) last name. I purposefully do not use the terms "surname," "sirname," or "family name," as they privilege the normalcy of patriarchal familial naming patterns. For its part, patrilineality denies mothers the ability to name their children, insisting that they affirm the primacy of the father. Sharon Lebell (1988: 20) exposes the interdependence of these two forms of nominal domination when she asserts that through patronymy "women are plugged into an artificial patrilineal scheme which confers intergenerational potency on the patronymic family name and on the male family figures, who are seen as the principal actors in the family's historical drama." Although it lies beyond the scope of this discussion, given that a wife's decision to keep her birth name disrupts the "natural" right of fathers to name children with the universal (monovocally male) "family" name, the question of children's names leads to increased pressure on women to participate in, and reproduce, patronymic naming practices. This chapter focuses on the processes constitutive of discrimination against women qua future wives of male citizens, which presumes the non-necessity of nominal autonomy/integrity for girls/women and perpetuates the inferior social value accorded to women's subjectivities as transhistorical protagonists within the family and society.

Patronymic naming practices impact on women of differing social locations inflected by nationality, class, race, and sexual orientation. With respect to the latter, contemporary naming laws have presumably applied to Canadian and Québécois same-sex spouses since *Hendricks* (2002), *Egale Canada* (2003), *Halpern* (2003), and the federal legalization of same-sex marriage in the Civil Marriage Act (2005). Same-sex marriage remains highly contested by patriarchal and religious fundamentalists in Canada, whose voices are disproportionately amplified within the minority Conservative government ("Canadian Conservatives Win," 2006). Honouring an election promise, Stephen Harper held a free vote on whether to reopen the debate on same-sex marriage (Bailey, 2006); his motion was defeated by 175 to 123 on 7 December 2006 (Bonoguore, 2006). To date, little research has been done on the meaning and types of naming practices within lesbian and gay marriages, an important area that requires further exploration; the subject, nonetheless, falls outside the scope of this chapter.

With respect to nationality, the following discussion invokes the term "citizen" for two reasons. First, I aim to suggest that the socio-political existence of each individual is, in some sense, constituted by the state and state discourse in law, much of which has had particularly devastating effects upon the integrity and liberty of women, notably women who are racialized, indigenous, and/or poor. Second, I aim to expose the ongoing contradiction within modern democracies whereby individuals can be subject, or subjected, to the law regardless of their effective access to self-government and political representation therein, and regardless of past colonizations. The realities of Aboriginal, Inuit, Innu, and Métis peoples, many of whom contest the legitimacy of Canadian and Québec laws, are some examples. Exposing these contradictions is of particular significance for white settler societies and for immigrant-receiving societies, wherein women's citizenship often remains legally dependent on the indigeneity/Aboriginal status and/or nationality/immigrant status of a male spouse (see Abu-Laban and Gabriel, 2002; Alia 1985, 1988, 1989; Backhouse, 1991, 1999; Bannerji, 2001; Bannerji, Mojab, and Whitehead, 2001; Boyd, 2002;

Cossman and Fudge, 2002; Hall 1995; Kobayashi 1995; Little, 1998; Monture-Angus, 1995, 1999; Shapiro, 1997; Strong-Boag et al., 1998; Taiaiake, 1999; Thobani, 2000; Tully, 1993; Turpel, 1996).

The minimal amount of research on the role of indigeneity, race and/or ethnicity as they intersect with (women's) marital naming (Alia 1985, 1988, 1989; Klymasz 1963; Monture-Angus 1995, 1999) poses several challenges in assessing the full implications of patronymy. Despite efforts to build post-colonial, multicultural/intercultural societies in Canada and Québec, it is possible that some women take their husband's name to escape racist attitudes or, conversely, that they proactively retain their birth name to affirm ties to their indigenous and/or ethnocultural heritage, despite the possibility of increased exposure to racism.

Regarding class, the few existing case studies (of predominantly white Canadian and American women) suggest that the decision to assert one's birth name occurs more often among women who are younger, highly educated, and who have higher incomes than women who exclusively use their husband's name after marriage (Fowler and Fuehrer, 1997: 315). These results may reflect methodological challenges (small sample size, recruitment of participants) as much as they reflect any inherent trend within a given economic class. Although some might assume that patronymic naming is only of concern to the equality rights of privileged, professional-class, straight women, I wish to argue that patronymy reflects modern binary assumptions of the primacy of male subjectivity over its female counterpart, and that it symbolically works to publicize state-registered heterosexuality and the patriarchal ordering of spouses within the family as the "norm" of contemporary sexual/familial organization. As such, it contributes to the marginalization and "othering" of the majority of women (and men) whose family and sexual practices stray from this invented tradition. As is commonly the case for many complex questions that deal with intersecting systems of oppression, it is extremely difficult to pinpoint *direct causal links* between domination and patronymic naming customs, given that the perceived and/or symbolic markers of inferiority borne by women both stem from and are constitutive of past and ongoing vulnerability to denigration and discrimination.

The goal of this inquiry is to expose the *structural domination* that is inscribed in naming laws in Canada and that works to deny or impose unjustified limits on women's liberty and diverse political subjectivities. Clearly, when engaging in discussions of "liberty," feminist theorists confront the fact that mainstream political philosophy has consistently contributed, either by sexist design or lack of intellectual rigour, to the exclusion of women's subjectivities. Although republican theorists have been no exception to this rule, the work of Philip Pettit, in *Republicanism: A Theory of Freedom and Government* (1997), restores hope that the application of old political philosophy tools by more rigorous thinkers might prove a worthy endeavour in the struggle against oppression. Indeed, the central contribution of feminist political theory to both the academy and contemporary democracies is its ability to expose the subtle workings of anti-democratic power and to re-invent the role of law and self-government as a means of eliminating oppressive practices. Although feminism and republicanism may seem strange bedfellows, I believe that their intellectual traditions can be strategic allies against the neoliberal revisionism of the empowering aspects of political belonging and democratic citizenship.

I will begin by outlining the central tenets of the neo-republican definition of "liberty" and its relationship to the concept of domination. Second, I will trace the genealogy of patronymy in the laws and practices governing women's names in Canada and Québec.[2] Third, I will propose a normative reading of the Canadian and Québécois laws on marital naming in light of the concept of liberty as non-domination, in order to expose the failure of laws in most Canadian provinces to take women's diverse subjectivities and liberty seriously. Ultimately, it is my hope that this discussion will pose a conceptual challenge to the heteronormative and patriarchal foundations of current state and social discourses on female citizens, and moreover, that it will contribute to alternative foundations for gendered relationships that recognize and protect the liberty, individuality, and diverse subjectivities of female and male citizens.

Liberty as Non-domination

My analysis of the strengths inherent in the republican notion of liberty as non-domination builds upon the arguments advanced by Philip Pettit in his important work *Republicanism: A Theory of Freedom and Government* (1997). Joining Pettit, this chapter seeks to contribute to the revival of republicanism as a much-needed alternative to the hegemonic force of liberal/neoliberal conceptions of citizenship. Defenders of liberalism perceived Pettit's failure to differentiate between its various strands (libertarianism, social liberalism, welfare state liberalism, neoliberalism) as a conspicuous silence. This is a critique for which I may be similarly vulnerable. Nonetheless, given my interest in liberalisms' normative influence on contemporary public policy and political culture *in practice,* rather than their normative foundations *in theory,* I have adopted Pettit's ascription of liberty as non-interference to "liberal" traditions founded on the notion of negative liberty.

In order to fully grasp the implications of liberty as non-domination, we must first define the notion of domination. Pettit (1997: 31) argues that the concept of freedom espoused by a wide variety of Roman (republican) philosophers was in fact "freedom as non-domination," not "freedom as non-interference." He returns to historical definitions of the citizen and the slave (*liber* and *servus*) in order to stress the fact that these terms referred to the condition of liberty in which citizens enjoyed autonomy and participation in self-government. Unlike slaves, citizens could not suffer from the arbitrary interference of another party. Pettit notes, "This opposition between slavery or servitude on the one hand and freedom on the other is probably the single most characteristic feature of the long rhetoric of liberty to which the experience of the Roman republic gave rise. It is significant, because slavery is essentially characterized by domination, not by actual interference" (31-32). Pettit traces the centrality of "domination" and "unfreedom" in discussions of liberty throughout the centuries, beginning with Algernon Sydney's statement in the late 1600s that "he is a slave who serves the best and gentlest man in the world, as well as he who serves the worst" (34-35). Accordingly, Pettit argues that any meaningful discussion of liberty and any political theory of government that aims to protect individual freedom must engage with and take the concept of domination seriously. Moreover, domination should be understood through the relationship of master to slave or master to servant wherein the dominating party has the ability to interfere on an arbitrary basis with the choices of the dominated (22). To illustrate this important nuance, Pettit observes that one could be in a master-servant relationship and yet not suffer interference should the goodwill and altruism of the master be such that the servant is allowed autonomy of action.

Distinguishing the conditions of liberty as non-domination from liberty as non-interference, Pettit makes the point that domination can exist as long as someone has the *ability* to interfere arbitrarily in one's affairs, regardless of whether such interference occurs in practice. Maurizio Viroli (2002: 36) illustrates the same point with concrete examples: "a wife who can be abused by her husband without being able to resist or demand restitution; workers who can be subjected to minor or major abuses from their employer or supervisor; a retiree who must depend on the whim of a functionary to obtain the pension to which he has a legitimate right; young scholars who know that their careers depend not on the quality of their work but on the whims of a senior professor."

Rejecting the view that legal interference from the state constitutes an infringement upon one's liberty, Pettit notes that republican conditions of liberty carve out a more sophisticated role of law in promoting egalitarian relations. Countering Thomas Hobbes' basic assertion that all law entails coercion and is therefore a limit to liberty, the republican view would be that "properly constituted law is constitutive of liberty" (Pettit, 1997: 35). Viroli (2002: 53) similarly notes that "a further reason for distinguishing between being subject to restraints and being dependent is that legislative measures that free some citizens from dependence restrict others in their freedom to act." In fact, the law necessarily interferes in the lives of its citizens through coercion; the republican view is that it may do so to the extent that it pursues the common interests of the polity (fostering non-domination) and when sanctioned by the citizenry through the democratic process. The notion of liberty as non-domination, therefore, has the potential to far exceed the minimal conditions tolerated by negative liberty. It is unhelpful to simply describe the presence or absence of state interference; rather, republican liberty attempts to inform what would constitute arbitrary undemocratic interference – namely, that which is inconsistent with the political foundations of respect for the autonomy and dignity of each citizen.

Most importantly for the discussion at hand, Pettit (1997: 69) states that non-domination is a form of power, one that "represents a control that a person enjoys in relation to her/his own destiny." More specifically, it "involves a sort of immunity or security against interference on an arbitrary basis." In a political arrangement that is genuinely based on non-domination, Pettit asserts, all individuals would be powerful in terms of shaping their own lives because they would not be dependent on luck or the benevolence of others to avoid the kinds of arbitrary exercises of power that are possible under a system based on liberty as non-interference.

Liberty as Non-interference

The notion of liberty as non-interference, Pettit (1997: 46) argues, "first appeared in the writings of authoritarians like Hobbes and Filmer, and achieved significant credibility with the writings of Bentham and Paley. An activist opponent of republican views on liberty, Paley promoted the idea that restraint of any kind, including the law, constituted an invasion of personal liberty. He charged that republicans viewed liberty as security against arbitrary interference, and therefore confused the means with the ends, stating 'they describe not so much liberty itself, as the safeguards and preservatives of liberty.'" Moreover, Paley held that defining liberty as non-interference was more scientific than emotionally laden claims of injustice; it did away with inflammatory talk of slavery and oppression and allowed for an empirical discussion of "liberty" as it is realized in degrees along a spectrum. Finally, Paley (quoted in Pettit, 1997: 47) stated that liberty as non-domination was simply an unrealistic goal: "Those definitions of liberty ought to be rejected, which, by making that essential to civil freedom which is unattainable in experience, inflame expectations that can never be gratified, and disturb the public content with complaints, which no wisdom or benevolence of government can remove."

If, as Paley suggests, it is impossible to craft a society wherein relations of domination are minimized, social justice activists worldwide might as well embrace their fate and go home. From the perspective of political theory,

Paley's curious defence of domination as *inevitable* likely reveals his personal investment in the status quo more than it calls into question the role of utopic thinking and activism. Indeed, the raison d'être of political philosophy, and notably of feminist theory, is its capacity to challenge undemocratic practices in order to propose alternative ideals of socio-political institutions that might advance respect for the integrity of all individuals constitutive of the political community. As Quentin Skinner (1998: 78-79) has astutely observed, "One legitimate aspiration of moral and political theory is surely to show us what lines of action we are committed to undertaking by the values we profess to accept. It may well be massively inconvenient to suggest that, if we truly value individual freedom, this commits us to establishing political equality as a substantive ideal. If this is true, however, what this insight offers us is not a critique of our principles as unduly demanding in practice; rather it offers us a critique of our practice as insufficiently attentive to our principles." Pettit likewise notes that our inability as a society to implement the principle of liberty as non-domination has little to do with any inherent flaws in the principle itself. Rather, it has only to do with the unwillingness of political leaders to be accountable to this principle in the establishment and structuring of political institutions that govern the power relationships between various actors within society. In the following section, I will illustrate this point by revealing the political apathy that has led to the tolerance of the linguistic effacement, via symbolic domination, of heterosexual married women's subjectivity as a result of ongoing male supremacist naming practices within contemporary Canadian society.

Marital Naming in Canada and Québec

First, it is helpful to situate Canadian legal/political culture and naming practices within heterosexual marriages in the context of those maintained in Anglo-American societies with similar traditions and legal heritage. Although the United States is arguably more conservative than Canada with respect to women's rights, a 1994 survey (cited in Brightman 1994: 910) showed that fully 90 percent of American women changed their names upon marriage and a mere 2 percent used their birth names exclusively.[3] Those women who retained their birth name tended to be younger, better educated, and better paid than those who did not (Fowler and Fuehrer, 1997: 315). Statistics Canada does not produce data on last name changes across Canada; conversations with its staff indicated that the standardized vital statistics form required for provincial marriage registrations does not track the occurrence, and they did not perceive this data as salient. A small body of literature exists on naming and family law trends in Anglo-American societies (see, for example, Alia 1985, 1988, 1989; Boivin, 1985; Lombard,

1984; Lebell, 1988; McCaughan, 1977; Mungall, 1977; Stannard, 1973, 1977, 1984; Steele, 2003). In addition, case studies have documented attitudes towards marital naming and the meanings that have been attached to it (for example, Embleton and King, 1984; Fowler and Fuehrer, 1997; Kline, Stafford, and Miklosovic, 1996; Scheuble and Johnson, 1993). A review of this literature revealed that the overwhelming majority of American and Canadian women still take their husband's name in marriage and that the reasons most commonly cited for doing so were social custom and/or the negative attitudes of others towards women who retained their "maiden name."

As will be shown in the following section, the messages and motivations lying behind patronymy had concrete goals relating to patriarchal family organization and property inheritance. Far from being abandoned in the modern era, they continue to bear consequences and must be linked to the legal framework of "choice" used in contemporary Canada. Understanding these connections can help us debunk the professed neutrality of contemporary naming laws and question the liberal mantra whereby "choice" is always empowering. Ultimately, the goal is to challenge the liberal myth that advances non-interference as the best philosophical foundation for contemporary laws, including those structuring the naming practices of marrying citizens.

Liberty as Non-interference and the Role of "Choice" in Canada

Historically, much confusion has surrounded the legality of a woman retaining her birth name after marriage. Dickenson (1997: 82-83) argues that the doctrine of coverture, articulated in *The Lawes Resolutions on Woman's Rights* (1632), was "the culmination and consequence of a long decline in women's civil rights, including their rights in property" that was legally confirmed throughout the seventeenth century in absolutist monarchies where female inheritance was barred. Although the social custom of patronymy predated this erosion of women's legal rights, it achieved the force of law through William Blackstone's *Commentaries on the Law of England (1765-69)*, in which he articulated the common law doctrine of coverture as follows: "The very being or legal existence of the woman is suspended during the marriage, or at least is incorporated and consolidated into that of the husband; under whose wing, protection and cover, she performs everything; and is called in our law-French a *feme covert, faemina viro co-operta;* and is said to be covert-baron, or under the protection and influence of her husband, her baron, or lord; and her condition during her marriage is called her coverture." During her coverture, a woman and her offspring fell under the protection of her husband as a means of ensuring that his legally recognized sons would inherit his wealth. No laws formally existed on the subject of an individual's name, other than the common law custom that allowed persons to take and consistently use any name they chose. However, in the nineteenth century, when married women began to assert their autonomy within the couple, the issue of their names began to be contested. As Lenore Weitzman (1981: 9) tellingly observes, as long as women "quietly accepted wifehood and the feminine sphere, their names were not an issue."

Few studies have examined the situation in Canada. However, Constance Mungall (1977) has documented Canadian administrative resistance to the retention of the birth name. In addition, Sheila Embleton and Ruth King's (1984: 14-15) study, among others, reveals that social resistance has influenced women's decisions to take their husband's name. In 1975, eight federal statutes required that women declare their marital status in order to register to vote in federal elections ("Federal Status Council's Report," 1975: 11). Furthermore, and despite the optional nature of taking a husband's name, married women who applied for passports in their birth name had to produce evidence to prove that they were known by that name. Although women were not formally required to take their husband's name upon marriage, the fallback position was that they automatically did so. In the *Legal Status of Married Women in Canada*, Margaret McCaughan (1977: 44) has observed that though the custom of patronymy had no legal authority, it was "tacitly implied in some legislation and administrative practices that a married woman's official name is that of her husband."

Open resistance by banks, creditors, public offices, newspapers, and judges to the legitimate and legal use of a woman's birth name after marriage contributed to creating a social reality wherein most men and women assumed it to be *illegal* for a woman to use her own name after marriage. Contributing to this social assumption, the *Globe and Mail* openly disregarded the wishes of Maureen McTeer, imposing, via newsprint, her husband's last name upon her in articles and photo captions ("Maureen McTeer Won't Disappear," 1976; Copes, 1976).[4] Against the backdrop of feminist struggles for the inclusion of gender equality guarantees, and of public debates on the adoption of the Charter of Rights and Freedoms, a Vancouver woman mused about the ridiculous fact that McTeer, wife of the leader of the opposition, still needed to "prove to the Passport Office that she is now who she was when she was born" (Sutherland, 1982: 7). In a 1983 divorce case, in violation of common law practice and Charter guarantees under section 28, Judge E.G. McNeely commanded that on the divorce decree the wife's name be changed to that of her husband. He decided that her birth name, Talariol, was but an "alias," despite her consistent common law use of this name, both before and after marriage ("Woman Challenges Judge," 1983). A woman's "maiden" name, like the individual identity of its bearer, was assumed to have suffered a legal death upon marriage, reducing her subjectivity to only one possible (wifely) identity – "Mrs. Him." Thus, a birth name used after marriage could only be illegal, fraudulent, or an alias at best.

In response to these forms of social, legal, and administrative resistance, some married women attempted to revert to their birth names by effecting a legal name change via the provincial Change of Name Act, which was created for non-marital contexts. Some provinces frustrated their efforts by making it a requirement of the Change of Name Act that all family members use the same last name (Mungall, 1977: 32-33). Outlining the sources of confusion in Canada, McCaughan (1977) notes that provisions for a *legal* change of name were introduced by the provinces, beginning with British Columbia in 1960 (*Change of Name Act*, R.C.B.C. 1960, c. 50). Under the BC law, neither husbands nor wives who shared a last name could unilaterally change it; in some provinces, it was impossible for a woman to revert to her birth name after she had customarily adopted that of her husband (McCaughan, 1977: 45). In the 1970s, in Manitoba, Nova Scotia, and British Columbia, a woman could apply to revert to her birth name, but only if she had the consent of her husband. The legal framework in Saskatchewan in 1976 was such that any woman who did not actively register her intention to retain her birth name within six months of marriage was assumed to have taken her husband's name (Mungall, 1977: 6).

Ironically, though married Canadian women never legally lost their right to use their birth names, they faced an informal patriarchal backlash against their assertion of individual autonomy when they attempted to do so. Ultimately, Canadian women mobilized in favour of formal legal changes in order to counter ongoing administrative practices and attitudes that suggested that a woman was legally obliged to use her husband's name after marriage. In the late 1970s to mid-1980s, a so-called gender-neutral framework of free choice was instituted in Canadian provinces outside of Québec: spouses could now choose to keep their names, to take the name of either spouse, or to join their last names to form a hyphenated compound. In some provinces, they could opt to use a new last name altogether. All of these changes would continue to be facilitated/subsidized by the state. In all circumstances other than marriage, those who wished to change their names legally had to apply through their province's Change of Name Act for the right to do so, as well as individually underwrite the administrative costs of the procedure; in 2007 this remains the legal standard in most Canadian provinces.

Liberty as Non-domination: Birth Name Permanence in Québec

One notable exception to the Anglo-American framework of non-interference and/or "free choice" for name changes upon marriage can be found in

Québec. Historically, in the French civil law tradition, the legal last name of any individual was that given at birth, and therefore if a woman sued a company or a person, or bought land, she did so under her birth name (Mungall, 1977: 5). However, due to the influence of British colonization and the use of the common law throughout North America, the custom of taking a husband's name in fact achieved the force of law in Québec (Brière, 1982: 10-11). With the Quiet Revolution, important developments in the status of women yielded higher divorce rates and subsequently increased bureaucratic costs associated with post-divorce changes of name. Moreover, Québécois couples strongly preferred common law relationships, to which customary/legal name change customs and processes did not apply (Belliveau, Oderkirk, and Silver 1994). Finally, in the late 1970s and early 1980s, feminist mobilization for concrete legal reforms to consolidate gender-egalitarian relations brought a wide range of family law regulations under review. In 1980, supported by Québec women's groups, such as the Fédération des femmes du Québec (see Boivin, 1985: 208; Brière, 1982: 471), and basing its preference for the twin principles of birth name permanence and spousal equality, the Québec government legislated that wherever a legal relation was involved, married women were *obligated* to use their birth name (*Loi instituant un nouveau Code civil et portant réforme du droit de la famille*, L.Q. 1980, c. 39, s. 7). Rejecting the adoption of a "gender-neutral" facade, the government changed Québec's family law so as to counter cultural presumptions of customary patronymy and the existing social obligation that effectively coerced *women* into abdicating their independent legal identity in favour of the wifely role associated with the "family" name of their male spouse.

The legal changes made by the Québec government in 1981 explicitly linked the loss of women's birth names, those under which they had established their legal and political personhood, to the loss of civil and political rights, and therefore of their right to equal recognition as individuals within the social contract. Aware that patronymy constrained women's choices, the government recognized that the framework of gender-neutrality, free choice, or non-interference that was being promoted in common law provinces was inconsistent with political commitments to achieving substantive equality between women and men within the family.

In the following section, I will place the theoretical concept of liberty as non-domination in dialogue with some of the documented socio-demographic realities of marrying heterosexual women in Canada, as a backdrop to the following questions: To what degree do women in Canada enjoy a choice with respect to their names? What power dynamics, if any, are masked by a gender-neutral framework? What role should the state play, in light of commitments to liberty as non-domination, for marrying heterosexual women?

The Theory and Practice of Liberty in Question

> Our names act as our ambassadors, traveling to places and times
> where we ourselves can't be, acting as the representatives of our
> words, deeds, thoughts, feelings, physical characteristics, and
> gestures.
>
> – Sharon Lebell (1988: 5)

What are the implications of the aforementioned realities in terms of wom-
en's status as rights-bearing members of the political community and of
their ability to enjoy liberty as non-domination? Pettit's (1997) analysis of
the citizen and the slave locates the common denominator of domination
and oppression in a state of "unfreedom" or "slavery" wherein one endures
the constant threat of interference and domination by a third party. This
could include the state, specific laws, expectations of a spouse, or patriarchal elements and norms within society that deny the democratic standing
and right to equality of an individual. Liberty as non-domination assumes
that all individuals require protection from arbitrary exercises of power that
use coercion to place unjustifiable (because inconsistent with democratic
principles) limits on their freedom to determine their lives. When this definition of coercion is accepted, the extent to which social pressures can work
to prevent heterosexual women from freely choosing to retain their birth
name becomes apparent. Indeed, for many women, the "choice" to take
their husband's name often stems largely from the unacceptability of, or
risks associated with, failing to do so and the perceived negative image of
themselves, as women and wives, that this might project to the outside
world.

   Embleton and King (1984) expose the investigative questioning and subtle coercion aimed at marrying women in Canada. The normative assumptions expressed in the inquiries of spouses and significant others put women
on notice as to the appropriate behaviour of those aspiring to become a
wife; as such, they informally coerce women to conform with traditional
roles that maintain the heterosexual, patriarchal, and patrilineal family structure of old. Some examples of the attitudes expressed by friends and family
of the women interviewed by Embleton and King include:

> "Don't you love your husband? If you really loved him you would be proud
> to bear his name"; "But what will you call the children? It would be odd if
> your name were different from theirs, and hyphenation is impractical";
> "But marriage will turn you into a new person, and you should show this
> by having a new name"; "That's just selfish"; "What does it matter anyway

– any name is as good as any other, so use his"; "People will think that you are just living together"; "People will think your husband is weak"; "People will stereotype you as one of those feminist extremists"; "A common sur- name binds a family together"; "But it's always been done that way." (14)

Given this, it would seem that keeping one's name equates with a lack of commitment to family, a lack of a state-recognized relationship, a lack of love for one's husband, or a lack of concern for one's future children. Painted as selfishness or as grounded in strident feminist convictions, it also sug- gests that the woman has selected a man who is weak. Thus, a marrying woman's "choice" effectively exposes her to harsh, if simplistic, judgments and crass stereotypes and can contribute to the social ridicule of her hus- band. A study by Philip Blumstein and Pepper Schwartz (1983: 17n2) of more than five thousand couples (married and unmarried, heterosexual, gay, and lesbian) confirmed the ongoing importance of gender and gender roles to the concept of marriage. In fact, they conclude by asserting that although the more egalitarian two-paycheque marriage is "emerging" in contemporary society, "the force of the previous tradition still guides the behavior of most modern marriages" (115). Laurie Scheuble and David Johnson (1993: 751) show that despite holding progressive views about women, many young male college students in the United States still expect a woman to follow the custom of patronymy, particularly if her husband or his relatives think she should do so. The message remains that a woman's right to liberty (as non-domination), and her power to determine her indi- vidual life path, remains disproportionately dependent upon the arbitrary interference and approval of others within the family.

In 1998, McGill sociologist Peta Tancred noted the return to conserva- tism in the face of rising divorce rates in Canada: "There is a fear that we have destroyed the family. This fits with a desire to rebuild it" (quoted in Nolen, 1998: C5). Indeed, in a *Globe and Mail* article, journalist Melanie Coulson (2003: F7) defended her *new* (husband's) name as the symbol of the *new* egalitarian family unit she was creating; yet she remained curiously silent as to why her husband had not changed his name to reflect this mu- tual commitment grounded in equality. Not only young women but nota- bly high-profile women become important symbolic targets for this kind of coercion. In the United States, Hillary Rodham's choice of last name sparked much discussion and controversy, leading to her eventual use of Rodham Clinton, and then simply Clinton (Brightman, 1994). Within the Canadian context, despite having been known as Laureen Teskey for over fifteen years of marriage to Stephen Harper, the wife of the Conservative prime minister recently announced to the media that she preferred to be known as "Mrs. Harper" ("Laureen: Just Call Me 'Mrs. Harper,'" 2006). For his part, Harper

234 Jackie F. Steele

himself has gone on record that it is "Laureen who has to be reigned in for public consumption" (Blatchford, 2006). *National Post* journalist Warren Kinsella (2006) recently suggested that most men are progressive (like him) in not caring what their wives call themselves. Yet he simultaneously asserted that it is *normal* for men to insist on naming their children as a means of affirming their "legitimacy" within the family. It would seem that the assertion of male supremacy has simply shifted to the power to name children, which is then rationalized as a form of "affirmative action" that compensates for men's inability to give birth; it also diverts attention from other means of securing legitimacy, such as active parenting. These neo-patriarchal pleas in favour of men's rights as fathers work to restore the undemocratic male privileges that were previously enshrined within family law. At the same time, they actively deny the ongoing (economic, social, and political) structural domination of women by men as a "social group" (see Iris Marion Young, 1990a, 1994), which reduces the negotiating power that individual wives/mothers exercise in practice, relative to husbands/fathers. Indeed, anecdotal evidence suggests that the vast majority of Canadian children still receive their father's name. During the first decade after the Québec reforms, more children received compound last names; however, a similar neo-patriarchal trend can be observed, despite the fact that all Québécois women retain their birth names after marriage. In fact, in 2007, only a small minority of Canadian and Québécois women within a heterosexual couple have had the power to confer their last names upon children they had borne.

The argument herein is that the law does not provide women with a genuine free choice: rather, it actually allows for them to be coerced by the bearers of anti-egalitarian, patriarchal values within society. By attempting to minimize the "interference" of the state in this public-cum-private decision, the liberal framework of choice in fact *legally invents* the premise for the arbitrary meddling of third parties in the decisions and choices of marrying heterosexual women. This eventuality is achieved by virtue of the law's implicit recognition (and subsidization) of the custom of patronymy and therefore of the possibility that the name of a marrying person (read: a woman) might change. Indeed, the law invites traditionalist spouses, in-laws, friends, and public administrative actors into a marrying woman's personal process of self-definition (Kline, Stafford, and Miklosovic, 1996: 605). Using the concept of privacy, rather than of liberty as non-domination, Anita Allen (1997: 72, 76) asserts the importance of decisional autonomy and the right to inviolate personality to foster the dignity and individuality of (male and female) citizens. In this light, this kind of permissive law does not legally protect the inviolability of women's names as the symbol of a complex and dynamic individuality, one granted legal and political standing, and constituted by multiple relationships. Instead, its impact upon heterosexual married women is such that they may be coerced into publicly affirming that their role as "Mrs. Him" is the single most important facet of their personhood. The process of renaming themselves with the symbolic discursive power of a new (post-wedding) name and identity becomes the means by which women are called upon to publicly profess loyalty to this singular role, indefinitely. This practice serves to hinder their ability to exist and evolve their subjectivity in their own voice, via an inviolate legal personality and name; moreover, it questions their right to continue and to develop loyalties to multiple (public and private) roles and relationships *even after marriage*. The change of name works to efface the original linguistic signifier that is granted to girls upon birth so as to accord them recognition within the political community. It replaces this important nominal marker of a complex human individuality, if female, with a monovocal and reified role or "status" of wifedom.

The framework of non-interference or "free choice" makes nominal self-mastery, liberty as non-domination, and individual self-determination more difficult for marrying heterosexual women in particular. Moreover, it leaves a pregnant silence as to the importance of all women's subjectivities, as informed by their non-spousal interpersonal relationships as sisters, daughters, mothers, colleagues, and friends that flow from the diversity of women's activities as caregivers, workers, soldiers, teachers, activists, volunteers, and artists. The subtle policing of marrying heterosexual women into the self-effacing roles of patriarchal wifehood/motherhood works to constitute a hegemonic norm of subordinate womanhood as the singular and "universal" historical figure or model within the family, human society, and history. Rather than being able to freely affirm their individual perspectives and corporeal realities/truths, the practical non-recognition of a woman's autonomous subjectivity and name (its signifier) places both individual women and women as a social group in the position of having to constantly fend off the discursive norms of a patriarchal gender system that sees them as mere appendages to male citizens. As Patricia Monture-Angus (1995: 3) has observed of the power of state labelling of "Status Indians," naming of this kind is derisory in that it contributes to a reality that authoritatively contradicts one's experiences and self-understandings. It denies the right to say "'I am!' – instead, you always find yourself saying, 'I am not!'"

The existing social science research and widespread anecdotal evidence point to a reality wherein a substantial majority of heterosexual marrying women in Canada automatically assume an obligation to change their names and/or "choose" to do so due to social pressure. This is not to deny the fact that a minority of women may also consciously choose their husband's name due to positive social reinforcement and pride at becoming a wife. As observed by Patricia Violi (1992: 175), we must be conscious of the reality whereby "even if women have a subordinate position in the patriarchal order, they nevertheless take part in it and often actively transmit it." Only a few women are situated in a socio-political and economic situation that affords them the autonomy and negotiating power required to retain their birth name without a husband's support and understanding (Fowler and Fuehrer, 1997: 318-19). At the same time, the legal creation of "choice" of last name remains largely irrelevant for marrying men, given that state and society have never obliged men to change their names to publicize commitment to their marital status and roles as husbands/fathers-to-be. In Québec, the law has purposefully eliminated what Suzanne Boivin (1985: 203) has termed "the emotional blackmail by the new spouse, or even by the community." Most importantly, it contributes to the production of egalitarian heterosexual identities and relationships between male and female spouses and citizens. As Violi (1992: 175) notes, "Without visible, non-patriarchal representations of women, a different form of subjectivity cannot be internalized." This, I argue, is the strength of the legal framework of birth name permanence, which protects women's liberty by institutionalizing relations of mutual non-domination between male and female subjectivities, be they in partnership within the family or in society at large. Given this, the Québec model represents a crucial step towards the decolonization of women's subjectivities from arbitrary anti-democratic gender systems based on male supremacy, and towards the positive legal constitution of democratic equality as the foundation of (heterosexual) spousal cooperation, wherein respect for the liberty, dignity, and inviolate personality of all citizens is the norm.

Conclusion

> My name is the symbol of my identity and must not be lost.
>
> –Lucy Stone (quoted in Arichi, 1999: 411)

The law plays a vital role in the constitution of meaning and worth within society. Charles Taylor (1992a: 25, 36) asserts that individuals from marginalized groups can suffer from a lack of recognition, a sort of *non*-recognition or *mis*-recognition of their selves, as a result of sexually, racially, or culturally discriminatory views and attitudes in society. Conversely, recognition from the state, society, and significant others serves as a crucial form of validation and affirmation of one's inherent worth, and promotes assurance of one's human potential and right to a life of dignity and equal respect. Demands for formal political recognition are never merely symbolic: rather, they alter in complex and often massive ways the social, economic, and political relations of power that constitute the present system of social cooperation (Tully, 2001: 15). The demand that legal frameworks of naming both structurally and practically empower women to retain their birth names after marriage is a demand for recognition of women as equals within the institution of marriage and in society generally.

In light of the goal of liberty as non-domination, I have argued that the symbolism of naming women promotes, as natural, the induction of all women, qua wives-to-be, into the role of a subordinate subjectivity called "wifehood." This gender system of spousal ordering is connected to the symbolism of naming children, which likewise defends, as natural, the appropriation of women's procreative labour by fathers. Both these aspects of naming act to strengthen the public recognition of male citizens as the main protagonists within the family by encouraging women to "choose" a public voice and subjectivity that references and brings honour to their husband's personhood, all the while effacing their own (often more significant) activities and contributions in terms of caregiving and unpaid procreative labour within the family and society. The issue of naming wives and children (in Canada) and of naming children (in Québec) continues to be highly contested. It exposes the arbitrary, and indeed undemocratic, forces that work to confer social recognition and power to male subjectivities through patriarchal gender systems that discursively define the norms of womanhood, the family, and citizenship.

I have argued that the perpetuation of patriarchal and patrilineal "name games" is not benign: rather, it announces a modern form of "customary" coverture, one that neoliberal discourse justifies as the apolitical, private choice of women. These state-sponsored, neo-patriarchal discourses and practices turn a blind eye to the contemptuous ways that women's democratic rights and freedoms are actively violated in contemporary times through legal precedents (*Trociuk,* 2003) that work to restore the primacy of fathers' rights over mother's rights.[5] The persistence of a legal framework that tolerates the private coercion of women, and the creation of new legal precedents that make women's citizenship rights *residual* to those enjoyed by male citizens, suggests that we have yet to fully implement the democratic principles that we as a society purport to defend, most notably in those instances when the rights of female and male citizens conflict.

Further research is required on the gendered politics of women's and children's names, and their complex relationships to neo-patriarchal, racist, and neo-colonial governance practices. This discussion has sought to explore several of the faces of this complex issue. I have argued for the usefulness, to feminists, of the concept of liberty as a democratic tool worth repatriating from malestream republican thought in the struggle to challenge impoverished notions of liberty as non-interference. The discursive power of liberty as non-domination may serve to advance the goals of progressive social movements as against neoliberal, neo-conservative, or so-called post-feminist discourses that aim to insulate, through privatization (state non-interference), the relations of domination sustaining patriarchal conceptions of marriage and family, and that wish to restore the primacy of the married heterosexual father/head of household as the basic unit of contemporary Canadian citizenship. Signalling a desire for a return to premodern and, indeed, authoritarian relations within the family, not only do these contemporary Canadian discourses and legal frameworks fly in the face of *constitutional* guarantees enshrined in the Charter of Rights and Freedoms, but they make a mockery of the ideal of democratic self-government itself by arbitrarily denying and limiting female citizens' practical enjoyment of equality, dignity, and liberty as non-domination.

12
Gendering Nation-States and/or Gendering City-States: Debates about the Nature of Citizenship

Caroline Andrew

The objective of this chapter is to discuss the gendering of the city-state as a part of, and at the same time an alternative to, gendering the nation-state. This chapter therefore engages with the debates about the nature of citizenship in the present day and the contribution made by feminist politics and feminist theorizing to these debates. Specifically, by considering developments in several Canadian cities, the discussion treats the relevance of multiple levels of citizenship and particularly the appropriateness of thinking about women's urban citizenship as one of the significant levels of citizenship in contemporary Canada.

These reflections are based on the observation of the political practices of women at the urban level, on the writings of feminist theorists of citizenship, and on the abundant recent literature on scalar politics, often referred to as the "rescaling" literature. In this way the chapter contributes to the main theme of this book – the importance of feminist theory and feminist politics to thinking about state processes, the nation-state, and citizenship.

The argument put forward here is that it is illuminating, and therefore useful, to think of urban citizenship, and that women are central to this understanding. Urban citizenship is linked to a politics of everyday life and to demands for services, programs, and rights that facilitate the complex lives of urban residents, particularly women, in negotiating the interfaces of public and private spheres as they connect paid employment, use of urban services, and family life. The assertion is not that cities or nations are not gendered but rather that their nature can be better understood by an explicit recognition and rendering visible of the connection between the roles played by women in city-states and the ways in which these urban centres function. In order to make its case, the chapter will look first at the rescaling literature and then discuss the conditions for thinking about urban citizenship. It will complete its argument by examining, in some detail, two examples of feminist political practices in Ottawa.[1]

Urban Citizenship and the Rescaling Literature

As the title of this chapter suggests, urban citizenship is both part of gendering the nation-state and an alternative to it. The dual role played by urban citizenship as both separate from and part of the nation-state can be understood from the analyses of the impact of globalization on the scales of political action and the ensuing debates as to the conditions of coexistence of different scales of political action. The literature on rescaling, or on the reconfiguration of scales of political action set in motion by the pressures of globalization, is useful to our understanding of the emerging level of the urban. Before the idea of women's urban citizenship is developed, however, it is important to look at the ways in which the rescaling literature understands shifts in political action.

The rescaling literature is in part a reaction to the dichotomous nature of studies on the impact of globalization: on one hand, these studies emphasize the power of transnational economic forces to reduce if not eliminate the authority of the nation-state; on the other, they stress the flourishing of local identity-based politics. "Yet," as Richard Howitt (2003: 139) puts it, "like all binaries, this one has its limits. Conflating the global/economic/ general and contrasting it with the local/cultural/specific obscures important dimensions that an alternative approach to scale might bring to critical geographical analysis, and responses built from it."

The rescaling literature attempts, in a variety of ways, to understand the manner in which the multiplicity of scales of political action emerge, operate, and interrelate. As Sally Randles and Peter Dicken (2004: 2012) note, "In fact there now exists among scale theorists remarkable consensus that scale is not a pregiven, taken-for-granted set of relationships but that it is constructed: produced by human interaction as both outcome and process of social relations occurring through space."

Sallie Marston's (2000: 237) important contribution to the rescaling literature was to argue for the consideration of social reproduction and therefore the inclusion of the scale of the household and "the home not as a private space, but as a unique form of public space." Following Marston's argument, scholars have also focused on the body as a significant political scale (see, in particular, Mills, 2005; Gabriel, 2005; and Willis, 2005).

Scalar analyses have also argued for the urban, regional, national, and global, as in the work of Neil Smith, or for the world economy, nation-state, and locality, as in that of Peter J. Taylor (Howitt, 2003: 139). Definitions of the various scales are fluid and numerous: at times the urban is co-terminous with the regional; at other times the word refers to centre-city activity (Brenner, 2004). In part, the variety of definitions springs from the paradox described by Howitt (2003: 151) – the "efforts to theorize scale in some way that divorces it from its geographical context" – but it also arises from the

desire to analyze scale as relational and as a "product of processes of negotiation and compromise" (Randles and Dicken, 2004: 2012).

This emphasis on the political, and conflictual, dimensions of scale has
led to conceptualizations of "jumping scale" and of "spaces of engagement
and the politics of scale." Neil Smith (1993) first described jumping scale as
a strategy of moving political issues upwards towards scales of political action seen to be more conducive to solutions. Since then, however, other
authors have applied the term to a variety of strategies by state and non-
state actors to move in all directions from one scale to another. The concept
of "spaces of engagement" (Cox, 1998) captures the same political processes
in ways that give less emphasis to individual actors or individual strategies
and more to the spaces in which the relations of power work themselves out.

In the rescaling debates, urban spaces are seen as central scales of political
action (Brenner, 2004; Marston, 2000), through both their economic and
cultural significance. The economic leadership of the large urban centres as
drivers of the global economy is coupled with their cultural centrality. It is for
this reason that the rescaling literature leads to theorizing urban citizenship.

At the same time, the rescaling debates have emphasized the importance
of recognizing the variability of specific circumstances. Globalization does
not create a universal set of political scales. The scales that are pertinent at
any one time and in a specific context relate to decisions being made by
state and civil society actors. There are structural conditions that impact on
the choice of scales, but there are also strategic decisions on the part of
actors, both state and non-state. The conclusion is that one must examine
specific cases in order to understand what levels of political action are central, for whom, and in what context.

To develop this example somewhat more concretely, one can look at the
scales of political action as they relate to the most recent urban demographic
development: the creation of a few large city-regions in Canada. Immigration and urbanization are creating city-regions, and an increasing number
of Canadians live in the largest metropolitan areas.

According to the 2001 census, 79.6 percent of Canada's nearly 30 million
inhabitants live in urban areas (Anderssen and Valpy, 2004: 288). The census definition of "urban" is very broad, covering all localities of more than
a thousand people. If only the largest urban centres are taken into account,
approximately 43 percent of the total population lives in Toronto (6,640,475
people, with the region defined as the extended Golden Horseshoe, which
stretches from Niagara Falls to Oshawa along the Great Lakes and north to
Barrie), Montreal (3,630,585 people in Montreal and surrounding area), and
the Vancouver area (2,635,380 people). If Ottawa-Gatineau, with a million
people, is added as the fourth-largest urban region, the figure rises to about
47 percent, or nearly half the total population of Canada.

Because these regions increasingly drive the Canadian economy, their problems – inadequate infrastructure, traffic congestion, housing shortages – are seen by policy-makers as constraints on economic development. This view has produced contradictory pressures. Both Ottawa and the provinces wish to eliminate what they see as impediments to economic growth; at the same time, however, both desire to offload some of their responsibilities to other levels of government, thus solving their own fiscal problems. These decentralization attempts – from Ottawa to the provinces, from the provincial to the municipal governments, and from the federal, provincial, and municipal governments to civil society – have not been accompanied by adequate financial compensation. The specific impact of these state decentralization processes on women, and particularly on groups of women doubly marginalized through poverty and racialization, has been analyzed in the Canadian context by Gerda Wekerle (2000) and Caroline Andrew (2003).

These pressures led to initiatives, particularly linked to decentralization, by state actors and had an impact on the opening up and strengthening of regional and local scales. For example, the Ontario government created regional health districts, and the Quebec government established regional development councils. At the same time, as Dominique Masson (2005) has shown in the case of Quebec, these initiatives in turn create strategic possibilities for social movement actors who can choose to invest in the new scale or to ignore it. Masson's research on the role of women's groups in the construction of a regional scale in Quebec politics gives support to the view that social movement actors do have a capacity to influence the way in which political struggles develop at a particular scale.

The capacity of actors to choose a scale includes the ability to jump scale, to move to a scale felt to be more strategically attractive. Many reasons can prompt actors to take this step: in the new scale, they may be seen as central rather than marginal players; state actors may move to a scale where they can limit (or expand, though this is less frequent in the recent neoliberal period) state activity; social movement actors may choose to operate in a new scale in hopes that the pressure generated there will extend to their regular scale (the "boomerang" strategy). An example of the boomerang strategy occurred when local women's groups in both Montreal and Ottawa used the International Union of Local Authorities' (IULA) Declaration on Women and Local Government, and the endorsement of this by the Federation of Canadian Municipalities, to put pressure on their municipal governments to take action (Andrew, Harewood, Klodawsky, and Willis, 2004: 49).

Thus, the argument is not about choosing one level of citizenship: rather, it is about multiple levels and potential moments in which one scale acquires particular importance, either through state actions, social movement politics, or a combination of the two.

Urban Citizenship and Gendering the City State in Canada

In writing about urban citizenship, James Holston (2001: 326) has elaborated three conditions that define it: "when the city is the primary political community, when urban residence is the criteria of membership and the basis of political mobilization and when rights-claims addressing urban experience and related civic performances are the substance of citizenship."

If we are to relate these three conditions to women, we must first address the definition of political community. In Canada, there is an underlying demographic reality, as was described earlier: Canada is a highly urbanized country with an ever-increasing percentage of the population living in the four largest urban regions of Toronto, Montreal, Vancouver, and Ottawa-Gatineau. More than this, these city-regions distinguish themselves by their ethnocultural diversity. The vast majority of recent immigrants to Canada settle in urban areas. Between 1996 and 2001, approximately 1.2 million immigrants came to Canada; of these, 46.1 percent settled in Toronto, 17.1 percent in Vancouver, and 12.1 percent in Montreal (Anderssen and Valpy, 2004: 290). During the 1996-2001 period, Ottawa-Gatineau followed Toronto and Vancouver as the third-most rapidly diversifying urban area.

However, as Yasmeen Abu-Laban and Judith A. Garber (2005: 547) have pointed out, although the national press does note the concentration of immigrants in the largest urban centres, "there is relatively little discussion of the role of cities" in its analysis of the 2001 census. Looking more seriously at the role of cities would have entailed examining municipal governments that can, and in some cases do, play significant roles in the integration of immigrants (Wong, 2004: 158). Indeed, the recent federal-Ontario agreement on immigrant settlement explicitly recognizes the role of municipalities in this process.

Women, particularly immigrant women, experience the urban reality in an especially intense fashion, as it is they who are largely responsible for knitting together public and private, family and school, neighbourhood and community. The research done on women's experience of immigration by Damaris Rose, Johanne Charbonneau, and Brian Ray underlines the very crucial role played by women in the processes of urban integration (Ray and Rose, 2000).

Although I would not go so far as to claim the city as *the* primary political community for immigrants, the urban is nonetheless strongly linked with immigrant and refugee women. This link is in part conflictual, one of struggle – a struggle to make ends meet, to negotiate the successful entry of family members into the new society, to make claims for services, and to develop the sense of entitlement necessary to confidently make such claims. But at the same time, it is a link of identity, a creation of new opportunities and new solidarities, even if initially it often exists between people, and within organizations, who belong to the same communities.

Indeed, for women the city has often represented a place of increased personal liberty. It meant the opportunity to leave social environments that were typically more dominated by traditional views and practices related to the place of women. Carolyn Strange (1995) discusses the movement of young women from the Ontario countryside to Toronto in the early twentieth century and the opportunities this represented. These opportunities included paid employment (even at low wages and in bad working conditions) but also greater choices about the use of free time. In the same vein, Elizabeth Wilson's *The Sphinx in the City* (1981) posits that women have been more at ease than men in the complexity and disorder of the city, that this has given them greater freedom to build their own paths through the interfaces of public and private, of home, employment, and services, of doing, creating, or buying services, of acting individually, as part of a family, as part of a neighbourhood, or as part of a group. Wilson's thesis is that urban planning has often involved the attempts of men to organize and control women precisely because women have profited from and enjoyed the creative chaos of urban spaces.

An additional argument about the importance of cities for women, and one specifically linked to municipal governments, is that many services that impact in a very significant way on the lives of women are the subject of municipal decisions. One of the most central is public transportation, a crucial service in terms of city life generally but one particularly significant for women. Studies (see, for example, Villeneuve, Frohn, and Trudelle, 2002-03: 366; Miller, 2000: 184-85) indicate that women use public transit more than men, and, as this use is linked to their lower incomes, poorer women use the service all the more frequently. The importance accorded to the development of public transport will therefore affect the lives of women, as will certain policy details concerning the ways in which the transit system functions. For example, many public transport systems in Canadian cities have initiated policies that allow passengers, in some cases only women, to exit a bus at a non-scheduled stop during the evening hours when it is dark. This policy is clearly advantageous to women, who may experience a sense of insecurity at night and who may limit their evening activities if they feel that their paths to and from the activities are potentially unsafe. However, even when such initiatives are in place, questions can arise concerning the extent to which the public is aware of them and how well they are applied in practice. To illustrate, I cite the following example from a project to which we will return below: Approximately 160 women participated in focus groups as part of the Working Group on Women's Access to Municipal Services in Ottawa. Although all indicated that they used Ottawa's bus system, only a tiny minority knew that they could ask to be let off between stops in the evening. Subsequent discussions with students at the University of Ottawa

confirmed the inadequacy of the information regarding the city's disembarkation policy. In addition, students who knew of the policy cited numerous
examples of when drivers had refused to follow it. Clearly, municipal government decisions concerning the overall resources and planning dedicated
to public transit are of vital importance to urban citizens; but so too are
those regarding the ways in which initiatives are advertised and implemented.

Public transport is not the only area of municipal decision making that is
central to women's lives. Zoning and urban planning decisions directly influence the relationship of residence to employment and of residence to
services. As studies have shown, women are more likely than men to seek
employment near their homes (in order to attempt to reconcile work and
family obligations) (Pratt and Hanson, 1991). Thus, mixed-use zones would
be more advantageous to women than the single-use segmented zones that
are typical of twentieth-century Canadian and American cities. Although it
dates from the 1960s, Jane Jacobs' *The Death and Life of Great American Cities*
(1961) remains essential reading on the advantages of mixed-use neighbourhoods for creating supportive environments in which work and family can
be reconciled. Because women are still the principal actors in this reconciliation, mixed-use neighbourhoods would greatly benefit them.

In addition, municipal governments deliver services, give grants, and establish agreements with groups in areas that impact on the lives of women
and particularly on those of women who are doubly marginalized, whether
through poverty, racial or ethnic origin, single-mother status, age, or disability. Depending on the municipal system and on the particular traditions of each municipality, these services and programs can vary widely.
Certainly, Toronto's grants to community associations through the program
titled "Breaking the Cycle of Violence" have made a major contribution to
women's groups. The program has funded numerous community-based projects relating to the elimination of violence against women and has been
proactive in funding projects that impact on the full diversity of women. In
addition, municipalities in Ontario have responsibility for daycare programs
and a wide range of social service programs. Therefore, insofar as they relate
to the specific nature of child care and social services, local decisions rather
than provincial ones are of importance to women in Ontario.

Do the dimensions catalogued above add up to the city as a primary political community, as James Holston outlines in his first criterion for urban
citizenship? Answering this question raises the problem of how one is to
proceed. Is a primary political community an entirely subjective entity, one
to be decided by asking people or by listening to their articulations regarding
it? Or are there objective elements relating to links between particular dimensions of political communities and the scales at which issues relating to
these dimensions can be addressed? This last query simply raises a further

question: To which scales should we refer? Should our choice be determined by which scales can best address these dimensions or by which scales the existing political system compels us to select? For example, at the present time, given the saliency of federal-provincial relations in Canadian politics, the municipal level of government is quasi-invisible and therefore almost certainly underestimated as a scale of political activity. In the absence of empirical data on women's declared primary political community, it is not possible to make a final judgment on this point. However, our argument has suggested that the city is a significant political community for women because municipal services significantly impact on the quality of their lives and because of the importance of women as builders of community within cities.

Moving on to the second condition established by Holston, namely, urban residence as a criterion for membership and as the basis of political mobilization, we find some interesting data on the greater acceptance of diversity by women in Canada that bear on the issue of political mobilization. The Centre for Research and Information on Canada (2003) has analyzed 2003 survey data on the acceptance of diversity, and the perception of discrimination, that indicate substantial differences between men and women. Women are far more likely than men to accept diversity and to recognize structural discrimination. On questions that asked whether people were judged on the basis of their ethnic background, women recognized prejudice to a greater extent than men. They were also much more likely (80 percent as compared to 68 percent for men) to recognize that a great deal of racism remains in Canada (6). Extrapolating from this survey, one could argue that women are more attuned to the current character of metropolitan life in Canada and to the characteristics that increasingly define the Canadian urban condition.

Finally, Holston's third criterion, that the substance of urban citizenship involves rights claims that connect with urban experience and civic performance, relates to the earlier point about the importance of urban policies to the daily lives of women. Although federal and provincial policies and decisions certainly influence the daily conditions of urban life, local policies are important here as well. They play a crucial role in the spatialization of activities (either through zoning, planning, or the direct provision and locating of services) and therefore the ways in which homes, jobs, urban services, and public spaces are connected. The connections can be physical, through transportation links, or virtual, through digital and telephone links. Given that women typically shoulder the bulk of domestic responsibilities, the links between various urban activities are particularly important for them. And given the fact that many have low incomes, public policies greatly affect their lives. Public transportation policy is especially important, but those relating to zoning, street lighting, and pedestrian traffic impact in a significant way on women's urban safety and their feelings of security.

Women's Political Practices: Examples from Ottawa

Two action-research projects in Ottawa illustrate Holston's third criterion for urban citizenship. The first was the Working Group on Women's Access to Municipal Services in Ottawa. This was created in 1998 when the then Regional Council of Ottawa-Carleton endorsed the International Union of Local Authorities' (IULA) Declaration on Women and Local Government and, at the same time, agreed to set up the working group in order to study the existing situation (as long as there was no expense to the municipal government). Funding was obtained from Status of Women Canada, and project staff were hired. The project consisted of conducting focus groups with women regarding their experiences of accessing municipal services. The focus groups, which were representative of the diversity of the female population, included immigrant and refugee women, women in emergency housing, elderly women, caregivers, and young women of immigrant families. Approximately 160 women took part in the focus groups, and the results illustrated the importance of municipal services for facilitating the complex interactions of home, work, and services in their lives. The focus group material illustrated two central points: first, inclusive public services can form the basis for a sense of participation and belonging; and second, the demands for improvements to these services were based on claims to equality on the grounds of gender, ethnocultural identity, age, immigration status, language, ability, and, importantly, the intersections of these. Women argued that information about city services should be disseminated through channels that they and other women used, and that it should be available in a variety of languages. Key city services should be easily accessible via public transit, and, wherever possible, should be located near each other so as to reduce travel time. The various types of urban services, and the ways in which these come together to influence women's urban experience, are central to the network of rights and responsibilities that form the substance of citizenship.

More specifically, the focus groups agreed that good information about the availability of services was important, that it should relate to women's lives, and that it should build on community networks. Another critical point was that the connections between public transit and essential city services should be improved. Criss-crossing the city in search of inconveniently situated services or, as was often the case, services whose locations revealed that accessibility for those dependent on public transit had never been taken into account, particularly disadvantaged women with small children.

The second project, the City for All Women Initiative, built on the first but focused more on civic performance. It too was funded by Status of Women Canada and also by the Trillium Foundation, as a partnership between the City of Ottawa, community-based women's groups, and representatives from the women's studies programs of Carleton University and the University of Ottawa. An initial survey of community-based women's groups in 2004 clearly indicated that training, and particularly training regarding how to have an impact on city hall, was felt to be needed. Thus, a first training session was organized that combined basic facts about municipal government structure with detailed information about techniques for making one's opinions known, including meetings with elected representatives and presenting briefs to committees. The initiative's time period coincided with that of local budget discussions in Ottawa. Deciding to participate in them, the women worked in small groups, with mentors, to prepare proposals for presentation to individual elected representatives and council committees.

The training was organized to provide information and develop skills but was also intended to build confidence and create a sense of group solidarity. In terms of ethnocultural origins, language, and age, the group was very diverse, and thus the training sessions were carefully structured to build solidarity around the respect for and celebration of diversity. The group motto was "Our opinions matter," and the sessions empowered the women to articulate their demands, based on the conditions of urban life and the perceived gaps in the city's capacity and/or willingness to meet their needs. The participants defined their needs in terms of the intersections of gender, ethnocultural identity, and family status; for the most part, they saw themselves as members of an ethnocultural community, as women, and, very often, as mothers. They worried about their children, their community, the women in their community, marginalized women and children in general, and, very specifically, the other participants in the project. They did articulate rights claims, basing these on their perception of the gaps between the level of services offered and that required for them to deal with the complexities of urban life and the successful integration of their families and their communities within the larger community of Ottawa.

In February 2005, the group presented a brief to the municipal council during the council's final hearings on the budget. It made an impressive presentation, due both to its visible diversity and its substantive content. The presentation began with a song composed by one of the women; in it, the group expressed its hope that the council members would listen but added that, if they did not, the group and the communities and organizations it represented would remember this at the next municipal election. This theme clearly resonated with the idea of rights based on the intersections of gender, ethnocultural identity, language, and age. Next, two group spokeswomen made representations in favour of reinstating the community grants program for the 2005 Ottawa city budget and against increases in fees for services. The arguments regarding the latter were eloquent testimony to the impact, for marginalized families and individuals, of such increases: raising the fees for recreational programs impedes the integration of children; increasing those for transit heightens the isolation of vulnerable community members. The group's demands were grounded in its desire for inclusion and participation in the community, and in its sense that because the city was required to treat all sectors of the population in an equitable fashion, it too was entitled to receive city services. The importance of these services to the lives of the women provides an illustration of Holston's argument about urban citizenship: the rights claims were related to civic performance and were based on a sense of entitlement to equitable treatment as participating citizens.

Clearly, a base exists for thinking about women's urban citizenship and therefore about gendering the city-state. This base builds on women's improved economic opportunities in urban areas, on their enhanced liberty in cities, on Canada's urban character and the growing difference between the increasingly diverse metropolitan areas and non-metropolitan Canada, on the greater recognition by women of structural discrimination combined with their greater support for diversity, and, finally, on the wide variety of urban policies in which gender is clearly relevant. The platform for considering women's urban citizenship also forms the base to argue for gendering the city-state as, if urban services are important to women's lives, being clearer about this and working to increase the quality of the services can only improve them.

This is particularly true for the intersections of gender, ethnocultural identity, immigration status, class, and age. Indeed, when we turn to the question of gendering the city-state as an alternative strategy to that of gendering the nation-state, the question on intersectionality is central. One can argue that creating political spaces that will be inclusive and equitable for the full diversity of women is more possible in Canada's cities than across the country or within a province or region. This is not to say that the national and provincial levels of government are irrelevant to the construction of an egalitarian politics, as, clearly, Ottawa and the provinces are responsible for areas that can set broad policies with important redistributive effects. But the municipal level in the large urban areas of Canada has two significant characteristics: first, due to the demographic importance of urban women, the political weight of groups representing their full diversity will be greater at this level; and second, the policy areas of municipal government can shape a whole range of dimensions of daily life that can be sensitive to the intersections of gender and ethnocultural diversity.

Municipal policies deal at a clearly "micro" level and can therefore be attuned to the intersections of diversity. For example, community grant programs can specifically accord priority to single mothers, Aboriginal-initiated projects, women, low-income residents, recent immigrant groups, and so on. These policies impact on women's lives because of the importance of urban services to the daily lives of women, and particularly because of the potential for political mobilization around the pivotal intersections of race, class, and gender, as illustrated by the City for All Women Initiative in Ottawa. Indeed, one can point to initiatives emerging across the major cities in Canada. Toronto is in the process of setting up a Working Group on the Status of Women and Gender Equity and Montreal has recently created a Council of Montreal Women (le Conseil des montréalaises). Vancouver had a Women's Task Force and the City Council has approved a Gender Equality Policy and a Gender Equality Action Plan but this was cancelled by the next municipal council. In all these cases, intersectionality is central. It is true that these initiatives are emerging after periods of cutbacks to municipal activities relating to women, and that progress in gendering city-states has clearly not been linear in Canada (Whitzman, 2002). The development of these initiatives is related to a variety of factors. These include the strength and unity of political mobilization from civil society, the existence of sympathetic elected representatives and of allies within the bureaucracy, the links to pertinent research, and the fiscal situation of the municipality.

However, the question remains regarding the compatibility of strategies aimed at gendering the city-state and the nation-state. That there are interesting possibilities for gendering the city-state does not necessarily eliminate the potential for gendering the nation-state; indeed, our earlier assertion that redistributive policies are important at the level of the nation-state argues for the compatibility of actions at different levels. This brings us back to the literature of rescaling and to the multiplicity of scales of political action. Strategies of jumping scale can also be multiple: community-based women's groups can use federal funding to mobilize locally; federal interest in the recognition of foreign credentials can be used to put pressure on municipal governments; and, indeed, global-local strategies offer interesting possibilities for gendering the city-state. There are a wide variety of international examples of gendering urban spaces that can be, and are being, used by Canadian urban gender equity activists (see, for example, Andrew, Harewood, Klodawsky, and Willis, 2004; Federation of Canadian Municipalities, 2004; Women in Cities International, 2004). Participating in international meetings in order to emphasize the importance of local gendering strategies and to increase the international visibility of the local Canadian examples is an urban strategy, using scale jumping to achieve its objectives.

International visibility can increase local visibility and local actors' sense of empowerment.

Conclusion

Gender is a crucial dimension to understanding state processes, be they of the city-state or the nation-state. Feminist practices at the local level have demonstrated the importance of urban policies for the lives of women and of political mobilization on the part of diverse groups of women to pressure for greater equity in the planning and delivery of urban services. Women's urban citizenship represents a significant scale for action relating to the politics of everyday life and the complex interrelations of public and private spaces, of work and family, and of the creation, use, delivery, and purchase of services, as all of these impact on diverse groups of women. This citizenship is one of the scales of political action in the twenty-first century; for the full diversity of women in Canada, it is an increasingly significant one.

Afterword: The Future of Feminism

Judy Rebick

In 1970 Canadian second-wave feminism emerged in its full glory in inter-action with the state through the Royal Commission on the Status of Women and the Abortion Caravan; its subsequent development focused increas-ingly on the state. Thus, it is not surprising that the rise of neoliberalism, or corporate globalization, with its turn away from the social programs so es-sential to feminist organizing, resulted in a serious decline of the women's movement.

Second-wave feminism in Canada may not be dead, but it has lost its influence and visibility for many of the reasons outlined in this excellent collection of essays. Many groups from second-wave feminism still remain and continue to do important work. For example, the recent push for a national child care campaign was led in large part by the same women who began the struggle in the 1960s and continued it through every broken promise. But like all social movements, the women's movement ebbs and flows, and today we are in more of an ebb than a flow.

Many women call themselves third-wave feminists. By "third wave" they mean a set of ideas that they see as quite different from those of the second wave. They are clearer from the outset on the intersection of various forms of domination, class, race, sex, and gender. They focus more on sexuality, although that is probably more a function of youth than of political differ-ence. They have adopted the LGBT (Lesbian, Gay, Bisexual, Transgendered) approach to sexual orientation and see second wavers as transphobic. They are more focused on cultural interventions than on political and social inter-ventions. In many ways, their development reflects the turn away from the state as a site of struggle, as outlined in so many of the chapters in this volume. I think third wavers do some interesting and important work, but they have not yet reached out to a wider layer of women in a way that is required to create a broad social movement.

My generation never called itself second wave. That was just a way for academics to distinguish between the two huge upsurges of women. The first wave won women the vote; the second gained them reproductive, economic, and legal rights. Feminist activism continued between the first and second waves, of course, and it perseveres today, but I don't yet see a mass movement dealing with gender issues. On the other hand, I think the division between generations exists in part because my generation has not made enough space for young women. The world is very different for young women today, and they should be in the lead of defining what a new feminism will look like.

Much conventional wisdom addresses the decline of the women's movement in Canada. Many blame it on identity politics. If feminists had only focused on what united women, they say, instead of on what divided them, the women's movement would have remained strong. It is true that the cross-class alliance of the women's movement was an important part of its power.

That there were a handful of women in positions of authority to promote the feminist agenda was critical to our success. But feminism would have betrayed its vision, and therefore lost its purpose, if it had continued to marginalize the poorest and most oppressed women to favour those more privileged.

In fact, the organizing of women of colour and their insistence that the women's movement belonged to them too breathed new life into a feminism that was co-opted by its own success at the end of the 1980s. As neoliberal globalization increased the gap between rich and poor, the challenge of maintaining a common vision among women became much greater. The global backlash against feminism and, in Canada, the federal state's funding cuts to women's groups made dealing with these difficulties even harder. The women's movement in Canada worked hard to find new ways to unite across differences. Today, the security state and the war on terror are further isolating already marginalized religious minorities and communities of colour.

As a number of chapters in this collection make clear, gender itself is becoming a contested notion under neoliberalism. As Janine Brodie says so eloquently on page 165 of this volume:

> Since then, however, the issue of gender equality has been progressively erased from official policy discourses and practices. This disappearance of gender coincides with the implementation of neoliberal governing practices in Canada and most advanced liberal democracies. Although the scope and degree of neoliberal policy reform vary widely among these states, neoliberalism has greatly influenced the framing of citizenship claims as well as relationships between the state and both the private sector (the economy and civil society) and the private sphere (the individual and the family) (Brodie, 1997; Clarke, 2004b). In the process, we have been submerged in a politics that seeks to reform and transform the irredeemably gendered

subjects of the post-war welfare state into genderless and self-sufficient market actors.

Carol Shields said it more poetically in her book *Unless* (2002: 99, emphasis in original): "*But we've come so far;* that's the thinking. So far compared with fifty or a hundred years ago. Well, no, we've arrived at the new millennium and we haven't 'arrived' at all. We've been sent over to the side pocket of the snooker table and made to disappear."

As gender disappears, and class and race divisions among women grow, it is increasingly difficult for women to self-identify as a group. It was that identification, captured in the phrase "sisterhood is powerful," that was so central to second-wave feminism. Women are still hungry for that identification and gender solidarity, but the ground for it has shifted.

In English Canada, we spent many years struggling with the differences among women. The efforts of marginalized women to be heard in feminism have been central to its development. Young feminists begin with the understanding of difference that took us many years of blood, sweat, and mostly tears to develop. But somehow, in creating a new comprehension of feminism that, in the words of bell hooks (quoted in Lewis, n.d.), embraced the "recognition of difference without attaching privilege to difference," we have stopped seeing what women have in common, feeding into the neoliberal drive to eliminate gender as a category.

The Quebec women's movement evolved quite differently from that of English Canada. The later arrival of neoliberalism in Quebec meant that the women's movement continued to grow and make gains well into the late 1990s, most significantly a truly universal child care program. The social service cuts that so devastated the women's movement in most provinces were not as great in Quebec. On the other hand, the struggles around racism that so defined the women's movement in English Canada in the late '80s and the 1990s have not played out in the same way in Quebec, in part because of the influence of the national question. So the Quebec women's movement has not achieved the diversity of its English-Canadian counterpart. Nevertheless, the more general impact of neoliberalism is also manifest in Quebec.

Despite our differences, women today continue to face common problems. Feminists fought for universal child care and for men to assume their full share of child rearing, but neither battle has yet been won. The reality today is that most women are working longer hours outside the home than they used to but are still taking primary responsibility within it. Whether they are pressured to overwork so as to advance in their profession or whether they are obliged to hold two or three part-time jobs, most women struggle with the crushing burden of paid work combined with the still excessive demands of labour in the home.

Although I agree that we need to regender our understanding of the state, as expressed in many of the chapters in this volume, I also believe that we must revisit the attention to the "private" sphere that was much more pronounced in the early years of the second wave. Women's equality will be possible only in a world that accepts nurturing and caring as important roles for both men and women. Gloria Steinem has said that her generation of feminists made it possible for women to do what men traditionally did; now it is time for the opposite to occur. Men who wish to spend more time with their children and enjoy their lives will be our allies in challenging a society that values career and money alone. Yet such men are still few and far between. Even in countries where government policy encourages men to take parental leave, as Paul Kershaw explains in Chapter 10 of this volume, the uptake is small.

We need a strategy that includes child care, a shorter work week, and improved parental leave for both men and women. But most of all, women must decide to stop carrying such an unfair share of the work of society. But as we learned in the second wave, the first step is to speak the name of the problem. In the 1960s, Betty Friedan (1963) spoke about the "problem with no name," thus sparking so much of the original second-wave activism. Today that problem is too much work, too much pressure, too little time. It's a problem that women share with men but suffer from much more. This problem is not about the state but about women's continuing predominance in the private sphere. A different kind of struggle is required, one that focuses much more on education and new kinds of relationships than it does on engaging with the state.

Another continuing and related problem is the intractable hold of men on power. Second-wave feminists put on armour to enter the battlefields created by patriarchy. To challenge the way in which power is practised, we need to challenge the men who hold it. In the 2005 Montreal roundtable to discuss my book about the Canadian women's movement, *Ten Thousand Roses,* journalist and filmmaker Francine Pelletier described the problem of the invisible glass ceiling. She said that although men initially welcome women into the workplace, they subsequently become uncomfortable with their presence and seek to marginalize them. It is difficult to name the problem because the men talk the talk of women's equality. Many young women in the audience nodded their heads in agreement. "It's so confusing," one young woman who works for an NGO told me. "We have strong feminists on our board, so how could our workplace be sexist? But it is. Women in leadership positions are always marginalized."

Both problems come from the fact that my generation of feminists failed to achieve its goal: to overturn the patriarchy. The system of male domination remains intact and is reinforced through male culture in the workplace, in politics, and in still too many families. This culture is not perpetrated solely by men. Many women in positions of power adopt the same methods of control as do their male colleagues. Our notions of leadership, for example, are still very masculinized. And certainly, the fact that so little value is placed on raising children or on caring for family, friends, and community is a sign that though, economically, we have moved radically from the family wage that allowed a male breadwinner to support a woman at home, in cultural terms, we have not moved very far at all.

At the beginning of the second wave, we were openly and actively challenging that male culture, but as our influence increased, we focused more and more on demands for reform and less and less on the deeper cultural and structural changes that would threaten patriarchy. Too many of us accepted a place within the patriarchal structures. In a 2004 interview I conducted with Frances Lankin, now the CEO of Toronto's United Way, she explained what happened to her feminist process once she became a minister in the Bob Rae government:

> I came into government having worked in a consensus model, and we tried to work in government that way. But, I had to move quickly to match the style of that world – very top down, directive, and not consensus oriented. People who knew me didn't understand how I could do it, but I did. I made it work and paid a price for that inside. I've found myself a lot in my life having to work in ways that I don't like. You get a strong training when you work in a male way of doing things, and it sometimes takes over how you are as a person. I sometimes wish I could have worked more in a women's collective and had more balance. I think this is why I've been successful in a man's world.
>
> I take pride in that but not in thinking that I've changed things to make it easier for women coming along. I think there's a lot of work for women to do to change the way in which institutions are run.

The pressure, as described by Lankin, to succeed as a woman in a traditionally male role almost always trumps the desire to change the way things are done to make room for other women. For one thing, all the hegemonic pressures push women in that direction; for another, we have no blueprint of any kind for making changes to deeply engrained hierarchical structures. The more power that resides in an organization, the harder it is to change.

How do we play the game but change the rules? As the poet Audre Lorde (1984: 110) so famously said, "The master's tools will never dismantle the master's house." But neither can we make change exclusively from the outside. The success of the second wave was in its ability to work both inside and outside the system: as some writers have put it, in and against the state. Once you are inside a system, however, the pressure to conform is tremendous.

Feminists of my generation started as kick-ass radicals but were slowly co-opted. Italian philosopher Antonio Gramsci (1971: 389-90) called this hegemony, the way that capitalism maintains its ideological hold.

We need to explore new ways of decision making that entail cooperation rather than domination, inclusion rather than elitism, and new kinds of leadership that involve empowering others rather than aggrandizing ourselves. We tried to do this in the second wave but generally failed. In my view we internalized too many patriarchal ways of operating to successfully create non-hierarchical organizations. Instead, as Jo Freeman states in her brilliant essay "The Tyranny of Structurelessness" (1972-73), we created informal power that was even more inaccessible to marginalized women than the formal structures of power themselves. Today we have the benefit of much more work, both academic and practical, in making decisions differently in realms ranging from popular education to participatory democracy. We know much more about creating egalitarian structures. Speaking truth to power, it turns out, is not enough. We must change the very nature of power.

A lot of young activists, seeing the dangers of co-option and the corruption of the existing political structures, choose to work completely outside of those structures. Young women ask me what I think of the impact of cyber feminism, for example. On the net you can communicate with large numbers of like-minded thinkers, developing ideas, debating issues, and even organizing protests. But unless we find ways to reach out to others who are not hooked into our networks, it is hard for me to see how we will effect change.

The World March of Women defined the priority of today's women's movement as fighting poverty and violence. Dealing with female poverty means dealing with neoliberalism, as several chapters in this collection make clear. With little or no discussion, welfare moms became part of the undeserving poor, and raising children was accorded even less economic and social value that it has had traditionally. When discussing why she should be a feminist, a young university professor recently asked me, "What's in it for me?" When you have access to privilege in a society that is so unequal, what's in it for you is the feeling that you are making a contribution to overcoming that inequity. Many people do see that need when it comes to solidarity with women and men in the developing countries but not so much within their own. The pressure, both financial and emotional, on poor women today is terrible. Racialized poor women or women in the sex trades face even greater marginalization and degradation. The horror that hundreds of Aboriginal women have disappeared, not only from Vancouver's Downtown Eastside but also across the country, illustrates that authorities still consider some women's lives to be dispensable.

Feminist strategies for protecting and empowering women have saved thousands of lives, and attitudes that blamed women for the violence directed against them have changed radically. Yet male violence continues almost unabated, in Canada as elsewhere. Although improving laws and their application is critical, that won't eliminate male violence. A new feminism needs to debate strategies for ending violence against women. My own view is that these discussions must include men. Men have been active in combating male violence through the all-male White Ribbon Campaign. Anti-violence feminists have been quite critical of that campaign, maintaining that it often takes up the space and financing desperately needed by women's groups. It is certainly irritating that when you google "violence against women," the White Ribbon Campaign comes up near the top. However, what I have in mind is not a male group that combats violence but a mixed discussion on the issue.

If we are to end violence against women, we must better understand how masculinization takes place and how it can be changed. From an early age, boys are still socialized to be aggressive, dominating, and competitive. There are few positive male role models in popular education. Boys still learn how to be men from patriarchal and often violent males, such as the heroes of team sports, action movies, and video games. And feminist men have to play a critical role in speaking out for a new masculinity that isn't based on the oppression of women.

Many young women identify as third-wave feminists. I see them as similar to the small group of women in the early and mid-1960s who identified as feminists. Years before the movement arose, women such as Simone de Beauvoir, Betty Friedan, and Doris Anderson were writing about the issues that would spawn it. Similarly, third-wave feminists are redefining feminism in new ways that focus on sexuality, the intersection of various forms of oppression, and the beauty myth. Not surprisingly, some of their ideas are a reaction to the excesses or absences of the generation before. They have also been heavily influenced by the postmodernism that has swept women's studies over the last number of years. To this old socialist feminist, the idea that intervening in strictly cultural arenas can change the world is highly idealistic and problematic. Without addressing the material reality of women, whether work time, child care, or violence, feminism will not find an echo among masses of women.

Nevertheless, sexuality and body image are central issues for feminism today. Several years ago, I had an e-mail conversation with Candice Steenburgen, a third-wave feminist academic, about sex. She told me, "We have no script about what equal sexual relationships look like." Second-wave feminists did challenge the male domination in relationships. However, though some individuals worked through their own relationships, we never really developed an understanding of what a new kind of equal relationship, whether heterosexual or lesbian, could be.

In her recent series about women and sex, Francine Pelletier (2005) reveals an incredibly broad diversity of women's sexual experience. She says that although women appear to have a lot of sexual agency today, you find something else when you dig deeper. She doesn't quite have the words to describe the lingering self-hatred that seems to remain from centuries of oppression and is fuelled by a massive industry designed to make us feel inadequate. We aren't thin enough, sexy enough, beautiful enough. We're too tall, too short, too loud, too quiet, too aggressive, too timid. What has changed is that no one now tells us we are too smart. Instead, the pressure today is to be smart, accomplished, *and* beautiful. And that pressure goes beyond youth with a terrifying explosion of cosmetic surgery.

As second-wave feminism began as a peace movement in Canada with the formation of the formidable Voice of Women (VOW), so peace must remain a central element of feminism. As VOW has always understood, women have the strongest interest in ending war. This is not solely because, increasingly, women and children suffer most from war and because mass rapes have become a generalized instrument of war. It is also because war is a central prop to patriarchy. A world in which women hold equal power with men will be a world in which war is no longer either a method of domination or a method of dispute resolution. And ecofeminism, an important part of the second wave, has taken on even more significance in this day and age. As Sandra Delaronde put it during the 2005 Winnipeg roundtable on *Ten Thousand Roses*, "Second wave feminism was focused on us as women and improving our status vis à vis men. Perhaps third wave feminism is about changing the world" (author's notes).

Indeed, most young feminists are more active in the global justice movement than in the women's movement. As a socialist feminist, I have always understood that women's equality can never be achieved in a capitalist system that is based on entrenched inequality. However, capitalism is not the only system of domination and inequality. The interlocking systems of capitalism, patriarchy, and colonialism produce the inequalities and injustice we seek to correct. Unless we challenge all those systems of domination, we will take two steps backward for every step forward. And the struggle to end this domination involves continuing engagement with the state but not in the almost exclusive focus that came to represent second-wave feminism. The personal is political too.

Notes

Introduction

1 Within Canada, these interventions have included *Changing Methods: Feminists Transforming Practice,* edited by Sandra Burt and Lorraine Code (1995), which takes as its focal point issues of method to show how feminism contributes to innovative research designs and political practice. As well, Isabella Bakker's edited 1996 volume *Rethinking Restructuring: Gender and Change in Canada* brings together chapters dealing with globalization, neoliberalism, and social citizenship. Caroline Andrew and Sanda Rogers' edited volume *Women and the Canadian State/Les femmes et l'état Canadien* (1997) uniquely unites both French- and English-language essays by academics, bureaucrats, and activists to address the Canadian state, focusing on the lessons to be learned from a critical evaluation of the 1970 tabling of the report of the Royal Commission on the Status of Women. The themes of gender, nation, and nationalism are interrogated in the 1998 volume edited by Veronica Strong-Boag et al., *Painting the Maple: Essays on Race, Gender and the Construction of Canada.* In *Malaises identitaires: échanges feministes autour d'un Québec incertain* (1999), editors Diane Lamoureux, Chantal Maillé, and Micheline de Sève examine the ambiguity of the interface between nationalism and feminism in the specific context of Quebec.

L. Pauline Rankin and Jill Vickers' co-written *Women's Movements and State Feminism: Integrating Diversity into Public Policy* (2001) is a policy research paper funded by Status of Women Canada that addresses the integration of diversity into the research, development, and analysis of public policy. As well, *Studies in Political Economy: Developments in Feminism* (2003), edited by Caroline Andrew et al., takes as its focal point the contribution that feminist political economy (and specifically the journal *Studies in Political Economy*) has made to understanding issues of production and reproduction, the workplace and the state, and public policy.

There are also a number of explicitly comparative contributions to the field of gender and politics. A very small sampling would include Dorothy McBride Stetson and Amy G. Mazur's edited volume *Comparative State Feminism* (1995), which covers a range of advanced capitalist countries, including Canada. More recently, Louise Chappell's 2003 *Gendering Government: Feminist Engagement with the State in Australia and Canada* engages in a sustained, explicit comparison of these two countries in the legal, electoral, parliamentary, and bureaucratic realms – a sweeping endeavour that won the American Political Science Association's 2003 Victoria Schuck Award for the best book in women and politics. As well, in *Gender, Politics and the State* (1998), editors Vicky Randall and Georgina Waylen include chapters that comparatively examine issues relating to gender and political organization in Britain, Ireland, Russia, China, and countries of Latin America. Editors Susan Baker and Anneke van Doorne-Huiskes' *Women and Public Policy: The Shifting Boundaries between the Public and Private Spheres* (1999) focuses mainly on public policy and gender in diverse locales, including Canada. Sylvia Bashevkin's *Welfare Hot Buttons* (2002) addresses the way social policy reform, and attention to child care issues and gender, has negatively impacted women in Britain, Canada, and the United States despite the rhetoric of "socially progressive" politicians. *Mainstreaming Gender, Democratizing the State?*, edited by Shirin M. Rai (2003), addresses a number of countries, including Canada, on how gender equality is or is not enhanced within state bureaucracies and public policies. Additionally, constitutions have also been a site of focus, such as in Alexandra Dobrowolsky and Vivien Hart's edited *Women Making Constitutions: New Politics and Comparative Perspectives* (2003), which examines gender and other forms of diversity in countries of the global South and North (including Canada), with a focus on constitutional change. Finally, Vanaja Dhruvarajan and Jill Vickers' edited work *Gender, Race and Nation: A Global Perspective* (2002) deals with issues of race and nation in Canada and internationally with an eye towards challenging the assumed homogeneity of the category "women" in both local and international contexts.

Chapter 1: Gendering the Hyphen
This chapter draws on a thirty-country study funded by the Social Sciences and Humanities Research Council of Canada. I wish to acknowledge the assistance of Judit Fabian and the advice of Professors Micheline de Sève and Pauline Rankin. For case details, please visit http://www.carleton.ca/genderandnation/.

1 I use "gender/nation" to draw attention to the interactive nature of relations between sex/gender regimes and national phenomena. Just as "gender" shapes "nation," so also nation shapes "gender."

2 Women in internal minority nations and in marginal Euro-American states such as Finland experienced positive gender/nation relationships. For example, Finnish women were well organized before they joined the struggle for independence from Russia. They gained the right to vote and run for office before Finland achieved independence. By 1907, a year after the new state was founded, they constituted 10 percent of the legislative representatives; in the early years of this century, their numbers rose to 38 percent. By contrast, the 10 percent threshold was not achieved in the United States until 1992 (Vickers, 2006a, 2006b).

3 For example, in some countries in the Middle East, the bodily features of sex are the main factors in sex/gender regimes, although discursive constructions are also involved. In Western societies, however, gender is increasingly multiple and performative in ways largely irrelevant to a Saudi woman who is still denied the right to vote or drive because she has a uterus. Therefore, the extent to which sex, as opposed to gender, marks specific regimes is variable and changes over time in each country – hence sex/gender regimes.

4 The conflict is explored in detail in Anthony D. Smith, *Nationalism and Modernism* (1998).

5 They are distinct from "tribes," which are based on kinship or blood ties.

6 It is important to stress that what is signified by "the West" varies. Empirically, gender/nation experiences varied between Western states (UK, US, France, Holland) and marginal Euro-American states (Finland, Norway, Canada).

7 "Feministas" is a term women in the Philippines have used since the nineteenth century to identify those working to change the status of women.

8 Although it is common to distinguish between liberal and republican theories of citizenship, the first-wave nation-states shared many elements of state design, and the state's role vis-à-vis capitalism and private property produced a common liberalism. Spain, Portugal, and Russia developed empires, but not, until recently, modern liberal-capitalist societies.

9 The dynamics in marginal Western countries, which often resulted in positive gender/nation experiences, are similar to those in modernizing anti-colonial national movements. Hroch (1993) asserts that in the (first-wave, original) dominant or "large" countries, nationhood was constituted through bourgeois struggles against their own aristocracy. It was in this "bourgeois revolution" that the private family was separated from the public sphere and women were excluded from active citizenship. This model of institutionalized, private patriarchy was imitated in (or imposed on) many countries. In many "small" European nations, including Norway, the Czech Republic, Finland, Estonia, and Slovakia, by contrast, nationhood developed through struggles against the domination of the large first-wave nation-states.

10 Talcott Parson's functionalism was built into the "civic culture" concept and used by social scientists to "explain" male dominance in Western democracies. Carol Pateman tracks the phenomenon in her essay "The Civic Culture" (1980). Feminist historians believe the eighteenth and nineteenth centuries saw a redefinition of the family, in which privileged women came to be understood as virtuous citizen-mothers or republican-mothers. Despite this extensive literature, modernist social science explains (privileged) women's confinement to the family in functional terms. Political scientists see this redefinition as part of the changing ideological legitimization (by both men and women) of women's forced exclusion from the public sphere, rights, and control of property (Vickers, 2006a).

11 In her famous "Remember the Ladies" letter to her husband, future US president John Adams, Abigail Adams noted that the private patriarchy in eighteenth-century America and Britain gave women no civil rights, leaving them without protection from tyrannical husbands. Although she did not mention suffrage, property rights, or legal equality in her (often misunderstood) petition to him as a founding father, she explicitly advocated for legal recourse against physical violence. Protection against physical abuse was not established in the new nation-state; but her petition reveals that the state did not provide security for women, especially not from their domestic partners. If women could not rely on states for security, in what sense were they citizens? See Edith B. Gelles (2002: 16-18).

12 Non-modernist explanations of nations and nationalisms offer little more insight about gender. Primordialists such as Pierre van den Berghe (1978, 1979) see nations as natural and derived from the "primordial" attributes of basic social and cultural phenomena, including kinship, religion, language, and ethnicity. Primordialists also see male dominance as natural. Perennialists such as Connor (1994) see national phenomena as long-term elements of historical development derived from ethnic ties, myths of origin, and familial metaphors, but most ignore gender. Much feminist scholarship, postmodern in its approach, employs deconstruction as its basic method, eschewing the possibility of causal theory. For example, Nira Yuval-Davis (1997) focuses on the current fragmentation of national identities. Ethno-symbolists concentrate on "the symbolic legacy of ethnic identities" of particular nations and on how nationalism works by reinterpreting symbols, myths, memories, and values to create new symbolic scripts for modern use (Anthony D. Smith, 1998: 223-25). Except for feminist postmodern accounts, therefore, those of non-modernists, like their modernist counterparts, ignore gender/nation experiences and diversity.

13 The reasons given for this exclusion centred on the belief that women's nature is sexual, nurturing, and emotional (Rousseau), or that the citizen-mother/republican-mother serves better at home, transmitting national culture (Locke, Jefferson, Montesquieu). Although less affluent women were economically active outside their homes, they lacked economic power because of their husbands' legal right to their wages and their inability to own property.

14 Globalization pushes nation-states to put in place modern laws and guarantees regarding the economy, including security of property rights and contracts. It has less impact on women's lives, however, especially regarding women's physical security or personal status laws. Feminization of the workforce (Kelly, Bayes, and Young, 2001) draws more women into the economy but without necessarily improving their security or their civil rights. Consequently, women are most often losers in relation to globalization.

15 Kumari Jayawardena (1986), Lois West (1997), and Sylvia Walby (1997) are among the few feminist authors who reject this thesis. Walby argues that though men and women may relate to different national projects, they may also relate differently to the same project.

16 What most Western women consider "feminist" reflects a modernist ideal including individualism, anti-natalism, universalism, secularism, pacifism, and the valorizing of public over domestic, especially as a site for politics (Dhruvarajan and Vickers, 2002). Women affiliated with their communities are not deemed "feminist."

17 We should not assume, however, that all anti-modern nationalisms are hostile to all of women's goals, including feminist goals. Mohandas K. Gandhi (1942) combined an anti-modern form of nationalism with a significant commitment to improving the status of women.

18 According to Merry Weisner (2000: 295), when early *nation*-states first emerged, the house-hold still "was widely regarded as part of the public realm," and women were seen as having public duties "even if they were not oath-swearing citizens." By the nineteenth century, however, the household in the West was seen as part of the private realm, through the privatization of the family under liberal ideology and the removal of many economic activities to the market.

19 In Vickers (2006a), I show how engagement with nationalism made it possible for women in Finland and Norway to make their nation-states more women-friendly. The text is posted on the project website.

Chapter 2: Gender and Nation in the Soviet/Russian Transformation

I thank Yasmeen Abu-Laban, Janet E. Johnson, Tatiana Zhurzhenko, and two anonymous reviewers for their helpful comments on an earlier draft of this chapter. I acknowledge the financial support of the Social Sciences and Humanities Research Council of Canada during the writing of this chapter.

1 The term "transition," as used in academic and policy circles, assumes a linear progression from state socialist economic and political structures to capitalism and liberal democracy through radical reforms. I use "transition" when referring to that specific meaning of the term. Otherwise I use the word "transformation" to capture the complexities of a process characterized by both continuity linked to the state socialist legacy and change resulting from neoliberal restructuring.

2 I use "patriarchal" to describe the emphasis in late Soviet and post-Soviet gender ideology on the need for women to pursue their "natural" role as mothers and for men to reassert their status in the public and private spheres.

3 To put this into context, Slavs made up 72.78 percent of the total population, according to the 1979 census (Rakowska-Harmstone, 1990: 88).

4 This perception of the West erases the diversity of family forms that exists in Western countries.

5 The Communist and Agrarian Parties together received about 20 percent of the votes, and Vladimir Zhirinovsky's fascist party won almost 23 percent (the largest number of any single party) (Urban and Gel'man, 1997: 193).

6 The Russian population has been declining since 1992. From 1988 to 1994, there was a reduction in births by two-thirds (Field, 2000: 13). Mortality has risen from 11.3 percent per 1,000 in 1985 to 15.4 percent per 1,000 in 1995 (16). Life expectancy among men dropped from 63.8 years in 1991 to 57.6 in 1995, and among women from 74.3 in 1991 to 71.2 in 1995 (Tikhomirov, 2000: 168).

7 For a more detailed gendered analysis of the Chechen wars, see Maya Eichler (2006).

Chapter 5: Feminist Ideals versus Bureaucratic Norms

1 Representatives from four women's groups and three legal organizations participated in the search conference. Two additional participants represented legal organizations working in the area of women's issues.

2 The commission did not advertise to recruit researchers from the outside. Rather, it approached experts identified through word-of-mouth recommendations.

3 Stephen P. Hoffert (1997: 1) defines meta-analysis as "a statistical method of quantitatively combining and synthesising results from individual studies."

Chapter 6: Framing Feminists

My thanks to David Laycock for his generous assistance with this chapter, as well as to Yasmeen Abu-Laban, Donley Studlar, and Linda Trimble. An earlier version appeared as "Populism and Public Choice in Australia and Canada: Turning Equality-Seekers into 'Special Interests,'" in *Us and Them: Anti-elitism in Australia,* ed. Marian Sawer and Barry Hindess (Perth: API Network, 2004).

1 Senator the Honourable Ian Campbell, interview on ABC Radio, 14 October 2005.

2 Francophone Canada has been more resistant to the discursive shifts described and analyzed here.

3   Audit of the *Australian*'s Opinion page undertaken by Gillian Evans, Political Science Program, RSSS, ANU, March 2005.
4   The federal director of the Australian Liberal Party, Brian Loughnane, was seconded as an adviser to Harper's campaign. The Australian Liberal Party had found this discourse so effective that for a brief period in 2000 it even issued a magazine called the *Mainstream.*

Chapter 7: Women's Rights and Religious Opposition

1   A number of states, including Ireland and Nigeria, have signed and ratified the treaty. Others, such as Kuwait, Oman, Sudan, the Syrian Arab Republic, and the United Arab Emirates, have taken the initial step of signing but not ratifying the statute, which means that it has no effect on their national laws. Other states, including Guatemala and Libya, have neither signed nor ratified the treaty. Although the US did not officially engage in the debates around gender, many US-based NGOs did. The official US position on the ICC has been extraordinary. After the Clinton administration signed on to the Rome Statute, the incoming Bush government withdrew US support and has remained strongly opposed to the court. Its hostility to the court has been such that since 2002, it has instigated forty bilateral immunity agreements (BIAs) with ICC-ratifying states to exclude US citizens and military personnel from the jurisdiction of the court when they are in the territory of these states. In many instances, such agreements were prefaced by threats that US aid to the ratifying state would cease if it failed to comply (for full details, see Coalition for the ICC, n.d.).
2   In other words, crimes committed by a national of a state party on the territory of a state that is not a party to the statute are also subject to the court's rules.
3   This latter category, yet to be defined under international law, will not come under the jurisdiction of the court until state parties to the ICC can agree on its meaning.
4   The full titles of these treaties are *The Convention of the Prevention and Punishment of the Crime of Genocide*, 9 December 1948, 78 UNTS 277; *Geneva Conventions I-IV*, 12 August 1949, and the *Protocol I and II to the Geneva Conventions of 12 August 1949*, June 1977; and *Convention against Torture and Other Cruel, Inhuman or Degrading Treatment or Punishment*, 10 December 1984, 1465 UNTS 85.
5   These states included, among others, the United Arab Emirates, Libya, Oman, Sudan, Lebanon, and Bahrain.
6   Canada is an exception here: in 1993 it became the first nation to accept sex-based persecution as a basis for claiming refugee status under its Immigration Review Board guidelines.

Chapter 8: Putting Gender Back In

The research for this chapter was supported by the Canada Research Chair Program in which I hold a Tier 1 Canada Research Chair in Political Economy and Social Governance. I would like to thank Yasmeen Abu-Laban, Lois Harder, and Malinda Smith for their helpful comments, and Michelle Brady and Victoria Miernicki for their research assistance.

Chapter 9: Citizenship in the Era of "New Social Risks"

This research was supported by a strategic grant from the Social Sciences and Humanities Research Council of Canada.

1   One of the striking differences that emerges from a comparison of the EU and Canada is that the EU has taken up – indeed, innovated in – many of the principles of the social investment perspective without completely sidelining the discourse of gender equality.
2   The citizenship-regime concept was developed in Jane Jenson and Susan D. Phillips (1996). It has also been used in, for example, Jane Jenson and Martin Papillon (2000), Deborah Yashar (1999), and Martin Papillon and Luc Turgeon (2003), among others.
3   Sylvia Bashevkin (1994) describes how in the 1980s the pan-Canadian women's movement was in many ways out of phase with those in other Anglo-American democracies that faced neoliberal governments. It continued to make progress on its legislative agenda, despite the rhetoric of neo-conservatism that dominated the government of the day, and was well entrenched in an institutionalized network of state, para-state, and civil society organizations.

4 In *Beyond Continuity,* Wolfgang Streeck and Kathleen Thelen (2005) argue that there are five forms of change; their chapters are organized around examples of each form.

5 This terminology is similar to that used by Gøsta Esping-Andersen (2002) in his report to the Belgian presidency of the EU. However, instead of employing his "welfare triangle" image of state/market/family, we prefer to use that of the "welfare diamond" so as to incorporate community into the state/market/family equation.

6 The change was so evident that Status of Women Canada, the remaining outpost of the "women's state" in Ottawa, issued a call for research reports in 1999 under the title of "Where Have All the Women Gone? Changing Shifts in Policy Discourses" (see, for example, Wiegers, 2002).

7 As a legacy of Mothers' Allowances, social assistance exempted the single mother from seeking employment because it regarded "her function in the home of greater social importance than her economic earnings" (Boychuk, 1998: 37). In Ontario, for example, lone mothers whose children were under sixteen were automatically exempted from all provincial employability programs until 1996. After that year, if their children were aged six or older, they were required to participate in Ontario Works in order to receive social assistance.

8 For the history of these patterns, see Deena White (2003). As Julia O'Connor, Ann S. Orloff, and Sheila Shaver (1999: 43) write, "Typically, liberalism's broader social policy content has been evoked with general references to Titmuss's ... model of residual social policy, in which public policy has a role only when market and family fail."

9 Although many reasons prompted NAC to help lead the forces of opposition, one involved fending off perceived incursions to equality rights won with great difficulty in the 1982 Constitution.

10 REAL stands for Realistic, Equal, and Active for Life. REAL Women is composed of women who support the traditional gender and family roles, and of right-wing, indeed, neoliberal, women opposed to the notion that the state should financially support advocacy groups at all. In particular, REAL Women was highly critical of the Secretary of State's Women's Program, which had become the site within the state for supporting feminism and groups promoting women's rights (Jenson and Phillips, 1996: 122).

11 Because NAC had joined others in excoriating the Meech Lake Accord, describing it as the work of "11 white men in suits," the charges of elitism or of being part of the "chattering classes" could constitute an attempt to discredit it politically.

12 The Old Age Security benefit was created in 1952 to provide a minimum level of income to seniors. In the 1980s it too was clawed back. But very visible opposition from seniors limited the effect, such that 95 percent of them still receive the full benefit. Therefore, analysts tend to describe it as quasi-universal (Boychuk, 2003: 13).

13 The Community Action Program for Children (CAPC) provides funds to community programs that target children who are "at-risk" of developmental delays or who live in poverty, have teen parents, suffer abuse, and so on. Aboriginal Head Start provides cultural education as well as remedial work. Also in 1992 the government announced the Child Development Initiative, centred on conditions of risk that threaten the health and well-being of children, especially the youngest, and set up a Children's Bureau.

14 What would eventually become Campaign 2000 began as the Child Poverty Action Group (CPAG), created in Toronto in 1983. In 1988 CPAG formed a child poverty coalition composed of seven organizations. Building on the momentum associated with the 1989 House of Commons decision to work to end child poverty by 2000, the coalition became Campaign 2000, made up of over seventy national, provincial, and community organizations (Dobrowolsky and Jenson, 2004: 169).

15 Not all organizations, even those with the word "poverty" in their name, were happy about refocusing all attention on child poverty. The National Anti-Poverty Organization (NAPO) feared that such a step would place categories of the poor in competition with each other (Dobrowolsky and Jenson, 2004: 169). Nor was the Canadian Labour Congress (CLC) particularly enthusiastic about the focus on low-income groups. Indeed, when its long-standing ally the Canadian Council for Social Development (CCSD) advocated a guaranteed income to fight poverty, the CLC's friendship cooled for a time. It preferred to emphasize job creation (Haddow, 1994).

16   Edward Greenspon and Anthony Wilson-Smith (1996: 232) describe the genesis of the CHST: "Closeted in Dodge's [DM Finance] twentieth-floor boardroom, the Finance officials designed a new system. In a late-night session with [finance minister] Martin they recommended lumping health, education and social assistance transfers into a single block fund, with its overall size determined by the federal government." The CHST reform had two goals: to control and to reduce spending. "In exchange Ottawa would loosen the conditions it placed on provincial use of the money" (232).

17   The anger and distrust generated by the unilateral measures of the 1995 budget infected intergovernmental discussions for years afterwards (Boismenu and Jenson, 1998).

18   In addition to the NCB, other initiatives to increase the income of lone-parent families and services for low-income families include the Federal Child Support Guidelines and the various agreements on developmental services.

19   Technically, the "new" money was supposed to come from the fact that the federal government had taken over part of social assistance expenditures. By providing income supplements (the Canada Child Tax Benefit and the National Child Benefit Supplement), federal spending could substitute for expenditures the provinces had previously made on social assistance, thereby freeing up money for alternative uses by provincial governments.

20   For a summary of the child care positions of these years, see Annis May Timpson (2001: 106) and Rianne Mahon and Susan D. Phillips (2002: 203-4).

21   Despite this, however, Canada lags behind other liberal welfare regimes, including the United States, in the actual amount of money made available to families with children (Mendelson, 2003).

22   At its founding in 1965, the Fédération des femmes du Québec (FFQ) included state-provided child care on its list of six basic demands. The theme was emphasized by many others through the 1970s and 1980s.

23   The United Kingdom has one of the longest traditions of longitudinal analysis of life situations, but other countries have enthusiastically invested in it as the "life-course perspective" has taken hold in social policy circles. Canada's NLSCY (National Longitudinal Survey of Children and Youth) is one example.

24   Peter Taylor-Gooby (2004) and his colleagues grouped European spending on the new social risks under three categories: services for the elderly and disabled, services for families, and active labour-market support. Comparing spending levels between 1980 and 1999, they found that across all four welfare regime types (Nordic, corporatist, liberal, and Mediterranean), spending had increased in all three of the categories. Although the rates and amounts differed, there were no exceptions to the trend (Taylor-Gooby, 2004: Table 1.1). Wage supplements, which have been adopted in a range of countries, are popular in liberal welfare regimes. For example, the United States' Earned Income Tax Credit (EITC), which supplements the income of those with low wages, cost Washington US$5.3 billion in 1990. It was enriched in 1996 in conjunction with the reforms to social assistance (welfare) instituted during the Clinton presidency. It now costs American taxpayers about US$30 billion a year. Other welfare regimes have also adopted the notion of supplementing earnings for workers with low-wage employment. The Canada Child Tax Benefit and the various provincial "child benefits" are Canadian examples.

25   These ideas are summarized in Jane Jenson and Denis Saint-Martin (2003: Table 2) and provide a synthetic presentation of the perspective. Denis Saint-Martin (2000) presents the Canadian versions of these ideas, and Ruth Lister (2003) summarizes them for Britain.

26   See, for example, Esping-Andersen (2002). Employing a social investment perspective, the OECD has become a major advocate for early learning and care, albeit not always for equality (Mahon, 2006).

Chapter 10: Care*fair*
This chapter is a condensed version of "Carefair: Choice, Duty and the Distribution of Care," *Social Politics* 13 (2006): 341-71.

1   For citizens who choose not to reproduce, "participation" in child rearing may simply mean recognizing the social value that flows from the child rearing of others by personally

subsidizing this work through taxation and accommodating in market and other civil society domains the flexibility that care provision requires.
2 I am indebted to Professor Anita Nyberg for providing data on Swedish parental leave in 2001.

Chapter 11: Republican Liberty, Naming Laws, and the Role of Patronymy
This chapter is dedicated to a sister "Lucy Stoner," Midorikawa Kaori, whose courage in pursuing the "gospel of individual sovereignty" in rural Nagano (Japan) and whose resilience against the hammers of patriarchal significant others inspired me to pursue this topic.

I wish to thank Caroline Andrew, Linda Cardinal, Doug Moggach, Stephanie Mullen, Marian Sawer, and Linda Trimble for their insightful comments on an earlier version, presented at the 2004 CPSA workshop entitled "Gendering the Nation-State." I wish to acknowledge the rigorous feedback received from the anonymous reviewers. Finally, my gratitude goes to Yasmeen Abu-Laban for her guidance and mentoring in support of this chapter.
1 See Judith Butler (1997); Catherine MacKinnon (1993); Mari Matsuda et al. (1999); Patricia Monture-Angus (1995); Dale Spender (1980); and Casey Miller and Kate Swift (1976).
2 Given that the common law framework used in the nine provinces and three territories differs from that adopted in Québec under the civil code, I will use the terms "Canada" and "Québec" to denote these two distinct juridico-political and cultural realities. When speaking of Canada, I am referring to the political/legal culture of predominantly English-speaking Canada and the ethnocultural groups who identify with that community and with the rule of the common law. When using the term "Québec," I am referring to the political/legal culture of predominantly French-speaking Québec and the ethnocultural groups who identify with that community and with the rule of the civil code.
3 As a somewhat ironic point of comparison, 98 percent of Japanese women also take their husband's name. However, in Japan, both spouses are legally obligated to share a single "family" name, the husband's or the wife's name (Arichi, 1999: 412). This legal framework is even more coercive for women, given that one of the spouses *must* undergo a name change and that very few husbands (2 percent) are willing to adopt their wife's name.
4 For American examples of newspapers that show open contempt for birth name retention, see Una Stannard (1977: 95) on the *Boston Post*'s urging that marriage "shut up" the mouth of Lucy Stone. Stone was the American pioneer of birth name retention after marriage. See also Stannard (56) for the *New York Times'* intentional mis-recognition and misnaming of Lucy Stone as "Lucy Stone Blackwell" in its published announcement of her death.
5 In its *Trociuk v. British Columbia* (2003) decision, the Supreme Court of Canada made unwed women vulnerable to the interventions of the biological father in naming their children. Historically, unwed mothers were prevented from bestowing the father's last name upon their children without his explicit permission. Fatherhood was understood to be social rather than biological, and the law ensured men's legal right to opt in or out of the responsibilities of fatherhood by virtue of this legal protection. At the same time, this practice served to stigmatize unwed mothers by making public, via the shared last name, the presence of a "bastard" child. An unintentional positive consequence of this practice in contemporary times has been that unwed mothers have retained the legal "right," by default, to name their children after themselves. The *Trociuk* case overturned the right of unwed mothers to name their children by unequivocally privileging the rights of biological fathers, as against those of mothers. The precedent established in *Trociuk* (2003) is that if unwed parents cannot agree on the child's last name, she or he will automatically receive a hyphenated last name consisting of both names in alphabetical order. Creating a new precedent within the common law, unmarried women are now also exposed to coercion with respect to children's names, by virtue of the ability of a former sexual partner (with whom pregnancy resulted) to take legal action to confer his last name on the child. It is unlikely that this precedent will be challenged in the near future, given that in September 2006, the Conservative Harper Government abolished the Court Challenges Program of Canada, which was created to provide financial support for costly test-cases aimed at advancing language and equality rights (see http://www.ccppcj.ca/e/ccp.shtml).

Chapter 12: Gendering Nation-States and/or Gendering City-States

1 It should be noted that I took part in both these projects and that therefore the analysis is that of a participant-observer. I acknowledge the involvement and intellectual contribution of Geneviève Allard, Suzanne Doerge, Pat Harewood, Fran Klodawsky, and Alette Willis, and the many other community and city representatives who were so wonderfully active in both projects. The analysis is my own, but it comes out of an intensely collective process, for which I am deeply grateful.

Bibliography

Abu-Laban, Yasmeen. 1998. "Keeping 'em Out: Gender, Race and Class Biases in Canadian Immigration Policy." In *Painting the Maple: Essays on Race, Gender and the Construction of Canada,* ed. Veronica Strong-Boag, Sherrill Grace, Avigail Eisenberg, and Joan Anderson, 69-82. Vancouver: UBC Press.

–. 2001. "Humanizing the Oriental: Edward Said and Western Scholarly Discourse." In *Revising Culture, Reinventing Peace: The Influence of Edward Said,* ed. Naseer Aruri and Muhammad A. Shuraydi, 74-85. New York and Northampton: Interlink.

–. 2004. "The New North America and the Segmentation of Canadian Citizenship." *International Journal of Canadian Studies* 29, 1: 17-40.

Abu-Laban, Yasmeen, and Christina Gabriel. 2002. *Selling Diversity: Immigration, Multiculturalism, Employment Equity and Globalization.* Peterborough: Broadview Press.

Abu-Laban, Yasmeen, and Judith A. Garber. 2005. "The Construction of the Geography of Immigration as Policy Problem: The United States and Canada Compared." *Urban Affairs Review* 40, 4: 520-61.

Agnew, Vijay. 1996. *Resisting Discrimination: Women from Asia, Africa and the Caribbean and the Women's Movement in Canada.* Toronto: University of Toronto Press.

Albrechtsen, Janet. 2002. "Dancing to the Ism of the World." *Quadrant* 46, 9 (September): 30-32.

Alford, Richard. 1988. *Naming and Identity: A Cross-Cultural Study of Personal Naming Practices.* New Haven: Hraf Press.

Al-Hibri, Azizah. 1999. "Is Western Patriarchal Feminism Good for Third World / Minority Women?" In *Is Multiculturalism Bad for Women?* ed. J. Cohen, M. Howard, and M. Nussbaum, 41-46. Princeton: Princeton University Press.

Alia, Valerie. 1985. "Women, Names, and Power." *Women and Language* 8: 34-36.

–. 1988. "Personal Names, Numbers and Northern Policy: Inuit Identity in Canada." In *Student Research in Canada's North: Proceedings of the National Student Conference on Northern Studies* (November 18-19, 1986), eds. Peter Adams and Peter Johnson, 417-19. Ottawa: Association of Canadian Universities for Northern Studies.

–. 1989. "Towards a Politics of Naming." Master's thesis. York University.

Allen, Anita. 1997. "The Jurispolitics of Privacy." In *Reconstructing Political Theory: Feminist Perspectives,* ed. Mary Lyndon Shanley and Uma Narayan, 68-83. Pennsylvania University Park: Pennsylvania State University Press.

Allen, Judith. 1990. "Does Feminism Need a Theory of the State?" In *Playing the State: Australian Feminist Interventions,* ed. Sophie Watson, 21-28. London: Verso.

Almond, Gabriel A. 1997. "The Political System and Comparative Politics: The Contribution of David Easton." In *Contemporary Empirical Political Theory,* ed. Kristen Renwick Monroe, 219-30. Berkeley and Los Angeles: University of California Press.

Althusser, Louis. 1971. "Ideology and Ideological State Apparatuses." In *Lenin and Philosophy, and Other Essays.* Trans. Ben Brewster, 123-73. New York: Monthly Review Press.

Ålund, Aleksandra, and Carl-Ulrik Schierup. 1991. *Paradoxes of Multiculturalism: Essays on Swedish Society.* Aldershot, UK: Avebury Academic Publishing.

American Medical Association. 1992. "Users' Guides to Evidence-Based Medicine." *Journal of the American Medical Association* 268, 17 (4 November): 2420-425.

Anderson, Benedict. 1991. *Imagined Communities: Reflections on the Origin and Spread of Nationalism.* Rev. ed. London: Verso.

Andersson, Erin, and Michael Valpy. 2004. *The New Canada.* A *Globe and Mail*/McClelland and Stewart Book.

Andrew, Caroline. 2003. "Women in the Urban Landscape." In *Out of the Ivory Tower,* ed. Andrea Martinez and Meryn Stuart, 189-204. Toronto: Sumach Press.

Andrew, Caroline, Pat Harewood, Fran Klodawsky, and Alette Willis. 2004. "Accessing City Hall." *Women and Environments International* 62-63: 49-50.

Andrew, Caroline, Pat Armstrong, Hugh Armstrong, Wallace Clement, and Leah F. Vosko, eds. 2003. *Studies in Political Economy: Developments in Feminism.* Toronto: Women's Press.

Andrew, Caroline, and Sanda Rogers, eds. 1997. *Women and the Canadian State/Les femmes et l'état canadien.* Montreal and Kingston: McGill-Queen's University Press.

Anthias, Floya. 1991. "Parameters of Difference and Identity and the Problems of Connections: Gender, Ethnicity and Class." *International Review of Sociology* 2: 29-51.

Anthias, Floya, and Nira Yuval-Davis, eds. 1989. *Woman-Nation-State.* London: Macmillan.

–. 1993. *Racialized Boundaries: Race, Nation, Gender, Colour and Class and the Anti-racist Struggle.* London and New York: Routledge.

Apter, Peter. 1989. *Nationalism.* London: Hodder and Stroughton.

Archibugi, Daniele, David Held, and Martin Köhler, eds. 1998. *Re-imagining Political Community: Studies in Cosmopolitan Democracy.* Stanford: Stanford University Press.

Arichi, Masumi. 1999. "Is It Radical? Women's Right to Keep Their Own Surnames after Marriage." *Women's Studies International Forum* 22: 411-15.

Arscott, Jane, and Manon Tremblay. 1999. "'Il reste encore des travaux à faire': Feminism in Canada and Québec." *Canadian Journal of Political Science* 32, 1: 125-51.

Arscott, Jane, and Linda Trimble. 1997. "In the Presence of Women: Representation and Political Power." In *In the Presence of Women: Representation in Canadian Governments,* ed. Jane Arscott and Linda Trimble, 1-17. Toronto: Harcourt.

Ashwin, Sarah. 2000. "Introduction: Gender, State and Society in Soviet and Post-Soviet Russia." In *Gender, State and Society in Soviet and Post-Soviet Russia,* ed. Sarah Ashwin, 1-29. London: Routledge.

–. 2006. "Dealing with Devastation in Russia: Men and Women Compared." In *Adapting to Russia's New Labour Market: Gender and Employment Behaviour,* ed. Sarah Ashwin, 1-31. London: Routledge.

Ashwin, Sarah, and Tatyana Lytkina. 2004. "Men in Crisis in Russia: The Role of Domestic Marginalization." *Gender and Society* 18, 2: 189-206.

Attwood, Lynne. 1996. "The Post-Soviet Women in the Move to the Market: A Return to Domesticity and Dependence?" In *Women in Russia and Ukraine,* ed. Rosalind Marsh, 255-66. Cambridge: Cambridge University Press.

Axtmann, Roland. 2004. "The State of the State." *International Political Science Review* 25, 3: 259-79.

Backhouse, Constance. 1991. *Petticoats and Prejudice: Women and the Law in Nineteenth-Century Canada.* Toronto: Women's Press for the Osgoode Society.

–. 1999. *Colour-Coded: A Legal History of Racism in Canada, 1900-1950.* Toronto: University of Toronto Press.

Baier, Annette. 1987. "The Need for More Than Justice." *Canadian Journal of Philosophy* supplementary 13: 41-56.

Bailey, Sue. 2006. "Harper Promises Gay Marriage Vote." *Canoes News,* 5 April. http://cnews.canoe.ca/CNEWS/Canada/2006/04/05/1521237-cp.html.

Baker, Susan, and Anneke van Doorne-Huiskes, eds. 1999. *Women and Public Policy: The Shifting Boundaries between the Public and Private Spheres.* Aldershot, UK: Ashgate.

Bakker, Isabella, ed. 1994. *The Strategic Silence: Gender and Economic Policy.* London: Zed Books in association with the North-South Institute.

–. 1996. *Rethinking Restructuring: Gender and Change in Canada.* Toronto: University of Toronto Press.

–. 2003. "Neo-liberal Governance and the Reprivatization of Social Reproduction: Social Provisioning and Shifting Gender Orders." In *Power, Production and Social Reproduction,* ed. Isabella Bakker and Stephen Gill, 66-80. London: Palgrave Macmillan.

Bakker, Isabella, and Stephen Gill, eds. 2003. *Power, Production and Social Reproduction.* London: Palgrave Macmillan.

Bannerji, Himani. 1995. *Thinking Through: Essays on Feminism, Marxism and Racism.* Toronto: Women's Press.

–. 2001. *Inventing Subjects: Studies in Hegemony, Patriarchy and Colonialism.* New Delhi: Tulika Books.

Bannerji, Himani, Shahrzad Mojab, and Judith Whitehead, eds. 2001. *Of Property and Propriety: The Role of Gender and Class in Imperialism and Nationalism.* Toronto: University of Toronto Press.

Banting, Keith. 1997. "The Social Policy Divide: The Welfare State in Canada and the United States." In *Degrees of Freedom: Canada and the United States in a Changing World,* ed. Keith Banting, George Hoberg, and Richard Simeon, 267-309. Montreal and Kingston: McGill-Queen's University Press.

Barbalet, J.M. 1988. *Citizenship: Rights, Struggle and Class Inequality.* Milton Keynes: Open University Press.

Barclay, Lesley, and Deborah Lupton. 1999. "The Experiences of New Fatherhood: A Sociocultural Analysis." *Journal of Advanced Nursing* 29, 4: 1013-20.

Barney, Darin, and David Laycock. 1999. "Right-Populists and Plebiscitary Politics in Canada." *Party Politics* 5: 317-39.

Barrett, Michele. 1980. *Women's Oppression Today: Problems in Marxist Feminist Analysis.* London: Verso.

Bashevkin, Sylvia. 1994. "Confronting Neo-conservatism: Anglo-American Women's Movements under Thatcher, Reagan and Mulroney." *International Political Science Review* 15: 275-96.

–. 1998. *Women on the Defensive: Living through Conservative Times.* Toronto: University of Toronto Press.

–. 2002. *Welfare Hot Buttons: Women, Work and Social Policy Reform.* Pittsburgh: University of Pittsburgh Press.

Basu, Aparna. 2000. "Women in Politics – India." In *Women's Politics and Women in Politics: In Honour of Ida Blom,* ed. Sølvi Sogner and Gro Hagemann. Universitetet i Bergen: Cappelen Akademisk Forlag.

Battle, Ken. 1993. "The Politics of Stealth: Child Benefits under the Tories." In *How Ottawa Spends 1993-1994: A More Democratic Canada...?* ed. Susan D. Phillips, 417-48. Ottawa: Carleton University Press.

–. 2001. "Relentless Incrementalism: Deconstructing and Reconstructing Canadian Income Security Policy." In *The Review of Economic Performance and Social Progress – The Longest Decade: Canada in the 1990s,* ed. Keith Banting, France St-Hilaire, and Andrew Sharpe, 183-229. Montreal: Institute for Research on Public Policy and Centre for the Study of Living Standards.

Battle, Ken, Sherri Torjman, and Michael Mendelson. 2003. "The 2003 Budget: Political Legacy Needs Policy Architecture." Ottawa: Caledon Institute of Public Policy, February.

–. 2006. *The Incredible Shrinking $1,200 Child Care Allowance: How to Fix It.* Ottawa: Caledon Institute of Social Policy. http://www.caledoninst.org/Publications/PDF/588ENG.pdf.

Bauman, Z. 2002. *Society Under Seige.* London: Polity.

Bayes, Jane H., Patricia Begne, Laura Gonzalez, Lois Harder, M.E. Hawkesworth, and Laura MacDonald. 2006. *Women, Democracy and Globalization in North America: A Comparative Study.* New York: Palgrave.

Beck, U., and E. Beck-Gernsheim. 2002. *Individualization: Institutionalized Individualism and Its Social and Political Consequences.* London: Sage.

Beckwith, Karen. 2003. "The Substantive Representation of Women: Newness, Numbers, and Models of Representation." Paper presented at the annual meeting of the American Political Science Association, Boston, 28-31 August.

Bedont, Barbara C. 1999. "Gender-Specific Provisions in the Statute of the ICC." In *Essays on the Rome Statute of the ICC,* ed. F. Lattanzi and W. Schabas, n.p. Naples: Editorial Scientifica. http://iccwomen.addr.com/recourses/genderprovs.html14.

Belliveau, Jo-Anne, Jillian Oderkirk, and Cynthia Silver. 1994. "Common-Law Union: The Québec Difference." In *Canadian Social Trends* (Summer), Statistics Canada, 8-13. Ottawa: Minister of Supply and Services.

Benner, Erica. 2001. "Is There a Core National Doctrine?" *Nations and Nationalism* 7, 2: 155-74.

Bettio, F., and J. Plantenga. 2004. "Comparing Care Regimes in Europe." *Feminist Economic* 10, 1 (March): 85-113.

Betts, Katharine. 1999. *The Great Divide: Immigration Politics in Australia.* Sydney: Duffy and Snellgrove.

Bhattacharya, Gargi, John Gabriel, and Stephen Small. 2002. *Race and Power: Global Racism in the Twenty-First Century.* London and New York: Routledge.

Billig, Michael. 1995. *Banal Nationalism.* London: Sage.

Blackburn, Robin. 1972. *Ideology in Social Science: Readings in Critical Social Theory.* London: Fontana.

Blanck, Dag, and Mattias Tydén. 1994. "Becoming Multicultural? The Development of a Swedish Immigrant Policy." In *Welfare States in Trouble: Historical Perspectives on Canada and Sweden,* ed. J.L. Granatstein and Sune Åkerman, 57-70. Toronto: Swedish-Canadian Academic Foundation.

Blatchford, Christie. 2006. "Teskey Will Breathe Life into 24 Sussex." *Globe and Mail Online,* 24 January. http://www.theglobeandmail.com/servlet/ArticleNews/TPStory/LAC/20060124/HARPERFAM24/National/Idx.

Blom, Ida, Karen Hagemann, and Catherine Hall. 2000. *Gendered Nations: Nationalisms and Gender Order in the Long Nineteenth Century.* New York and Oxford: Berg.

Blumstein, Philip, and Pepper Schwartz. 1983. *American Couples: Money, Work, Sex.* New York: William Morrow.

Boismenu, Gérard, and Jane Jenson. 1998. "A Social Union or a Federal State? Intergovernmental Relations in the New Liberal Era." In *How Ottawa Spends, 1998-99: Balancing Act: The Post-deficit Mandate,* ed. Leslie Pal, 56-79. Ottawa: Carleton University Press.

Boivin, Suzanne. 1985. "The Surname of the Married Woman and of Children." In *Family Law in Canada: New Directions,* ed. Elizabeth Sloss, 195-210. Ottawa: Canadian Advisory Council on the Status of Women.

Bonoguore, Tenille. 2006. "House Votes Not to Re-open Same-Sex Marriage Debate." *Globe and Mail Online,* 7 December. http://www.theglobeandmail.com/servlet/story/RTGAM.20061207.wsamesex07/BNStory/National/home.

Bonoli, Giuliano. 2005. "The Politics of the New Social Policies: Providing Coverage against New Social Risks in Mature Welfare States," *Policy and Politics* 33, 3: 431-49.

Boon, Kirstin. 2001. "Rape and Forced Pregnancy under the ICC Statute: Human Dignity, Autonomy, and Consent." *Columbia Human Rights Law Review* 32: 624-75.

Boychuk, Gerard. 1998. *Patchworks of Purpose: The Development of Provincial Social Assistance Regimes in Canada.* Montreal and Kingston: McGill-Queen's University Press.

–. 2003. *A History of Canadian Social Architecture: The Logics of Policy Development.* Report F 36. Ottawa: Canadian Policy Research Networks. http://www.cprn.org.

Boyd, Susan, ed. 2002. *Challenging the Public/Private Divide: Feminism, Law, and Public Policy.* Toronto: University of Toronto Press.

Braidotti, Rosi. 1992. "On the Female Feminist Subject, or: From 'She-Self' to 'She-Other.'" In *Beyond Equality and Difference: Citizenship, Feminist Politics, Female Subjectivity,* ed. Gisela Bock and Susan James, 177-92. London: Routledge.

Brenner, Neil. 2004. "Urban Governance and the Production of New State Spaces in Western Europe 1960-2000." *Review of International Political Economy* 11, 3: 447-88.

Bridger, Sue, Rebecca Kay, and Kathryn Pinnick. 1996. *No More Heroines? Russia, Women and the Market*. London: Routledge.

Brière, Germain. 1982. "Les effets du mariage, selon la conception du législateur Québécois de 1980." *Revue générale de droit* 13: 10-11.

Brightman, Joan. 1994. "Why Hillary Chooses Rodham Clinton." *American Demographics* 16: 910.

Brodie, Janine. 1997. "Meso-Discourses, State Forms, and the Gendering of Liberal-Democratic Citizenship." *Citizenship Studies* 1, 2: 223-42.

–. 2002. "The Great Undoing: State Formation, Gender Politics, and Social Policy in Canada." In *Western Welfare in Decline: Globalization and Women's Poverty*, ed. Catherine Kingfisher, 90-111. Philadelphia: University of Pennsylvania Press.

–. 2007. "Canada's 3-D's: The Rise and Decline of the Gender-Based Policy Capacity." In *Remapping Gender in the New Global Order*, ed. Marjorie Cohen and Janine Brodie, 166-84. London: Routledge.

Brown, Wendy. 1995. *States of Injury: Power and Freedom in Late Modernity*. Princeton: Princeton University Press.

Brush, L.D. 2002. "Changing the Subject: Gender and Welfare Regime Studies." *Social Politics* 9, 2 (Summer): 161-86.

Buckley, Mary. 1989. *Women and Ideology in the Soviet Union*. Ann Arbor: University of Michigan Press.

Buchanan, James M., and Gordon Tullock. 1962. *The Calculus of Consent: Logical Foundations of Constitutional Democracy*. Ann Arbor: Ann Arbor Paperbacks.

Burt, Sandra. 1995. "Gender and Public Policy: Making Some Difference in Ottawa." In *Gender and Politics in Contemporary Canada*, ed. François-Pierre Gingras, 86-105. Toronto: Oxford University Press.

Burt, Sandra, and Lorraine Code, eds. 1995. *Changing Methods: Feminists Transforming Practice*. Peterborough: Broadview Press.

Burt, Sandra, and Elizabeth Lorenzin. 1997. "Taking the Women's Movement to Queen's Park: Women's Interests and the New Democratic Government of Ontario." In *In the Presence of Women: Representation in Canadian Governments*, ed. Jane Arscott and Linda Trimble, 202-27. Toronto: Harcourt.

Buss, Doris. 1998. "Robes, Relics and Rights: The Vatican and the Beijing Conference on Women." *Social and Legal Studies* 7, 3: 339-63.

Buss, Doris, and Didi Herman. 2003. *Globalizing Family Values: The Christian Rights in International Politics*. Minneapolis: University of Minnesota Press.

Butler, Judith. 1990. *Gender Trouble*. New York: Routledge.

–. 1997. *Excitable Speech: A Politics of the Performative*. New York: Routledge.

–. 2004. *Undoing Gender*. London: Routledge.

Bystydzienski, Jill M., ed. 1992. *Women Transforming Politics: Worldwide Strategies for Empowerment*. Bloomington: Indiana University Press.

–. 1995. *Women in Electoral Politics: Lessons from Norway*. Westport, CT: Praeger.

Caiazza, Amy. 2002. *Mothers and Soldiers: Gender, Citizenship, and Civil Society in Contemporary Russia*. New York: Routledge.

Cairns, Alan. 1990. "Reflections on Commission Research." In *Commissions of Inquiry*, ed. P. Pross, I. Christie, and J. Yogis, 87-108. Toronto: Carswell.

Canada Employment Insurance Commission. 2003. *Employment Insurance: 2002 Monitoring and Assessment Report*. Hull: Human Resources Development Canada, Strategic Policy, Labour Market Policy Directorate.

Canada-Nova Scotia. 2005. *Moving Forward on Early Learning and Child Care*. Agreement-in-Principle between the Government of Canada and the Government of Nova Scotia. http://www.sdc.gc.ca/en/cs/comm/sd/news/agreements_principle/index.shtml.

"Canadian Conservatives Win Minority Government." 2006. *Christian Post*, 26 January. http://www.christianpost.com/article/americas/205/section/canadian.conservatives.win. minority.government/1.htm.

Canovan, Margaret. 1981. *Populism*. New York: Harcourt Brace Jovanovich.

–. 1996. *Nationhood and Political Theory.* Cheltenham and Northhampton: Edward Elgar.
–. 2002. "Making Sense of Populism." In *Democracies and the Populist Challenge,* ed. Yves Mény and Yves Surel, 25-54. Houndmills, UK: Palgrave.
Carson, Fiona. 2001. "Feminism and the Body." In *The Routledge Companion to Feminism and Postfeminism,* ed. Sarah Gamble, 117-28. London and New York: Routledge.
Catholic Family and Human Rights Institute. 1999. "Protection for Families Dropped from the New International Criminal Court." *Friday Fax,* 17 December, 3-5.
Centre for Research and Information on Canada. 2003. *A New Canada: An Identity Shaped by Diversity.* CRIC Papers, No. 11. Montreal: Centre for Research and Information on Canada.
Change of Name Act, R.C.B.C. 1960, c. 50.
Chappell, Louise. 2002. "The 'Femocrat' Strategy: Expanding the Repertoire of Feminist Activists." *Parliamentary Affairs* 55: 85-98.
–. 2003. *Gendering Government: Feminist Engagement with the State in Australia and Canada.* Vancouver: UBC Press.
–. 2004. "The Contentious Politics of Women's Human Rights: Religious and Cultural Challenges to Women's Equality in the International Arena." Paper presented at the annual meeting of the American Political Science Association Conference, Chicago, 3 September. http://www.allacademic.com/meta/p61158_index.html.
–. 2006. "Contesting Women's Rights: The Emergence of a Conservative Patriarchal Counternetwork." *Global Society* 20: 491-520.
Charlesworth, Hilary, and Christine Chinkin. 2000. *The Boundaries of International Law: A Feminist Analysis.* Manchester: Manchester University Press.
Chatterjee, Partha. 1986. *Nationalist Thought and the Colonial World.* London: Zed Books.
–. 1989. "Colonialism, Nationalism and the Colonized Woman." *American Ethnologist* 16: 622-33.
Childs, Sarah. 2001. "In Their Own Words: New Labour Women and the Substantive Representation of Women." *British Journal of Politics and International Relations* 3, 2: 173-90.
–. 2004a. "A Feminised Style of Politics? Women MPs in the House of Commons." *British Journal of Politics and International Relations* 6: 3-19.
–. 2004b. *New Labour's Women MPs: Women Representing Women.* London and New York: Routledge.
–. 2006. "The House Turned Upside Down? The Difference Labour's Women MPs Made." In *Representing Women in Parliament: A Comparative Study,* ed. Marian Sawer, Manon Tremblay, and Linda Trimble, 152-68. London: Routledge.
Citizenship and Immigration Canada. 2001a. *A Look at Canada.* Ottawa: Minister of Public Works and Government Services.
–. 2001b. *Planning Now for Canada's Future: Introducing a Multi-year Planning Process and the Immigration Plan for 2001 and 2002.* Ottawa: Communications Branch, Citizenship and Immigration Canada. http://www.cic.gc.ca/english/pub/anrep01.html.
–. 2002. *A Newcomer's Introduction to Canada.* Ottawa: Minister of Public Works and Government Services.
Civil Marriage Act, Statutes of Canada S.C. 2005, c. 33. http://canada.justice.gc.ca/en/news/nr/2005/doc_31376.html.
Clarke, John. 2004a. *Changing Welfare, Changing States: New Directions in Welfare Policy.* London: Sage.
–. 2004b. "Dissolving the Public Realm? The Logic and Limits of Neo-liberalism." *International Journal of Social Policy* 33, 1: 27-48.
Coalition for the ICC. N.d. "US and the ICC." http://www.iccnow.org/documents/usandtheicc.html.
Cohn, Carol, and Cynthia Enloe. 2003. "A Conversation with Cynthia Enloe: Feminists Look at Masculinity and the Men Who Wage War." *Signs* 28, 4: 1187-207.
Cole, David. 2002-03. "Their Liberties, Our Security: Democracy and Double Standards." *Boston Review* (December-January). http://www.bostonreview.net/BR27.6/cole.html.
Collins, Patricia Hill. 1991. *Black Feminist Thought: Knowledge, Consciousness, and the Politics of Empowerment.* New York and London: Routledge.

–. 1994. "Shifting the Center: Race, Class, and Feminist Theorizing about Motherhood." In *Mothering: Ideology, Experience, and Agency,* ed. Evelyn Nakan Glenn, Grace Chang, and Linda R. Forcey, 45-65. New York: Routledge.

Coltrane, Scott. 1996. *Family Man: Fatherhood, Housework and Gender Equity.* New York: Oxford University Press.

Connell, R.W. 1987. *Gender and Power: Society, the Person and Sexual Politics.* Cambridge: Polity Press.

–. 1990. "The State, Gender and Sexual Politics: Theory and Appraisal." *Theory and Society* 19, 5: 507-44.

Connor, Walker. 1994. *Ethno-nationalism: The Quest for Understanding.* Princeton: Princeton University Press.

–. 1990. "When Is a Nation?" *Ethnic and Racial Studies* 13, 1: 92-103.

Cook, Judith, and Mary Margaret Fonow. 1986. "Knowledge and Women's Interests: Issues of Epistemology and Methodology in Feminist Sociological Research." *Sociological Inquiry* 56, 4: 2-29.

Copelon, Rhonda. 2000. "Gender Crimes as War Crimes: Integrating Crimes against Women into International Law." *McGill Law Journal* 46: 217-40.

Copes, Debby. 1976. "Call Me Ms." *Globe and Mail,* 26 February.

Cossman, Brenda, and Judy Fudge, eds. 2002. *Privatization, Law, and the Challenge to Feminism.* Toronto: University of Toronto Press.

Coulson, Melanie. 2003. "A Feminist by Any Other Name." *Globe and Mail,* 5 July, F7.

Courchene, Thomas J. 1994. *Social Canada in the Millennium: Reform Imperatives and Restructuring Principles.* Toronto/Ottawa: C.D. Howe Institute/Renouf.

Cowell-Meyers, Kimberly. 2001. "Gender, Power and Peace: A Preliminary Look at Women in the Northern Ireland Assembly." *Women and Politics* 23, 3: 55-88.

Cox, Kevin. 1998. "Spaces of Engagement, Spaces of Dependence and the Politics of Scale, or: Looking for Local Politics." *Political Geography* 17, 1: 1-23.

Dacks, Gurston, Joyce Green, and Linda Trimble. 1995. "Road Kill: Women in Alberta's Drive toward Deficit Elimination." In *The Trojan Horse: Alberta and the Future of Canada,* ed. Trevor Harrison and Gordon Laxer, 271-80. Montreal: Black Rose.

Dahlerup, Drude. 1987. "Confusing Concepts – Confusing Reality: A Theoretical Discussion of the Patriarchal State." In *Women and the State,* ed. Anne Showstack Sassoon, 93-127. London: Hutchison.

–. 1988. "From a Small to a Large Minority: Women in Scandinavian Politics." *Scandinavian Political Studies* 11, 4: 275-98.

Daly, M. 2002. "Care as a Good for Social Policy." *Journal of Social Policy* 31, 2: 251-70.

Daly, M., and C. Saraceno. 2002. "Social Exclusion and Gender Relations." In *Contested Concepts in Gender and Social Policies,* ed. B. Hobson, J. Lewis, and B. Sim, 84-107. Cheltenham, UK: Edward Elgar.

Delacourt, Susan. 2001. "Put Off by Parliament." *Elm Street:* 53-62.

Deutsch, Karl W. 1953. *Nationalism and Social Communication: An Inquiry into the Foundations of Nationality.* New York: John Wiley.

Dhruvarajan, Vanaja, and Jill Vickers, eds. 2002. *Gender, Race and Nation: A Global Perspective.* Toronto: University of Toronto Press.

Dickenson, Donna. 1997. *Property, Women and Politics: Subjects or Objects?* New Brunswick, NJ: Rutgers University Press.

Dieng, A. 2002. "International Criminal Justice: From Paper to Practice – A Contribution from the International Criminal Tribunal for Rwanda to the Establishment of the International Criminal Court." *Fordham International Law Journal* 25: 688-707.

Dobrowolsky, Alexandra. 1998. "'Of Special Interest': Interest, Identity and Feminist Representational Activism." *Canadian Journal of Political Science* 31, 4: 707-42.

–. 2001. "Intersecting Identities and Inclusive Institutions: Women and a Future Transformative Politics." *Journal of Canadian Studies* 35, 4: 240-61.

–. 2004. "The Chrétien Legacy and Women: Changing Policy Priorities with Little Cause for Celebration." *Review of Constitutional Studies* 9, 1: 171-98.

Dobrowolsky, Alexandra, and Vivien Hart, eds. 2003. *Women Making Constitutions: New Politics and Comparative Perspectives.* Basingstoke and New York: Palgrave Macmillan.

Dobrowolsky, Alexandra, and Jane Jenson. 2004. "Shifting Representations of Citizenship: Canadian Politics of 'Women' and 'Children.'" *Social Politics* 11, 2: 154-80.

–. 2005. "Social Investment Perspectives and Practices: A Decade in British Politics." In *Social Policy Review 17,* ed. Martin Powell, Linda Bauld, and Karen Clarke, 203-30. Bristol, UK: Policy Press.

Dobrowolsky, Alexandra, and Evangelia Tastsoglou, eds. 2006. *Women, Migration and Citizenship: Making Local, National and Transnational Connections.* Aldershot, UK: Ashgate.

Donkor, Martha. 2004. "Education and Training Options for Women in Canada." In *Calculated Kindness: Global Restructuring, Immigration and Settlement in Canada,* ed. Rose Baaba Folson, 44-60. Winnipeg: Fernwood.

Dovi, Suzanne. 2002. "Preferable Descriptive Representatives: Will Just Any Woman, Black or Latino Do?" *American Political Science Review* 96, 4: 729-43.

Dufour, Pascale, and Isabelle Giraud. 2004. "Transnationalisation des mouvements féministes: quels impacts sur la lutte des femmes? Le cas de la Marche mondiale des femmes." Paper presented at the "Congrès international Genre et militantisme," Université de Lausanne, Lausanne, 26-27 November.

Dymond, Tim. 2004. "A History of the 'New Class' Concept in Australia." In *Us and Them: Anti-elitism in Australia,* ed. Marian Sawer and Barry Hindess, 57-76. Perth: API Network.

Easton, David. 1957. "An Approach to the Analysis of Political Systems." *World Politics* 9, 3: 383-400.

Egale Canada Inc. v. Canada (Attorney General), [2003] B.C.J. No. 994 (C.A.).

Eggebeen, David J., and Chris Knoester. 2001. "Does Fatherhood Matter for Men?" *Journal of Marriage and Family* 63 (May): 381-93.

Eichler, Margrit. 1993. "Frankenstein Meets Kafka: The Royal Commission on New Reproductive Technologies." In *Misconceptions: The Social Construction of Choice and the New Reproductive and Genetic Technologies,* ed. Gwynne Basen, Margrit Eichler, and Abby Lippman, 196-222. Hull: Voyageur.

Eichler, Maya. 2005. "Explaining Post-Communist Transformations: Economic Nationalism in Ukraine and Russia." In *Economic Nationalism in a Globalizing World,* ed. Eric Helleiner and Andreas Pickel, 69-87. Ithaca: Cornell University Press.

–. 2006. "Russia's Post-Communist Transformation: A Gendered Analysis of the Chechen Wars." *International Feminist Journal of Politics.* 8, 4 (December): 486-511.

EIRR. 2001a. Maternity, Paternity and Parental Benefits across Europe: Part 2. *European Industrial Relations Review* 330 (July): 15-18.

–. 2001b. Maternity, Paternity and Parental Benefits across Europe: Part 3. *European Industrial Relations Review* 331 (August): 13-17.

Elshtain, Jean Bethke. 1981. *Public Man, Private Woman: Women in Social and Political Thought.* Princeton: Princeton University Press.

–. 1987. *Women and War.* New York: Basic Books.

Embleton, Sheila, and Ruth King. 1984. "Attitudes towards Maiden Name Retention." *Onomastica Canadiana* 66: 11-22.

Enloe, Cynthia. 1989. *Bananas, Beaches and Bases: Making Feminist Sense of International Politics.* Berkeley: University of California Press.

Eremitcheva, Galina, and Elena Zdravomyslova. 2001. "Die Bewegung der Soldatenmütter – Eine zivilgesellschaftliche Initiative: Der Fall St. Petersburg." In *Zivilgesellschaft und Gender-Politik in Rußland,* ed. M. Ritter. Frankfurt: Campus Verlag.

Esping-Andersen, Gøsta, ed. 2002. *Why We Need a New Welfare State.* Oxford: Oxford University Press.

Esping-Andersen, Gøsta. 1999. *Social Foundations of Postindustrial Economies.* London: Oxford University Press.

Etzioni, Amitai. 1996. *The New Golden Rule: Community and Morality in a Democratic Society.* New York: Basic Books.

Evans, Sara. 1999. *Born for Liberty: A History of Women in America.* New York: Free Press.

Facio, Alda. 1999. "Integrating Gender into the World's First Permanent Criminal Court." http://www.iccwomen.org/archive/resources/bplus5/part1.htm.

–. 2004. "All Roads Lead to Rome but Some Are Bumpier Than Others." In *Global Issues: Women and Justice,* ed. Sharon Pickering and Caroline Lambert. Sydney: Federation Press.

Fanon, Franz. 1963. *The Wretched of the Earth.* New York: Grove Press.

–. 1967. *Black Skins, White Masks.* New York: Grove Press. (Orig. pub. 1952.)

"Federal Status Council's Report Saves Harsh Words for Indian Act." 1975. *Globe and Mail,* 1 October, 11.

Federation of Canadian Municipalities and Femmes et Ville, Montreal. 2004. *A City Tailored to Women.* Ottawa: Federation of Canadian Municipalities.

Feijoo, Maria Del Carmen. 1998. "Democratic Participation and Women in Argentina." In *Women and Democracy: Latin America and Eastern Europe,* ed. Jane S. Jaquette and Sharon L. Wolchik, 29-46. Baltimore: Johns Hopkins University Press.

Fenwick, Helen. 2002. "Responding to 11 September: Detention without Trial under the Anti-terrorism Crime and Security Act 2001." In *Superterrorism: Policy Responses,* ed. Lawrence Freedman, 80-104. Oxford: Blackwell.

Ferguson, Kathy E. 1984. *The Feminist Case against Bureaucracy.* Philadelphia: Temple University Press.

Field, Mark G. 2000. "The Health and Demographic Crisis in Post-Soviet Russia: A Two-Phase Development." In *Russia's Torn Safety Net: Health and Social Welfare during the Transition,* ed. Mark G. Field and Judyth L. Twigg, 11-42. New York: St. Martin's Press.

Finkle, Jason L., and C. Alison McIntosh. 1994. "The New Politics of Population." *Population and Development Review* 20: 3-34.

Flanagan, Tom. 2000. *First Nations? Second Thoughts.* Montreal and Kingston: McGill-Queen's University Press.

Flax, Jane. 1990. "Postmodernism and Gender Relations in Feminist Theory." In *Feminism/Postmodernism,* ed. Linda J. Nicholson, 39-62. New York and London: Routledge.

Flint, David. 2003. *The Twilight of the Elites.* Melbourne: Freedom.

Folbre, N. 2001. *The Invisible Heart: Economics and Family Values.* New York: New Press.

Folson, Rose Baaba. 2004. "Representation of the Immigrant." In *Calculated Kindness: Global Restructuring, Immigration and Settlement in Canada,* ed. Rose Baaba Folson, 21-32. Winnipeg: Fernwood.

Fowler, Rebekah, and Ann Fuehrer. 1997. "Women's Marital Names: An Interpretive Study of Name Retainers' Concepts of Marriage." *Feminism and Psychology* 7: 315-20.

Francis, Babette. 1994. "Some More Equal." http://www.endeavourforum.org.au.

Frank, Thomas. 2002. *One Market under God.* London: Vintage.

Fraser, Nancy. 1994. "After the Family Wage: Gender Equity and the Welfare State." *Political Theory* 22, 4 (November): 591-618.

Freeman, Jo. 1972-73. "The Tyranny of Structurelessness." *Berkeley Journal of Sociology* 17: 151-65.

Friedan, Betty. 1963. *The Feminine Mystique.* New York: Random House.

Friedman, Elisabeth Jay. 2003. "Gendering the Agenda: The Impact of the Transnational Women's Rights Movement at the UN Conferences of the 1990s." *Women's Studies International Forum* 26, 4: 313-31.

Friedman, Milton, and Rose Friedman. 1980. *Free to Choose.* London: Secker and Warburg.

Frostfeldt, Asa. 2000. "Beijing Plus Five: Much Work Left to Be Done." *Human Rights Tribune* 7, 2-3. http://64.26.129.97/tribune/viewArticle.asp?ID=2568.

Fukuyama, Francis. 2000. *The Great Disruption: Human Nature and the Reconstitution of the Social Order.* New York: Simon and Schuster.

Gabriel, Christina. 2005. "International Labour Mobility and the Politics of Scale." Paper presented at the *Studies in Political Economy* conference "Towards a Political Economy of Scale," Toronto, 3-5 February.

Gabriel, Christina, and Laura Macdonald. 1994. "NAFTA, Women and Organising in Canada and Mexico." *Millennium: Journal of International Studies* 23, 3: 535-62.

Gal, Susan, and Gail Kligman. 1997. *Reproducing Gender: Politics, Public, and Everyday Life after Socialism.* Princeton: Princeton University Press.
–. 2000. *The Politics of Gender after Socialism: A Comparative-Historical Essay.* Princeton: Princeton University Press.
Gandhi, Mohandas K. 1942. *Women and Social Injustice.* Ahmedabad: Navajivan Publishing.
Gapova, Elena. 2004. "Conceptualizing Gender, Nation, and Class in Post-Soviet Belarus." In *Post-Soviet Women Encountering Transition: Nation Building, Economic Survival, and Civic Activism,* ed. Kathleen Kuehnast and Carol Nechemias, 85-102. Baltimore: Johns Hopkins University Press.
Gelles, Edith B. 2002. *Abigail Adams.* New York and London: Routledge.
Gellner, Ernest. 1983. *Nations and Nationalism.* Oxford: Basil Blackwell.
Giddens, Anthony. 1999. *The Third Way.* Cambridge: Polity Press.
Gilligan, Carol. 1982. *In a Different Voice: Psychological Theory and Women's Development.* Cambridge, MA: Harvard University Press.
–. 1987. "Moral Orientation and Moral Development." In *Women and Moral Theory,* ed. E.F. Kittay and D.T. Meyers. Totowa, NJ: Rowman and Littlefield.
Goldsmith, Marlene, ed. 1998. *Social Justice: Fraud or Fair Go?* Canberra: Menzies Research Centre.
Goldstein, Joshua S. 2001. *War and Gender: How Gender Shapes the War System and Vice Versa.* Cambridge: Cambridge University Press.
Golts, Aleksander. 2004. "The Social and Political Condition of the Russian Military." In *The Russian Military: Power and Policy,* ed. Steven E. Miller and Dimitri Trenin, 73-94. Cambridge, MA: MIT Press.
Goodman, Ellen. 2001. "What's in a Name? Just ask my Plumber." *Guardian Weekly,* 13-19 September, 35.
Gotell, Lise, and Janine Brodie. 1991. "Women and Parties: More Than an Issue of Numbers." In *Party Politics in Canada,* 6th ed., ed. Hugh G. Thorburn, 53-67. Scarborough: Prentice-Hall.
Government of Canada. 1995. *The Employment Equity Act.* Ottawa: Department of Justice. http://laws.justice.gc.ca/en/E-5.401/50293.html.
Government of Quebec. 2001. *Rapport Annuel 2000-2001.* Quebec City: Ministère de la Famille et de l'Enfance.
Gramsci, Antonio. 1971. *Selections from the Prison Notebooks.* Edited by Q. Hoare and G.N. Smith. New York: International Publishers.
Green, Joyce. 2001. "Canaries in the Mines of Citizenship: Indian Women in Canada." *Canadian Journal of Political Science* 34, 4: 715-38.
Greenfeld, Liah. 1992. *Nationalism: Five Roads to Modernity.* Cambridge, MA: Harvard University Press.
–. 2004. "Is Modernity Possible without Nationalism?" In *The Fate of the Nation-State,* ed. Michael Seymour, 38-50. Montreal and Kingston, London and Ithaca: McGill-Queen's University Press.
Greenspon, Edward, and Anthony Wilson-Smith. 1996. *Double Vision: The Inside Story of the Liberals in Power.* Toronto: Doubleday.
Grey, Sandra. 2002. "Does Size Matter? Critical Mass and New Zealand's Women MPs." *Parliamentary Affairs* 55: 19-29.
–. 2006. "The 'New World'? The Substantive Representation of Women in New Zealand." In *Representing Women in Parliament: A Comparative Study,* ed. Marian Sawer, Manon Tremblay, and Linda Trimble, 134-51. London: Routledge.
Guest, Dennis. 1985. *The Emergence of Social Security in Canada.* 2nd rev. ed. Vancouver: UBC Press.
Guibernau, Monserrat. 1999. *Nations without States.* Cambridge: Polity Press.
Guttman, Amy. 2005. "Revisiting Representation." Paper presented at the annual meeting of the American Political Science Association Roundtable "Mobilizing Representation 40 Years after Pitkin," Washington, 31 August to 3 September.
Haddow, Rodney. 1994. "Canadian Organized Labour and the Guaranteed Annual Income." In *Continuities and Discontinuities: The Political Economy of Social Welfare and Labour Market*

Policy in Canada, ed. Andrew Johnson, Stephen McBride, and Patrick Smith, 350-66. Toronto: University of Toronto Press.

Hajjar, Lisa. 2004. "Religion, State Power, and Domestic Violence in Muslim Societies: A Framework for Comparative Analysis." *Law and Social Inquiry* 29: 1-38.

Hall, Peter A., and David Soskice, eds. 2001. *Varieties of Capitalism: The Institutional Foundations of Comparative Advantage.* Oxford: Oxford University Press.

Hall, Stuart. 1996. "The West and the Rest: Discourse and Power." In *Modernity: An Introduction to Modern Societies,* ed. Stuart Hall, David Held, Don Hubert, and Kenneth Thompson, 184-227. Oxford: Blackwell.

Hall, Stuart, David Held, Don Hubert, and Kenneth Thompson, eds. 1996. *Modernity: An Introduction to Modern Societies.* Oxford and Malden, MA: Blackwell.

Halpern v. Canada (Attorney General), [2003] O.J. No. 2268 (C.A.).

Hankivsky, Olena. 2004. *Social Policy and the Ethic of Care.* Vancouver: UBC Press.

Hanson, Pauline. 1996. First Speech, *Commonwealth of Australia Parliamentary Debates.* House of Representatives, 10 September.

–. 1997. *Pauline Hanson – The Truth.* Ipswich: Private Printer.

–. 1998. ABC News. 16 July.

Haraway, Donna. 1991. *Simians, Cyborgs, and Women: The Reinvention of Nature.* New York: Routledge.

Harper, Stephen, and Tom Flanagan. 1996-97. "Our Benign Dictatorship." *Next City* 2, 2 (Winter): 34.

Hatfield, M. 2004. "Vulnerability to Persistent Low Income." *Horizons: Policy Research Initiative* 7, 2: 19-26.

Haubrich, Dirk. 2003. "September 11, Anti-Terror Laws and Civil Liberties: Britain, France and Germany Compared." *Government and Opposition* 38, 1 (January): 3-28.

Hawkesworth, Mary E. 2001. "Democratization." In *Gender, Globalization and Democratization,* ed. Rita Mae Kelly, Jane H. Bayes, and Mary E. Hawkesworth, 223-36. Lanham, MD: Rowman and Littlefield.

Hayek, Friedrich A. 1976. *Law, Legislation and Liberty.* Vol. 2. *The Mirage of Social Justice.* London: Routledge and Kegan Paul.

Held, David, Anthony McGrew, David Goldblatt, and Jonathan Perraton. 1999. *Global Transformations: Politics, Economics and Culture.* Stanford: Stanford University Press.

Hendricks v. Québec (Attorney General), [2002] J.Q. No. 3816 (S.C.).

Henry, Frances, and Carol Tator. 2002. *Discourses of Domination: Racial Bias in the Canadian English-Language Press.* Toronto: University of Toronto Press.

Herd, Graeme P. 2003. "Russia's Demographic Crisis and Federal Instability." In *Russia's Regions and Regionalism: Strength through Weakness,* ed. Graeme P. Herd and Anne Aldis, 41-62. London: RoutledgeCurzon.

Herr, Ranjoo S. 2003. "The Possibility of Nationalist Feminism." *Hypatia* 18, 3: 135-60.

Hinterhuber, E.M. 2001. "Between Neotraditionalism and New Resistance: Soldiers' Mothers of St. Petersburg." *Anthropology of East Europe Review* 19, 1: 1-13. http://condor.depaul.edu/~rrotenbe/aeer/.

Hobson, Paul, and France St-Hilaire. 2000. "The Evolution of Federal-Provincial Fiscal Arrangements: Putting Humpty Together Again." In *Canada: The State of the Federation 1999/2000 – Towards a New Mission Statement for Canadian Fiscal Federalism,* ed. Harvey Lazer. Kingston: Institute of Intergovernmental Relations.

Hojgaard, Lis. 1997. "Working Fathers – Caught in the Web of the Symbolic Order of Gender." *Acta Sociologica* 40: 245-62.

Holston, James. 2001. "Urban Citizenship and Globalization." In *Global City-Regions: Trends, Theory, Policy,* ed. A. Scott, 325-48. Toronto: Oxford University Press.

Holy See. 1998. "Intervention of the Holy See Diplomatic Conference of Plenipotentiaries on the Establishment of an International Criminal Court." Working Group on War Crimes. http://147.222.27.5/people.dewolf/hs.html.

Honig, Bonnie. 1999. "My Culture Made Me Do It." In *Is Multiculturalism Bad for Women? Susan Moller Okin with Respondents,* ed. Joshua Cohen, Matthew Howard, and Martha C. Nussbaum, 35-40. Princeton: Princeton University Press.

House of Commons Debates. 1996. 30 April, 2115.

House of Representatives Standing Committee on Community Affairs. 1991. *"You Have Your Moments": A Report on Funding of Peak Health and Community Organisations.* Canberra: Australian Government Publishing Service.

Howard, John. 1994. "Some Thoughts on Liberal Party Philosophy in the 1990s." *Quadrant* (July-August): 22, 25.

–. 1995. "The Role of Government: A Modern Liberal Approach." Menzies Research Centre National Lecture Series, Menzies Research Centre, Canberra, Australia, 6 June.

–. 1998. Transcript of Radio Interview with Alan Jones on 2UE, 873 AM, 16 March.

Howitt, Richard. 2003. "Scale." In *A Companion to Political Geography,* ed. J. Agnew, K. Mitchell, and G. Toal, 138-57. Oxford: Blackwells.

Hroch, Misolav. 1993. "From National Movements to the Fully-Formed Nation: The Nation-Building Process in Europe." *New Left Review* 198: 3-20.

Huntington, Samuel. 1993. "The Clash of Civilizations?" *Foreign Affairs* 72, 3 (Summer): 22-49.

–. 1996. "The West Unique Not Universal." *Foreign Affairs* 75, 6: 28-48.

Ignatieff, Michael. 1993. *Blood and Belonging: Journey into the New Nationalism.* Toronto: Penguin Books.

Integrationsverket. 2001. *Sweden: A Pocket Guide.* Norrköping, Sweden: Swedish Integration Board.

International Criminal Court. 2002. ICC Judges, Facts and Background, Resumes. http://www.iccnow.org/building_the_court/judges/statusofnominations/resumes.html.

Inter-Parliamentary Union. 2007. "Women in National Parliaments." http://www.ipu.org/wmn-e/world.htm.

Issoupova, Olga. 2000. "From Duty to Pleasure? Motherhood in Soviet and Post-Soviet Russia." In *Gender, State and Society in Soviet and Post-Soviet Russia,* ed. Sarah Ashwin, 30-54. London: Routledge.

Jacobs, Jane. 1961. *The Death and Life of Great American Cities.* New York: Random House.

Jacoby, Tami Amandai. 1999. "Feminism, Nationalism and Difference: Reflections on the Palestinian Woman's Movement." *Women's Studies International Forum* 22, 5: 511-22.

Jayawardena, Kumari. 1986. *Feminism and Nationalism in the Third World.* London: Zed Books.

Jenson, Jane. 1986. "Gender and Reproduction: Or, Babies and the State," *Studies in Political Economy* 20: 9-46.

–. 1994. "Commissioning Ideas: Representation and Royal Commissions." In *How Ottawa Spends, 1994,* ed. Susan D. Phillips, 39-70. Ottawa: Carleton University Press.

–. 2001. "Rethinking Equality and Equity: Canadian Children and the Social Union." In *Democratic Equality: What Went Wrong?* ed. Ed Broadbent, 111-29. Toronto: University of Toronto Press.

–. 2004a. *Canada's New Social Risks: Directions for a New Social Architecture.* Report FI43. Ottawa: Canadian Policy Research Networks. http://www.cprn.org.

–. 2004b. "Family Responsibility or Investing in Children: Shifting the Paradigm." *Canadian Journal of Sociology/Cahiers canadiens de sociologie* 29, 2: 169-92.

Jenson, Jane, and Martin Papillon. 2000. "Challenging the Citizenship Regime: The James Bay Cree and Transnational Action." *Politics and Society* 28, 2 (June): 245-64.

Jenson, Jane, and Susan D. Phillips. 1996. "Regime Shift: New Citizenship Practices in Canada." *International Journal of Canadian Studies* 14 (Fall): 111-36.

Jenson, Jane, and Denis Saint-Martin. 2003. "New Routes to Social Cohesion? Citizenship and the Social Investment State." *Canadian Journal of Sociology* 28, 1: 77-99.

Jenson, Jane, and Mariette Sineau, eds. 2001. *Who Cares? Women's Work, Child Care and Welfare State Redesign.* Toronto: University of Toronto Press.

Jessop, Bob. 2001. "Bringing the State Back In (Yet Again): Reviews, Revisions, Rejections, and Redirections." *International Review of Sociology* 11, 2: 149-73.

Joachim, Jutta. 2003. "Framing and Seizing Opportunities: The UN, NGOs, and Women's Rights." *International Studies Quarterly* 47: 247-74.

Johns, Gary. 1996. "Cult of Rights Rejected." *Age,* 4 March, 23.

Johnson, Carol. 2001. "Labor and the Left." In *Left Directions: Is There a Third Way?* ed. Paul Nursey-Bray and Carol Bacchi. Perth: University of Western Australia Press.

Joseph, Saud. 1997. "The Public/Private – The Imagined Boundary in the Imagined Nation: The Lebanese Case." *Feminist Review* 57: 73-92.

Kandiyoti, Deniz. 1991. "Identity and Its Discontents: Women and the Nation." *Millennium: Journal of International Studies* 20, 3: 429-43.

–. 1994. "Identity and Its Discontents: Women and the Nation." In *Colonial Discourse and Post-Colonial Theory: A Reader,* ed. Patrick Williams and Laura Chrisman, 376-91. New York: Columbia University Press.

Kanter, Rosabeth Moss. 1977. "Some Effects of Proportion on Group Life: Skewed Sex Ratios and Responses to Token Women." *American Journal of Sociology* 82: 965-90.

Kaplan, Gisella. 1997. "Feminism and Nationalism: The European Case." In *Feminist Nationalism,* ed. Lois West, 3-40. London and New York: Routledge.

Kathlene, Lyn. 1994. "Power and Influence in State Legislative Policymaking: The Interaction of Gender and Position in Committee Hearing Debates." *American Political Science Review* 88: 560-76.

Katznelson, Ira, and Helen V. Milner. 2002. "American Political Science: The Discipline's State and the State of the Discipline." In *Political Science: The State of the Discipline,* ed. Ira Katznelson and Helen V. Milner, 1-32. New York: W.W. Norton and the American Political Science Association.

Kay, Rebecca. 2000. *Russian Women and Their Organizations: Gender, Discrimination, and Grassroots Women's Organizations, 1991-96.* New York: St. Martin's Press.

–. 2002. "A Liberation from Emancipation? Changing Discourses on Women's Employment in Soviet and Post-Soviet Russia." *Journal of Communist Studies and Transition Politics* 18, 1: 51-72.

Kaye, Miranda, and Julia Tolmie. 1998. "Discoursing Dads: The Rhetorical Devices of Fathers' Rights Groups." *Melbourne University Law Review* 22: 162-94.

Keck, Margaret, and Kathryn Sikkink. 1998. *Activists beyond Borders: Advocacy Networks in International Politics.* Ithaca: Cornell University Press.

Kedourie, Elie. 1960. *Nationalism.* New York: Frederick A. Praeger.

Kelly, Rita Mae, Jane H. Bayes, and Brigett Young, eds. 2001. *Gender, Globalization and Democratization.* Lanham: Rowan and Littlefield.

Kerber, Linda. 1980. *Women of the Republic: Intellect and Ideology in Revolutionary America.* Chapel Hill: University of North Carolina Press.

Kershaw, Paul. 2005. *Carefair: Rethinking the Responsibilities and Rights of Citizenship.* Vancouver: UBC Press.

Kershaw, Paul, Jane Pulkingham, and Sylvia Fuller. Forthcoming. "Expanding the Subject: Violence, Care and (In)Active Male Citizenship." *Social Politics.*

Kiblitskaya, Marina. 2000. "'Once We Were Kings': Male Experiences of Loss of Status at Work in Post-communist Russia." In *Gender, State and Society in Soviet and Post-Soviet Russia,* ed. Sarah Ashwin, 90-104. London: Routledge.

Kingwell, Mark. 1996. *Dreams of Millennium: Report from a Culture on the Brink.* Toronto: Viking.

Kinsella, Warren. 2006. "What's in a Name?" *Canada.com Online,* 20 April. http://www.warrenkinsella.com/sourcefiles/natpost_042006.pdf.

Kirkham, Della. 1998. "The Reform Party of Canada: A Discourse on Race, Ethnicity and Equality." In *Racism and Social Inequality in Canada: Concepts, Controversies and Strategies of Resistance,* ed. Vic Satzewich, 243-68. Toronto: Thompson Educational Publishing.

Klein, Seth, and Andrea Long. 2003. *A Bad Time to Be Poor.* Vancouver: Canadian Centre for Policy Alternatives/Social Planning and Research Council of BC.

Kline, Susan, Laura Stafford, and Jill Miklosovic. 1996. "Women's Surnames: Decisions, Interpretations and Associations with Relational Qualities." *Journal of Social and Personal Relationships* 13: 593-617.

Klymasz, Robert. 1963. "The Canadianization of Slavic Surnames: A Study in Language Contact," *Names* 2: 81, 81-105.

Kobayashi, Audrey. 1995. "Challenging the National Dream: Gender Persecution and Canadian Immigration Law." In *Nationalism, Racism and the Rule of Law*, ed. P. Fitzpatrick, 61-74. Aldershot, UK: Dartmouth Publishing.

Kuehnast, Kathleen, and Carol Nechemias, eds. 2004. *Post-Soviet Women Encountering Transition: Nation Building, Economic Survival, and Civic Activism*. Baltimore: Johns Hopkins University Press.

Kukhterin, Sergei. 2000. "Fathers and Patriarchs in Communist and Post-communist Russia." In *Gender, State and Society in Soviet and Post-Soviet Russia*, ed. Sarah Ashwin, 71-89. London: Routledge.

Kunz, J., and J. Frank. 2004. "Poverty: Thy Name Is Hydra." *Horizons: Policy Research Initiative* 7, 2: 4-8.

Kymlicka, Will. 1995. *Multicultural Citizenship*. Oxford: Oxford University Press.

–. 1999. "Liberal Complacencies." In *Is Multiculturalism Bad for Women?* ed. J. Cohen, M. Howard, and M. Nussbaum, 31-34. Princeton: Princeton University Press.

Lamoureux, Diane, Chantal Maillé, and Micheline de Sève, eds. 1999. *Malaises identitaires: échanges féministes autour d'un Québec incertain*. Montreal: Éditions du Remue-ménage.

Lamphere, Louise. 1993. "The Domestic Sphere and Women and the Public World of Men: The Strengths and Limitations of an Anthropological Dichotomy." In *Gender in Cross-Cultural Perspective*, ed. Caroline B. Brettell and Carolyn F. Sargent, 67-77. Englewood Cliffs: Prentice Hall.

Lapidus, Gail Warshofsky. 1978. *Women in Soviet Society: Equality, Development, and Social Change*. Berkeley: University of California Press.

Larner, Wendy. 2003. "Neoliberalism?" *Environment and Planning D: Society and Space* 21: 509-12.

Larner, Wendy, and David Craig. 2005. "After Neoliberalism? Community Activism and Local Partnerships in Aotearoa New Zealand." *Antipode* 37, 3: 402-24.

Lasch, Christopher. 1995. *The Revolt of the Elites and the Betrayal of Democracy*. New York: W.W. Norton.

Latham, Mark. 2001a. "ABC's Exercise in Symbolism." *Daily Telegraph*, 9 July, 21.

–. 2001b. "The Truth Is Out There, Somewhere." *Daily Telegraph*, 25 June, 21.

Lauber, Sabina. 2001. "Where to Now? International Women's Rights." *Alternative Law Journal* 26, 1: 16-21.

"Laureen: Just Call Me 'Mrs. Harper.'" 2006. *Canoe News Online*, 26 January. http://cnews.canoe.ca/CNEWS/Canada/2006/01/26/1412905-cp.html.

Laycock, David. 2002. *The New Right and Democracy in Canada: Understanding Reform and the Canadian Alliance*. Don Mills, ON: Oxford University Press.

Lebell, Sharon. 1988. *Naming Ourselves, Naming Our Children: Resolving the Last Name Dilemma*. Freedom, CA: Crossing Press.

Lee, R.S. 2002. "An Assessment of the ICC Statute." *Fordham International Law Journal* 25: 750-66.

Lewis, Jone Johnson. N.d. "Women Voices: Quotations by Women – bell hooks." http://womenshistory.about.com/library/qu/blquhook.htm.

Lieven, Anatol. 1999. *Chechnya: Tombstone of Russian Power*. New Haven: Yale University Press.

Lifesite. 1998. "International Criminal Court Approved." Lifesite Special Report, 19 July. http://www.lifesite.net.ldn/1998/jul/98071b.html.

–. 2000. "Radical Feminists Laud International Criminal Court." 9 March. http://www.lifesite.net.ldn/2000/mar/00030905.html.

Lister, Ruth. 1993. "Tracing the Contours of Women's Citizenship." *Policy and Politics* 21, 1: 3-16.

–. 1997. *Citizenship: Feminist Perspectives*. Houndmills, UK: Macmillan.

–. 2003. "Investing in the Citizen-Workers of the Future: Transformations in Citizenship and the State under New Labour." *Social Policy and Administration* 37, 5: 427-43.

–. 2004. *Poverty*. Cambridge: Polity Press.

Little, Margaret. 1998. *No Car, No Radio, No Liquor Permit: The Moral Regulation of Single Mothers in Ontario, 1920-1997*. Toronto: Oxford University Press.

Loi instituant un nouveau Code civil et portant réforme du droit de la famille, L.Q. 1980, c. 39 (*An Act to Establish a New Civil Code and to Reform Family Law*).

Lombard, Frederica. 1984. "The Law on Naming Children: Past, Present and Occasionally Future." *Names* 32: 129-37.

Lorde, Audre. 1984. *Sister Outsider: Essays and Speeches*. Freedom, CA: Crossing Press.

Lovenduski, Joni. 2002. "Feminizing Politics." *Women: A Cultural Review* 13, 2: 207-30.

Lovenduski, Joni, and Pippa Norris. 2003. "Westminster Women: The Politics of Presence." *Political Studies* 51: 84-102.

Lupton, Deborah, and Lesley Barclay. 1997. *Constructing Fatherhood: Discourses and Experiences*. London: Sage.

Macdonald, Laura. 2003. "Gender and Canadian Trade Policy: Women's Strategies for Access and Transformation." In *Feminist Perspectives on Canadian Foreign Policy*, ed. Claire Turenne Sjolander, Heather A. Smight, and Deborah Stienstra, 40-54. Toronto: Oxford University Press.

Mackey, Eva. 2002. *The House of Difference: Cultural Politics and National Identity in Canada*. Toronto: University of Toronto Press.

MacKinnon, Catherine. 1989. *Toward a Feminist Theory of the State*. Cambridge, MA: Harvard University Press.

–. 1993. *Only Words*. Cambridge, MA: Harvard University Press.

Macklin, Audrey. 2001. "Borderline Security." In *The Security of Freedom: Essays on Canada's Anti-terrorism Bill*, ed. Ronald J. Daniels, Patrick Macklem, and Kent Roach, 383-404. Toronto: University of Toronto Press.

Mahon, Rianne. 2004. "Early Child Learning and Care in Canada: Who Rules? Who Should Rule?" Discussion paper prepared for "Child Care for a Change," Canadian Council on Social Development conference on childcare in Canada, Winnipeg, 12-14 November. http://www.ccsd.ca/pubs/2004/cc/mahon.pdf.

Mahon, Rianne. 2006. "The OECD and the Work/Family Reconciliation Agenda: Competing Frames." In *Children, Changing Families and Welfare States*, ed. Jane Lewis, 173-99. Cheltenham, UK: Edward Elgar.

Mahon, Rianne, and Susan D. Phillips. 2002. "Dual-Earner Families Caught in a Liberal Welfare Regime? The Politics of Child Care Policy in Canada." In *Child Care Policy at the Crossroads: Gender and Welfare State Restructuring*, ed. Sonya Michel and Rianne Mahon, 191-218. New York: Routledge.

Mallon, John. 2000. "Evangelicals, Rabbi Support Vatican at UN." *Inside the Vatican*. http://www.c-fam.org/HolySee/voicesoftruth.html#11.

Mandell, Nancy, ed. 1998. *Feminist Issues: Race, Class and Sexuality*. 2nd ed. Scarborough: Prentice Hall.

Mansbridge, Jane. 1999. "Should Blacks Represent Blacks and Women Represent Women? A Contingent 'Yes.'" *Journal of Politics* 61, 3: 628-57.

Marshall, Katherine. 2003. "Benefiting from Extended Parental Leave." *Perspectives on Labour and Income* 3, 3 (March): 5-11.

Marshall, T.H., ed. 1964. *Class, Citizenship, and Social Development*. Garden City, NY: Doubleday.

Marston, Sallie. 2000. "The Social Construction of Scale." *Progress in Human Geography* 24, 2: 219-42.

Masson, Dominique. 2005. "Constructing Scale/Contesting Scale." Paper presented at the *Studies in Political Economy* conference "Towards a Political Economy of Scale," Toronto, 3-5 February.

Matsuda, Mari, Charles Lawrence, Richard Delgado, and Kimberlé Williams Crenshaw, eds. 1999. *Words That Wound: Critical Race Theory, Assaultive Speech and the First Amendment*. Boulder: Westview Press.

Matthews, Jill Julius. 1984. *Good and Mad Women: The Historical Construction of Femininity in Twentieth-Century Australia*. Sydney: George Allen and Unwin.

"Maureen McTeer Won't Disappear in Clark's Shadow." 1976. *Globe and Mail*, 24 February.

McCaughan, Margaret. 1977. *The Legal Status of Married Women in Canada*. Toronto: Carswell.

McClintock, Anne. 1993. "Family Feuds: Gender, Nationalism and the Family." *Feminist Review* 44: 61-81.

–. 1995. *Imperial Leather: Race, Gender and Sexuality in the Colonial Context.* New York: Routledge.

–. 1997. "'No Longer in a Future Heaven': Gender, Race and Nationalism." In *Dangerous Liaisons: Gender, Nations and Postcolonial Perspectives,* ed. Anne McClintock, Aamir Mufti, and Ella Shohat, 89-112. Minneapolis: University of Minnesota Press.

McDonald, Marci. 2004. "The Man behind Stephen Harper." *Walrus* (October): 34-48.

McIntosh, Mary. 1978. "The State and the Oppression of Women." In *Feminism and Materialism: Women and Modes of Production,* ed. Annette Kuhn and Ann Marie Wolpe, 254-89. London: Routledge and Kegan Paul.

McKeen, Wendy. 2001. "Writing Women Out: Poverty Discourse and Feminist Agency in the 1990's National Social Welfare Policy Debate." *Canadian Review of Social Policy* 48: 19-33.

–. 2004. *Money in Their Own Name: The Feminist Voice of Poverty, 1970-1995.* Toronto: University of Toronto Press.

McLaughlin, Janice. 2003. *Feminist Social and Political Theory: Contemporary Debates and Dialogues.* Houndmills, UK, and New York: Palgrave Macmillan.

Mead, Lawrence M. 1986. *Beyond Entitlement: The Social Obligations of Citizenship.* New York: Free Press, Macmillan.

–, ed. 1997. *The New Paternalism.* Washington, DC: Brookings Institute Press.

Meehan, Elizabeth. 1993. *Citizenship and the European Union.* London: Sage.

Mendelson, Michael. 2003. *Child Benefits Levels in 2003 and Beyond: Australia, Canada, the UK and the US.* Ottawa: Caledon Institute of Social Policy. http://www.caledoninst.org.

Meshcherkina, Elena. 2000. "New Russian Men: Masculinity Regained?" In *Gender, State and Society in Soviet and Post-Soviet Russia,* ed. Sarah Ashwin, 105-17. London: Routledge.

Migrationsverket. 2004. *Statistics on Our Activities.* http://www.migrationsverket.se/english.jsp.

Miliband, Ralph. 1969. *The State in Capitalist Society.* New York: Basic Books.

Mill, John Stuart. 1975. *On Liberty.* Edited by D. Spitz. New York: W.W. Norton.

Miller, Casey, and Kate Swift. 1976. *Words and Women.* Garden City, NY: Anchor Press.

Miller, Eric J. 2000. "Transportation and Communication." In *Canadian Cities in Transition,* 2nd ed., ed. Trudi Bunting and Pierre Filion, 173-97. Don Mills: Oxford University Press.

Mills, Lisa. 2005. "Body Politics: Maternal Health and the Politics of Scale in Mexico." Paper presented at the *Studies in Political Economy* conference "Towards a Political Economy of Scale," Toronto, 3-5 February.

Ministry of Foreign Affairs. 2001. *Sweden in 2000: A Country of Migration – Past Present and Future.* Stockholm: Ministry of Foreign Affairs.

Mishra, Ramesh. 1999. *Globalisation and the Welfare State.* Cheltenham, UK: Edward Elgar.

Moghadam, Valentine M., ed. 1994. *Gender and National Identity: Women and Politics in Muslim Societies.* London and Atlantic Highlands, NJ: Zed Books.

–. 2005. *Globalizing Women: Transnational Feminist Networks.* Baltimore: Johns Hopkins University Press.

Mohanty, Chandra Talpade. 2003. *Feminism without Borders: Decolonizing Theory, Practicing Solidarity.* Durham and London: Duke University Press.

Molyneux, Maxine. 1996. "Women's Rights and the International Context in the Post-Communist States." In *Mapping the Women's Movement,* ed. Monica Threlfall, 232-59. London: Verso.

Monture-Angus, Patricia. 1995. *Thunder in My Soul: A Mohawk Woman Speaks.* Halifax: Fernwood.

–. 1999. "Standing against Canadian Law: Naming Omissions of Race, Culture and Gender." In *Locating Law: Race, Class, Gender Connections,* ed. Elizabeth Comack, 76-94. Halifax: Fernwood.

Morton, F.L., and Rainer Knopff. 2000. *The Charter Revolution and the Court Party.* Peterborough: Broadview.

Morton, Ted. 1998. "New-Egalitarians: The Real Threat to Human Rights." *Calgary Herald,* 19 December.

Moshan, Brook Sari. 1998. "Women, War, and Words: The Gender Component in the Permanent International Criminal Court's Definition of Crimes against Humanity." *Fordham International Law Journal* 22: 154-84.

Mouffe, Chantal. 1992. "Feminism, Citizenship and Radical Democratic Politics." In *Feminists Theorize the Political,* ed. Judith Butler and Joan W. Butler, 369-84. New York and London: Routledge.

Muhtadie, L. 2004. "Child Poverty Rate Seen at Highest since 1996." *Globe and Mail Update,* 24 November. http://www.theglobeandmail.com.

Mungall, Constance. 1977. *Changing Your Name in Canada: How to Do It Legally.* Vancouver: International Self-Counsel Press.

Murav, Harriet. 1995. "Engendering the Russian Body Politic." In *Post-Communism and the Body Politic,* ed. Ellen E. Berry, 32-56. New York: New York University Press.

Myles, John, and Paul Pierson. 1997. "Friedman's Revenge: The Reform of 'Liberal' Welfare States in Canada and the United States." *Politics and Society* 25, 4: 443-72.

Myles, John, and Jill Quadagno. 2000. "Envisioning a *Third Way:* The Welfare State in the Twenty-First Century." *Contemporary Sociology* 29, 1: 157-67.

Nahan, Mike. 2000. "From the Editor." *IPA Review* 53, 3 (September): 2.

Nairn, Tom. 1972. *The Breakup of Britain.* London: New Left Books.

–. 1974. "Scotland and Europe." *New Left Review* 83: 57-82.

–. 1977. *The Breakup of Britain: Crisis and Neo-nationalism.* London: Verso.

–. 1979. *The Break-up of Great Britain: Crisis and Neo-nationalism.* London: New Left Books.

National Citizens' Coalition (NCC). 2007. http://nationalcitizens.ca.

National Council of Welfare. 2004. *Poverty Profile 2001.* Report No. 122. Ottawa: Ministry of Public Works and Government Services.

Neale, Palena R. 1998. "The Bodies of Christ as International Bodies: The Holy See, Wom(b)an and the Cairo Conference."*Review of International Studies* 24: 101-18.

Nikolic-Ristanovic, V. 2002. *Social Change, Gender, and Violence: Post-communist and War-Affected Societies.* Dordrecht: Kluwer Academic Publishers.

Nolen, Stephanie. 1998. "Private Lives: Name-Change Revival," *Globe and Mail,* September 2, C5.

Nordlinger, Eric. 1981. *On the Autonomy of the Democratic State.* Cambridge, MA: Harvard University Press.

O'Brien, Mary. 1981. *The Politics of Reproduction.* London: Routledge and Kegan Paul.

O'Connor, Julia, Ann S. Orloff, and Sheila Shaver. 1999. *States, Markets and Families: Gender, Liberalism and Social Policy in Australia, Canada, Great Britain and the United States.* Cambridge: Cambridge University Press.

Ohmae, Kenichi. 1990. *The Borderless World: Power and Strategy in the Interlinked Economy.* New York: HarperBusiness.

Okin, Susan Moller. 1991. "John Rawls: Justice as Fairness – for Whom?" In *Feminist Interpretations and Political Theory,* ed. Mary Lyndon Shanley and Carole Pateman, 181-98. University Park: Pennsylvania State University Press.

–. 1998. "Feminism and Multiculturalism: Some Tensions." *Ethics* 108: 661-84.

–. 1999. "Is Multiculturalism Bad for Women?" In *Is Multiculturalism Bad for Women?* ed. J. Cohen, M. Howard, and M. Nussbaum, 7-26. Princeton: Princeton University Press.

O'Lary, Brendan. 1996. "Political Science." In *The Social Science Encyclopedia.* 2nd ed., ed. Adam Kuper and Jessica Kuper. London and New York: Routledge.

Olson, Kevin. 2002. "Recognizing Gender, Redistributing Labor." *Social Politics* 9, 3: 380-410.

O'Neill, Brenda. 2003. "On the Same Wavelength? Feminist Attitudes across Generations of Canadian Women." In *Women and Electoral Politics in Canada,* ed. Manon Tremblay and Linda Trimble, 178-91. Toronto: Oxford University Press.

Organization of Islamic Conference. 2000. "On Slanderous Campaigns Waged by Certain Non-governmental Organizations (NGOs) against a Number of OIC Member States

Targeting the Islamic Shari'a under the Mantle of Human Rights Protection." 62/9-P(IS). http://www.oic-un.org.

Orloff, A. 2003: "Social Provision and Regulation: Theories of States, Social Policies, and Modernity." Paper presented at the annual meeting of Research Committee 19 on Poverty, Social Welfare and Social Policy, International Sociological Association, University of Toronto, Toronto, August.

Otto, Dianne. 1996. "Holding Up Half the Sky, but for Whose Benefit? A Critical Analysis of the Fourth World Conference on Women." *Australian Feminist Law Journal* 6: 7-28.

Pal, Leslie. 1997. *Beyond Policy Analysis: Public Issues Management in Turbulent Times.* Scarborough: ITP Nelson.

–. 1993. *Interests of State: The Politics of Language, Multiculturalism, and Feminism in Canada.* Montreal and Kingston: McGill-Queen's University Press.

Papillon, Martin, and Luc Turgeon. 2003. "Nationalism's Third Way? Comparing the Emergence of Citizenship Regimes in Quebec and Scotland." In *The Conditions of Diversity in Multinational Democracies,* ed. A-G Gagnon, M. Guibernau, and F. Rocher, 315-41. Montreal: Institute for Research on Public Policy.

Pascall, Gillian, and Nick Manning. 2000. "Gender and Social Policy: Comparing Welfare States in Central and Eastern Europe and the Former Soviet Union." *Journal of European Social Policy* 10, 3: 240-66.

Pateman, Carol. 1980. "The Civic Culture: A Philosophic Critique." In *The Civic Culture Revisited,* ed. Gabriel A. Almond and Sidney Verba, 57-102. Boston and Toronto: Little, Brown.

–. 1988a. "The Patriarchal Welfare State." In *Democracy and the Welfare State,* ed. Amy Guttman, 231-60. Princeton: Princeton University Press.

–. 1988b. *The Sexual Contract.* Oxford: Polity Press.

Paterson, S., P. Levasseur, and T. Teplova. 2004. "I Spy with My Little Eye ... Canada's National Child Care Benefit." In *How Ottawa Spends 2004-05: Mandate Change in the Paul Martin Era,* ed. G.B. Doern, 131-50. Montreal and Kingston: McGill-Queen's University Press.

Pearson, Mark, and Peter Scherer. 1997. "Balancing Security." *OECD Observer* 205 (April-May): 6-9.

Peck, Jamie, and Adam Tickell. 2002. "Neoliberalizing Space." *Antipode* 34, 3: 380-404.

Pelletier, Francine. 2005. "Sex, Truth, and Videotape." CBC Broadcast. Virage Productions.

Peterson, V. Spike. 1999. "Sexing Political Identities: Nationalism as Heterosexism." *International Feminist Journal of Politics* 1, 1: 34-65.

Peterson, V. Spike, and Anne Sisson Runyan. 1993. *Global Gender Issues.* Boulder: Westview Press.

Pettit, Philip. 1997. *Republicanism: A Theory of Freedom and Government.* Oxford: Clarendon Press.

Pettman, Jan. 1996. *Worlding Women: A Feminist International Politics.* London and New York: Routledge.

Phillips, Anne. 1995. *The Politics of Presence.* Oxford: Clarendon.

–. 1997. "Why Worry about Multiculturalism?" *Dissent* (Winter): 57-63.

Pickel, Andreas, and Jacqui True. 1999. "Global Forces, Transnational Linkages and Local Actors: Towards a New Political Economy of Post-Socialist Transformation." Paper presented at the American Association for the Advancement of Slavic Studies, St. Louis, Missouri, 18-21 November.

Pierson, Paul. 2000. "Increasing Returns, Path Dependence and the Study of Politics." *American Political Science Review* 94: 251-67.

–. 2004. *Politics in Time: History, Institutions and Social Analysis.* Princeton: Princeton University Press.

Pierson, Paul, and Theda Skocpol. 2002. "Historical Institutionalism in Contemporary Political Science." In *Political Science: State of the Discipline,* ed. Ira Katznelson and Helen V. Milner, 693-721. New York: W.W. Norton.

Pilcher, Jane, and Imelda Whelehan. 2004. *Key Concepts in Gender Studies.* London: Sage.

Pinnick, K. 1997. "When the Fighting Is Over: The Soldiers' Mothers and the Afghan Madonnas." In *Post-Soviet Women: From the Baltic to Central Asia,* ed. M. Buckley, 143-56. Cambridge: Cambridge University Press.

Pitkin, Hannah. 1967. *The Concept of Representation.* Los Angeles: University of California Press.

Pocock, J.G.A. 1992. "The Ideal of Citizenship since Classical Times." *Queen's Quarterly* 99, 1: 33-55.

Policy Research Initiative. 2005. *Social Capital as a Public Policy Tool.* Ottawa: Privy Council Office.

Popenoe, David. 1996. *Life without Father.* New York: Free Press.

Posadskaya, Anastasia, ed. 1994. *Women in Russia: A New Era in Russian Feminism.* London: Verso.

Pratt, G., and S. Hanson. 1991. "On the Links between Home and Work." *International Journal of Urban and Regional Research* 15: 55-74.

Puwar, Nirmal. 2004. "Thinking about Making a Difference." *British Journal of Politics and International Relations* 6: 65-80.

Rai, Shirin M. 2003. *Mainstreaming Gender, Democratizing the State? Institutional Mechanisms for the Advancement of Women.* Manchester and New York: Manchester University Press.

Rakowska-Harmstone, Teresa. 1990. "Nationalities and the Soviet Military." In *The Nationalities Factor in Soviet Politics and Society,* ed. Lubomyr Hajda and Mark Beissinger, 72-94. Boulder: Westview Press.

Randall, Vicky, and Georgina Waylen, eds. 1998. *Gender, Politics and the State.* London and New York: Routledge.

Randles, Sally, and Peter Dicken. 2004. "'Scale' and the Instituted Construction of the Urban: Contrasting the Cases of Manchester and Lyon." *Environment and Planning A* 36: 2011-32.

Rankin, L. Pauline. 2000. "Sexualities and National Identities: Re-imaging over Nationalism." *Journal of Canadian Studies* 35, 2: 176-96.

Rankin, L. Pauline, and Jill Vickers (with the research assistance of Anne-Marie Field). 2001. *Women's Movements and State Feminism: Integrating Diversity into Public Policy.* Ottawa: Status of Women, Canada.

Ray, Brian, and Damaris Rose. 2000. "Cities of the Everyday: Social-Spatial Perspectives on Gender, Difference and Diversity." In *Canadian Cities in Transition,* ed. T. Bunting and P. Filion, 502-24. 2nd ed. Don Mills: Oxford University Press.

REAL Women of Canada. 1998. "The International Criminal Court: World Nightmare." http://www.realwomenca.com/newsletter/1998_May_Jun/article_9.html.

–. 2003. "Statements on Equal Pay for Work of Equal Value and Child Care." http://www.realwomenca.com.

Rebick, Judy. 2005. *Ten Thousand Roses: The Making of a Feminist Revolution.* Toronto: Penguin Canada.

Rebick, Judy, and Kiké Roach. 1996. *Politically Speaking.* Vancouver: Douglas and McIntyre.

Reis, Elisa P. 2004. "The Lasting Marriage between Nation and State Despite Globalization." *International Political Science Review* 25, 3: 251-57.

Rivkin-Fish, Michelle. 2003. "Anthropology, Demography, and the Search for a Critical Analysis of Fertility: Insights from Russia." *American Anthropologist* 105, 2: 289-301.

Robertson, Geoffrey. 2000. *Crimes against Humanity: The Struggle for Global Justice.* Melbourne: Penguin.

Rome Statute of the International Criminal Court. 1998. UN Doc. A/Conf. 183/9. http://www.un.org/law/icc/statute/romefra.htm.

Royal Commission on New Reproductive Technologies. 1993. *Final Report: Proceed with Care.* Ottawa: Minister of Government Services.

Said, Edward. 1979. *Orientalism.* New York: Vintage Books.

Saint-Martin, Denis. 2000. "De l'État-providence à l'État d'investissement social?" In *How Ottawa Spends 2000-2001: Past Imperfect, Future Tense,* ed. Leslie A. Pal, 33-58. Toronto: Oxford University Press.

Salmenniemi, Suvi. 2003. "Renegotiating Citizenship: Gender and Civil Society in Contemporary Russia." Paper presented at the 5th European Feminist Research Conference, Lund, Sweden, 20-24 August. http://www.5thfeminist.lu.se/filer/paper_571.pdf.

Sanchez, Laura, and Elizabeth Thomson. 1997. "Becoming Mothers and Fathers: Parenthood, Gender and the Division of Labor." *Gender and Society* 11, 6: 747-72.

Sassoon, Anne Showstack. 1987. "Introduction: The Personal and the Intellectual, Fragments and Order, International Trends and National Specificities." In *Women and the State*, ed. Anne Showstack Sassoon, 15-42. London: Hutchison.

Sawer, Marian. 1997. "A Defeat for Political Correctness?" In *The Politics of Retribution: The 1996 Federal Election*, ed. Clive Bean, S. Bennett, M. Simms, and J. Warhurst. Sydney: Allen and Unwin.

–. 2000. "Parliamentary Representation of Women: From Discourses of Justice to Strategies of Accountability." *International Political Science Review* 21, 4: 361-80.

–. 2002. "Governing for the Mainstream: Implications for Community Representation." *Australian Journal of Public Administration* 61: 39-49.

–. 2003. *The Ethical State: Social Liberalism in Australia*. Melbourne: Melbourne University Press.

–. 2004. "The Impact of Feminist Scholarship on Australian Political Science." *Australian Journal of Political Science* 39, 3: 553-66.

–. 2006. "'When Women Support Women ...' EMILY's List and the Substantive Representation of Women in Australia." In *Representing Women in Parliament: A Comparative Study*, ed. Marian Sawer, Manon Tremblay, and Linda Trimble, 103-19. London: Routledge.

Scalmer, Sean, and Murray Goot. 2004. "Elites Constructing Elites: News Limited's Newspapers 1996-2002." In *Us and Them: Anti-elitism in Australia*, ed. Marian Sawer and Barry Hindess. Perth: API Network.

Scheuble, Laurie, and David Johnson. 1993. "Marital Name Change: Plans and Attitudes of College Students." *Journal of Marriage and Family* 55: 747-54.

Service, Robert. 1997. *A History of Twentieth-Century Russia*. Cambridge, MA: Harvard University Press.

Shapiro, Michael. 1997. "Narrating the Nation, Unwelcoming the Stranger: Anti-immigration Policy in Contemporary 'America.'" *Alternatives* 22: 1-34.

Sharpe, Sydney. 1994. *The Gilded Ghetto: Women and Political Power in Canada*. Toronto: HarperCollins.

Shields, Carol. 2002. *Unless: A Novel*. London and New York: Random House Canada.

Silver, Cynthia. 2000. "Being There: The Time Dual-Earner Couples Spend with Their Children." *Canadian Social Trends* 57 (Summer): 26-29.

Simeon, Richard. 1987. "Inside the Macdonald Commissions." *Studies in Political Economy* 22: 167-79.

Singh, Jyoti Shankar. 1998. *Creating a New Consensus on Population: The International Conference on Population and Development*. London: Earthscan.

Skinner, Quentin. 1998. *Liberty before Liberalism*. Cambridge: Cambridge University Press.

Skocpol, Theda. 1979. *States and Social Revolutions*. Cambridge and New York: Cambridge University Press.

–. 1985. "Bringing the State Back In: Strategies of Analysis in Current Research." In *Bringing the State Back In*, ed. Peter B. Evans, Dietrich Rueschneyer, and Theda Skocpol, 3-37. Cambridge and New York: Cambridge University Press.

Sluga, Glenda. 1998. "Identity, Gender and the History of European Nations and Nationalisms." *Nations and Nationalism* 4: 87-111.

Smart, C. 1995. *Law, Crime, and Sexuality*. London: Sage.

Smith, Anthony D. 1991. *National Identity*. Harmondsworth: Penguin.

–. 1998. *Nationalism and Modernism*. London and New York: Routledge.

Smith, Neil. 1993. "Homeless/Global: Scaling Places." In *Mapping the Futures: Local Cultures, Global Change*, ed. Jon Bird, Barry Curtis, Tim Putnam, George Robertson, and Lisa Tickner, 87-119. New York: Routledge.

Spalter-Roth, Roberta, and Heidi Hartmann. 1999. "Small Happinesses: The Feminist Struggle to Integrate Social Research with Social Activism." In *Feminist Approaches to Theory and*

Methodology: An Interdisciplinary Reader, ed. Sharlene Hesse-Biber, 206-24. Oxford: Oxford University Press.

Spees, Pam. 2003. "Women's Advocacy in the Creation of the International Criminal Court: Changing the Landscapes of Justice and Power." *Signs* 28, 4: 1233-256.

Spelman, Elizabeth V. 1988. *Inessential Woman: Problems of Exclusion in Feminist Thought*. Boston: Beacon Press.

Spender, Dale. 1980. *Man Made Language*. London: Routledge and Kegan.

Sperling, Valerie. 1999. *Organizing Women in Contemporary Russia: Engendering Transition*. Cambridge: Cambridge University Press.

Squires, Judith. 1999. "Rethinking the Boundaries of Political Representation." In *New Agendas for Women*, ed. Sylvia Walby, 169-89. London: Macmillan.

Stannard, Una. 1973. *Married Women vs. Husbands: The Case for Wives Who Keep Their Own Name*. San Francisco: Germainbooks.

–. 1977. *Mrs. Man*. San Francisco: Germainbooks.

–. 1984. "Manners Make Laws: Married Women's Names in the United States." *Names* 32: 114-28.

Stasiulis, Daiva, and Nira Yuval-Davis. 1995. *Unsettling Settler Societies: Articulations of Gender, Race, Ethnicity and Class*. London: Sage.

Statement of Claim. 1991. Reprinted in 1993 in *The Social Construction of Choice and the New Reproductive and Genetic Technologies*, ed. Gwynne Basen, Margrit Eichler, and Abby Lippman. Hull: Voyageur Publishing.

Statistics Canada. 2000. *Women in Canada 2000: A Gender-Based Statistical Report*. Ottawa: Statistics Canada, Housing, Family and Social Statistics Division.

Steele, Jackie. 2003. "Naming: The Inequality. Women as Citizens or Women as 'Wives/ Mothers-to-Be': Marriage Law, 'Surnames' and the Politics of Recognition in Canadian, Québécois and Japanese Societies." Master's thesis, Carleton University.

Stetson, Dorothy McBride, and Amy G. Mazur, eds. 1995. *Comparative State Feminism*. Thousand Oaks, CA: Sage.

Stevens, Jacqueline. 1999. *Reproducing the State*. Princeton: Princeton University Press.

Stoler, Ann Laura. 1997. "Making Empire Respectable: The Politics of Race and Sexual Morality in Twentieth-Century Colonial Cultures." In *Dangerous Liaisons: Gender, Nations and Postcolonial Perspectives*, ed. Anne McClintock, Aamir Mufti, and Ella Shohat, 344-73. Minneapolis: University of Minnesota Press.

Strange, Carolyn. 1995. *Toronto's Girl Problem*. Toronto: University of Toronto Press.

Stratigaki, M. 2004. "The Cooptation of Gender Concepts in EU Policies: The Case of 'Reconciliation of Work and Family.'" *Social Politics* 11, 1: 30-56.

Streeck, Wolfgang, and Kathleen Thelen, eds. 2005. *Beyond Continuity: Institutional Change in Advanced Political Economies*. Oxford: Oxford University Press.

Strong-Boag, Veronica, Sherrill Grace, Avigail Eisenberg, and Joan Anderson, eds. 1998. *Painting the Maple: Essays on Race, Gender and the Construction of Canada*. Vancouver: UBC Press.

Studlar, Donley, and Ian McAllister. 2002. "Does a Critical Mass Exist? A Comparative Analysis of Women's Legislative Representation since 1950." *European Journal of Political Research* 41: 233-53.

Sutherland, Ann. 1982. "Equality of Women." *Globe and Mail*, 7 January, 7.

Swan, Peter, and M. Bernstam. 1987. "Brides of the State." *IPA Review* 41 (May-July): 22-25.

Swerdlow, Joel. 1998. "Making Sense of the Millennium." *National Geographic* 193, 1 (January): 2-11.

Swers, Michele. 2001. "Research on Women in Legislatures: What Have We Learned, Where Are We Going?" *Women and Politics* 23, 1-2: 167-85.

Taiaiake, Alfred. 1999. *Peace, Power, Righteousness: An Indigenous Manifesto*. Don Mills: Oxford University Press.

Tarrow, Sidney. 2001. "Transnational Politics: Contention and Institutions in International Politics." *Annual Review of Political Science* 4: 1-20.

Taylor, Charles. 1992a. *Multiculturalism and "The Politics of Recognition."* Edited by Amy Gutmann. Princeton: Princeton University Press.

–. 1992b. "The Politics of Recognition." In *Multiculturalism and "The Politics of Recognition"*, ed. Amy Gutmann, 25-73. Princeton: Princeton University Press.

Taylor-Gooby, Peter. 1991. *Social Change, Social Welfare and Social Science*. Toronto: University of Toronto Press.

–, ed. 2004. *New Risks, New Welfare: The Transformation of the European Welfare State*. Oxford: Oxford University Press.

Temkina, Anna, and Anna Rotkirch. 1997. "Soviet Gender Contracts and Their Shifts in Contemporary Russia." In *Russia in Transition: The Case of New Collective Actors and New Collective Actions*, ed. Anna Temkina, 183-207. Helsinki: Kikimora Publications.

Temkina, Anna, and Elena Zdravomyslova. 2001. "Die Krise der Männlichkeit im Alltagsdiskurs: Wandel der Geschlechterordnung in Rußland." *Berliner Debatte Initial* 12, 4: 78-90.

Teplova, Tatyana. 2003. "Russian Welfare State: Towards a Neofamilialist Type." Paper presented at the International Sociological Association annual meeting of the Research Committee on Poverty, Social Welfare, and Social Policy, Toronto, 21-24 August. http://individual.utoronto.ca/RC19_2003/papers.html.

Thelen, Kathleen. 2003. "How Institutions Evolve." In *Comparative Historical Analysis in the Social Sciences*, ed. James Mahoney and Dietrich Rueschemeyer, 208-40. New York: Cambridge University Press.

Thobani, Sunera. 2000. "Closing Ranks: Racism and Sexism in Canada's Immigration Policy." *Race and Class* 42: 35-55.

Thomas, Sue. 1991. "The Impact of Women on State Legislative Policies." *Journal of Politics* 53: 958-76.

–. 1994. *How Women Legislate*. New York: Oxford University Press.

Tikhomirov, Vladimir. 2000. *The Political Economy of Post-Soviet Russia*. New York: St. Martin's Press.

Timpson, Annis May. 2001. *Driven Apart: Women's Employment Equality and Child Care in Canadian Public Policy*. Vancouver: UBC Press.

Tohidi, Nayrereh. 1994. "Modernity, Islamization and Women in Iran." In *Gender and National Identity: Women and Politics in Muslim Societies*, ed. Valentine Moghadam, 110-47. London and New Jersey/Karachi: Zed Books/Oxford University Press.

–2003. "Women's Rights in the Muslim World: The Universal-Particular Interplay." *HAWWA* 1, 2: 152-88.

Towns, Ann. 2003. "Understanding the Effects of Larger Ratios of Women in National Legislatures: Proportions and Gender Differentiation in Sweden and Norway." *Women and Politics* 25, 1-2: 1-29.

Townson, Monica. 2005. *Poverty Issues for Canadian Women*. Prepared for Gender Equality Consultations. Ottawa: Status of Women Canada.

Tremblay, Manon. 1992. "Quand les femmes se distinguent: féminisme et représentation politique au Québec." *Revue canadienne de science politique* 25: 65-88.

–. 1997. "Quebec Women in Politics: An Examination of the Research." In *In the Presence of Women: Representation in Canadian Governments*, ed. Jane Arscott and Linda Trimble, 228-51. Toronto: Harcourt Bace.

–. 1998. "Do Female MPs Substantively Represent Women? A Study of Legislative Behaviour in Canada's 35th Parliament." *Canadian Journal of Political Science* 31, 3: 435-65.

–. 2003. "Women's Representational Role in Australia and Canada: The Impact of Political Context." *Australian Journal of Political Science* 38, 2: 215-38.

Tremblay, Manon, and G. Boivin. 1990-91. "La question de l'avortement au Parlement Canadien: de l'importance de genre dans l'orientation des débats." *Revue juridique la femme et le droit* 4: 459-76.

Tremblay, Manon, and Réjean Pelletier. 2000. "More Feminists or More Women? Descriptive and Substantive Representations of Women in the 1997 Canadian Federal Elections." *International Political Science Review* 21, 4: 381-405.

Trimble, Linda. 1993. "A Few Good Women: Female Legislators in Alberta, 1972-1991." In *Standing on New Ground: Women in Alberta*, ed. Catherine A. Cavanaugh and Randi R. Warne, 87-118. Edmonton: University of Alberta Press.

–. 1997. "Feminist Politics in the Alberta Legislature, 1972-1994." In *In the Presence of Women: Representation in Canadian Governments,* ed. Jane Arscott and Linda Trimble, 128-53. Toronto: Harcourt.

–. 1998. "Who's Represented? Gender and Diversity in the Alberta Legislature." In *Women and Political Representation in Canada,* ed. Manon Tremblay and Caroline Andrew, 257-89. Ottawa: University of Ottawa Press.

–. 2003. "Women and the Politics of Citizenship." In *Reinventing Canada: Politics of the 21st Century,* ed. Janine Brodie and Linda Trimble, 131-50. Toronto: Prentice Hall.

Trimble, Linda, and Jane Arscott. 2003. *Still Counting: Women in Politics across Canada.* Peterborough: Broadview Press.

Trociuk v. British Columbia (Attorney General), [2003] 1 S.C.R. 835.

True, Jacqueline. 2000. "Engendering Transformations: Re-constructing State and Civil Society in the Post-Socialist Czech Republic." PhD diss., York University, Toronto.

Tully, James. 1993. "Rediscovering America: The Two Treatises and Aboriginal Rights." In *An Approach to Political Philosophy: Locke in Contexts,* ed. James Tully, 137-78. Cambridge: Cambridge University Press.

–. 2001. "Introduction." In *Multinational Democracies,* ed. Alain Gagnon and James Tully, 1-34. Cambridge: Cambridge University Press.

Turpel, Mary Ellen. 1996. "The Cultural Non-homogeneity of Québec: Secessionism, Indigenous Legal Perspectives and Inseparability." In *Self-Determination: International Perspectives,* ed. Donald Clark and Robert Williamson, 284-90. London: Macmillan.

Urban, Michael, and Vladimir Gel'man. 1997. "The Development of Political Parties in Russia." In *Democratic Changes and Authoritarian Reactions in Russia, Ukraine, Belarus, and Moldova,* ed. Karen Dawisha and Bruce Parrot. Cambridge: Cambridge University Press.

Vakhnina, L. 2002. "Zashchitit' synovei: ob organizatsii soldatskikh materei." *Informatsionnyi Biulleten' Pravleniia obshchestva "Memorial."* http://www.memo.ru/about/bull/b25/6.htm.

van den Berghe, Pierre. 1978. "Race and Ethnicity: A Sociobiological Perspective." *Ethnic and Racial Studies* 1, 4: 401-11.

–. 1979. *The Ethnic Phenomenon.* New York: Elsevier.

van Dijk, Teun. 1995. "Discourse Semantics and Ideology." *Discourse and Society* 6, 2: 243-89.

–. 1991. *Racism and the Press.* London: Routledge.

Vandelac, Louise. 1993. "The Baird Commission from 'Access' to 'Reproductive Technologies' to the 'Excesses' of Practitioners of the Art of Diversion and Relentless Pursuit." In *Misconceptions: The Social Construction of Choice and the New Reproductive and Genetic Technologies,* ed. Gwynne Bassen, Margrit Eichler, and Abby Lippman, 253-72. Hull: Voyageur.

Verdery, Katherine. 1996. *What Was Socialism and What Comes Next?* Princeton: Princeton University Press.

Vickers, Jill. 1994. "Notes toward a Political Theory of Sex and Power." In *Power/Gender: Social Relations in Theory and Practice,* ed. H.L. Radtke and Hendrickus S. Stam, 179-93. London, Thousand Oaks, CA, and New Delhi: Sage.

–. 1997. *Reinventing Political Science: A Feminist Approach.* Halifax: Fernwood.

–. 2000. "Feminisms and Nationalisms in English Canada." *Journal of Canadian Studies* 35, 2: 128-48.

–. 2002. "Feminists and Nationalisms." In *Gender, Race and Nation,* ed. Vanaja Dhruvarajan and Jill Vickers, 273-94. Toronto, Buffalo, and London: University of Toronto Press.

–. 2003. "In Search of the Citizen-Mother." Paper presented at the annual meeting of the Canadian Political Science Association. Halifax, 1 June.

–. 2006a. "Bringing Nations In: Some Methodological and Conceptual Issues in Connecting Feminisms with Nationhood and Nationalisms." *International Journal of Feminist Politics* 8, 1: 84-109.

–. 2006b. "In Search of Women-Friendly Democracy: Gender/Nation Relations in Modern Nation-States." Davidson Dunton Research Lecture, Carleton University, Ottawa, 27 March.

Vickers, Jill, Pauline Rankin, and Christine Appelle. 1993. *Politics as If Women Mattered.* Toronto: Toronto University Press.

Villeneuve, Paul, Winnie Frohn, and Catherine Trudelle. 2002-03. "Femmes, pouvoir local et politiques municipals à Québec." *Espaces, Populations, Sociétés:* 361-72.

Violi, Patricia. 1992. "Gender, Subjectivity and Language." In *Beyond Equality and Difference: Feminist Politics Female Subjectivity*, ed. Gisela Bock and Susan James, 164-76. London: Routledge.

Viroli, Maurizio. 2002. *Republicanism*. New York: Hill and Wang.

Voronina, Olga. 1994. "The Mythology of Women's Emancipation in the USSR as the Foundation for a Policy of Discrimination." In *Women in Russia: A New Era in Russian Feminism*, ed. Anastasia Posadskaya, 37-56. London: Verso.

Voyer, J.P. 2004. "Poverty and Exclusion: New Perspectives, New Approaches." *Horizons* 7, 2: 1-2.

Wagner, Claudia. 2000. *Rußlands Kriege in Tschetschenien: Politische Transformation und militärische Gewalt*. Munster: LIT Verlag.

Walby, Sylvia. 1994. "Is Citizenship Gendered?" *Sociology* 28, 2: 379-95.

–. 1997. *Gender Transformations*. London and New York: Routledge.

–. 2002. "Gender, Nations and States in a Global Era." *Nations and Nationalisms* 6, 4: 523-40.

–. 2004. "The European Union and Gender Equality: Emergent Varieties of Gender Regimes." *Social Politics* 11, 1: 4-29.

Walsh, Peter. 1990. "New Class Is Just More of the Same." *Australian Financial Review*, 28 August, 13.

Wängnerud, Lena. 2000. "Testing the Politics of Presence: Women's Representation in the Swedish Riksdag." *Scandinavian Political Studies* 23, 1: 67-91.

Warbrick, Colin, and Dominic McGoldrick. 2001. "The Preparatory Commission for the International Criminal Court." Current Developments: Public International Law. *International and Comparative Law Quarterly* 50: 420-35.

Warren, Mark E. 2005. "Citizen Representatives." Paper presented at the annual meeting of the American Political Science Association Roundtable "Mobilizing Representation 40 Years after Pitkin," Washington, 31 August to 3 September.

Weir, Fred. 2002. "In Russia, an Army of Desertion." *Christian Science Monitor*, 30 September. http://www.csmonitor.com/2002/0930/p01s02-woeu.htm.

Weisner, Merry. 2000. *Women and Gender in Early Modern Europe*. 2nd ed. Cambridge: Cambridge University Press.

Weitzman, Lenore. 1981. *The Marriage Contract: Spouses, Lovers, and the Law*. New York: Free Press.

Wekerle, Gerda. 2000. "Women's Rights to the City: Gendered Spaces of a Pluralistic Citizenship." In *Democracy, Citizenship and the Global City*, ed. Engin Isin, 203-17. London: Routledge.

Weldon, S. Laurel. 2002. "Beyond Bodies: Institutional Sources of Representation for Women in Democratic Policymaking." *Journal of Politics* 64, 4: 1153-74.

West, Lois, ed. 1997. *Feminist Nationalism*. New York and London: Routledge.

Westin, Charles, and Elena Dingu-Kyrklund. 1997. *Reducing Immigration, Reviewing Integration: An Account of the Current Facts, Figures and Legislation concerning Multiculturalism in Sweden*. Stockholm: CEIFO. Centrum för forskning om internationell migration och etniska relationer/Centre for Research in International Migration and Ethnic Relations.

White, Deena. 2003. "Social Policy and Solidarity: Orphans of the New Model of Social Cohesion." *Canadian Journal of Sociology* 28, 1: 51-76.

White, Linda A. "From Ideal to Pragmatic Politics: National Child Care Advocacy Groups in the 1980s and 1990s." In *Changing Child Care: Five Decades of Child Care Advocacy and Policy in Canada*, ed. Susan Prentice, 97-115. Halifax: Fernwood.

White, Stuart. 2000. "Review Article: Social Rights and the Social Contract – Political Theory and the New Welfare Politics." *British Journal of Political Science* 30: 507-32.

Whitworth, Sandra. 1994. *Feminism and International Relations: Towards a Political Economy of Gender in Interstate and Non-governmental Institutions*. New York: St. Martin's Press.

Whitzman, Carolyn. 2002. "The 'Voice of Women' in Canadian Local Government." In *Urban Affairs, Back on the Policy Agenda*, ed. C. Andrew, K. Graham, and S. Phillips, 93-118. Montreal and Kingston: McGill-Queen's University Press.

"Who's Obstructionist? Arabs Ask." 1998. *Terraviva: The Conference Daily Newspaper*. http://www.ips.org.iss/tv020703.htm.

Wiegers, Wanda. 2002. *The Framing of Poverty as "Child Poverty" and Its Implications for Women.* Report in the research program "Where Have All the Women Gone? Changing Shifts in Policy Discourses." Ottawa: Status of Women Canada.

Williams, Melissa. 1998. *Voice, Trust and Memory: Marginalized Groups and the Failings of Liberal Representation.* Princeton: Princeton University Press.

Willis, Alette. 2005. "Rescaling World Peace: Modeling the Global Community at Pearson College." Paper presented at the *Studies in Political Economy* conference "Towards a Political Economy of Scale," Toronto, 3-5 February.

Wilson, Elizabeth. 1981. *The Sphinx in the City.* Berkeley: University of California Press.

Wilson, Fiona, and Bodil Folke Frederickson, eds. 1995. *Ethnicity, Gender and the Subversion of Nationalism.* London: Frank Cass.

Wilton, Shauna. 2000. "Manitoba Women Nurturing the Nation: The Manitoba IODE and Maternal Nationalism, 1913-1920." *Women and Nationalisms: Canadian Experiences. Journal of Canadian Studies/Revue d'études canadiennes* 35, 2: 149-65.

Wishlow, Kevin. 2001. "Rethinking the Polarization Thesis." In *Saskatchewan Politics Into the Twenty-First Century,* ed. H.A. Leeson, 169-97. Regina: University of Regina.

Wodak, Ruth, Rudolf de Cillia, Martin Reisigl, and Karin Liebhart. 1999. *The Discursive Construction of National Identity.* Edinburgh: Edinburgh University Press.

"Woman Challenges Judge over Use of Maiden Name." 1983. *Globe and Mail,* 17 October, 5.

Women in Cities International. 2004. *Women's Safety Awards 2004: A Compendium of Good Practices.* Montreal: Women in Cities International.

Women-Church Convergence. N.d. "Equal Is as Equal Does." http://www.catholicsforchoice.org/articles/.

Women's Caucus for Gender Justice. 1998. "The Crime of Forced Pregnancy." http://www.iccwomen.org/icc/iccpc/rome/forcedpreg.html.

-. 1999. "Excluding Crimes against Women from the ICC Is Not an Option." http://iccwomen.addr.com/reports.marpaneleng.htm.

-. 2000. *Recommendations and Commentary to the Elements Annex and Rules of Procedure and Evidence.* Submitted to the Preparatory Commission for the International Criminal Court. 12-30 June. http://www.iccwomen.org/icc/iccpc062000pc/elementsannex.html.

Women's Initiatives for Gender Justice. 2006. "Three Women Elected to the Bench of the ICC." http://www.iccwomen.org/news/2006_01_26.php.

Wong, Baldwin. 2004. "Diversity and Access." In *Our Diverse Cities,* ed. C. Andrew, 158-59. Ottawa: Metropolis.

Yalnizyan, A. 2005. *Canada's Commitment to Equality: A Gender Analysis of the Last Ten Federal Budgets (1995-2005).* Ottawa: Canadian Feminist Alliance for International Action.

Yashar, Deborah. 1999. "Democracy, Indigenous Movements, and the Postliberal Challenge in Latin America." *World Politics* 52, 1: 76-104.

Yeatman, Anna. 1993. "Voice and Representation in the Politics of Difference." In *Feminism and the Politics of Difference,* ed. Sneja Gunew and Anna Yeatman, 228-45. Halifax: Fernwood.

-. 1994. *Postmodern Revisionings of the Political.* London: Routledge.

Yoder, Janice D. 1991. "Rethinking Tokenism: Looking beyond Numbers." *Gender and Society* 5, 2: 178-92.

Young, B. 2003. "Financial Crises and Social Reproduction: Asia, Argentina and Brazil." In *Power, Production and Social Reproduction,* ed. Isabella Bakker and Stephen Gill, 103-21. London: Palgrave Macmillan.

Young, Iris Marion. 1989. "Polity and Group Difference: A Critique of the Ideal of Universal Citizenship." *Ethics* 99, 2: 250-74.

-. 1990a. *Justice and the Politics of Difference.* Princeton: Princeton University Press.

-. 1990b. *Throwing Like a Girl and Other Essays in Feminist Philosophy and Social Theory.* Indianapolis: Indiana University Press.

-. 1994. "Gender as Seriality: Thinking about Women as a Social Collective." *Signs* 19, 3: 713-38.

–. 2000. *Inclusion and Democracy.* Oxford: Oxford University Press.

Young, Lisa. 1997. "Fulfilling the Mandate of Difference: Women in the Canadian House of Commons." In *In the Presence of Women: Representation in Canadian Governments,* ed. Jane Arscott and Linda Trimble, 82-103. Toronto: Harcourt.

Yurchak, Alexei. 2002. "Muzhskaia ekonomia: ne do glupostei kogda kar'eru kuësh'" In *O Muzhe(n)stvennosti,* ed. Sergei Ushakin, 245-67. Moscow: Novoe literaturnoe obozrenie.

Yuval-Davis, Nira. 1991. "The Citizenship Debate: Women, Ethnic Processes and the State." *Feminist Review* 39: 58-68.

–. 1997. *Gender and Nation.* London and Thousand Oaks, CA: Sage.

–. 1998. "Gender and Nation." In *Women, Ethnicity and Nationalism: The Politics of Transition,* ed. Rick Wilford and Robert L. Miller, 23-35. London and New York: Routledge.

Zhurzhenko, Tatiana. 2001. *Sotsial'noe vosproisvodstvo i gendernaia politika v Ukraine.* Kharkov: Folio.

–. 2004. "Staraia ideologiia novoi sem'i: demograficheskii natsionalism Rossii i Ukrainy." In *Semeinye uzy: Modeli dlia sborki (kniga 2),* ed. Sergei Ushakin, 268-96. Moscow: Novoe literaturnoe obozrenie.

Index

Embleton, Sheila, 229, 232
embryo research, 107
employment. *See* labour
Employment Insurance (Canada), 211
Endeavour Forum (Australia), 134
enforced pregnancy, 152-54
enforced prostitution, 157
Enloe, Cynthia, 2
enslavement, of women, 155, 157
EOC. See *Elements of Crime Annex*
equality: in Australia, 15, 125-28, 132-35;
in Canada, 15-17, 61, 67, 69-71, 73-74,
130-35, 165, 185, 189-90, 197-98, 202;
market populism perspective on, 125,
132-35; means to achieving, 10; naming
laws and, 231, 237; neoliberalism and,
186; new class and, 122; populism and,
15; in Quebec, 231; as same treatment,
132-35; in Soviet Union, 49-50; in
Sweden, 61, 69-71, 73-74; transnational
advocacy involving, 159
Esping-Andersen, Gøsta, 166, 173
Europe, welfare states in, 173-74
Evangelical Protestantism, 142
evidence-based medicine (EBM), 98,
108-12

Facio, Alda, 151, 152
family: in Canada, 69-70, 73-74; poverty
in, 177; religious conservatism and, 148,
155; in Soviet Union, 50; in Sweden, 68,
71, 73-74; violence in, 154-56; welfare
state and, 168, 174. *See also* caregiving;
children; motherhood; naming laws;
patriarchy
Family Allowances (Canada), 189, 192-93
Fanon, Franz, 37-40, 42-43
Fédération des femmes du Québec, 231
Federation of Canadian Municipalities,
242
femininity, in Russia, 56
feminism: in Australia, 127; and bureaucracy, 98-100, 118; in Canada, 192; and
Catholic Church, 143; channels for
actions of, 257; controversial issues in,
38; cyber, 257; first-wave, 253; future of,
18, 252-59; and International Criminal
Court, 139-40, 149-61; legislative
representation of, 87; market populism
perspective on, 121, 127, 130-31, 134,
138; and nationalism, 21-25, 27, 32-33,
37-39; and race, 253; and religion, 161;
and reproductive technologies, 97-119;
second-wave, 252-59; third-wave, 252,
258; waves of, 18, 252-53; Western vs
non-Western, 22, 24-25, 38, 262n16.

See also feminist research; feminist
scholarship
Feminism without Borders (Mohanty), 2-3
feminist research: in bureaucratic context,
97-98, 100; dual vision of, 100; quantitative approach vs, 110; on reproductive
technologies, 100-101. *See also* feminist
scholarship
feminist scholarship: boundaries as subject
of, 2-3; and citizenship, 8-11; contributions of, 5-12, 224; and the nation,
11-12, 61-62; and political change, 18;
political science discipline and, 4-5; on
religion, 160-61; significance of, 2; and
the state, 6-8; on transnational activism,
141-42. *See also* feminist research
feministas, 25, 261n7
feminization of poverty, 171, 177, 182,
194
femocrats, 99, 125
Ferguson, Kathy E., 98-99
Filmer, Robert, 226
Finland, 21, 25, 28, 31, 261n2
First Nations, 130
First Nations? Second Thoughts (Flanagan),
130
first-wave feminism, 253
Flanagan, Tom, 130-31
Focus on the Family, 148
Folbre, Nancy, 168
Folson, Rose Baaba, 65
forced pregnancy. *See* enforced pregnancy
Fourth World Conference on Women
(FWCW, Beijing, 1995), 142, 148, 151,
158
France, 31
Frank, Thomas, 120
Fraser, F.C., 107
Fraser Forum (magazine), 125
Fraser Institute, 124, 130, 131
Fraser, Nancy, 203, 209-10
Free to Choose (Friedman and Friedman),
122
Free Trade Agreement (FTA), 192
freedom. *See* liberty
Freeman, Jo, 257
French Revolution, 26
Friedan, Betty, 171, 255, 258
Friedman, Milton, 124; *Free to Choose*,
122
Friedman, Rose, *Free to Choose*, 122
Frum, David, 123
Fukuyama, Francis, *The Great Disruption*,
172
FWCW. *See* Fourth World Conference on
Women

Locke, John, 9
lone-parent families. *See* single mothers
A Look at Canada (Citizenship and
Immigration Canada), 60, 65, 70, 72
Lorde, Audre, 256
Lorenzin, Elizabeth, 82
Lovenduski, Joni, 86
Lupton, Deborah, 211, 217

Mackey, Eva, 63
MacKinnon, Catherine, 6
Manitoba, 230
Manitoba Centre for Health Policy and
Evaluation, 112
Manning, Preston, 130, 133
marital naming policies. *See* naming laws
market populism: in Australia, 125-28; in
Canada, 128-32; and elites, 121-23, 126-
28, 130-31, 133; and equality, 132-35;
and new class, 122-24, 126-28, 133; and
NGOs, 135-37; and special interests, 124-
29, 132-36; strategy of, 120-21; target of,
121; think-tanks and, 124-25, 130, 131,
136
marriage: concept of, 233; social policy
and, 172. *See also* naming laws
Marshall, T.H., 9
Marston, Sallie, 240
Martin, Paul, 194
Marxism, 5-7
Masson, Dominique, 242
McAllister, Ian, 81, 83
McCaughan, Margaret, 230; *Legal Status of
Married Women in Canada*, 229
McClintock, Anne, 12, 39, 41, 61
McCutcheon, Susan, 104
McDonald Commission on Canada's
Economic Prospects, 111, 114, 119
McIntosh, Mary, 7
McKeen, Wendy, 175
McLachlin, Beverley, 131
McMaster University, Centre of Clinical
Epidemiology and Biostatistics, 112
McNeely, E. G., 229
McTeer, Maureen, 102-4, 106, 229
Mead, Lawrence M., 206-8, 217, 218
media, and market populism, 124-25, 129,
131
Meech Lake Accord, 192
Melikian, Gennadii, 55
men and masculinity: and caregiving, 203-
4, 210-19, 255; and life satisfaction, 217-
18; military and, 52, 58; naming laws
and, 232-34, 236; in Russia, 53-54, 58; in
Soviet Union, 50-52; and violence, 258;
welfare state and, 125. *See also* gender

Men's Equalization Inc. (Canada), 134-35
men's rights, 134-35
Men's Rights Agency (Australia), 134-35
Meshcherkina, Elena, 54
meta-analysis, 108, 263n3
Miliband, Ralph, 6
militarization: patriarchy and, 42-43; in
Russia, 57-58. *See also* war
Mill, John Stuart, 215
minorities, and caregiving, 216
modernity and modernization: in anti-
colonial countries, 29-30; anti-modern
tendencies and, 36, 38, 262n17; characteristics of, 31; individualism and, 31-
32; nation/nationalism and, 24, 30-32;
nation-states and, 24, 26, 32; the West
and, 26-27; women and, 27-32, 39-41
Moghadam, Valentine, 38
Mohanty, Chandra Talpade, *Feminism
without Borders*, 2-3
Monture-Angus, Patricia, 235
moral hazard argument: for caregiving,
210-15; for employment duties, 206-7
Morton, Ted, 130-31; *The Charter
Revolution and the Court Party*, 130
motherhood: in Russia, 55, 57-58; in
Soviet Union, 46, 50
Mouffe, Chantal, 10
Mullen, Michelle, 107
Mulroney, Brian, 176, 193
multicultural citizenship, 10
multiculturalism: in Canada, 129;
integration policies and, 64; and
women's oppression, 62
Multilateral Agreement on Investment,
136
Mungall, Constance, 229
Murdoch, Rupert, 125, 131
Muslim women, in Soviet Union, 50-52

Nairn, Tom, 40
naming laws, 17, 220-23, 227-38; for
children, 221-22, 234, 237, 267n5; class
and, 223; and equality, 231, 237; history
of Anglo-American, 228-29; and identity,
220-21, 229, 234-36; indigeneity/race/
ethnicity and, 223; liberty and, 221, 223,
227-38; patriarchy and, 220-22, 228, 234-
35, 237-38; political nature of, 220; same-
sex marriage and, 222; social pressure
and, 229-30, 232-36; structural domination of, 223
nation and nationalism: anti-modern, 38,
262n17; in Canada, 192; definition of,
24; feminism and, 21-25, 27, 32-33,
37-39; feminist scholarship on, 11-12,

Pitkin, Hannah, 80
Poland, 24, 142
Policy (journal), 125
Policy Research Initiative (PRI) (Canada),
175, 178-83
political correctness, 123
political parties, 15
political scale: in Canada, 246; cities and,
240-42; gendering strategies and, 250-51;
globalization and, 240-42; literature on,
239-42; in Quebec, 242
political science: citizenship as subject of,
8-9; feminist scholarship and, 4-5; nation-
state as subject of, 4-5; state as subject
of, 5-6
Popular Sector (Canada), 192
populism: characteristics of, 120; history
of, 120; and policy, 15, 120-38; strategies
of, 120. *See also* market populism
post-colonial countries: anti-modern/
Western elements of, 36; women in,
27-28, 34-37. *See also* anti-colonial
countries
post-neoliberalism: neoliberalism vs, 16,
186, 198; and social investment state,
174-75
Poulantzas, Nicos, 6
poverty: child, 176-78, 193-94, 198, 200;
gender and, 171, 177-78, 182-83, 194,
257; individualization and, 179-83;
persistent, 180-83, 181(tab)
power: gender and, 255-57; non-
domination as, 226
pregnancy, enforced, 152-54
prenatal diagnosis, 107
PRI. *See* Policy Research Initiative
private/public divide: functionalist
explanation of, 262n10; laissez-faire
state and, 167; in nineteenth century,
262n10, 263n18; social contract and, 9;
Western preoccupation with, 34;
women's role in, 255
Progressive Conservative Party (Canada),
128-29
pro-life organizations: and International
Criminal Court, 147-48, 157; and
women, 140, 142, 153-54
proportions theory of representation,
83-84, 92
prostitution, enforced, 157
public choice theory, 121, 124-25, 127,
133, 137
public opinion, privileging of, 137
public transportation, 244-45
public/private divide. *See* private/public
divide

Putin, Vladimir, 57-59
Puwar, Nirmal, 91

Qatar, 147, 151
Quadrant (journal), 123
qualitative research approach, 109-10
quantitative method, 108-12
Quebec: constitutional accords and, 192;
equality in, 231; feminism in, 21, 45,
254; naming laws in, 230-31, 234, 236;
parental leave policy in, 212; political
scale in, 242; as state, 24; women in,
44-45, 63
Quebec Pension Plan, 189

race: in Canada, 66-67; caregiving and,
216; feminism and, 253; gender and
perception of, 246; poverty and, 181; in
Sweden, 68; visible minorities, 66-68,
127
Racism and the Press (van Dijk), 69
Rae, Bob, 256
Rakowska-Harmstone, Teresa, 52
Randles, Sally, 240
Rankin, L. Pauline, 33
rape, 157
rational action theory, 121
Ray, Brian, 243
REAL Women (Realistic, Equal, Active for
Life) (Canada), 134, 148, 192, 265n10
Rebick, Judy, 18; *Ten Thousand Roses*, 255
Reform Party (Canada), 122, 126, 128-31,
191-92
regional citizenship, 10
Regional Council of Ottawa-Carleton,
247
Reis, Elisa P., 35
religion: conservatism in, 140-43, 147-49,
151-61; feminist scholarship on, 160-61;
nation-states and, 26-27, 35; and
patriarchy, 143, 161; and secularization,
36. *See also* Catholic Church; Islam
rent seekers, 121, 125, 133
representation: burden of, 92; defining,
85-88, 93-95; descriptive, 79-80, 92, 94;
men's responsibility for, 85, 92-93;
numbers-based theories of, 80-85, 92;
substantive, 80, 92; of women in
politics, 14-15, 79-96; Young's concept
of, 85-88, 93-95, 94(fig)
reproductive technologies: in Canada, 15,
97-119; debates over, 97; feminist research
on, 100-101; legal issues in, 112-13;
policy research on, 112-14; quantitative
research approach to, 108-12; social/
ethical issues in, 113-14